Theory and Practice of Public Sector Reform

"This book fills a gap in thought leadership on public sector reform. It consolidates current theory, themes, and perspectives from leading scholars, thereby raising consciousness of the too neglected reform pulse of public management."

—John K. Wilkins, *York University, Canada*

Theory and Practice of Public Sector Reform offers readers differing theoretical perspectives to help examine the process of public sector reform, combined with an overview of major trends in the core areas of the functioning of the public sector. The book consists of three parts, the first addresses a number of conceptual and theoretical perspectives on public sector reform. It shows how different ways of looking at reform reveal very different things. The second part addresses major changes in specific areas of public sectors—'objects of reform.' Part three focuses on the study of public sector reform.

Aimed at academics, researchers and advanced students, this edited collection brings together many of the most eminent academics in the area of Public Policy and Management seeking to link to theory in part one and insights into specific thematic areas in part two, offering readers a display of theoretical perspectives to look at public sector reform.

Steven Van de Walle is Research Professor at the Public Governance Institute, KU Leuven, Belgium, and Professor of Public Management at Erasmus University Rotterdam, the Netherlands.

Sandra Groeneveld is Professor of Public Management at the Institute of Public Administration of Leiden University, the Netherlands.

Routledge Critical Studies in Public Management

Edited by Stephen Osborne

For a full list of titles in this series, please visit www.routledge.com

The study and practice of public management has undergone profound changes across the world. Over the last quarter century, we have seen

- increasing criticism of public administration as the over-arching framework for the provision of public services,
- the rise (and critical appraisal) of the 'New Public Management' as an emergent paradigm for the provision of public services,
- the transformation of the 'public sector' into the cross-sectoral provision of public services, and
- the growth of the governance of inter-organizational relationships as an essential element in the provision of public services

In reality these trends have not so much replaced each other as elided or co-existed together—the public policy process has not gone away as a legitimate topic of study, intra-organizational management continues to be essential to the efficient provision of public services, whilst the governance of inter-organizational and inter-sectoral relationships is now essential to the effective provision of these services.

Further, whilst the study of public management has been enriched by contribution of a range of insights from the 'mainstream' management literature, it has also contributed to this literature in such areas as networks and inter-organizational collaboration, innovation and stakeholder theory.

This series is dedicated to presenting and critiquing this important body of theory and empirical study. It will publish books that both explore and evaluate the emergent and developing nature of public administration, management and governance (in theory and practice) and examine the relationship with and contribution to the over-arching disciplines of management and organizational sociology.

Books in the series will be of interest to academics and researchers in this field, students undertaking advanced studies of it as part of their undergraduate or postgraduate degree and reflective policy makers and practitioners.

Theory and Practice of Public Sector Reform

Edited by Steven Van de Walle
and Sandra Groeneveld

Routledge
Taylor & Francis Group

NEW YORK AND LONDON

First published 2016
by Routledge
711 Third Avenue, New York, NY 10017

and by Routledge
2 Park Square, Milton Park, Abingdon, Oxon OX14 4RN

First issued in paperback 2018

*Routledge is an imprint of the Taylor & Francis Group,
an informa business*

Library of Congress Cataloging-in-Publication Data
Names: Van de Walle, Steven, editor. | Groeneveld, Sandra,
  1972– editor.
Title: Theory and practice of public sector reform / edited by Steven
  Van de Walle and Sandra Groeneveld.
Description: New York : Routledge, 2016. | Includes bibliographical
  references and index.
Identifiers: LCCN 2016009854 | ISBN 9781138887411
  (hardback : alk. paper) | ISBN 9781315714141 (ebook)
Subjects: LCSH: Public administration. | Administrative agencies—
  Reorganization. | Civil service reform. | Organizational change.
Classification: LCC JF1351 .T512 2016 | DDC 352.3/67—dc23
LC record available at https://lccn.loc.gov/2016009854

ISBN 13: 978-1-138-34082-4 (pbk)
ISBN 13: 978-1-138-88741-1 (hbk)

Typeset in Sabon
by Apex CoVantage, LLC

Contents

PART II
Objects of Reform

PART III
Studying and Practicing Reform

129

237

Tables and Figures

Tables

Figures

Contributors

Victor Bekkers is Professor of Public Administration and Public Policy at Erasmus University Rotterdam, the Netherlands.

Geert Bouckaert is Professor at the KU Leuven Public Governance Institute, Belgium. He also is President of the International Institute of Administrative Sciences (IIAS).

Tom Christensen is Professor of Public Administration and Policy at the University of Oslo, Norway. He also has adjunct appointments at University of Bergen and Renmin University.

Sandra Groeneveld is Professor of Public Management at the Institute of Public Administration of Leiden University, the Netherlands.

Christopher Hood is Gladstone Professor of Government Emeritus and Emeritus Fellow of All Souls College Oxford, UK.

Erik-Hans Klijn is Professor of Public Administration at Erasmus University Rotterdam, the Netherlands.

Joop Koppenjan is Professor of Public Administration at Erasmus University Rotterdam, the Netherlands.

Ben Kuipers is Associate Professor at the Institute of Public Administration of Leiden University (The Netherlands), consultant and owner of Performability, and co-founder of the Public Leadership Foundation.

Per Lægreid is Professor at the Department of Administration and Organization Theory, University of Bergen, Norway.

Mirko Noordegraaf is Professor of Public Management at the Utrecht School of Governance (USG), Utrecht University, the Netherlands.

Johan P. Olsen is Professor Em. at Arena, Centre for European Studies, University of Oslo, Norway.

B. Guy Peters is Maurice Falk Professor of Government, University of Pittsburgh, US.

Kim Putters is Director of the Netherlands Institute for Social Research (SCP) and Professor of Healthcare Policy and Governance at Erasmus University Rotterdam, the Netherlands.

Tiina Randma-Liiv is Professor of Public Management and Policy at Tallinn University of Technology, Estonia.

Rod Rhodes is Professor of Government at the University of Southampton, UK.

Arthur Ringeling is Emeritus Professor of Public Administration at Erasmus University Rotterdam, the Netherlands.

Christoph Reichard is Emeritus Professor of Public Management at Potsdam University, Germany.

Bram Steijn is Professor of HRM in the Public Sector at Erasmus University Rotterdam, the Netherlands.

Richard J. Stillman is Professor of Public Administration at the School of Public Affairs, University of Colorado Denver, US.

Lars Tummers is Associate Professor at Utrecht University, the Netherlands. He is also affiliated to Erasmus University Rotterdam and Arizona State University.

Frans-Bauke Van der Meer is Associate Professor at Erasmus University Rotterdam, the Netherlands.

Joris van der Voet is Assistant Professor of Public Management at Leiden University, the Netherlands.

Steven Van de Walle is Research Professor at the Public Governance Institute, KU Leuven, Belgium, and Professor of Public Management at Erasmus University Rotterdam, the Netherlands.

Sandra van Thiel is Professor of Public Management at the Department of Public Administration and Director of the Institute for Management Research at Radboud University, Nijmegen, the Netherlands.

1 Introduction

Theory and Practice of Public Sector Reform

Steven Van de Walle
and Sandra Groeneveld

Introduction

Written by some of the most prominent public management researchers, this book introduces different theoretical perspectives on public sector reform and outlines key reform trends in a number of areas. It also reflects on the practice of studying public sector reforms and on the practice of reform itself. As such, the book aims to offer a broad introduction to public sector reform.

This book was written for a special occasion, namely the retirement of Prof. Walter Kickert. However, it is not your ordinary *liber amicorum*, which tends to only attract attention from friends, colleagues and the writers of individual chapters. Instead, we wanted to compile a volume on the study of public sector reform that is relevant for students of reform. However, one characteristic of a *liber amicorum* remains. All authors are in one way or another related to the person to whom this book is dedicated. This selection process has resulted in an impressive list of public management scholars who have worked with Walter Kickert.

Walter Kickert's influence on public management and public sector reform research cannot be overestimated. We distinguish three major achievements. A first major achievement is his contribution to introducing systems theory and systems thinking into public management, which is undeniably associated with his unusual background. He graduated from the University of Utrecht in experimental physics, and by being a research assistant at Queen Mary University of London, among other influences, he began to explore the use of 'fuzzy set theory' for the study of decision-making (Kickert, 1978). In 1979, he defended his dissertation on the 'Organisation of Decision-Making: A Systems-Theoretical Approach' (Kickert, 1980) at the Department of Organisation Sciences at the Eindhoven University of Technology. Subsequently, he worked at the Catholic University of Nijmegen (now Radboud University) on topics such as government planning and its limitations (Kickert, 1986), and as a public official at the Dutch Ministry of Education and Sciences. The choice of topic for his inaugural lecture ('Complexity, Self-steering and Dynamics') at his appointment as Professor of Public Management at the Department of Public Administration, Erasmus University Rotterdam, demonstrates how his background has been very conducive to the study of public sector reform. One observes a strong influence of systems thinking combined with a certain disbelief in government planning (see, e.g., Kickert, 1993). As such, his work stood in sharp contrast to the then dominant Dutch school of rational policy making, culminating in the classic book 'Managing Complex Networks,' edited together with Klijn and Koppenjan (Kickert, Klijn, & Koppenjan, 1997), who also contributed a chapter to the current volume. In the 1990s, one can see his work moving towards the study of public sector reforms, with a focus on reform processes (traces of which can still be seen in his current work on change management, see Kickert, 2014; Kuipers et al., 2014) and on steering relations through a focus on autonomous agencies, a direct result of his earlier work on planning and decision-making (Kickert, 1995; Kickert & Verhaak, 1995).

Gradually, Kickert became a comparativist. His attention to what was happening outside his own country is his second major achievement. Kickert fits clearly within a European tradition of public administration, but he always evaded a narrow focus on his own country (Kickert, 2005). He became interested in less frequently studied countries (see, e.g., Kickert, 2007a, b). His focus in recent decades has mainly been on Southern European countries at a time when most scholars were interested in the other—mainly English-speaking—countries. His recent work on the fiscal crisis also has a very explicit comparative dimension (Kickert & Randma-Liiv, 2015). His excellent knowledge of languages and his multinational German/Belgian background made such an international outlook logical, although he himself—only partly in jest—explains it by referring to the travel opportunities that go along with comparative research. His attention to international public management is also visible in his work on the study of public management in Europe and the US (Kickert & Stillman, 1999; Kickert, 2007c).

Third, Kickert's work is one of the early examples of Dutch public management research becoming truly international. He started publishing in English and internationally already in the late 1970s, then still an anomaly in Dutch academic public administration; indeed, most European public administration scholarship was still very nationally oriented. He would also later become deputy editor of Public Administration. His writings helped in making the Dutch model of public management more widely known outside the Netherlands (Kickert & Van Vught, 1995; Kickert, 1997a; Kickert, 2003). At the same time, he was (and remains) critical about tendencies in the discipline towards high-volume publishing. In 2012, Walter Kickert received the IRSPM Routledge Prize for Outstanding Contribution to Public Management Research.

This book was written during a period of reform and change, both in the public sector, facing the fiscal crisis, and in the department where Walter was working. The latter reorganization allowed the editors, neither of whom has experience within the public sector, to experience a structural reform, with all of its rhetoric, politicking, stagnation and garbage cans. It is this reform and the subsequent departure of both editors that is to be blamed for a serious delay in the publication. Just as in real-world public sector reforms, university reforms do not go as planned.

Purpose and Structure of the Book

This book combines theory and practice of reform. Many academic works on public sector reforms focus on a specific topic or analyze specific country cases. Other books try to compare across a specific region or take a specific theoretical approach to public sector reform. What we felt was lacking was a book that could introduce readers to the most commonly used theories to explain how and why the public sector and public sector organizations change, as well as provide students of reform with an overview of major reform trends, without going into the minutiae of specific national reform programs. The book has three main parts. Part One offers seven different theoretical perspectives on public sector reform, while Part Two discusses key reform trends in six domains. Part Three elaborates on the practice of reform and of studying reform.

Part 1: Theoretical Perspectives

Part One of the book presents seven theoretical perspectives for looking at public sector reform. Much of the reform literature is atheoretical or largely dependent on a single theoretical perspective. In Part One, we present readers with a variety of perspectives that should help students of reform to analyze reform projects from different angles. The perspective that is taken determines what is seen. Each chapter outlines the key ideas behind the theory and applies the perspective to reforms. This part of the book starts with a number of classic perspectives. First, Johan Olsen introduces the institutional perspective—currently one of the most popular ones in public management scholarship. Christen and Lægreid offer a variation through their transformative perspective. Van Thiel then introduces another classic perspective, the principal agent perspective, which is foundational to New Public Management. We proceed with two more recent perspectives now common in public sector reform scholarship. First, Bekkers and Tummers introduce the innovation theory perspective, and Van der Voet, Kuipers and Groeneveld show how a change management perspective may help in understanding public sector reform. Christopher Hood's cultural theory perspective takes us again in a very different direction, as does Rod Rhodes with his introduction to the interpretative perspective.

Through presenting these very different alternative approaches for understanding public sector reform, we want to broaden reform students' toolkit for analyzing what is happening when actors announce reforms, promote reforms, reform and assess reforms.

Part 2: Objects of Reform

Part Two of the book focuses on objects of reform—that which is to be reformed. Public sector reform touches upon the core building blocks of the public sector: organizational structures, people and finances. Each of the chapters presents and discusses a set of major transformations in a specific domain and aims to give readers a fairly comprehensive overview of the key reforms that have taken place in Western public sectors. Van de Walle starts by discussing structural reforms in the public sector and the alternation of structural disaggregation and reaggregation. This alternation is visible in trends towards outsourcing, agencification and privatization, and in the current attention to mergers, departmentalization and public sector coordination. B. Guy Peters subsequently discusses changes in political administrative relations and how these have been affected by reform. More specifically, he shows how the pendulum of power between bureaucrats and politicians has swung many times. First, managers received more autonomy, but politicians were striking back, and politicization and patronage appear to have resurfaced. Klijn and Koppenjan introduce the shift towards network governance in the public sector and the new managerial tasks that have emerged as a consequence of this trend. Groeneveld and Steijn identify key trends in the management of human resources. Underlying these trends is a shift from career- to position-based civil service systems and the individualization of human resource management. The financial crisis has created a trend towards downsizing to decrease the size of the public sector.

The role of professional workers in the public sector has also changed, argues Mirko Noordegraaf. He discusses not only the changing nature of professional work but also the emergence of reform professionals. Finally, Randma-Liiv and Bouckaert analyze key trends in public financial management, starting with the modernization of the financial cycle, including a move to accrual accounting, participatory budgeting and the linking of finances to performance. Subsequently, they also show how the fiscal crisis has changed public finance structures and decision making.

Part 3: Studying and Practicing Reform

The third part of the book offers a reflection on the study and practice of public sector reform. First, Putters reflects on public sector reform as practice by showing how social trends and public sector reforms co-exist, making successful top-down planned reform unlikely. Stillman reminds us that different countries have different state traditions and that this influences both how scholars study administrative reforms and how reforms are shaped. Finally, Van der Meer, Reichard and Ringeling show how to become a student of reform and why it is important for students who are or wish to become public managers, professionals or academics in the field of public management to study public sector reforms.

References

Kickert, W.J.M. (1978). *Fuzzy theories on decision making: A critical review*. Boston: Kluwer.

Kickert, W.J.M. (1980). *Organisation of decision making: A systems-theoretical approach*. Amsterdam: Elsevier Science Ltd.

Kickert, W.J.M. (1986). *Overheidsplanning: theorieën, technieken en beperkingen*. Assen: Van Gorcum.

Kickert, W.J.M. (1993). Autopoiesis and the science of (public) administration—essence, sense and nonsense. *Organization Studies, 14*(2), 261–278.

Kickert, W.J.M. (1995). Steering at a distance: A new paradigm of public governance in Dutch higher education. *Governance, 9*(1), 135–157.

Kickert, W.J.M. (1997a). Public governance in the Netherlands, an alternative to Anglo-American 'managerialism'. *Public Administration Review, 75*(4), 731–752.

Kickert, W.J.M. (Ed.). (1997b). *Public management and administrative reform in Western Europe*. Cheltenham: Edward Elgar.

Kickert, W.J.M. (2003). Beyond public management: Shifting frames of reference in administrative reforms in the Netherlands. *Public Management Review, 5*(3), 377–399.

Kickert, W.J.M. (2005). Distinctiveness in the study of public management in Europe: A historical-institutional analysis of France, Germany and Italy. *Public Management Review, 7*(4), 537–563.

Kickert, W.J.M. (2007a). Distinctive characteristics of state and administrative reform in Southern Europe. In H. Hill (Ed.), *Modernizing government in Europe* (pp. 191–212). Baden-Baden: Nomos Verlag.

Kickert, W.J.M. (2007b). Public management reforms in countries with a Napoleonic state model: France, Italy and Spain. In C. Pollitt, S. van Thiel and V. Homburg (Eds.), *New public management in Europe: Adaptation and alternatives* (pp. 26–51). Houndmills: Palgrave Macmillan.

Kickert, W.J.M. (Ed.). (2007c). *The study of public management in Europe and the US: a competitive analysis of national distinctiveness*. London: Routledge.

Kickert, W.J.M. (2014). Specificity of change management in public organizations: Conditions for successful organizational change in Dutch ministerial departments. *American Review of Public Administration, 44*(6), 693–717.

Kickert, W.J.M., Klijn, E.H., & Koppenjan, J.F.M. (Eds.). (1997). *Managing complex networks: Strategies for the public sector*. London: Sage.

Kickert, W.J.M., & Randma-Liiv, T. (2015). *Europe managing the crisis: The politics of fiscal consolidation*. London: Routledge.

Kickert, W.J.M., & Stillman, R.J. (Eds.). (1999). *The modern state and its study: New administrative sciences in a changing Europe and United States*. Cheltenham: Edward Elgar.

Kickert, W.J.M., & van Vught, F.A. (Eds.). (1995). *Public policy & administration sciences in the Netherlands*. Hemel Hempstead: Prentice Hall and Harvester Wheatsheaf.

Kickert, W.J.M., & Verhaak, F.O.M. (1995). Autonomizing executive tasks in Dutch central government. *International Review of Administrative Sciences, 61*(4), 531–548.

Kuipers, B.S., Higgs, M.J., Kickert, W.J.M., Tummers, L.G., Grandia, J., & van der Voet, J. (2014). The management of change in public organisations: A literature review. *Public Administration, 92*(1), 1–20.

Part I

Perspectives on Public Sector Reform

2 An Institutional Perspective

Johan P. Olsen

Introduction

Contemporary debates regarding public sector reform hark back to old and still unresolved questions in political-administrative theory: how important are institutions of government and what are their ordering effects? What are the dynamics through which governmental institutions emerge and are maintained, transformed or eliminated (compare Christensen & Lægreid, this volume)? To what extent and under what conditions are forms of government a matter of deliberate design and reform (compare Van Thiel, this volume)? Is it possible to establish good government from reflection and choice rather than by accident and force (Mill, 1861/1962: 1; Hamilton & Madison, 1787/1964: 1)? The aim of this chapter is to contribute to a research agenda and theoretical understanding of political-administrative organization and organizing. Based on an institutional approach, this chapter asks what explanatory power established institutions have, compared to actors and deliberate design and the wider societal conditions.[1]

Public sector reforms are here primarily connected to comprehensive changes in European political-administrative orders—arrangements of institutions—rather than to incremental modifications in single institutions. The reason is simple. We live in an era of reform (Kickert & Van der Meer, 2011). There are attempts to reinvent government (Osborne & Gaebler, 1992) and shifts in politics-administration and state-society relations. Traditional public sector values are challenged by attempts to introduce a private management culture (Kickert & Jørgensen, 1995a,b; Kuipers et al., 2014: 13). The welfare state is in trouble. There are budget deficits, financial crises, austerity policies and new poverty. A social-democratic order is seen to be replaced by a neo-liberal order (Dahrendorf, 1988; Sejersted, 2005). European integration and globalization are accompanied by separatist movements.

In contrast to public sector reforms celebrating private enterprise and competitive markets, it is assumed that an adequate understanding of the dynamics of political-administrative institutions must take into account the specific characteristics of the public sector (March & Olsen, 1995: 247–248). In contrast to approaches that give primacy to technical-managerial concerns, the chapter concerns the basic normative principles on which democracies are organized, debates and struggles over how normative ideals are to be understood and translated into institutional arrangements and how established institutions contribute to organized rule, orderly change and civilized co-existence.

In the literature, it is commonplace to assume that institutions are excessively static and that institutionalism cannot make sense of change because it is overly structural and does not grant purposeful actors a proper role (Olsen, 2009a; Peters, 2012). Here, it is argued that such assumptions are mistaken. It is also held that if the future of democracies depends on the quality of their political-administrative institutions, then it may be worthwhile to examine the democratic-instrumental vision that citizens and their representatives can and should use to decide how they are to be organized and governed. It may be useful to study the possibilities and limitations of governing through deliberately changing institutional arrangements and thereby achieve intended and desired effects, including the role of established institutions in such processes (Olsen, 2010).

First, two competing perspectives to institutionalism are sketched—an actor-centered and a society-centered approach. Then, an institutional approach is outlined, featuring the ordering effects of institutions and their role in balancing order and change. Finally, there is a discussion of what an institutional approach may contribute in an era of comprehensive European reforms.

'Institution' as Study Object and Analytical Concept

What is called an 'institution' in everyday language (a parliament, ministry, court, or political party) has long been an important *study object* for students of politics and public administration. The *analytical concept* of an institution is also central in political science-public administration, and in recent decades there has been increasing interest in how institutional reforms can be understood and to what extent, in what respects, through what processes, under what conditions and why institutions make a difference.

There is, however, a multitude of perspectives used to make sense of institutions. Competing approaches prioritize different analytical units—what is attributable to political actors, societal processes and existing institutional arrangements (Olsen, 1992; Goodin, 1996; Rhodes, Binder & Rockman, 2006; Peters, 2012). Approaches differ in how they understand the nature of institutions; their ordering effects and the processes that translate structures into political effects; and change and the processes that translate human behavior into structures and establish, sustain, transform or eliminate institutions. Different approaches conceive governmental institutions as instruments of command, coercion and redistribution, as instruments for regulating and facilitating efficient exchange and as vehicles for defining appropriate behavior (March & Olsen, 1989).

The institutional approach used here competes with two other interpretations of public sector reform. The first is a rational actor perspective, which regards political life as organized by exchange among calculating, self-interested actors maximizing their expected utility (compare Van Thiel, this volume). The second is a society-centered perspective that regards political institutions and behavior as arising from societal forces, rather than society as being governed by politics.

Within an *actor-centered frame,* explanatory factors are located in the characteristics of individual decision-makers, their goals, understandings and resources. Institutions are a result of deliberate decisions, and political-administrative leaders use them as tools to achieve pre-determined ends. Institutional design entails two assumptions: institutional form is a significant determinant of performance, and human choices are important determinants of institutional forms (Olsen, 1997). Institutions may be the product of decisions by a unitary actor or a winning coalition. In both cases: (a) Reformers are assumed to know what they want. They have clear, consistent and stable objectives over the time period studied. (b) They understand how alternative institutional forms affect performance and know what it takes to achieve their objectives. (c) They have the power to do what is needed to achieve a desired outcome.

This approach is an instrumentalist celebration of institutional engineering—human will, understanding and control. The basic ideas are consistent with democratic ideals assuming the primacy of politics. Citizens and their elected representatives deliberately establish new institutional structures and re-arrange existing ones. A challenge for empirical research is to identify who the actors are, what they are attempting to achieve, what is the actual latitude for purposeful institutional design under varying conditions and what are the effects of changing power relations.

Within a *society-centered frame,* explanatory factors are located in the objective characteristics of an institution's environment. Institutions are reflections of circumstances. They are social organisms that evolve over time as an unplanned consequence of historical processes. A standard argument is that institutions survive and flourish because they are well-adapted to their functional (Goodin, 1996) or normative environments (Meyer & Rowan, 1977). In the latter perspective, symbols and legitimacy are more important than performance. 'Institution' refers to cultural-cognitive models external to specific organizational forms. There is diffusion of global templates, with convergence and isomorphy as a result. Institutional change can be better predicted from knowledge of the world environment than from an understanding of internal structure (Jepperson & Meyer, 1991: 226). A third version of an environmental perspective conceives institutions as the result of chance and coincidence. In 'organized anarchies', characterized by ambiguous goals, uncertain understanding and limited control, reform efforts become a unintended confluence of actors, problems, solutions and decision-making opportunities and 'garbage can' processes (Cohen, March & Olsen, 1972; March & Olsen, 1983).

Environmental determinism assumes that political institutions adapt fairly quickly to changes in human purposes and external conditions. A key process is experiential learning and rational adaptation. Another is competitive selection. Institutions that do not match their functional and normative environments lose legitimacy and support and are eliminated. A challenge for empirical research is to explore institutional abilities to adapt spontaneously to environmental changes and environmental effectiveness in eliminating non-adaptive and sub-optimal institutions.

An institutional approach does not understand institutions as an epiphenomenon of individual actors or environmental forces. It goes beyond portraying institutional change as a simple reflection of differences in the comparative functional efficiency or normative match of alternative forms, or as a product of chance events. Institutions are partly autonomous. Explanatory factors are located in institutional structures and processes. Key distinctions between competing perspectives are (a) the extent to which institutions are seen as having some degree of autonomy and independent effects and (b) the extent to which an approach regards institutionalized rules and identities as being reproduced with some reliability, at least partly independent of deliberate design and reform efforts, as well as of environmental stability or change.

An Institutional Approach

Institutionalism, then, connotes a specific approach to the public sector and political life, a set of theoretical ideas and hypotheses concerning the relationships among institutional characteristics, political agency and societal change. An institutional approach holds that political life is not voluntaristic (caused by human intentions), deterministic (caused by external forces and laws) or random (governed by the laws of chance). Political institutions are neither completely static nor in constant flux.

A core assumption is that the organization of political life has an independent explanatory power. Institutions create temporary and imperfect order in political and social life. They have durable and independent effects and some robustness with respect to individual actors and environments. Action is driven by a conception of identity and a logic of appropriateness. Meaning, including understandings of history and self, is constructed through political and social processes. Institutions are markers of a polity's identity, traditions and visions, and history is inefficient. It matches institutions, behavior and contexts in ways that take time and have multiple, path-dependent equilibria. However, institutions also facilitate change and have dynamics of their own.[2]

In contrast with an older, law-inspired institutionalism that used formal-legal rules as proxies for political organization, action and outcomes, the new institutionalism is behavioral. Theoretical ideas are required to be consistent with empirical observations of actual practices and outcomes. Institutionalism offers an interpretation of how '*living*' political-administrative institutions can be conceptualized, to what degree they have independent and endurable impacts, and the processes through which they emerge, are maintained and change.

An institution is an enduring collection of rules and organized practices, embedded in structures of meaning and resources that are relatively invariant in the face individual turnover and changing external circumstances (March & Olsen, 2006). Repertoires of constitutive rules and standard operating procedures prescribe appropriate behavior for specific roles in specific situations. Structures of meaning, involving standardization, homogenization and authorization of common purposes, vocabularies, ways of reasoning and accounts, explain, justify and legitimate behavioral rules. Structures of resources (budgets, staffs and equipment) create capabilities for acting. Resources are routinely tied to rules and worldviews, empowering and constraining actors differently and making them more or less capable of acting according to codes of behavior.

Institutionalization implies

- Increasing clarity and agreement about behavioral rules, including the allocation of formal authority and accountability. The standardization and formalization of practice reduce uncertainty and conflict concerning who does what, when and how. As some ways of acting are perceived to be natural and legitimate, there is less need to use incentives or coercion to make people follow prescribed rules.
- Increasing consensus concerning how behavioral rules are to be explained and justified, with a common vocabulary, expectations and success criteria. There is a decreasing need to explain and justify why modes of action are appropriate in terms of problem-solving and normative validity.
- The supply of resources becomes routinized and 'taken for granted.' Less effort is needed to obtain or mobilize the resources required for acting in accordance with prescribed rules of appropriate behavior. Public sector reforms are called for, or old rules are ignored.

As corollary, de-institutionalization implies that identities, roles, authority, explanations, justifications and resources become contested. There is increasing uncertainty, disorientation and conflict. New actors are mobilized. There are demands for new explanations and justifications of existing practices. Outcomes are more uncertain, and it is necessary to use more incentives or coercion to make people follow prescribed rules.

A polity, a society organized and integrated politically, is a configuration of institutions that defines the setting within which governing and politics take place. For some time, the key setting has been the sovereign, territorial state. Hobbes assumed that for individuals in a state of nature—without institutions that command general consent and are observed—life would be solitary, poor, nasty, brutish and short. His solution was Leviathan, government based on centralization and absolute independent authority (Hobbes, 1651/1962). In contrast, an institutional approach holds that contemporary democracies are not founded upon a coherent set of normative and organizational principles. Polities are composite and mixed orders with institutional differentiation. They are characterized by the co-existence of several interdependent, yet relatively autonomous, self-organizing and resourceful institutions. Institutions have separate origins and histories, different missions and internal and external organization. They operate according to different repertoires of behavioral logics and standard operating procedures and are the guardians of competing values, interests, worldviews and groups. There are several, not necessarily synchronized and coordinated, processes of change. A challenge is to provide a better understanding of the ordering effects of institutions, how they structure political-administrative and social life, and how they both facilitate continuity and change, including public sector reform.

The Ordering Effects of Institutions

An institutional approach recognizes that governing usually implies intervention in and through formal organizations and that formally organized institutions under ordinary conditions operate on the basis of rules, roles, practices and standard operating procedures (March & Simon, 1958). Governmental organizations can usually do only what they are trained to do and know how to do, and government can deliver only what large-scale organizations are capable of doing and motivated to do. It is, therefore, important to understand *the processes through which institutional structures are translated into behavior.*

Governments impact behavior and outcomes through coercion, incentives and persuasion and by shaping collective and individual identities and interpretations of the world. To the degree that institutions generate beliefs in a legitimate order, they simplify governing by ensuring that many things are taken as given. They give order to social relations, reduce flexibility and variability in behavior and restrict the possibilities of a one-sided pursuit of self-interest (Weber, 1978: 40–43). For an institutional approach, a key question is, then, which organizational forms are legitimate in a specific culture, beyond their substantive performance (Selznick, 1957), that is, whether political life is organized in a way that people accept as natural and appropriate, reasonable and just.

Legitimate rules and practices specify what is normal, must be expected, can be relied upon and what makes sense in a community. Institutions facilitate sense-making and guide and stabilize expectations. They dampen conflicts over resource allocations, and some of the capabilities of institutions come from their effectiveness in substituting rule-bound behavior for individually autonomous behavior. Two challenges arise for institutionalism: to specify how variations in institutional forms influence (a) conduct, behavior and performance, and (b) peoples' inner states of mind, and their moral and intellectual qualities, identities and belongings, such that they become carriers of rules and practices.

Impacting Conduct

Institutions are concentrations of resources and collective action capabilities. They prescribe how authority and power are constituted, exercised, legitimated, controlled and redistributed. Institutions provide codes of appropriate conduct and define basic rules for resolving conflicts. They organize and stabilize attention, information, responsibility and accountability, and they empower and constrain actors by regulating the use of institutionalized and private resources. Institutions affect allocations of advantages and burdens, but they do not determine action and performance in detail. Politics matter, and the legitimacy of democratic institutions is partly based on the expectation that they will provide open-ended processes without determinate outcomes. The same organizational arrangement can have different consequences under different conditions, and different arrangements can produce the same effects (March & Olsen, 1989, 2006; Brunsson & Olsen, 1993; Egeberg, 2012).

The logic of appropriateness is an interpretation of human action. To act appropriately is to proceed according to the institutionalized rules and practices of a collectivity and mutual understandings of what is true, reasonable, natural, right and good. Actors seek to fulfill the obligations and duties encapsulated in a role, an identity and membership in a community. Rules are followed because they are perceived to be adequate for the task at hand and to have normative validity.

Institutionalism assumes that political life is not solely organized around policy making, the aggregation of predetermined preferences and resources. Consistent with an old strand in the study of political-administrative life, institutionalism holds that politics and administration involves a search for collective purpose, direction, meaning and belonging (March & Olsen, 1976, 1989). In routine situations, rule-based action may reflect, almost mechanically, prescriptions embedded in institution-specific rules, professional norms, laws or constitutions. Defining a role and achieving it can, however, require time and energy, thought and capability. For example, courts of law illustrate that following rules can be a complicated cognitive process involving thoughtful, reasoning behavior. Such reasoning is not primarily connected to the anticipation of consequences and incentives. Actors use criteria of similarity and congruence, rather than likelihood and expected value. The core behavioral proposition of institutionalism is that, humans generally take reasoned action by attempting to answer three elementary questions: what kind of a situation is this? What kind of person am I (are we)? What does a person such as I (we) do in a situation such as this—what kind of behavioral prescriptions follow from matching the facts of the situation with the relevant rules (March & Olsen, 1989)?

The clarity, consistency and acceptance of rules and identities are variables, as are the familiarity with and understanding of situations and the behavioral implications of matching rules. There may be more or less time for analysis and decision-making. Prescriptions may be straightforward or unclear, and hence actors have a difficult time interpreting which historical experiences are relevant for current situations. They may struggle with how to classify themselves and others—who they are, what they are and who they want to be—and what the classifications imply in a specific situation. Institutionalized authority and resources may be adequate, or they may be overpowered by non-institutionalized resources and informal processes.

These problems are particularly challenging in compound polities in which several institutions structured according to different principles and behavioral logics provide competing analyses and prescriptions for the same area of action. Processes and outcomes depend on which identities and rules are activated and which are considered primary and secondary. For example, a variety of factors impact the relations between a logic of appropriateness and a logic of consequentiality, the salience of different logics and the institutional conditions under which each is likely to dominate. Political actors may subsume one logic as a special case of another. They may establish a hierarchy among logics or be governed by the relative prescriptive clarity of different logics. The resources available for acting in accordance with different logics may be decisive. Actors may use different logics for different purposes, and changing logics of action may result from specific experiences (March & Olsen, 1998). A key task for institutionalists is to improve the understanding of the conditions under which actors are motivated by and capable of complying with rules of appropriateness and the factors that strengthen or weaken the relationship between rules and actions.

Impacting Identities and Mentalities

Whereas institutions affect behavior through external opportunity and incentive structures, they also have the potential to constitute actors and shape their character, models of the world, preferences, commitments, resources and action capabilities. Human nature is changing and variable, not fixed and universal (March & Olsen, 1989). Identities are endogenous, not exogenous, and identification is a fundamental mechanism in group integration (March & Simon, 1958).

Institutions integrate a political community and provide its members with a shared sense of identity and constitutive socio-cultural belongings. They offer a sense of reason, justice, purpose, and emotional ties. Actors may, for example, internalize beliefs in the common good, citizenship and civic virtue; in ethical ideas about the just society, rights and duties; and in how to simultaneously make collective decisions and maintain peaceful co-existence. There are culturally defined purposes to be sought and modes of appropriate procedures for pursuing purposes, and there is no perfect positive correlation between effectiveness and normative validity (Merton, 1942). Legitimacy, therefore, depends not only on demonstrating that actions accomplish appropriate objectives but also on actors behaving in accordance with appropriate procedures ingrained in a culture.

In brief, institutions make us who we are, as president, minister, bureaucrat, judge and citizen. They do so in legal terms (Dworkin, 1986: vii) and in behavioral terms (March & Olsen, 1989). Key issues for institutionalists are: what are the processes of collective reasoning, experience, education and socialization by which a political community learn identities and roles? How are standards of appropriateness created, changed, evoked and interpreted? How are they organized into political identities and roles, such as democrats and law-abiding, non-corrupt rulers and ruled?

Internalization takes place in a variety of institutional settings—ordinary work-situations, higher education, civil society and politics. Politics involves public justification and criticism of identities, and normative and organizational principles, and public authorities in democracies are supposed to contribute to the development of a democratic culture. Nevertheless, institutions have limited legitimacy in fashioning identities and mentalities. To avoid problems of conformity and totalitarianism, democracies have to combine free personal choices with legitimate normative bonds and community. They have to strike a balance between the collectivist notion of a sovereign people and the individualistic notion of the sovereign individual, between rulers and ruled guided by community norms or by the calculation of expected self-interest.

This implies a need to study the types of humans selected and formed by different types of institutions and to specify the mechanisms by which different rules of appropriateness evolve and are legitimized, reproduced, modified and replaced. An adequate understanding of the effects of institutional structure and political order also presupposes an understanding of how institutional arrangements change over time: the processes underlying structural change, the role of deliberate design and reform, what factors lead to different forms of order and which institutional characteristics favor change or make institutions resistant to change.

Order and Change

Institutions are simultaneously creating order and change. They are not static and do not always favor continuity over breaks with the past. Change is a constant feature of institutions as they respond to experience and evolve routines for addressing reform proposals and external events. Political orders are more or less settled. Some are more vulnerable than others, and institutional decay and breakdowns exist. There are multiple paths of change, and change can be not only rapid and direct but also contested and unsuccessful (March, 1981; March & Olsen, 2006; Olsen, 2009a). Institutionalism approaches these issues by arguing, first, that history is 'inefficient' and that there is a need to identify factors that create frictions in adaptation and selection and, second, that there is a need to explore intra- and inter-institutional sources of change.

Historical Inefficiency

The democratic vision, that citizens and their elected representatives choose how they are to be organized and governed, is frustrated by a variety of factors. Governmental institutions and public sector reforms are not simple tools for the people and their representatives. In contrast with standard equilibrium models, assuming that institutions reach a unique organizational form conditional on current functional and normative circumstances, and thus independent of their historical path, institutionalism holds that the matching of institutions, behaviors and contexts requires time and has multiple, path-dependent equilibria (March & Olsen, 1989).

Rules develop in response to history, but that development is not uniquely optimal in any meaningful sense. Institutionalism holds that key behavioral mechanisms encoding experience into rules and routines are history-dependent and guarantee neither improvement nor increasing survival value. Observation and interpretation of experience and institutional memories, retrieval and responses are affected by institutional arrangements, and adaptation is less continuous and precise than assumed by standard equilibrium models (March, 2010). A better understanding of historical inefficiency requires the detailed exploration of possible frictions in processes of institutional design and reform, institutional abilities to adapt spontaneously to changing circumstances, and environmental effectiveness in eliminating suboptimal institutions and identities.

Public sector reformers are neither omnipotent nor impotent. They are institutional gardeners more than engineers or the pawns of the great historic necessities (Olsen, 1997, 2007: Ch.8). They reinterpret codes of behavior, affect causal and normative beliefs, foster identities and engagement, develop organized capabilities and improve adaptability. Nevertheless, institutions are defended by insiders and validated by outsiders and cannot be changed arbitrarily. The more institutionalized an area, the more resilient are its structures against reform efforts and environmental change, and resistance is strongest when change threatens institutional identities.

Comprehensive public sector reforms are long-term efforts. It is easier to change formal-legal arrangements than established power-relations, culture and behavior and to achieve intended and desired effects. Many, more or less tightly coupled, change-processes may be involved. Causal chains are often complex, long and contingent (Weaver & Rockman, 1993). Reformers may face ambiguous goals, causal uncertainty, modest control and unclear responsibility and accountability-relations (Cohen, March & Olsen, 1972; Olsen, 2014; Christensen & Lægreid, 2007). Comprehensive reform requires strong organizational capabilities to stabilize attention, mobilize resources and cope with resistance (March & Olsen, 1983). Attempts to re-constitute government through comprehensive reform often create stalemates, confrontations and crises. Radical reorganization of a polity with a single scheme at a specific point in time is unlikely to be politically digestible, except under special conditions.

Reforms can lead to unexpected and undesired outcomes and demands for new reforms (Brunsson & Olsen, 1993). A reform that is perceived as a success in the short run may be assessed as a fiasco in the long run. Similarly, short-term fiascos may, from the perspective of a longer horizon, be ultimately assessed a success (March & Olsen, 1983). Incremental, piecemeal and slow changes can generate long-term accumulation and major changes when they have a consistent direction (Kickert & Van der Meer, 2011). How quickly institutions will arise and adapt to reforms and environmental changes or dissolve depends on what ties the component units together and what keeps them apart. Institutions integrated primarily through calculated benefits and continuous performances are likely to adapt or be eliminated more rapidly than institutions integrated through identity-based community and shared traditions (Weber, 1978).

Internal Dynamics

The assumption that structures persist unless there are external irritants or shocks underestimates intra- and inter-institutional dynamics and sources of change. Institutions prescribe and proscribe, accelerate and delay change. Change can be driven by explicit rules, pressures from institutional ideals (such as 'democracy') that are unlikely to be fulfilled in practice, internal loss of faith in institutions and by intra- and inter-institutional tensions. Institutions facilitate change within the possibilities and constraints of the identity, history and internal dynamic of an institution and political order. They impede change that transcends the possibilities and constraints of an identity, history and internal dynamic. In the first case, change tends to be incremental and continuous. In the latter, it tends to be episodic and dramatic (March & Olsen, 1989; Olsen, 2009a, b).

Reforms have become routine in many organizations (Brunsson, 2009). In democracies, change is routinized through periodic elections and facilitated and legitimized through institutionalized opposition and freedom of expression. While concepts of institution and order assume some internal coherence and consistency, integration is imperfect and tensions and disputes are endemic. For example, a bureaucracy is constituted by hierarchical loyalty to elected leaders, to *Rechtsstaat* rules and to professional knowledge and expertise—principles that are not always easy to reconcile (Olsen, 2006, 2008).

Political-administrative orders are never fully accepted by the entire society. The coherence of orders and the scopes and modes of institutionalized activity vary across political systems, policy areas and historic time (Eisenstadt, 1965; Goodin, 1996). Political-administrative and social orders are constituted by a collection of institutions that fit more or less into a coherent system, and there are competing ideas regarding the role of different institutions as part of a larger order. Most political-administrative orders function through a mix of co-existing, partly inconsistent organizational and normative principles, behavioral logics and legitimate resources. The coherence of an order can be threatened by strong identifications with subunits or roles, and institutions organized upon competing principles can create problems for one another (Orren & Skowronek, 2004; Olsen, 2007, 2010).

One hypothesis is that democracies work comparatively well *because* their political-administrative orders are not well-integrated (Olsen, 2010). In everyday life, inconsistencies and tensions are buffered by institutional specialization, separation, sequential attention, local rationality, slack resources and norms of conflict avoidance (Cyert & March, 1963). Political-administrative orders cope with competing normative and organizational principles through institutional separation of behavioral logics, hierarchy among competing logics, sequencing logics and differences in prescriptive clarity (March & Olsen, 1998). These mechanisms help democracies cope with issues that create conflicts and stalemates at moments of comprehensive public sector reform when demands for consistency and coherence are stronger (Olsen, 2007: Ch.9). Certain periods are characterized by institutional confrontations and transformations. Nevertheless, there are radical intrusions and attempts to achieve control over other institutional spheres and stern institutional defense against invasions of alien norms. Changing patterns of authority and power follow from, and affect, inter-institutional processes of separation and integration, de-coupling or re-coupling. Arguably, Europe is now in such a situation.

Europe in an Era of Reform

Europe is currently an institutional (re-)building site involving reforms of relations between levels of government and between institutional spheres. The future political-administrative organization of Europe is impacted by institution-building, reforms at the European level and by New Public Management (NPM) and post-NPM inspired reforms at the national and local level. The reforms affect the role of the European Union and its inter-institutional relations, the role of regions, the sovereign territorial state, local government, democratic quality and the welfare state. Reforms also provide a site for theoretical speculations and empirical studies of public sector reforms, the malleability of political-administrative institutions and the explanatory power of established institutions. It is, however, beyond the scope of this chapter to discuss how useful an institutional approach is for making sense of current European transformations. The chapter is primarily theoretical-conceptual, and the less heroic aspiration is now to make a few comments on the possibilities and limitations of governing through institutional reform and for understanding the nature of reform processes (Olsen, 2010).

Consider the role of deliberate reform. Many studies conceive leadership as a key factor in the development of political-administrative institutions. Nevertheless, change management often involves facilitating and guiding change more than hierarchical command and control (Baez & Abolafia, 2002; Boin & Christensen, 2008; Kuipers et al., 2014). Actors holding key positions in key institutions can succeed in changing formal arrangements and practices even under inhospitable conditions. However, the final outcome is not necessarily what was originally desired (Gornitzka & Metz, 2014). The evolving multi-level Union administration (Egeberg, 2006), the emergence of European agencies (Egeberg, Martens & Trondal, 2012) and the European political-administrative order at large are not the result of any grand plan, even if there are elements of deliberate design and reform (Olsen, 2002, 2007, 2010).

In the words of a former President of the European Commission:

'we are talking about a highly differentiated, highly complex, multi-layered system of decision-making in which it is almost a miracle when we arrive at a final outcome or resolution that is exactly as it was originally planned. The EU lacks a clear system of leadership. There is no directoire, there are only shifting coalitions. I prefer to look at the EU as a very complex reality or system in which governments make what they believe to be rational choices but that afterwards enter into a highly complex system of unintended consequences and feedback, and in which the institutions themselves have a lot of autonomy.'
(Barroso, 2007: 4)

As expected from by an institutional approach, well-entrenched institutions and identities have not changed easily. Facing European-level developments, New Public Management doctrines and post-NPM reforms reasserting the political center, 'whole of government', coordination and accountability rather than rolling back the state, existing institutional arrangements have shown considerable resilience (Christensen & Lægreid, 2007, 2015; Olsen, 2010; Verhoest & Lægreid, 2010; Dahlström, Peters & Pierre, 2011). Global prescriptions of reform have consistently been interpreted and responded to differently depending on national institutional arrangements, resources and historical traditions. Reform practices and performance have varied across countries and regions (Christensen & Lægreid, 2007, 2012; Kickert & Van der Meer, 2011; Pollitt & Bouckaert, 2011). The territorial state is transformed, but it has not withered. Compared to rhetoric concerning deliberate reforms based on calculations of expected utility, political-administrative reality has changed less, more slowly and often in unexpected ways. Institutional self-dynamics have, however, facilitated change. Examples are claims regarding a democratic deficit and the European Parliament's appeals to democracy as parliamentary government. European-level institutions have become increasingly important explanatory factors, as they have acquired identities and resources of their own (Olsen, 2010: 110–111).

A hypothesis is that European integration has succeeded *because* practice has not followed the Union's strategic actor rhetoric. Integration and cooperation have not been based on a process whereby, first, substantive operational goals have been formulated and, then, tailor-made institutions have been designed. The Union has been involved in an institutional search process without agreement on a political philosophy or a constitutional theory that set out the purposes and ends of institutional arrangements. The EU has formulated acceptable procedures, rules, timetables and fairly general targets and aspirations, without agreeing on any desired 'end state' of the Union. The EU has developed codes of behavior, affected causal and normative beliefs, fostered identities and engagement, developed organized action capabilities and improved adaptability (Olsen, 2010).

A complication for public sector reformers in general is that there is no single 'bottom-line', as suggested by private enterprise templates. It might be possible to govern by calculating the costs and benefits of alternative institutional forms under relatively simple and stable conditions. Political-administrative actors, however, also must act when they do not know exactly what they want and when comprehension and control are limited, time is short, and the consequences of possible actions are uncertain. Reforms in democratic orders often take place under such conditions, and theorizing public sector reform requires going beyond assumptions of clear and stable goals and perfect understanding and control. Comprehensive reforms are often compromises among multiple, vague, inconsistent and changing goals. Political aspirations might be impossible to meet within existing competences and resources.

In democracies, reformers' discretion is constrained by institutions and professions that regard themselves as guardians of different 'red lines', defining what is appropriate or acceptable. Reformers have to consider what is acceptable to popular opinion and the political community, legal rules and principles, core values and traditions of a culture, the available economic and staff resources, scientific truths and professional expertise, powerful organized interests and reactions in financial markets and military and religious communities. They need to reconcile institutional identities and missions with responsiveness to shifting political leadership and changing societies. In brief, reformers face the issue of how contradictory demands and success criteria can be integrated. Rather than assuming a coherent preference function, a variety of criteria may be treated as independent constraints (Cyert & March, 1963).

This interpretation affects how reforms are conceived by an institutional approach—what they are seen to be all about. Whereas public sector reformers have primarily relied upon changing external incentives and controls, increased complexity, ambiguity, uncertainty and volatility make external control more difficult. An institutional approach, therefore, calls attention to processes of internalization, reforms as political pedagogy and political spaces in which the demos can discuss how they want to be politically organized and governed (March & Olsen, 1995). Reform processes are (also) symbolic acts. They involve a search for meaning and battles over peoples' minds (March & Olsen, 1976, 1993). Reformers can demonstrate good intentions by making formal changes without behavioral or substantive effects (Meyer & Rowan, 1977), and the literature typically says more about form and process than content and impact (Toonen, 2012: 574). The latter type of knowledge is 'patchy and contested' (Christensen & Lægreid, 2012: 585). Results are promised or expected, but systematic evaluations of major structural change are rare (Verhoest & Lægreid, 2010: 294). An analysis of 133 articles on change management in public organizations concludes that actual results are not documented in any detail (Kuipers et al., 2014: 13, 16).

Conclusion

Assumptions concerning the explanatory power of institutions and a focus on institutional sources of continuity and change in political-administrative orders do not deny the importance of political agency and environmental driving forces. An improved understanding of the dynamics of institutions and identities requires devoting attention to several 'imperfect' and disjointed processes of change, not a focus on a single mechanism and a coherent and dominant process. Reformers are unlikely to eliminate chance, coercion, incremental adaptation or breakdowns. There is a need to further examine the tension and interaction between purposeful actors and their reform-efforts, societal environments and historically developed institutions and political orders, based upon realistic assumptions of how institutions are structured, how they work and how they are transformed.

Notes

1. Thanks to Morten Egeberg, Sandra Groeneveld, Torben Beck Jørgensen, Per Lægreid, James G. March and Steven Van de Walle for helpful comments.
2. For an expanded discussion of institutions, institutionalization and the distinction between the rule-driven logic of appropriateness and the logic of consequentiality, assuming self-regarding actors calculating expected utility, see below and March and Olsen 1984, 1989, 1998, 2006; Olsen 1992, 1997, 2007, 2009a, b, 2010.

References

Baez, B., & Abolafia, M.Y. (2002). Bureaucratic entrepreneurship and institutional change: A sense-making approach. *Journal of Public Administration Research and Theory, 12*(4), 525–552.

Barroso, J.M. (2007). Q and A with President Barroso. *EUSA Review Forum, 20*(4), 1–5.

Boin, A., & Christensen, T. (2008). The development of public institutions: Reconsidering the role of leadership. *Administration & Society, 40*(3), 271–297.

Brunsson, N. (2009). *Reform as routine: Organizational change and stability in the modern world.* Oxford: Oxford University Press.

Brunsson, N., & Olsen, J.P. (1993). *The reforming organization.* London: Routledge.

Christensen, T., & Lægreid, P. (2012). Administrative reforms in Western democracies. In B.G. Peters and J. Pierre (Eds.), *The Sage handbook of public administration* (pp. 577–589). 2nd edition. Los Angeles: Sage.

Christensen, T., & Lægreid, P. (Eds.). (2007). *Transcending new public management: The transformation of public sector reforms.* Aldershot: Ashgate.

Cohen, M.D., March, J.G., & Olsen, J.P. (1972). A garbage can model of organizational choice. *Administrative Science Quarterly, 17*, 1–25.

Cyert, R.M., & March, J.G. (1963). *A behavioral theory of the firm.* 2nd edition 1992. Englewood Cliffs, NJ and Oxford: Prentice-Hall and Basil Blackwell.

Dahlström, C., Peters, B.G., & Pierre, J. (Eds.). (2011). *Steering from the centre: Strengthening political control in Western democracies.* Toronto: University of Toronto Press.

Dahrendorf, R. (1988). *The modern social conflict: An essay on the politics of liberty.* London: Weidenfeld and Nicolson.

Dworkin, R. (1986). *Law's empire.* Cambridge, MA: Harvard University Press.

Egeberg, M. (2012). How bureaucratic structure matters: An organizational perspective. In B.G. Peters and J. Pierre (Eds.), *Handbook of public administration* (pp. 157–168). London: Sage.

Egeberg, M. (Eds.). (2006). *Multilevel union administration: The transformation of executive politics in Europe.* Houndmills: Palgrave Macmillan.

Egeberg, M., Martens, M., & Trondal, J. (2012). Building executive power at the European level: On the role of European agencies. In M. Busuioc, M. Groenleer and J. Trondal (Eds.), *The agency phenomenon in the European Union* (pp. 19–41). Manchester: Manchester University Press.

Eisenstadt, S.N. (1965). Bureaucracy, bureaucratization, markets, and power structure. In S.N. Eisenstadt (Ed.), *Essays in comparative institutions* (pp. 175–215). New York: Wiley.

Goodin, R.E. (1996). Institutions and their design. In R.E. Goodin (Ed.), *The theory of institutional design* (pp. 1–53). Cambridge: Cambridge University Press.

Gornitzka, Å., & Metz, J. (2014). European institution building under inhospitable conditions—the unlikely establishment of the European Institute of Innovation and Technology. In M.H. Chou and Å. Gornitzka (Eds.), *Building the knowledge economy of Europe* (pp. 111–130). Cheltenham: Edward Elgar.

Hamilton, A.J., & Madison, J. (Eds.). (1964) [1787–88]. *The federalist papers.* New York: Pocket Books.

Hobbes, T. (1962) [1651]. *Leviathan.* London: Fontana Library.

Jepperson, R.L., & Meyer, J.W. (1991). The public order and the construction of formal organizations. In W.W. Powell and P.J. DiMaggio (Eds.), *The new institutionalism in organizational analysis* (pp. 204–231). Chicago: University of Chicago Press.

Kickert, W.J.M., & Jørgensen, T.B. (1995a). Introduction: Managerial reform trends in Western Europe. *International Review of Administrative Sciences, 61*, 499–510.

Kickert, W.J.M., & Jørgensen, T.B. (1995b). Conclusion and discussion: Management, policy, politics and public values. *International Review of Administrative Sciences, 61*, 577–586.

Kickert, W.J.M., & Van der Meer, F.B. (2011). Small, slow, and gradual reform: What can historical institutionalism teach us? *International Journal of Public Administration, 34*, 475–485.

Kuipers, B.S., Higgs, M., Kickert, W., Tummers, L., Grandia, J., & Van der Voet, J. (2014). The management of change in public organizations: A literature review. *Public Administration, 92*(1), 1–20.

Lægreid, P., & Verhoest, K. (Eds.). (2010). *Governance of public sector organizations: Proliferation, autonomy and performance.* London: Palgrave Macmillan.

March, J.G. (1981). Footnotes to organizational change. *Administrative Science Quarterly, 2*, 563–577.

March, J.G. (2010). *The ambiguities of experience.* Ithaca, NY: Cornell University Press.

March, J.G., & Olsen, J.P. (1976). *Ambiguity and choice in organizations.* Bergen: Universitetsforlaget.

March, J.G., & Olsen, J.P. (1983). Organizing political life: What administrative reorganization tells us about government. *American Political Science Review, 77*, 281–297.

March, J.G., & Olsen, J.P. (1984). The new institutionalism: Organizational factors in political life. *American Political Science Review, 78*, 734–749.

March, J.G., & Olsen, J.P. (1989). *Rediscovering institutions: The organizational basis of politics.* New York: Free Press.

March, J.G., & Olsen, J.P. (1995). *Democratic governance.* New York: Free Press.

March, J.G., & Olsen, J.P. (1998). The institutional dynamics of international political orders. *International Organizations, 52*(4), 943–969.

March, J.G., & Olsen, J.P. (2006). Elaborating the 'new institutionalism'. In R.A.W. Rhodes, S.A. Binder and B.A. Rockman (Eds.), *The Oxford handbook of political institutions* (pp. 3–20). Oxford: Oxford University Press.

March, J.G., & Simon, H.A. (1958). *Organizations.* 2nd edition 1993. New York and Cambridge, MA: Wiley and Blackwell.

Merton, R.K. (1942). A note on science and technology in a democratic order. *Journal of Legal and Political Sociology, 1*(1–2), 115–126.

Meyer, J.W., & Rowan, B. (1977). Institutionalized organizations: Formal structure as myth and ceremony. *American Journal of Sociology, 83*, 340–363.

Mill, J.S. (1962) [1861]. *Considerations on representative government.* South Bend: Gateway.

Olsen, J.P. (1992). Analysing institutional dynamics. *Staatswissenschaften und Statspraxis, 2*, 247–271.

Olsen, J.P. (1997). Institutional design in democratic contexts. *The Journal of Political Philosophy, 5*(3), 203–229.

Olsen, J.P. (2002). Reforming European institutions of governance. *Journal of Common Market Studies, 40*(4), 581–602.

Olsen, J.P. (2006). Maybe it is time to rediscover bureaucracy? *Journal of Public Administration Research and Theory, 16*(1), 1–24.

Olsen, J.P. (2007). *Europe in search for political order.* Oxford: Oxford University Press.

Olsen, J.P. (2008). The ups and downs of bureaucratic organization. *Annual Review of Political Science, 11*, 13–37.

Olsen, J.P. (2009a). Change and continuity: An institutional approach to institutions of democratic government. *European Political Science Review, 1*(1), 3–32.

Olsen, J.P. (2009b). Democratic government, institutional autonomy and the dynamics of change. *West European Politics, 32*(3), 439–465.

Olsen, J.P. (2010). *Governing through institution building: Institutional theory and recent European experiments in democratic organization.* Oxford: Oxford University Press.

Olsen, J.P. (2014). Accountability and ambiguity. In M. Bovens, R.E. Goodin and T. Schillemans (Eds.), *The Oxford handbook of public accountability* (pp. 106–123). Oxford: Oxford University Press.

Orren, K., & Skowronek, S. (2004). *The search for American political development.* Cambridge: Cambridge University Press.

Osborne, D., & Gaebler, T. (1992). *Reinventing government: How the entrepreneurial spirit is transforming the public sector.* Reading, MA: Addison-Wesley.

Peters, B.G. (2012). *Institutional theory in political science: The new institutionalism.* 3rd revised edition. New York: Continuum.

Pollitt, C., & Bouckaert, G. (2011). *Public management reform: A comparative analysis—NPM, governance and the Neo-Weberian state.* 3rd edition. Oxford: Oxford University Press.

Rhodes, R.A.W., Binder, S.A., & Rockman, B.A. (Eds.). (2006). *The Oxford handbook of political institutions.* Oxford: Oxford University Press.

Sejersted, F. (2005). *Sosialdemokratiets tidsalder. Norge og Sverige i det 20. århundre.* Oslo: Pax.

Selznick, P. (1957). *Leadership in administration.* New York: Harper & Row.

Toonen, T.A.J. (2012). Administrative reform: Analytics. In B.G. Peters and J. Pierre (Eds.), *The Sage handbook of public administration* (pp. 565–576). 2nd edition. Los Angeles: Sage.

Verhoest, K., & Lægreid, P. (2010). Organizing public sector agencies: Challenges and reflections. In P. Lægreid and K. Verhoest (Eds.), *Governance of public sector organizations: Proliferation, autonomy and performance* (pp. 276–297). London: Palgrave Macmillan.

Weaver, R.K., & Rockman, B.A. (Eds.). (1993). *Do institutions matter? Government capabilities in the United States and abroad.* Washington, DC: Brookings.

Weber, M. (1978). In G. Roth and C. Wittich (Eds.), *Economy and society.* Berkeley: University of California Press.

3   A Transformative Perspective

Tom Christensen and Per Lægreid

Introduction

Public reform processes are often characterized by complexity and hybridity in terms of the problems they address, the solutions they offer and the actors involved (Pollitt & Bouckaert, 2011). This applies particularly to broad reforms encompassing whole political-administrative systems that may include cross-sectoral and multi-level features, particularly if they are related to 'wicked issues' such as immigration, poverty,. internal security and public health (Christensen & Lægreid, 2011). Such reforms will involve many diverse actors as well as complex goal structures, problems and solutions, uncertain means-ends relations and ambiguous values, resulting in prolonged decision-making trajectories. Often, these types of reforms are also hybrid, meaning that complexity is compounded by inconsistency. They typically have to address permanent tensions between centralization and decentralization, between coordination and specialization, between integration and fragmentation and among efficiency, fairness and resilience (Hood, 1991). Normally, there are no optimal solutions to such tensions. One has to accept trade-offs that are subject to contextual constraints in systems with conflicting principles of organization. Compound and composite administrative reforms are multi-dimensional and represent mixed, coexisting orders that balance interests, values and power relations (Olsen, 2010).

To analyze complex and hybrid reforms, we need analytical tools that can grasp this type of dynamic. One such analytical point of departure is organizational theory, which encompasses instrumental and institutional elements (Peters, 2012; Olsen, this volume). A transformative approach builds on such a basis and examines how environmental factors, polity features and cultural factors constrain and enable active and deliberate administrative reform processes and designs (Christensen & Lægreid, 2001, 2007; Christensen, Lægreid, Roness & Røvik, 2009). The transformative elements are the result of the interaction of environmental features, internal administrative cultural features and structural constraints and in a dynamic way transcend the established structures and cultures. These features represent broad sets of contexts that allow us to understand reform processes and effects in different ways. A transformative approach applies a meso-level theoretical approach, which is an intermediate perspective between a macro-level generic approach and a micro-level individual approach. Meso-level theory focuses on organizations as intermediate bodies situated between individuals and the overall political-administrative system. Such an approach accounts for contextual features and presupposes that organizations have institutional features, meaning that the organizations do not simply or straightforwardly adapt easily to either new governance signals from political and administrative executives or to new external pressures. In studying public decision-making processes in general and reform processes more specifically, this approach accounts for the various contextual features (Christensen & Lægreid, 2013). There is no single best theory to explain reform processes and effects in all situations, at all times and everywhere (Pollitt, 2004). We therefore combine structural, cultural and environmental perspectives as our set of contextual factors.

Accordingly, the following research questions will be emphasized: what are the major elements and dynamics of the transformative approach? How can we use this approach to empirically examine public reforms? What are examples from different countries of the use of this approach?

A Transformative Approach

Our point of departure is that the organizational and institutional dynamics of reforms can best be understood and interpreted as a complex mixture of environmental pressure, historical institutional context and polity features (Christensen & Lægreid, 2001). These factors define the leeway or constraints that political and administrative leaders face in adopting and implementing reforms. They can both further and hinder reforms, resulting in complex and changing patterns of influence, learning and effects.

Environmental Pressure

One school of thought regards the implementation of modern reforms primarily as a response to *external pressure*. Pressure from the environment can in some cases be rather deterministic (Olsen, 1992), whereby the reform is a collection of ideas that have survived selection processes and, therefore, proven their strength. In other cases, the leadership is able to influence, shape and handle reforms rather easily. Here, pressure can come either from the technical or from the institutional environment; in the latter case, myths and symbols in the environment exert pressure on countries and public organizations to act in a manner regarded as appropriate and hence taken for granted (Meyer & Rowan, 1977). The institutional environment addresses the world of ideas and dominating values in the environment. In contrast to this soft world of fads and rituals, the technical environment is more the hard-core instrumental environment related to technological

Table 3.1 Types of environmental pressure related to reforms

	Technical environment	*Institutional environment*
Strong pressure	Deterministic adaptation	Isomorphic adaptation (coercive, normative, mimetic)
Weaker pressure	Optional and negotiable adaptation	Pragmatic adaptation from different organizational fields

features, financial and economic conditions and market pressure (Meyer & Rowan, 1977) (see table 3.1).

'Deterministic adaptation' reflects the 'there is no alternative' (TINA) argument. It is characterized by adaptation to strong actors in the technical 'task environment', actors upon which one is rather dependent (Thompson, 1967). An example of this is New Zealand's introduction of NPM as a response to financial crises and market pressure (Aberbach & Christensen, 2001).

Isomorphic adaptation is similar in that the environmental pressure is also strong, but the adaptation is informed more by myths, symbols, fads and fashions coming from the environment. DiMaggio and Powell (1983) distinguish between coercive normative and mimetic isomorphy. This type of adaptation is presented as modern and rational and uses 'window-dressing' and 'image-building' at 'front-stage' with a view to increasing leaders' legitimacy without actually changing much of the instrumental activities within the organizations involved. Brunsson (1989) labels such a strategy, involving loose coupling between 'talk' and action, 'double-talk' or 'hypocrisy'. Although public organizations may differ considerably internally, they appear outwardly similar because they display the same types of myths, symbols or fashions.

Optional or negotiable adaptation means that the technical pressure to reform is not particularly strong, implying stronger internal actors, and can hence be decided on and negotiated in different ways, leading to a broader spectrum of reform implementation (March & Olsen, 1983). Reforms can be negotiated and compromises reached across levels and sectors. The difference between this type and a deterministic adaptation is that the former often involves compromises and is hence less clear, but it will often also lead to more legitimacy because more people participate in the reform process (Mosher, 1967).

Pragmatic adaptation means that the pressure from the institutional environment is not very strong. Instead of isomorphic adaptation to strong environmental pressure driven by broad myths, organizational leaders can choose narrower reform elements from different organizational fields, pragmatically opt for some but not others, and edit or translate them in different ways, thus creating variety and using what Røvik (2002) labels institutional standards or recipes. This type of reform may encompass broad families of reform elements with internal variety.

Cultural Factors

Another view holds that reforms are primarily a product of the *national historical-institutional context and traditions*. Different countries have different historical-cultural traditions, and their reforms are 'path dependent', meaning that national reforms have unique features that are influenced by the normative context that became established in institutions' formative years (Krasner, 1988; March & Olsen, 1989). The paths to reform that are taken reflect the main features of national institutional processes, where cultural 'roots' determine the path or route followed, in a gradual adaptation to internal pressure and pressure from the local 'task environment' (Selznick, 1957). This view emphasizes institutional autonomy and internal values and dynamics over external pressure and tends to predict small, slow and gradual reforms (Kickert & Van der Meer, 2011).

When public organizations are exposed to reform processes, the reforms are subject to a cultural compatibility test. The greater the consistency between the values underlying the reforms and the informal norms and values of the existing administrative system, the more likely the reforms are to be successfully implemented (Brunsson & Olsen, 1993). The institutional leadership may have a divided role in reforms. On the one hand, it will have to carry the 'historical baggage' or 'administer the necessities of history' (March, 1994), meaning being sensitive to cultural traditions and guarding and furthering historical paths. On the other hand, leaders will participate in gradually changing cultural traditions to adapt to a new and changed environment and context. This endeavor may involve critical elements such as mission statements, the embodiment of purpose activities, the socialization and training of new members of an organization and changing the attitudes of existing ones (Selznick, 1957).

A distinction can be drawn between societal culture and administrative/organizational culture (Verhoest, 2011). Societal culture might include egalitarian or elitist dimensions, individualism or collectivism (Hofstede, 2001). An administrative culture may be based either on the Germanic '*Rechtsstaat*' culture based on bureaucratic merit, on the entrepreneurial and pluralist Anglo-American culture or on the patronage-based Mediterranean culture (Ongaro, 2009). A further option is the Scandinavian tradition, with a strong welfare state orientation (Painter & Peters, 2010). Thus, national distinctiveness is important (Kickert, 2008). Cultural features may also either reflect polity features or modify their effect. The strength of the pressure from the cultural factors depends not only on how consistent the pressure from different broader or narrower cultural features is but also on how compatible the cultural constraints are with the reforms or policy means and measures.

Polity Features

A further dimension along which countries differ is their *constitutional arrangements and political-administrative structures*, factors that help to explain how they handle reform processes (Weaver & Rockman, 1993; Olsen & Peters, 1996). The main features of the polity, the election system, the form of government and the formal structure of decision-making within the political-administrative system and arrangements with stakeholders in the private sector (corporatism) may all influence a country's capacity to adopt and implement public reforms (Christensen, 2003). Accordingly, it is assumed that political and administrative leaders will use the structural design of public entities to fulfill public goals (Egeberg, 2012). Major preconditions for this are that the leaders have a relatively large degree of control over change or reform processes, including implementation, and that they score high on rational calculation or means-ends thinking (Dahl & Lindblom, 1953; Aberbach & Christensen, 2014). There are two major versions of this view—a hierarchical one and a negotiational one—with the former emphasizing an unambiguous command structure and clear goals, while the latter focuses on heterogeneity and conflicts and negotiations between different interests (March & Olsen, 1983).

Complex and Dynamic Logic of Actions

Political and administrative leaders have varying amounts of leeway to launch and implement reforms via administrative design and an active administration policy. This is related to the dynamic context or constraints stipulated by the components of the transformative approach. Leaders' identities, resources and capacity for rational calculation and political control are constrained by environmental, historical-institutional and polity features, in dynamic combinations. Thus, adaptation to external pressure is not only a matter of environmental determinism but may also have intentional elements connected to the actions of the political-administrative leadership, professional groups or consulting firms that 'certify' certain 'prescriptions', represent 'double-talk' or 'hypocrisy' or engage in negotiations (Brunsson, 1989). Public leaders' conscious national application of internationally inspired reforms can, however, mean that only selected reform elements are imitated instead of entire reform packages (often labelled 'institutional standards'), leading to variation across countries (Røvik, 2002). Furthermore, the political ability to control reform processes can be affected by polity and structural factors such that the political leadership's capacity and attention can either be enhanced or hindered by negotiation processes or by a lack of compatibility with historical-institutional norms (Brunsson & Olsen, 1993; Christensen & Peters, 1999).

While nationally based reforms have unique features, they are also influenced by international trends. The main reform ideas, solutions, methods of implementation and practice coming from outside change when they encounter different political-administrative and historical-cultural contexts. A type of 'editing' of reform ideas occurs as they are put into operation and come face to face with existing national ideas and practice

(Sahlin-Andersson, 1996); alternatively, a reform 'virus' manages to penetrate a country's administration only after a certain period of time (Røvik, 2011).

Thus, the transformative approach is not merely a matter of combining and blending different perspectives but also concerns *translation*: co-evolution, dynamic interplay and processes of mutual dependency among reforms, structural features and culture and environmental pressure. The reforms are constrained by structural, cultural and environmental features, but they may equally contribute to changing such features. Reforming the public administration is a twofold process in which it is important to draw a clear distinction between reforms and their determinants (cf. Jacobsson, Lægreid & Pedersen, 2004). Reforms are both a product of cultural, structural and environmental features and a cause of changes in those features. Translation transforms both what is translated and those who translate it (Lægreid & Roness, 1999). There are co-evolutionary and mutually affecting processes. National administrations have the potential to transform reform ideas in widely different ways. Some of these may be regarded as strategic adaptations (Oliver, 1991), others as determined by the situation or the process, while still others may be seen as an expression of how robust existing administrations are.

Context is important in a transformative approach (Christensen & Laegreid, 2013). One important contextual feature is tasks. The type of task is primarily a structural variable, but it can also be a cultural variable, whereby certain traditions or norms exist that determine how public tasks are performed (Christensen et al., 2009). It is an example of a more specific contextual feature. The type of tasks might be understood as a moderator affecting the response of executives to external pressure. At one extreme, reform or change may be furthered by a combination of diffuse tasks with low salience and visibility of effects that are performed over a long period of time and are small in scale. Reforms and change will be much more difficult to implement, by contrast, if tasks are salient, have specific and visible effects, are performed over a short period of time and are very broad and ambitious.

A transformative approach denies both the optimistic position that willful political reform actors have full, comprehensive insight into and power over reform processes and the fatalistic position that they have no ability to influence reforms through political choice (Olsen, 1992; Olsen & Peters, 1996; Lægreid & Roness, 1999). Instead, it offers an intermediate position. Political and administrative executives are assured a degree of maneuverability, but their influence is constrained by environmental factors, polity features and historical-institutional context. The transformative approach adds complexity and hybridity to our understanding of administrative reform processes and transcends established structures and cultures, which makes the story less elegant, although more realistic.

Using the Transformative Approach to Analyze Public Sector Reforms

A transformative approach can be applied in three different ways, reflecting different analytical-methodological perspectives. First, we can begin with international doctrines, ideas and reform movements and examine how they are filtered, modified, translated and interpreted by two national processes: domestic political-administrative culture and instrumental choices made by political and managerial executives (Olsen, 1992). Second, we can focus on administrative reforms as a complex interaction among various structural, cultural and environmental features that might constrain and enable deliberate design on the part of actors. Beginning with design and conscious reforms, one can examine how they are transformed when they encounter cultural constraints and external pressure. Third, one can take cultural features as a starting point and examine how the conditions emphasized within the other perspectives (instrumental design and external pressure) are translated and filtered within established norms and rules.

The different components of the transformative approach can work together and influence one another in a supplementary manner, meaning both giving partial explanation on different aspects of the reforms and having different interpretations of the entire set of reforms (Christensen et al., 2009). If we begin with *environmental factors,* we can, in principle, first study the sources of environmental pressure, such as international organizations and consulting firms as carriers of reform ideas (Sahlin-Andersson, 2001). However, one can also study the environmental pressure from the receiving end by considering how various countries or individual public organizations respond to that pressure.

If one combines these two sources of information, it is possible to answer many important questions with different types of data. First, one can study whether external pressure is technical or institutional. Is it related to mandatory changes in hierarchical relationships? Second, it is crucial to study the timing and spread of reforms. Is it possible to identify the source(s) of the pressure and to trace how reform solutions or concepts are spread across and within countries and organizations (Sahlin-Andersson & Engwall, 2002)? Have these concepts spread slowly or rapidly, where have they spread, and have they changed in the process (Czarniawska & Sevon, 1996)? Third, one may study the content of the environmental pressure exerted on countries or individual public organizations. How are international or national concepts received and handled? Are they accepted, but kept at the top of the organization as symbolic features (Brunsson, 1989)? Are they implemented with instrumental effects (Pollitt & Bouckaert, 2011)?

Turning to the *cultural factors,* they can be of two types: national cultural historical traditions or trajectories or administrative-cultural factors more related to specific public organizations. The main data sources revealing the importance of these factors are historical accounts of the development, trajectories and path-dependencies of cultures and identities (Painter & Peters, 2010; Verhoest, 2011). What is unique and typical of the culture of a national system or individual public organizations? These can be either academic or professional accounts or accounts from leaders who have had long careers in public organizations, enabling them to trace historical-cultural paths of development. When we focus on historical-cultural paths, we are able to study whether these paths are characterized by continuity over time, whether elements are eventually added or removed, whether critical junctures lead in new directions, whether they are homogeneous paths or characterized by heterogeneity and sub-cultures and what the main driving forces behind them are. Path dependency might matter (Krasner, 1988), as might layering, displacement, drift and convergence (Mahoney & Thelen, 2010).

When we consider cultural factors, it is also important to discuss the dynamics between environmental pressure and cultural features. Does strong technical environmental pressure change cultural features? Do political and administrative leaders have more leeway in adapting to this type of pressure? Do reform myths or standards from the institutional environment contribute to changing internal culture or will they support or further existing cultural features? The relevant sources for revealing such dynamics are national political and administrative leaders and their experiences and views on the interaction between environmental pressure and cultural development.

The third set of factors in the transformative perspective is *polity features*. Overall, what is the relevance for a reform trajectory of the type of political system, the election system and the number of and balance between political parties? What is the relevance for reform processes of how the relationship between the political and administrative leadership is organized? What are the implications of the degree of homogeneity in the administrative system? Overall, one can conclude that Anglo-Saxon systems with their 'elective dictatorships' will have more capacity and potential control in adopting and implementing reforms than non-Westminster systems with several parties or different types of presidential systems (Hood, 1996).

It is also important to examine the dynamics between polity factors and environmental and cultural factors. Overall, a political system of the Westminster type, in which there is a close relationship between the political and administrative leadership and the administrative apparatuses are homogeneous, will more easily integrate and implement reforms coming from the technical and institutional environments because such systems potentially score high on capacity and control (Pollitt & Bouckaert, 2011). Such features may be strengthened if reformers are able to control or divert environmental pressure and avoid internal cultural resistance. By contrast, adopting and implementing reforms is supposedly most problematic in non-Westminster systems with complicated coalition features, a high degree of negotiation among political and administrative leaders and with civil service unions, cultural and structural heterogeneity, cultural resistance and a lack of control over external reform symbols.

Examples of the Relevance of the Transformative Approach

Three types of examples of how the transformative approach can be applied will be discussed in the following: first, the general spread of NPM and post-NPM as major reform waves; second, a comparative example of this spreading process; and, third, some specific examples from the Norwegian reform context.

General Spread of Reforms

Our point of departure is NPM as a global reform movement that began in the 1980s. It was inspired by a broad neo-liberal ideology and a particular set of economic theories and normative values, the main focus of which was on increasing efficiency (Boston, Martin, Pallot & Walsh, 1996). However, the process of reform has not been the same everywhere. Whereas some countries may have mainly used NPM ideas from outside, in others, the reform process might have resulted more from national or local initiatives that subsequently acquired an NPM label (Pollitt & Bouckaert, 2011; Lægreid, 2015). Thus, the spread of NPM, as well as of subsequent post-NPM reforms, is understood as a complex process going through different stages and packaged in different ways in different countries, with each country following its own reform trajectory within a broader framework (Christensen & Lægreid, 2011).

NPM originated in certain Anglo-Saxon countries and international organizations, such as the Organization for Economic Co-operation and Development (OECD), where a type of reform myth took hold, became ideologically dominant and diffused across the globe (Meyer & Rowan, 1977; Czarniawska & Sevon, 1996). This diffusion process implied isomorphic elements—i.e., it created pressure for similar reforms and structural changes in many countries (DiMaggio & Powell, 1983). Isomorphism can be seen as a deterministic, natural process engendered by dominant and shared norms and values. NPM may also be regarded as the optimal solution to widespread technical problems—i.e., it is adopted to solve problems created by a lack of instrumental performance or by economic competition and market pressure. In this instance, NPM reforms are adopted not because of their ideological hegemony but because of their technical efficiency.

Myths and diffusion are associated not only with NPM reforms but also with post-NPM reforms. The counter-myths that attracted support for a new generation of reforms highlighted the negative aspects of NPM, contending that NPM had undermined the welfare state, benefited few people, weakened political control, created mistrust, reduced legitimacy and produced ambiguity and less transparency (Christensen & Lægreid, 2007). The images associated with the 'whole-of-government' or 'joined-up government' initiatives that have characterized post-NPM reforms readily bring to mind the idea of repairing and reassembling something that is broken, has fallen apart or become fragmented (Gregory, 2003). The advantages of an integrated governmental apparatus are taken for granted.

Some studies construe post-NPM reforms as a return to the cultural norms and values of the traditional Weberian and centralized system, while others emphasize that NPM has created a new trajectory that makes it difficult to return to the 'good old days'—i.e., NPM has a constraining effect on post-NPM reforms (Christensen & Lægreid, 2007). There is also a co-evolution between administrative reform and administrative culture. In the first instance, the domestic administrative culture may constrain reform processes, whereas in the second instance, the reforms may strike back and change the administrative culture. It is also important to analyze whether some countries have consciously redesigned cultural features as a part of post-NPM reforms, while paying less attention to other reform features.

Will the distinction between Westminster and non-Westminster systems also explain national differences in post-NPM reforms? Will trail-blazing NPM countries find it easier to reverse course and impose centralizing and coordinative reforms, or will such features explain why post-NPM reforms have not been more extreme? Will Scandinavian countries, having long been hesitant to implement NPM reforms, continue further down that path than the trailblazers, simply because they have finally committed themselves to doing so? Alternatively, will they find it easier to reverse course because the NPM measures implemented have not yet become entrenched and are thus more easily abandoned in favor of post-NPM reforms?

A Comparative Example

Comparing briefly the development of modern reforms in Norway, Sweden, Australia and New Zealand reveals both similarities and differences (Christensen & Lægreid, 2001, 2007). Whereas Norway and Sweden belong to a Scandinavian reform trajectory of laggards, maintainers or modernizers, New Zealand and Australia are more radical NPM frontrunners (Christensen & Lægreid, 2001). Environmental characteristics raise questions concerning turbulence and insecurity that create a need for substantial changes in the public sector or lead to the adoption of international myths of modernity. Apparently, New Zealand and, to a somewhat lesser extent, Australia felt that they were experiencing an economic crisis in the early 1980s, and that facilitated pressing for comprehensive civil service reforms intended to roll back the state (Evans, Grimes, Wilkinson & Teece, 1996). Sweden also experienced a fiscal crisis, but it came later and was not as strong as those in Australia and New Zealand. The answer in Sweden was to modernize the state and to make it more efficient rather than to minimize it (Pollitt & Bouckaert, 2011).

The economic crisis in New Zealand posed a need for reform that had been accumulated but not met during Muldoon's tenure as prime minister (Massey, 1995). The pressure from the environment was defined as deterministic, in a sort of 'worst case scenario' thinking. In Australia, it was argued that without major surgery, the country would end up as a banana republic (Campbell & Halligan, 1992). In addition, being a member of the family of Anglo-American countries may have made it easier for Australia and New Zealand to imitate or build on some reform elements from the US and Britain (Hood, 1996). In Norway, there was no obvious economic crisis that could legitimate comprehensive public reforms.

What was the role of the cultural-institutional tradition—i.e., the norms and values that characterize the political-administrative system (March & Olsen, 1989)? The historical-institutional context in Norway and Sweden is characterized by a strong statist tradition, normative homogeneity, egalitarian and collectivistic values, mutual trust between political and administrative leaders, incremental changes, the balancing of many considerations, a de-emphasis on economic factors in the civil service and a policy style of peaceful co-operation and revolution in slow motion (Olsen, Roness & Saeten, 1982; Olsen, 1996; Christensen & Peters, 1996). All this suggests that NPM will be implemented more slowly, reluctantly and in a modified form because of a lack of cultural compatibility.

New Zealand is also a relatively small country, building on some of the same values as Norway, with the state as a collective vehicle for popular action; however, the former is likely more polarized and culturally heterogeneous, and its statist tradition has weakened since the 1980s with stronger elitist and individualistic values (Boston et al., 1996). This leaves us with a somewhat mixed picture: on the one hand, long-term cultural incompatibility with NPM and on the other, a system that, from a short-term perspective, is becoming more culturally receptive to NPM reforms.

Australia also has a statist tradition, but it is a larger, federative and more heterogeneous one, with much more varied cultural traditions and a greater degree of tension between political and administrative leaders, making it more likely that certain parts of the system will be compatible with NPM-oriented reforms. In contrast to Norway, mistrust characterized the relationship of the Labour governments in Australia and New Zealand with their civil servants for periods in the 1970s.

In contrast to the public interest culture and confrontational style of the Anglo-American reform movement vis-à-vis interest groups, the Norwegian and Swedish policy style was traditionally more legalistic and *Rechtsstaat*-oriented and was distinguished by co-operation and mutual understanding in a tripartite collaboration. Traditionally, Norway and Sweden have been described as archetypes of a corporate-pluralistic state (Olsen, 1983); however, traditional co-operative, corporatist arrangements and close links between the labour parties and the trade unions were also politically important in Australia and New Zealand.

The four countries also differ in the characteristics of their polities. The two-party Westminster system used in Australia and New Zealand made the forceful implementation of reforms more likely than in Norway and Sweden, where the multi-party system and minority governments tended to result in negotiations and parliamentary turbulence (Christensen & Peters, 1999). In addition, the Westminster system likely also offers greater opportunity for strong political leaders to act as reform entrepreneurs than the multi-party system in Norway and Sweden, with its formally weaker prime minister. In contrast to the other three countries, Australia has a federative system. Federalism may modify features of the Westminster system and implies parallel systems that both compete with and imitate one another, thus leading to substantial variety and a greater possibility of reform from below rather than from above.

Combining the three sets of independent variables in the transformative approach may highlight some variety among the four countries. New Zealand has taken the most dramatic NPM reform path because of a combination of an economic crisis and elective dictatorship (Mulgan, 1992), whereas the cultural tradition has made the journey less understandable and more problematic in some ways. In Australia, the NPM reforms emerged against a background of tension and conflict between political leaders and the civil service and experimentation with reform in some states, forcefully led by the prime minister as a political entrepreneur (Campbell & Halligan, 1992). However, the road taken was a more cautious one than in New Zealand because of greater heterogeneity and corporatist features. In Sweden, the process of public management reforms has been incremental but continuous since the early 1980s, and in the 1990s the emphasis shifted toward increasing organizational autonomy and saving public expenditures, a development intensified by the financial crises of the early 1990s. In Norway, NPM reforms were introduced late and in an incremental and reluctant way because of low cultural compatibility and relatively weak political-instrumental power, which made civil servants more important change agents than political leaders (Christensen, 2003). The diversity of the post-NPM processes has similar features to NPM.

Contemporary Norwegian Reforms

The third set of examples relates to two comprehensive contemporary public reforms in Norway, which have combined NPM and post-NPM features in a complex and hybrid manner. How can these reforms be related to the transformative approach?

The 2002 *hospital reform* combined three different and partly inconsistent elements. The central government took over ownership of the hospitals from the counties, a typical post-NPM feature, but authority was then decentralized and delegated to regional and local health authorities, and daily activities have many performance management features. The latter two reform elements were thus typical NPM, reflecting a compromise. Actors desiring more centralization and professional leadership because regional hospital processes were too political gained more influence, but this was balanced by a greater regional and local focus on efficiency and the retention of strong professional groups in the hospitals (Lægreid, Opedal & Stigen, 2005).

The *welfare administration reform* was decided in 2005 and implemented through 2010, but revised in 2008. The major features of the reform that merged the central employment and pension agencies and established a partnership arrangement with locally based social services in an effort to make a central and local hierarchy collaborate were both typical post-NPM endeavors. The original reform proposed strong local offices with 'one door' (also known as a one-stop shop), whereas the reorganization moved resources to the regional level, made the pension administration more separate and addressed economies of scale, professional quality, impartiality and the rights of clients. The reform was influenced by international post-NPM trends but was more internally anchored. Uncharacteristically, it was initiated by the parliament, because the services were too fragmented, but the political-administrative leadership was opposed to it and attempted to prevent it. A new minister, the reform entrepreneur, made a compromise; his solution was partial, an effort to make both the central and local authorities happy. The reform represented a new path that was partly revised back toward the old one (Christensen, Fimreite & Lægreid, 2013).

Conclusion

A transformative approach implies that we have to use three sets of explanatory factors to understand the development of reform processes—environmental, cultural and polity. In a dynamic interaction, these factors explain why reform initiatives and implementations differ around the world (Christensen & Lægreid, 2001; Pollitt, Van Thiel & Homburg, 2007; Pollitt & Bouckaert, 2011). Thus, diverse empirical realities contrast with ideas of 'generic' public management, 'global recipes' and simple models of administrative reforms. The organization of the public administration is becoming increasingly complex and multi-functional, even hybrid, with different organizational principles resulting from multiple contextual factors working together in a complex mix (Christensen & Lægreid, 2007; Lægreid & Verhoest, 2010; Olsen, 2010).

We cannot take it for granted that leaders, as reform entrepreneurs, have sufficient resources, cognitive capacity or power to act as rational actors. Often, their attempts at organizational design are constrained by various polity, culture and environmental features. We support the claim that context matters (March, 2008), but there is still no good theory of contextual factors that specifies the conditions under which different contexts matter (Pollitt, 2003). It is challenging to explain how complex and hybrid institutions and reforms based on mixed political orders and partly competing organizational principles can be understood (Olsen, 2010). Rather than decontextualized generic theories, we need theories of the middle-range that account for cultural trajectories, polity features and environmental constraints.

Administrative reforms must be matched carefully with the needs, traditions and resources of each political system (Olsen, 2006). Reforms that do not take the historical institutional context into consideration tend to produce new reforms rather than increased performance. Our argument is that global myths or prescriptions for administrative reforms have been interpreted and responded to differently depending on national and sector-specific institutional arrangements and historical traditions (Lægreid & Verhoest, 2010). In recent years, the enthusiasm for some of the NPM-related reforms has gradually waned. There has been a rediscovery of historical-institutional context and the Neo-Weberian state (Olsen, 2006; Pollitt & Bouckaert, 2011). This development signals a need to take the domestic administrative and institutional context into consideration when designing and implementing administrative reforms.

References

Aberbach, J.D., & Christensen, T. (2001). Radical reform in New Zealand: Crisis, window of opportunity and rational actors. *Public Administration, 79*(2), 403–422.

Aberbach, J.D., & Christensen, T. (2014). Why reforms so often disappoint. *American Review of Public Administration, 44*(1), 3–16.

Boston, J., Martin, J., Pallot, J., & Walsh, P. (1996). *Public management: The New Zealand model*. Auckland: Oxford University Press.

Brunsson, N. (1989). *The organization of hypocrisy*. Chichester: Wiley.

Brunsson, N., & Olsen, J.P. (1993). *The reforming organization*. London: Routledge.

Campbell, C., & Halligan, J. (1992). *Political leadership in an age of constraints*. Pittsburgh: University of Pittsburgh Press.

Christensen, T. (2003). Narrative of Norwegian governance: Elaborating the strong state. *Public Administration, 14*(4), 163–190.

Christensen, T., Fimreite, A.L., & Lægreid, P. (2013). Joined-up government for welfare administration reform in Norway. *Public Organization Review*, online first.

Christensen, T., & Lægreid, P. (2011). Complexity and hybrid public administration—theoretical and empirical challenges. *Public Organization Review, 11*, 407–423.

Christensen, T., & Lægreid, P. (2013). Context and administrative reforms—a transformative approach. In C. Pollitt (Ed.), *Context in public policy and management: The missing link?* (pp. 131–156). Cheltenham: Edward Elgar.

Christensen, T., & Lægreid, P. (Eds.). (2001). *The new public management: The transformation of ideas and practice*. Aldershot: Ashgate.

Christensen, T., & Lægreid, P. (Eds.). (2007). *Transcending new public management: The transformation of public sector reforms*. Aldershot: Ashgate.

Christensen, T., Lægreid, P., Roness, P.G., & Røvik, K.A. (2009). *Organization theory and the public sector*. London: Routledge.

Christensen, T., & Peters, B.G. (1999). *Structure, culture and governance: A comparative analysis of Norway and the United States*. Lanham, MD: Rowman & Littlefield.

Czarniawska, B., & Sevon, G. (Eds.). (1996). *Translating organizational change*. Berlin: Walter de Gruyter.

Dahl, R.A., & Lindblom, C.E. (1953). *Politics, economics, and welfare*. New York: Harper & Row.

DiMaggio, P.J., & Powell, W.W. (1983). The iron cage revisited: Institutional isomorphism and collective rationality in organizational fields. *American Sociological Review, 48*(2), 147–160.

Egeberg, M. (2012). How bureaucratic structure matters: An organizational perspective. In B.G. Peters and J. Pierre (Eds.), *Handbook of public administration* (pp. 116–126). 2nd edition. London: Sage.

Evans, L., Grimes, A., Wilkinson, B., & Teece, D. (1996). Economic reform in New Zealand 1984–1995: The pursuit of efficiency. *Journal of Economic Literature, 34*(December), 1856–1902.

Gregory, R. (2003). All the king's horses and all the king's men: Putting New Zealand's public sector together again. *International Public Management Review, 4*(2), 41–58.

Hofstede, G. (2001). *Culture's consequences: Comparing values, behaviours, institutions and organizations across nations*. Thousand Oaks: Sage.

Hood, C. (1991). A public management for all seasons? *Public Administration, 69*(1), 3–19.

Hood, C. (1996). Exploring variations in public management reform of the 1980s. In H.A.G.M. Bekke, J.L. Perry and T.A.J. Toonen (Eds.), *Civil service systems* (pp. 268–287). Bloomington: Indiana University Press.

Jacobsson, B., Lægreid, P., & Pedersen, O.K. (2004). *Europeanization and transnational states: Comparing Nordic central governments*. London: Routledge.

Kickert, W.J.M. (Ed.). (2008). *The study of public management in Europe and the US*. London: Routledge.

Kickert, W.J.M., & Van der Meer, F.B. (2011). Small, slow, and gradual reform: What can historical institutionalism teach us? *International Review of Public Administration, 34*, 475–485.

Krasner, S. (1988). Sovereignty: An institutional perspective. *Comparative Political Studies, 21*, 66–94.

Lægreid, P. (2015). A public management for all seasons? Revisited. In E.C. Page, M. Lodge and S.J. Balla (Eds.), *The Oxford handbook of classics of public policy* (pp. 541–558). Oxford: Oxford University Press.

Lægreid, P., Opedal, S., & Stigen, I. (2005). The Norwegian hospital reform: Balancing political control and enterprise autonomy. *Journal of Health Politics, Policy and Law, 30*(6), 1035–1072.

Lægreid, P., & Roness, P.G. (1999). Administrative reform as organized attention. In M. Egeberg and P. Lægreid (Eds.), *Organizing political institutions* (pp. 301–330). Oslo: Scandinavian University Press.

Lægreid, P., & Verhoest, K. (Eds.). (2010). *Governance of public sector organizations: Proliferation, autonomy and performance*. London: Palgrave Macmillan.

Mahoney, J., & Thelen, K. (Eds.). (2010). *Explaining institutional change: Ambiguity, agency and power*. Cambridge: Cambridge University Press.

March, J.G. (1994). *A primer on decision-making*. New York: Free Press.

March, J.G. (2008). *Explorations in organizations*. Stanford: Stanford University Press.

March, J.G., & Olsen, J.P. (1983). Organizing political life: What administrative reorganization tells us about governance. *American Political Science Review, 77*(2), 281–297.

March, J.G., & Olsen, J.P. (1989). *Rediscovering institutions*. New York: Free Press.

Massey, P. (1995). *New Zealand: Market liberalization in a developed economy*. Basingstoke: Palgrave Macmillan.

Meyer, J.W., & Rowan, B. (1977). Institutionalized organizations: Formal structure as myth and ceremony. *American Journal of Sociology, 83*(September), 340–363.

Mosher, F. (Eds.). (1967). *Democracy and the public service.* New York: Oxford University Press.

Mulgan, R. (1992). The elective dictatorship in New Zealand. In H. Gold (Ed.), *New Zealand politics in perspective* (pp. 513–532). Auckland: Longman.

Oliver, C. (1991). Strategic responses to institutional processes. *Academy of Management Review, 16,* 145–179.

Olsen, J.P. (1983). The dilemmas of organizational integration in government. In J.P. Olsen (Ed.), *Organized democracy* (pp. 148–187). Bergen: Universitetsforlaget.

Olsen, J.P. (1992). Analyzing institutional dynamics. *Statswissenschaften und Staatspraxix, 2,* 247–271.

Olsen, J.P. (2006). Maybe it is time to rediscover bureaucracy. *Journal of Public Administration Research and Theory, 16*(1), 1–24.

Olsen, J.P. (2010). *Governing through institution building.* Oxford: Oxford University Press.

Olsen, J.P., & Peters, B.G. (1996). *Lessons from experience: Experimental learning in administrative reforms in eight democracies.* Oslo: Scandinavian University Press.

Olsen, J.P., Roness, P.G., & Sæten, H. (1982). Norway: Still peaceful coexistence and revolution in slow motion? In J.J. Richardson (Ed.), *Policy style in Western Europe* (pp. 47–79). London: Allen & Unwin.

Ongaro, E. (2009). *Public management reform and modernization: Trajectories of administrative reform in Italy, France, Greece, Portugal and Spain.* London: Edward Elgar.

Painter, M., & Peters, B.G. (Eds.). (2010). *Tradition and public administration.* Houndmills: Palgrave.

Peters, B.G. (2012). *Institutional theory in political science: The new institutionalism.* 3rd revised edition. New York: Continuum. 3.

Pollitt, C. (2003). *The essential public manager.* Maidenhead: Open University Press.

Pollitt, C. (2004). Theoretical overview. In C. Pollitt and C. Talbot (Eds.), *Unbundled government* (pp. 319–341). New York: Routledge.

Pollitt, C., & Bouckaert, G. (2011). *Public management reform: A comparative analysis: New public management, governance and the Neo-Weberian state.* 2nd edition. Oxford: Oxford University Press.

Pollitt, C., Van Thiel, S., & Homburg, V. (Eds.). (2007). *New public management in Europe.* Basingstoke: Palgrave.

Røvik, K.A. (2002). The secrets of the winners: Management ideas that flow. In K. Sahlin-Andersson and L. Engwall (Eds.), *The expansion of management knowledge: Carriers, flows and sources* (pp. 113–144). Stanford: Stanford University Press.

Røvik, K.A. (2011). From fashion to virus: An alternative theory of organizations' handling management ideas. *Organizational Studies, 32*(5), 631–653.

Sahlin-Andersson, K. (1996). Imitating by editing success. In B. Czarniawska and G. Sevon, (Eds.), *Translating organizational change* (pp. 69–92). New York: De Gruyter.

Sahlin-Andersson, K. (2001). National, international and transnational construction of new public management. In T. Christensen and P. Lægreid (Eds.), *New public management: The transformation of ideas and practice* (pp. 43–72). Aldershot: Ashgate.

Sahlin-Andersson, K., & Engwall, L. (2002). Carriers, flows and sources of management knowledge. In K. Sahlin-Andersson and L. Engwall (Eds.), *The expansion of management knowledge: Carriers, flows and sources* (pp. 3–32). Stanford: Stanford University Press.

Selznick, P. (1957). *Leadership in administration.* New York: Free Press.
Thompson, J.D. (1967). *Organizations in action.* New Brunswick: McGraw Hill.
Verhoest, K. (2011). The relevance of culture for NPM. In T. Christensen and P. Lægreid (Eds.), *The Ashgate research companion to new public management* (pp. 47–64). Farnham: Ashgate.
Weaver, R.K., & Rockman, B. (Eds.). (1993). *Do institutions matter?* Washington, DC: Brooking Institution.

4   A Principal-Agent Perspective

Sandra van Thiel

Introduction

Principal-agent theory is frequently used in research on public sector reforms, as it enables researchers to explain both the adoption of specific reforms, the implementation of such reforms and their ensuing success or failure (see e.g., Broadbent, Dietrich & Laughlin, 1996; Van Thiel, 2001; Thatcher & Sweet, 2002; Brown, Potoski & Van Slyke, 2007). In this chapter, I will first discuss the origins and key concepts of principal-agent theory and then apply it to a specific type of public sector reform: the creation of quasi-autonomous organizations (quangos).

However, the use of principal-agent theory in research on the public sector has not been without criticism (cf. Waterman & Meier, 1998; Laffont & Martimort, 2002; Miller, 2005). Principal-agent theory originated as an economic model developed for market situations and private organizations, and as such it does not always fit with traditions and typical characteristics of the public domain and public sector organizations. These criticisms will also be addressed in this chapter, including a number of adaptations that could or should be made when applying this perspective to the public sector and to public sector reforms.

Origins of Principal-Agent Theory

Principal-agent theory is one of the three theories in neo-institutional economics (NEI) (Gibbons & Roberts, 2012). NEI aims to predict the conditions under which the production of goods is best achieved either through the market mechanism or, when markets fail to reach an optimum, through organizations (or businesses). Particularly in the case of collective goods, markets will fail to achieve efficient and equitable production. Collective goods are goods for which exclusive production and consumption for a single buyer is not possible. The classic example is the protection that an army offers to a nation: individual citizens cannot be excluded from it, even if individuals have not paid the taxes used to fund the costs of the army. In many cases, the government has taken it upon itself—or the citizens expect it to do so—to organize and carry out the production of such goods (see De Swaan, 1988, for additional examples such as sewerage and charity services). However, this need not always be the case. Collective goods can be provided through market mechanisms, as the example of the US hiring private security companies in Iraq demonstrates. However, production of collective goods through markets requires regulation or intervention by the government. In sum, if the government does not produce collective goods by itself, it will be involved in the regulation of provision by other means, including through the market. Neo-institutional economic theories offer insights into when and how governments should choose which option.

For example, *property rights theory* offers a solution to market failure through the distribution of property rights associated with the production of goods (Jensen & Meckling, 1976). The classic example here concerns the environmental pollution that privately owned factories produce, in addition to the goods that they intend to sell in the market. By assigning the 'property right on pollution' to the private company, the company becomes responsible for the costs of cleaning the environment or the air (Coase theorem). A market for property rights has to be designed to compensate for market failures. This is where government has a role. In this example, independent agencies such as the US Environmental Protection Agency or the Dutch Emission Authority are responsible, on authority of the government, for ensuring that the collective good of a clean and healthy living environment is guaranteed for all citizens—while they can still purchase commercial goods in the market, such as clothes and cars.

Transaction cost theory (TCE), the second strand within neo-institutional economics, refers to a different mechanism (Williamson, 1979, 2005). Each transaction in the market between supply and demand parties leads to additional costs, so-called transaction costs. These are the costs of negotiations, drawing contracts, ensuring compliance with the contract, seeking information about potential suppliers and buyers, and so forth. Transaction costs are high when (1) specific assets are involved, (2) deals are struck at a high frequency, and (3) there is considerable uncertainty regarding, for example, continuity of delivery. Specific assets refer to specialist knowledge or materials that are needed for the production of goods. Not only will this influence the actual price of goods, but the need to invest in such assets creates risks for the producer (so-called sunk costs or investments), while the buyer is highly dependent on the producer because such specific assets are not widely available. Consider, for example, the rare earth metals that are necessary for the production of high-tech products; countries that possess such metals can manipulate their prices by reducing or increasing their availability. In such circumstances, transaction cost theory (Williamson, 1979, 2005) stipulates that it is more efficient for a company to 'hierarchically integrate' companies that possess these specific assets instead of purchasing them in the market. A similar mechanism can be observed in the public domain when governments have to decide whether to provide a particular service themselves or outsource it to the market (cf. the army example above). The other two conditions in the transaction cost model are high frequency and high uncertainty. Both follow a similar line of reasoning: when such costs are too high, it is more efficient to integrate than to transact in the market.

An important assumption underlying TCE in particular is Herbert Simon's concept of bounded rationality. Whereas most traditional economic theories assume that all players in a market (buyers and sellers) have full and perfect information, and can, therefore, make the optimal choice, neo-institutional economic theorists assume that the players either do not have full information or do not have the capacity to process all information. Hence, they will not always make the optimal choice. We will return to this point below.

Principal-agent theory is the third branch of NEI (Pratt & Zeckhauser, 1991; Laffont & Martimort, 2002; Besley, 2006). It describes the situation in which the production of specific goods is charged to a third party: the principal hires an agent to do the work. Originally, principal-agent theory was developed to model the relationship between shareholders and the managers of private sector companies, but real life examples also abound, for example, when one hires a builder to perform construction work on one's house (as one is unable to perform the work due to a lack of skills and/or time). Examples in the public domain will be discussed below, for example, regarding the relationship between a government or political principal (e.g., a ministry) that hires an agent (e.g., a quango) to execute a particular public task. Principals hire agents because the latter are experts that have specific knowledge (assets) required for the job and are, therefore, much better able to perform the work and do so at a more cost-efficient price. However, there are a number of assumptions underlying the principal-agent model that could make the outcomes less optimal. This will be explained in the next section, as well as some potential remedies.

Key Concepts of Principal-Agent Theory

As explained above, the core of principal-agent theory consists of a simple, dyadic model of two actors: the *principal* who hires the *agent* to perform a certain task. Together, they draw up a *contract* that stipulates under which conditions the agent will perform its task, for example, what the agent will deliver (output), when or under which conditions (time), and for what reward (budget). Principals will hire agents for those tasks that they cannot perform themselves, either because of a lack of time or priority or because of a lack of skills and expertise. The agent is an expert and, therefore, is expected to be able to do a good job and to do so for lower costs than if the principal did it himself. However, this also means that the agent has more information about the task at hand, for example, what it requires in terms of money, time and investments. This *information asymmetry* creates uncertainty with the principal: how can he be certain that agent will do a good job?

The principal's uncertainty rests on an important assumption of the theory. The reader should recall that principal-agent theory is an economic theory and, therefore, based on a model of rationality and utility maximization. Actors are assumed to pursue specific objectives; this is the principle of *opportunism*. In the principal-agent model, the objectives of the principal and the agent are assumed to be divergent: the principal wants the agent to produce as many of the required goods or services as possible for the lowest price possible, whereas the agent is expected to want to produce as little as possible for the highest possible price. This *goal divergence* creates two problems, which are exacerbated by information asymmetry.

First, how can the principal be certain that he has selected the best agent for the job? This is known as the problem of *adverse selection* and results from the fact that agents can conceal information about their (in-)competence. In a market with imperfect information, or when principals suffer from *bounded rationality*, principals cannot always make the optimal choice. (Moreover, in the public sector, many agents are monopolists, as we will see below, and hence there is often little or no choice.) The second problem arises when a principal has selected an agent and is known as *moral hazard*. It is the risk that the agent's performance is suboptimal, either because the agent has charged too high a price for his services or produces less output than possible (this is also known as shirking). Again the information asymmetry is used to conceal information from the principal, in this case regarding the agent's true performance. In both cases, the use of an agent will lead to less efficiency gains than the principal had anticipated. This loss of efficiency is known as the *residual loss*.

To remedy the information asymmetry and residual loss, principals can use two instruments: monitoring and incentives. *Monitoring* can refer both to the collection of additional information by the principal, for example, by instigating audits or external evaluations, and to imposing accountability requirements upon the agent, forcing him to deliver overviews and reports on production, budgets and so forth. The collection and processing of this information will, however, lead to more additional costs for the principal, so-called *monitoring costs*. The alternative instrument is to give *incentives* to the agent, stimulating the agent's performance and rewarding 'good' behavior (i.e., in line with the wishes of the principal). For example, the principal can allow the agent to retain a surplus of the budget that was set in the contract. This implies that the principal knows that it would have been possible to set a lower budget, but as long as the surplus is lower than the monitoring costs and residual loss would have been, this option remains the most efficient solution to the principal-agent problem.

A third 'remedy' is often mentioned, although it is technically speaking not a remedy: *bonding activities*. Agents have a strong incentive to maintain good relations with their principals, to ensure continuity in the contractual agreements and being hired to do a certain job. To this end, agents will invest in their relationship with the principal and in their own reputation as a good, or the best, agent. For example, agents may offer special deals (discounts, preferential treatment) or invest in (positive) external assessments to convince the principal of their outstanding performance. However, such activities will all lead to additional costs (*bonding costs*), which come essentially out of the budget that the principal has paid in the past and, therefore, can add to the costs mentioned thus far. However, it can be vital for an agent to engage in bonding activities, for example, when the agent has invested in specific knowledge or assets to execute the task at hand. Only new and more assignments from the principal will make such investments (or *sunk costs*) worthwhile.

Two further concepts are important here. First, residual loss, monitoring costs and bonding costs together form *agency costs*. To this we could even add the transaction costs (cf. above) that the principal will have to make to hire an agent, such as the costs of negotiating the contract. The second is *ex post haggling,* which refers to the situation in which a principal, for example, based on information obtained through monitoring, seeks to end or change a contract with an agent, potentially to negotiate a better (lower) price. (This is quite common in the public domain, as we will see below.) The existence of this risk does make agents more opportunistic; to protect themselves from potentially worse conditions, agents will have an even stronger incentive to conceal information from the principal than they did before closing a contract.

Applying Principal-Agent Theory to Public Sector Reform

Now that the key concepts of the theory have been explained, we can examine how the theory can be applied to the topic of this book: public sector reform. First, principal-agent theory can be used to *explain the adoption of certain reforms*. Consider, for example, the decision of governments to outsource or hive large numbers of tasks: this mirrors the essence of the principal's decision to hire an agent to perform a specific task. Contracting out literally implies setting up a contract to specify which task has to be performed and under which conditions. Together with the other two strands of NEI, principal-agent theory can predict, based on task characteristics, for example, whether a government will decide to contract out certain activities, as in the case of non-specific assets and low transaction costs. Simple, high-volume tasks, such as the nearly mechanical implementation of detailed policies, are one example of tasks that could easily be contracted out, as often occurs in the field of social benefits (cf. Van Thiel, 2012). However, not all predictions based on NEI have proven true thus far (see, e.g., Domberger & Jensen, 1997; Macher & Richman, 2008; Warner & Bel, 2008). This shows that the political decisions to adopt reforms are not always based on economic (rational) considerations (cf. Van Thiel, 2001; Miller, 2005).

Another example of the use of principal-agent theory when studying public sector reforms can be found in the increased use of performance indicators (Van Dooren, Bouckaert & Halligan, 2015). Performance indicators are used to many ends (Behn, 2003), to improve results, to increase transparency, to enhance motivation and to extend accountability. From a principal-agent perspective, the rise of performance measurement can be explained as an increase in monitoring, which is necessary to compensate for the loss of control by the principal as increasing numbers of tasks are performed by (quasi-independent) agents. Interestingly, there is little research on the costs of all these new monitoring devices or on what is done with the results of monitoring. Pollitt and Dan (2013) collected over 500 studies into the effects of NPM reforms in 23 countries and found that most studies were performed by academics rather than by practitioners. There appears to be a general lack of interest among governments (principal) in the performance of the agents who implement policies, deliver public services and perform public tasks. In terms of the principal-agent model, this means that information asymmetry continues to exist and can lead to moral hazard behavior and adverse selection.

A third illustration of the use of a principal-agent perspective on public sector reform concerns the structural disaggregation of units of governments— the fourth principle of NPM according to Hood (1991; cf. James & Van Thiel, 2011). These disaggregated units are usually granted a certain degree of autonomy, either legally (becoming an independent or statutory body), managerially (for example, regarding personnel and financial decisions), or both. There are many examples of such quasi-autonomous organizations, or quangos for short, such as the Non-Departmental Public Bodies in the UK, ZBOs in the Netherlands, and public establishments in France, Italy and Portugal (for an overview of 30 countries, see Verhoest, Van Thiel, Bouckaert & Lægreid, 2012). In most parliamentary democracies, quangos are managed—or steered—by parent ministries ('t Hart & Wille, 2006; Van Thiel & Yesilkagit, 2011). Only in some cases does parliament itself play a direct role, for example, in the case of the AAIs in France (Lafarge, 2012) and in case of the US (Peters, 2012). Below, I will apply the principal-agent model to the relationship between a parent ministry and a quango in the Netherlands to illustrate in greater detail how principal-agent theory can be used to study this public sector reform (cf. Van Thiel & Pollitt, 2007; James & Van Thiel, 2011; Tonkiss, Van Thiel, Verhoest & Skelcher, 2015).

Quangos were established in large numbers in the 1980s and 1990s but have existed in the Netherlands for a much longer time (Greve, Flinders & Van Thiel, 1999; Van Thiel, 2001). Under the influence of NPM, their number increased because they were expected to be able to execute public tasks in a more businesslike and hence efficient manner (Kickert, 2001). The growth in the number of quangos led to an intense political debate, in which politicians and political parties expressed dissatisfaction with their perceived loss of political and/or ministerial control, the poor quality of regulation underlying the establishment of many quangos, and the general fragmentation of the public sector, which made it difficult to oversee how many and which organizations were active in a given policy sector (Yesilkagit & Van Thiel, 2012). This dissatisfaction can be regarded as indicative of the uncertainty of a principal, as described above. Several attempts have been made to restore control, including creating a new type of quango (*agentschap*) with full ministerial accountability and a charter law for ZBOs, the most frequent type of quango at that time (circa 2000). However, considerable time was required before most ministries developed adequate instruments to fulfill their role as principal in a satisfying way—for quangos and ministries alike (evaluation studies reveal substantial friction in the relations between ministries and quangos on this topic, cf. De Leeuw, 2013).

As the principal, parent ministries are responsible for assigning a public task (policy implementation, public service delivery, regulation) to a quango and drawing up a 'contract'. These contracts have many names: covenant, letter of intent, subsidy decisions, management contract, and so forth. Unfortunately, most of these contracts have not been made public. Being a principal also includes paying the quango for services rendered and monitoring the quango and its performance to be able to make decisions on continuation of the task and the quango. Ministries are, therefore, in effect multiple principals. Most Dutch ministries currently use a model for the different roles that was originally developed for an *agentschap* in the economic policy sector but is now applied to all types of quangos. It discerns three roles for a ministry in its principal-agent relationship with quangos: the sponsor, the owner and the overseer (Van Thiel & Pollitt, 2007; Tonkiss et al., 2015). The sponsor formulates the policies that form the basis for a quango's task and negotiates the terms of the contract. The 'owner' is responsible for safeguarding the continuity of the quango and financial viability. The overseer is in charge of monitoring quangos. However, not all ministries use this model, and those ministries that do use it make different choices regarding which ministerial units are assigned which role—and whether roles are assigned to the same or different units (directorates). A few ministries have developed a document in which they describe how they have designed their relationship with quangos, and why (see, e.g., Ministry of Infrastructure and Environment). The most common model shows that the sponsor role is assigned to a policy unit, the ownership rests with a financial unit, and the overseer can be, for example, an audit unit or an independent regulator or inspectorate. Ministries also differ in their intensity of relationships: some ministries have little to no contacts; others have frequent interactions (Van Thiel, 2006; Van Thiel & Hendriks, 2014; Tonkiss et al., 2015). There are also different instruments in place, ranging from informal meetings to legislation. Commonly used instruments include performance indicators, monthly management reports, evaluations and audits. In some cases, quangos have taken it upon themselves to develop such instruments to account for their performance, as not all ministries have been equally active in monitoring them. Such activities can clearly be labeled 'bonding' but could also be interpreted as a 'reversal of control' (see below).

Quangos have no direct relations with parliament; the parent minister is held accountable in parliament. (This reflects another principal-agent relationship: between parliament and the minister. However, let us not complicate matters too much here). In the case of ZBOs, ministerial accountability is limited, although no one knows to what extent. Common practice dictates that the parent minister is responsible for the policies that a ZBO implements, the decision to charge this task to a ZBO, and for monitoring the ZBO. However, in practice, ministers can be held (politically) accountable for everything—and there are examples of political debates on issues that are likely more the responsibility of a ZBO than of a minister (such as the remodeling costs of UWV, a ZBO in charge of social benefits).

In sum, the principal-agent model can be fitted quite easily to the relationship between parent ministry and quango: the quango is the expert in performing a particular task, there is a contractual arrangement between ministry and quango and monitoring is applied to counter the loss of information resulting from the fact that quangos are autonomous and often at arm's length from the ministry. There are different types of monitoring, ranging from audits by the parent ministry, to external evaluations and inspections by independent inspectorates or regulators (often quangos themselves). Even the use of incentives can be found in this example: most ZBOs are allowed to retain their surplus, although more recently agreements have been made to prevent ZBOs from accumulating excessive capital reserves from public funds (e.g., a cap can be implemented, or existing reserves can be used to reduce tariffs for customers). Quangos have also engaged in bonding activities, as is apparent from the Charter on Public Accountability that a number of quangos have signed, agreeing to be publicly scrutinized by an independent peer review committee. The charter also prescribes a governance code to which all members have to adhere.

There are, however, considerable differences between parent ministries and how they design and maintain their relationship with quangos. Two recent reports have criticized ministries for this (POC, 2012; De Leeuw, 2013), but the highly decentralized Dutch politico-administrative system does not foster much uniformity. The Home Office has not proven particularly effective thus far in harmonizing arrangements, or even sharing information and practices—as, for example, the coordinating ministries in the UK and Flanders have been able to do (Tonkiss et al., 2015). Dutch ministries are silos; they prefer to join forces with their 'own' quangos than with other ministries (Van Ammers & Van Thiel, 2012). In the next section, we will see that this *silo-ization* can create new problems because quangos increasingly work for more than one principal.

Criticism of the Use of Principal-Agent Theory in the Public Sector

The illustrations above show that principal-agent theory offers a powerful and elegant model that can be used to explain the adoption of a specific reform (such as contracting out) and the implementation thereof (i.e., the relationship between parent ministries and quangos). Moreover, the underlying assumptions concerning rational behavior and the emphasis on efficiency and businesslike ways of working (e.g., with contracts) fit with the basic tenets of the NPM ideology that has spawned so many public management reforms (Boston, 1995). This likely also explains why scholars who study this type of reform have resorted so frequently to the principal-agent model. However, the application of principal-agent theory to the public sector is not without problems or criticism. The most generic, or paradigmatic, criticism relates to the fact that the model does not take the institutional context into account (Davis, Schoorman & Donaldson, 1997; Waterman & Meier, 1998) when predicting the behavior of decision-makers (and in aggregate form organizations). Although principal-agent theory allows certain conditions or restrictions to be included in the model, it is true that the focus is on rational decision-making with little eye for the context. However, such paradigmatic discussions are beyond the scope of this chapter. Instead, I will focus on a number of problems that can occur once a scholar has decided to apply principal-agent theory to public sector topics.

Self-Interest and Goal Divergence

Principal-agent theory is an economic model and was originally developed to model the relationship between shareholders and managers. In economic theories, the basic model of man assumes a rational actor, in pursuit of individual objectives within the boundaries of preferences, resources and constraints. Driven by this utility maximization, actors are expected to behave opportunistically, which is usually translated as self-interested behavior. Several scholars object to the idea that public servants are driven by self-interest; instead, public servants are concerned about the public or general interest, that of all citizens and society as a whole (Perry & Wise, 1990; Bozeman, 2007; Van der Wal, De Graaf & Lasthuizen, 2008). In the public domain, values such as profitability and efficiency are much less important to individuals and organizations than, for example, values such as equity and empathy. This does not mean that the mechanism of opportunism is not present in the public domain, however. James (2003), for example, demonstrated that civil servants, working in ministries, can support the structural disaggregation of government units because it enables them to focus more on the task they consider most important (policy making) while other, less important tasks (policy implementation) are hived off. However, the opportunism of public servants is directed toward goals other than profitability, the primary goal in the private sector. However, the criticism of this assumption of principal-agent theory is more profound: opponents argue that there is no goal divergence between principals and agents in the public sector. Public servants want the same thing—to serve the public's interests—as their (political) principals. If this is indeed true, the risks of moral hazard and adverse selection would be severely reduced, although not eliminated, as information asymmetry and bounded rationality continue to exist.

This criticism could be solved by using an alternative model: the principal-steward model (Schillemans, 2013). Stewardship theory is an economic theory, just like principal-agent theory, but with one important difference: the model assumes that the steward has the same objectives as the principal. It was developed by Davis et al. (1997) but has yet to be tested extensively (see Tosi, Brownlee, Silva & Katz, 2003; Van Slyke, 2007 for some exceptions). While there remains information asymmetry between a principal and a steward, the lack of goal divergence will substantially reduce the risks of adverse selection and moral hazard. Hence, there would also be less need to impose monitoring. Intense monitoring could actually create new problems, as the basis for the 'contract' between principal and steward is found in mutual trust (Davis et al., 1997: 25–26). A principal has to demonstrate trust in the steward to achieve an optimal result; monitoring is considered an expression of distrust and could lead to friction and a loss of performance/efficiency by the steward. Therefore, using a stewardship model as the basis for a relationship between a principal and, for example, a quango will only be sensible if both parties agree to the same principles, such as trust and ex post accountability based on results (cf. Kickert, 2001). Principals should respect the professional expertise and autonomy of the steward; otherwise, there is no sound basis for a good relationship. In return, the steward will perform well and display good behavior (cf. bonding as mentioned above).

Unfortunately, in practice, we see many examples in which political principals do not trust quangos, want to change the terms of contracts, or engage in ex post haggling in light of changing political or economic conditions. Elsewhere, I have labeled this the 'empty nest syndrome' (Van Thiel, 2011), the dysfunctional relationship between ministries and quangos after separation in the event that ministries cannot relinquish direct control and continue meddling in daily affairs (Pollitt, 2005). A well-known example concerns the director of the UK Prison Service who was going to be fired after the escape of a number of IRA-prisoners. This was not in line with the contract that was drawn up with the director and the organization, and the director went to court (with success). Other examples show that political principals often choose to 'restructure' or merge (reshuffle) quangos, for no apparent reason other than altering the conditions of working (i.e., the contract) or reducing uncertainties concerning quango performance. In the Dutch case, the number of ZBOs will be reduced by 50%. Both the report and the Cabinet's letter on this topic, however, do not mention any justification for this decision, such as poor performance, lack of compliance or increasing control (cf. Flinders & Skelcher, 2012, on a similar operation in the UK). This is indicative of the distrust and uncertainty of political principals vis-a-vis quangos and, hence, of a line of thinking that accords better with principal-agent than principal-steward thinking.

The actual extent to which a high degree of goal convergence exists in this field, however, is questionable. First, most policy decisions (on new policies and decisions on which agent will implement them) are often highly contested and, therefore, ambiguous; there is always room for interpretation and discretionary authority by the agents who implement the policies (Elmore, 1979; Torenvlied, 2000). The agent's professional expertise and politicians' intentions may not always coincide. Moreover, politicians come and go, whereas public servants/organizations stay on, at least in Weberian systems. In sum, politics and politicians may have a discontinuous but disturbing effect on what agents do, and goal convergence, therefore, may be less present than opposing scholars assume. A second counterargument against opponents of principal-agent theory can be found in so-called capture (Gilardi & Maggetti, 2010); agents, particularly when operating at arm's length from the government, may become more attuned to the objectives of the individuals/organizations that they have to interact with when implementing policies than with the politicians who developed the policy. Several examples of captures have been discovered in the wake of the financial crisis, when regulatory authorities (quangos) responsible for regulating the financial market were found to be more attuned with the objectives of banks and financial organizations than with the government's objectives of independent regulation.

In sum, whereas there is merit to the idea that public servants are not self-interested, this does not immediately imply that there is (full) goal convergence between principals and agents in the public domain. Moreover, information asymmetry and bounded rationality also remain present. Students and researchers should bear this in mind when applying principal-agent theory to public sector topics and public sector reforms.

Contracts and Ex Post Haggling

In addition to the above, the private sector origin of principal-agent theory is criticized for two more reasons. First, a contract between a principal and an agent in the public sector is usually not as legally binding as contracts in the private sector. Most contracts between ministries and quangos, therefore, are not referred to as contracts but more often as covenants, letters of intent, subsidy decisions and management contracts (Tonkiss et al., 2015). Consequently, it is not always easy to ensure that parties remain faithful to the agreements or to prevent ex post haggling. It is not uncommon for political principals to want to change 'contracts' drawn up by their predecessors or to alter them when political circumstances have changed, for example, when new budget cuts have to be made (Binderkrantz & Christensen, 2009).

This makes principals less reliable partners (see also below), but agents in the public domain usually have no (legal) means to enforce the original contract. Moreover, according to the second criticism, most public sector agents are monopolists, meaning that political principals often have no real choice when selecting an agent (recall the problem of adverse selection). Therefore, even if contracts are broken, principals and agents have no real alternative and are in fact dependent on one another. This situation has been labeled a bilateral monopoly. The fact that principals often have only one agent to negotiate with also means that the agent can have considerable say in the terms of the contract; the agent, therefore, can use this advantage to its benefit and include safety options in the event of political changes. White (1991) has referred to the 'reversal of control' between principals and agents in such cases, when the agent can essentially dictate the terms of a contract. Finally, a lack of competitors also means that most public sector agents cannot go bankrupt; the sunk costs are simply too high to allow an agent to be dissolved (hence, public sector organizations have very long lifespans; see Kaufman, 1976). Therefore, although the agent cannot enforce a contract, the lack of alternative agents diminishes the power of principals to end a contract unilaterally.

At present, principal-agent theory does not enable scholars to formulate assumptions or hypotheses on these situations or about potential solutions. Moreover, the model only pays attention to the opportunism of the agent, not of the principal. To better fit the model with the characteristics of the public domain, the model should be further elaborated in these respects.

Multiple Principals

A third major line of criticism of applying principal-agent theory to public sector topics concentrates on the principal. The model assumes that there is one principal. However, in practice, in the public domain there are often multiple principals, either in the case of one principal holding multiple roles simultaneously or in the case of there actually being more than one principal (Van Thiel & Verhof, 2012). The first type of multiplicity refers to the fact that governments (political principals) have multiple roles: they develop policies, decide which agent has to implement the policy, monitor that agency, fund it and evaluate both the agent and the policy, which could lead to adjustments and new decisions. This mixture of roles can lead to conflicts. To give an example: the Dutch Minister of Economic Affairs is responsible for gas extraction in Groningen. This function is performed by a state-owned company, the shares of which are owned by the Ministry of Finance. In recent years, a number of earthquakes occurred as a result of gas extraction. The Minister of Economic Affairs has to find a solution for the damage to the houses of the citizens of Groningen and the consequent decline in house prices. Finally, the same minister is also in charge of supervising the gas companies (by an independent regulator, a quango).

Moreover, gas extraction creates high profits for the Dutch state, and agreements have been made regarding how much revenues have to be gained for the benefit of all Dutch citizens. This is also the responsibility of the Minister of Economic Affairs. In short, the minister (principal) has multiple roles and is dealing with multiple agents. However, principal-agent theory does not allow for such multiplicity within one actor. The same problem is found in the second case of multiplicity: when agents work for more than one principal, for example, for multiple ministries (as in the case of shared services, Van Thiel & Verhof, 2012), when they implement European regulation that has been transposed by the national government (Egeberg & Trondal, 2009), or in the case of the US, where Congress and the President both can be the principal for agents that make or implement policies (McCubbins, Noll & Weingast, 1989). In both types of multiplicity, cross-pressure is created (Moe, 1987), different, potentially contradicting, steering signals can lead to confusion, overlap or a shortage of steering (e.g., monitoring) for the agent. This adds to the existing problems of information asymmetry, adverse selection and moral hazard.

The existence of multiple principals creates a theoretical challenge for principal-agent theory, as it is still based on a dyadic model. Within each principal-agent relationship, problems such as moral hazard can occur, but the addition of multiple principals creates additional problems. For example, if there is more than one principal, who will pay for the monitoring costs? Opportunistic behavior between principals (free-rider behavior) can only be solved by improving the coordination between principals (Dixit, 2002). Turf wars, bureau-politics and silo-ization between political principals such as parliament, ministries and ministerial directorates make such solutions very difficult to achieve.

Conclusion

This chapter has argued that the principal-agent perspective can explain both the adoption and the implementation of public sector reforms. The adoption of reforms such as contracting out mirror the basic dilemma in principal-agent theory: when to choose which agent for a specific task. The example of the relationship between parent ministries and quangos shows how the principal-agent model can be used to describe the actual practice of public sector organizations at arm's length. The popularity of principal-agent theory in research on public sector reforms can be attributed to the fit between the underlying assumptions of many NPM reforms and to the simplicity of the dyadic model between two utility-maximizing actors. However, this theory was not developed for the public domain, and consequently, it does not always fit well with the typical characteristics of public sector organizations. Several criticisms were mentioned, such as the assumed goal divergence between the agent and the principal. It is unclear whether such divergence actually exists in the public domain. In the event of goal convergence, stewardship theory could be a good alternative to principal-agent theory. A second important criticism concerns the fact that in the public domain contracts are not as legally binding as their counterparts in the private domain, and the former are, therefore, much more vulnerable to ex post haggling, particularly by political principals who regularly respond to changing political conditions. However, principal-agent theory does not devote much attention to the opportunistic behavior of principals. Third, it was noted that there are often multiple principals in the public domain, either because there is more than one principal (such as the national and EU governments) or because one principal fulfills multiple roles (such as policy maker, financer and overseer). At present, principal-agent theory does not describe such situations or the risks that could be associated with them and the solutions to remediate these risks. This is definitely an area for further research and theory development. At the root of these criticisms lies the disturbing role of politics; principals' decisions to hire agents to execute public tasks may be based on entirely different motives than economic rationality. This severely damages the applicability of principal-agent theory to public sector reform and warrants that researchers further adapt and elaborate on this elegant but simple model.

References

Behn, R.D. (2003). Why measure performance? Different purposes require different measures. *Public Administration Review, 63*(5), 586–606.

Besley, T. (2006). *Principled agents? The political economy of good government.* Oxford: Oxford University Press.

Binderkrantz, A., & Christensen, J.G. (2009). Governing Danish agencies by contract: From negotiated freedom to the shadow of hierarchy. *Journal of Public Policy, 29*, 55–78.

Boston, J. (1995). Lessons from the Anitpodes. In B. O'Toole and G. Jordan (Eds.), *The next steps: Improving management in government* (pp. 161–177). Aldershot: Dartmoor.

Bozeman, B. (2007). *Public values and public interest: Counterbalancing economic individualism.* Washington: Georgetown University Press.

Broadbent, J., Dietrich, M., & Laughlin, R. (1996). The development of principal-agent, contracting and accountability relationships in the public sector: Conceptual and cultural problems. *Critical Perspectives on Accounting, 7*(3), 259–284.

Brown, T.L., Potoski, M., & Van Slyke, D.M. (2006). Managing public service contracts: Aligning values, institutions and markets. *Public Administration Review, 66*(3), 323–331.

Davis, J.H., Schoorman, F.D., & Donaldson, L. (1997). Toward a stewardship theory of management. *The Academy of Management Review, 22*(1), 20–47.

De Leeuw, J. (2013). *Onderzoek naar de herpositionering van zbo's.* Report. Den Haag: ABD Top Consult.

De Swaan, A. (1988). *In care of the state: Health care, education and welfare in Europe and the USA in the modern era.* New York and Cambridge: Oxford University Press and Polity Press.

Dixit, A. (2002). Incentives and organizations in the public sector: An interpretative review. *The Journal of Human Resources, 37*(4), 696–727.

Domberger, S., & Jensen, P. (1997). Contracting out by the public sector: Theory, evidence, prospects. *Oxford Review of Economic Policy, 13*(4), 67–78.

Egeberg, M., & Trondal, J. (2009). National agencies in the European administrative space: Government driven, commission driven or networked? *Public Administration, 87*(4), 779–790.

Elmore, R.F. (1979). Backward mapping: Implementation research and policy decisions. *Political Science Quarterly, 94*(4), 601–616.

Flinders, M., & Skelcher, C. (2012). Shrinking the quango state: Five challenges in reforming quangos. *Public Money and Management, September, 32*(5), 327–334.

Gibbons, R., & Roberts, J. (Eds.). (2012). *The handbook of organizational economics*. Princeton: Princeton University Press.

Gilardi, F., & Maggetti, M. (2010). The independence of regulatory authorities. In D. Levi-Faur. (Ed.), *Handbook on the politics of regulation* (pp. 201–214). Cheltenham: Edward Elgar.

Greve, C., Flinders, M.V., & Van Thiel, S. (1999). Quangos: What's in a name? Defining quasi-autonomous bodies from a comparative perspective. *Governance, 12*(1), 129–146.

Hood, C. (1991). A public management for all seasons? *Public Administration, 69*(3), 3–19.

James, O. (2003). *The executive agency revolution in Whitehall: Public interest versus bureau-shaping perspectives*. Basingstoke: Palgrave MacMillan.

James, O., & Van Thiel, S. (2011) [2010]. Structural devolution and agencification. In T. Christensen and P. Lægreid (Eds.), *Ashgate research companion to new public management* (pp. 209–222). Aldershot: Ashgate Publishing Ltd.

Jensen, M.C., & Meckling, W.H. (1976). Theory of the firm: Managerial behavior, agency costs and ownership structure. *Journal of Financial Economics, 3*(4), 305–360.

Kaufman, H. (1976). *Are government organizations immortal?* Washington: Brookings Institution Press.

Kickert, W.J.M. (2001). Public management of hybrid organizations: Governance of quasi-autonomous executive agencies. *International Public Management Journal, 4*, 135–150.

Lafarge, F. (2012). France. In K. Verhoest, S. Van Thiel, G. Bouckaert and P. Lægreid (Eds.), *Government agencies: Practices and lessons from 30 countries* (pp. 98–109). Basingstoke: Palgrave MacMillan.

Laffont, J.-J., & Martimort, D. (2002). *The theory of incentives: The principal-agent model*. Princeton: Princeton University Press.

Macher, J.T., & Richman, B.D. (2008). Transaction cost economics: An assessment of empirical research in the social sciences. *Business and Politics, 10*(1).

McCubbins, M.D., Noll, R.G., & Weingast, B.R. (1989). Structure and process, politics and policy: Administrative arrangements and the political control of agencies. *Virginia Law Review, 75*(2), 431–482.

Miller, G.J. (2005). The political evolution of principal-agent models. *Annual Review of Political Science, 8*, 203–225.

Moe, T.M. (1987). An assessment of the positive theory of 'congressional dominance'. *Legislative Studies Quarterly, 12*(4), 475–520.

Perry, J., & Wise, L.R. (1990). The motivational bases of public service. *Public Administration Review, 50*(3), 367–373.

Peters, B.G. (2012). The United States. In K. Verhoest, S. Van Thiel, G. Bouckaert and P. Lægreid (Eds.), *Government agencies: Practices and lessons from 30 countries* (pp. 69–76). Basingstoke: Palgrave MacMillan.

POC: Parlementaire Onderzoekscommissie. (2012). *Verbinding verbroken? Onderzoek naar de parlementaire besluitvorming over de privatisering en verzelfstandiging van overheidsdiensten*. Eerste Kamer, vergaderjaar 2012–2013, B en C.

Pollitt, C. (2005). Ministries and agencies: Steering, meddling, neglect and dependency. In M. Painter and J. Pierre (Eds.), *Challenges to state capacity: Global trends and comparative perspectives* (pp. 112–136). Basingstoke: Palgrave MacMillan.

Pollitt, C., & Dan, S. (2013). Searching for impacts in performance-oriented management reform: A review of the European literature. *Public Performance & Management Review, 37*(1), 7–32.

Pratt, J.W., & Zeckhauser, R.J. (Eds.). (1991). *Principals and agents.* Boston: Massachusetts & Harvard Business School Press.

Schillemans, T. (2013). Moving beyond the clash of interests: On stewardship theory and the relationships between central government departments and public agencies. *Public Management Review, 15*(4), 541–562.

't Hart, P., & Wille, A. (2006). Ministers and top officials in the Dutch core executive: Living together, growing apart? *Public Administration, 84,* 121–146.

Thatcher, M., & Sweet, A.S. (2002). Theory and practice of delegation to non-majoritarian institutions. *West European Politics, 25*(1), 1–22.

Tonkiss, K., Van Thiel, S., Verhoest, K., & Skelcher, C. (2015). *How are arm's length relationships instrumentalised in Europe? Analysing plural principals in three countries.* Paper presented at the 73rd. Mid-West Political Science Association Conference, Chicago, 16–19 April 2015.

Torenvlied, R. (2000). *Political decisions and agency performance.* Dordrecht: Springer.

Tosi, H.L., Brownlee, A.L., Silva, P., & Katz, J.P. (2003). An empirical exploration of decision-making under agency controls and stewardship structure. *Journal of Management Studies, 40*(8), 2053–2071.

Van Ammers, M., & Van Thiel, S. (2012). Kaderwet Zelfstandige Bestuursorganen: het einde van Raden van Toezicht als toezichthouders bij ZBO's? *Bestuurswetenschappen, 66*(4), 35–54.

Van der Wal, Z., De Graaf, G., & Lasthuizen, K. (2008). What's valued most? Similarities and differences between the organizational values of the public and private sector. *Public Administration, 86*(2), 465–482.

Van Dooren, W., Bouckaert, G., & Halligan, J. (2015). *Performance management in the public sector.* Adbingdon: Routledge.

Van Slyke, D. M. (2007). Agents or stewards: Using theory to understand the government-nonprofit social service contracting relationship. *Journal of Public Administration Research and Theory, 17*(2), 157–187.

Van Thiel, S. (2001). *Quangos: Trends, causes and consequences.* Aldershot: Ashgate Publishing Ltd.

Van Thiel, S. (2006). Styles of reform: Differences in agency creation between policy sectors in the Netherlands. *Journal of Public Policy, 26*(2), 115–139.

Van Thiel, S. (2011). The empty nest syndrome: Dutch ministries after the separation of policy and administration. In S. Van de Walle and S.M. Groeneveld (Eds.), *New steering concepts in public management* (pp. 25–40). Bingly: Emerald Group Publishing Ltd.

Van Thiel, S. (2012). Comparing agencies across countries. In K. Verhoest, S. Van Thiel, G. Bouckaert and P. Lægreid (Eds.), *Government agencies: practices and lessons from 30 countries* (pp. 18–26). Basingstoke: Palgrave MacMillan.

Van Thiel, S., & Hendriks, R. (2014). Aansturing van zelfstandige bestuursorganen door ministeries: stijlverschillen. *Bestuurswetenschappen, 68*(4), 53–68.

Van Thiel, S., & Pollitt, C. (2007). The management and control of executive agencies: An Anglo-Dutch comparison. In C. Pollitt, S. Van Thiel and V. Homburg (Eds.), *New public management in Europe: Adaptation and alternatives* (pp. 52–70). Basingstoke: Palgrave MacMillan.

Van Thiel, S., & Verhof, D. (2012). *Serving two masters: The plural principal problem in agency management.* Paper presented at EGPA Conference, Bergen, Norway, 5–8 September 2012.

Van Thiel, S., & Yesilkagit, K. (2011). Good neighbours or distant friends: Trust between Dutch ministries and their executive agencies. *Public Management Review, 13*(6), 783–802.

Verhoest, K., Van Thiel, S., Bouckaert, G., & Lægreid, P. (Eds.). (2012). *Government agencies: Practices and lessons from 30 countries*. Basingstoke: Palgrave MacMillan.

Warner, M.E., & Bel, G. (2008). Competition or monopoly? Comparing privatization of local public services in the US and Spain. *Public Administration, 86*(3), 723–735.

Waterman, R.W., & Meier, K.J. (1998). Principal-agent models: An expansion? *Journal of Public Administration, Research & Theory, 8*(2), 173–202.

White, H.C. (1991). Agency as control. In J.W. Pratt and R.J. Zeckhauser (Eds.), *Principals and agents* (pp. 187–213). Boston: Massachusetts & Harvard Business School Press.

Williamson, O.E. (1979). Transaction-cost economics: The governance of contractual relations. *Journal of Law and Economics, 22*(2), 233–261.

Williamson, O.E. (2005). Transaction cost economics. In C. Menard and M.M. Shirley (Eds.), *Handbook of new institutional economics* (pp. 41–65). Dordrecht: Springer.

Yesilkagit, K., & Van Thiel, S. (2012). The Netherlands. In K. Verhoest, S. Van Thiel, G. Bouckaert and P. Lægreid (Eds.), *Government agencies: Practices and lessons from 30 countries* (pp. 179–190). Basingstoke: Palgrave MacMillan.

5 An Innovation Perspective[1]

Victor Bekkers and Lars Tummers

Introduction

Many people believe that the public sector is not innovative (Borins, 2002). Related to this, New Public Management propagandists argue that government organizations should be exposed to competition. Competition incentivizes employees to develop and implement new and creative ideas, which ultimately improve or even develop services (Osborne & Gaebler, 1992). However, not everyone agrees with this. Other scholars argue that innovation in the public sector is alive and lively (see, for instance, Damanpour & Schneider, 2009; Osborne & Brown, 2013; Walker, 2014). They cite various examples. For instance, governments have introduced forms of electronic government, making use of internet and social media to improve the quality of public services. Furthermore, one-stop shops (physical and online) have been erected, allowing citizens to obtain various services at one location. This can improve citizen satisfaction and citizen-state interactions more generally. Such innovations are highly visible. However, there are public innovations that are less visible and less appealing then electronic gadgets. In this chapter, our aim is to provide a more all-encompassing innovation perspective, focusing especially on innovation's relationship with public sector reform (Kickert, 1997b; Pollitt & Bouckaert, 2011).

As will be discussed in greater detail below, we define public sector innovation as 'the introduction of new elements into a public service—in the form of new knowledge, a new organization and/or new management or processual skills—that represent discontinuity with the past' (based on Osborne & Brown, 2005: 4). We focus on innovation and give special attention to one approach to innovation: *'social'* innovation. Social innovation is being embraced by many politicians and policy makers. For instance, President Obama has established a Social Innovation Fund. This fund combines public and private resources to grow promising community-based solutions that have evidence of results in any of three priority areas: economic opportunity, healthy futures and youth development.[2] Social innovation is an inspiring but weakly conceptualized concept (Mulgan, 2006; 2009). It is intended to develop long-lasting outcomes that address societal needs, such as youth employment, the ageing of the population and the regeneration of urban neighborhoods and rural areas. This is achieved by fundamentally changing the relationships, positions and rules between the stakeholders involved, via a process of open participation and collaboration.

From a public sector reform perspective, social innovation seems to be an interesting approach. It is a particular perspective on how the public sector should be reformed. Reforms should be achieved via 'social innovation'. First, social innovation implies that end users, such as citizens, should be involved in the process of developing solutions. Hence, it is less 'top-down' than many other approaches proclaimed in a welfare state tradition (Pierson, 2001). According to the European Commission (2011: 30), 'social innovation mobilizes each citizen to become an active part of the innovation process.' Second, it is intended to fundamentally change the roles of various stakeholders in service delivery. For instance, in healthcare, it is possible that under the previous arrangement, citizens/patients were passive users of a service and the physician decided which nurse to hire, whereas citizens can make more active decisions and have a personal budget as a result of social innovation. They can choose which type of help, from which organization, they obtain. Such a reform fundamentally alters the relations between stakeholders.

Hence, it appears that innovations (and social innovations in particular) are indeed taking place in and with public sector organizations, reforming the public sector and beyond. It is, therefore, important to deepen our understanding of this phenomenon. In this chapter, we will first analyze the background of innovation as a relevant concept to study public sector reform (section 2). In section 3, we will specifically consider the notion of 'social innovation', given its increasing importance for contemporary reform. In section 4, we will address a number of relevant drivers of and barriers to innovation processes in the public sector. In the final section, we will draw conclusions and discuss future research opportunities when studying innovation in the public sector.

Innovation: Theory and Concepts

Innovation as an Object

Definitions of innovation abound, each emphasizing different aspects of the concept. Schumpeter, who argued that innovation is the motor of economic change, was one of the first to describe various types of innovation. Innovation, according to him, is a matter of *doing things differently*. An innovation is, for instance, introducing a new product with which citizens are not yet familiar or introducing a new product attribute. This description of innovation is well-aligned with the layman's understanding of innovation. However, Schumpeter (1934) also regards as innovations 'opening up new markets' and adjusting the new organization of an industry, such as creating a monopoly position or the breaking up of a monopoly position. Related to the work of Schumpeter, Rogers (2003: 35) defines an innovation as 'an idea, practice, or object perceived as new by an individual or other unit of adoption.' Hence, Rogers also stresses the novelty aspect of innovations. However, according to Rogers, something need not be objectively 'new' but has to be *perceived* as new.

When studying innovation, it is important to recognize the difference between innovation and the related concepts of creativity and change. Creativity can be seen as an intellectual thought process of generating ideas that are new and potentially useful (Shalley, Zhou & Oldham, 2004). Creativity is the precursor of innovation. As Amabile, Conti, Coon, Lazenby & Herron (1996: 1154) note, 'All innovation begins with creative ideas. Successful implementation of new programs, new product introductions, or new services depends on a person or a team having a good idea—and developing that idea beyond its initial state.' The distinction between innovation and change is to be found in the degree of radicalness (Osborne & Brown, 2005: 4). Change is a general term, whereas innovation is a specific form of change, namely *discontinuous* change. Innovation represents a qualitative break from the past. Hence, innovation concerns a specific type of change.

We follow Osborne and Brown (2005: 4) and define public sector innovation as the introduction of new elements into a public service—in the form of new knowledge, a new organization and/or new management or processual skills—that represent discontinuity with the past. This definition highlights a) the novelty aspect (in line with both Schumpeter and Rogers) and b) the discontinuity aspect (differentiating innovation from change) and c) shows that the elements really should be introduced before it constitutes an innovation (showing the difference between a creative idea and innovation).

The definition of the public sector innovation is very broad. A number of scholars have, therefore, classified innovations into various types (Schumpeter, 1942; Mulgan & Albury, 2003; Windrum & Koch, 2008). When these types are applied to the public sector, a classification can be proposed (based on Bekkers, Edelenbos & Steijn, 2011: 15–16). This is shown in table 5.1.

The classification serves as a helpful analytical tool to understand various types of innovations. However, we recognize that the boundaries are not clear-cut. Real-life innovations can have characteristics of various types. A public management reform can, for instance, be intended to introduce teleworking in organizations, to improve efficiency (less office space needed) and attract younger workers (who are accustomed to working from various locations and on a varying time schedule). From an innovation perspective, teleworking can be regarded as an organizational and technological innovation. However, it can be accompanied by a 'conceptual innovation': a paradigm shift by managers that employees do not need to be monitored directly to determine whether they are doing their work.

Table 5.1 Classifying six types of public sector innovations

Type of innovation	Description	Example
Product or service innovation	Focused on the creation of new public services or products	Creation of the youth work disability benefits
Technological innovation	Focused on the invention of new information and communication and other technologies	Data mining techniques related to 'big data'
Process innovations	Focused on the development and re-design of the quality and efficiency of internal and external policy process, public service delivery and administrative processes	Development of 'one-stop shop' by a municipality, where citizens can get various services at one location
Organizational innovation	Focused on creating new organizational forms, the introduction of new management methods and techniques, and new working methods	Introducing teleworking in a public sector organization
Governance innovation	Focused on the development of new forms and processes of governance in order to address specific societal problems	The governance practice that attempts to enhance the self-regulating and self-organizing capacities of citizens
Conceptual innovation	Focused on the introduction of new concepts, frames of reference or even new paradigms that help to reframe the nature of problems and solutions	The introduction of the paradigm that when looking at a person's work (dis)ability, insurance physicians no longer analyze what people cannot do, but instead analyze what they still *can* do, hence focusing on work ability potential instead of disability

Innovation as a Local Process

In addition to studying innovation as an *object*, we can also analyze innovation as a *process*. Indeed, Joseph Schumpeter (1942) describes innovation as a process of creative destruction in which 'new combinations of existing resources' are achieved. In his view, innovation cannot be separated from entrepreneurship. They are two sides of the same coin. He defines entrepreneurship as 'Die Durchsetzung neuer Kombinationen': the will and ability to achieve new combinations that have to compete with established combinations.

Such an innovation process does not take place in a vacuum: it is locally embedded in a specific context, such as a specific country or policy sector with a specific state and governance tradition, a specific time, specific power relations and so forth (Osborne & Brown, 2005; Bekkers et al., 2011).

Castells calls these environments 'innovation milieus' (Castells, 1996: 3). It is important to recognize the influence of the specific environment in which innovation processes take place. Regarding public management reform, Hansen (2011) shows that the adoption of New Public Management reforms is heavily dependent on the context. For example, such adoption is positively related to organizational size and negatively related to the extent to which managers have a classical bureaucratic rule orientation.

Based upon the importance of local embeddedness, some scholars argue that we should study innovation from an ecological perspective (Greenhalgh, Robert, Macfarlane, Bate & Kyriakidou, 2004; Bason, 2010; Osborne & Brown, 2011). This ecological perspective emphasizes that innovation processes are shaped by the local and, thus, are dependent on institutionally embedded exchanges between relevant actors. During these exchanges, actors learn from one another and share resources such as knowledge and staff. The advantage of such an ecological approach is that is makes it possible to account for characteristics, such as a) the various governance traditions that are used in various countries, b) the role of politics and c) relevant policy sector and network characteristics.

In this way, this ecological perspective can be directly connected to studying public sector reform from a comparative perspective, taking into account state and governance traditions (Loughlin & Peters, 1997). For instance, Kickert (1997a, b) argues that the 'managerial' approach to public administration as developed in, among other countries, the US, the United Kingdom and New Zealand is ill-suited to the particular state and governance traditions of the Netherlands. Here, a 'public governance' approach is more appropriate. Hence, from an ecological perspective, it becomes possible to understand why certain public management reforms are well-suited to certain contexts but not to others.

Diffusion and Adoption of Innovations

When an innovation has been implemented (in a local environment), one organization or group of organizations can use it. However, public sector innovation does not stop here. The innovation literature also discusses the diffusion and adoption of innovations by other organizations. This can be considered a process that is only loosely coupled with the innovation process itself. That is why Damanpour and Schneider (2009) argue that, in essence, two types of processes can be identified: innovation *generating* activities and innovation *adopting* activities.

The diffusion of an innovation is defined as 'a process in which an innovation is communicated through certain channels over time among the members of a social system' (Rogers, 2003: 5). This is highly related to scaling up, which can be described as efforts to increase the use of innovations by other actors (Simmons & Shiffman, 2007). When innovation diffusion succeeds, various others 'adopt' the innovation. Innovation adoption is 'the voluntary and/or coercive process through which an organization passes from first knowledge of an innovation, to forming an attitude towards the innovation, to a decision to adopt or reject, to implementation of the new idea, and to confirmation of this decision' (Rogers, 2003: 20).

Although diffusion and adoption is a vivid theme in the business administration literature (see, for instance, Ghoshal & Bartlett, 1988), hardly any systematic attention has been devoted to this critical aspect of innovation in the public sector (Greenhalgh et al., 2004). However, there are some studies focusing on the stages of the adoption process (Albury, 2005). Here, one important concept is the 'adopter categories', as developed by Rogers (2003). Rogers offers a classification of social members of a social system on the basis of their innovativeness. Innovations are first adopted by the 'innovators', then 'early adopters', then the 'early majority', then the 'late majority' and, finally, 'the laggards'. Such categories are often used. However, following Greenhalgh et al. (2004: 598), we must note that these 'have been extensively misapplied as explanatory variables. There is little empirical support for these stereotypical and value-laden terms, which fail to acknowledge the adopter as an actor who interacts purposively and creatively with a complex innovation.'

The diffusion and adoption of innovations can be linked to public management reform. Public management reforms—especially NPM—have spread across many organizations, sectors, countries and even continents (Pollitt & Bouckaert, 2011). Hence, its 'scaling-up' process has been quite 'successful'. However, these reforms are adopted in various ways. Some countries, such as New Zealand, adopted far more characteristics of NPM than did others (such as Belgium or France). Furthermore, other countries were even less enthusiastic and did not adopt many of the NPM aspects (such as Germany). This can be related to the state and governance tradition in Germany that is strongly rooted in the '*Rechtsstaat*' (compare Olsen, this volume; Christensen & Laegreid, this volume).

Social Innovation in the Public Sector

Social innovation is potentially an even fuzzier concept than innovation. One central reason for this is that the literature on social innovation is dominated by 'grey literature', such as policy advisory reports, applied research memoranda and normative 'to-do' lists, whereas the empirical base is weak. The European Union (2010, based on Murray, Caulier-Grice & Mulgan, 2010: 3) states that social innovations are new ideas (products, services and models) that simultaneously meet social needs (more effectively than alternatives) and create new social relationships or collaborations. Hence, the argument is that social innovations are both good for society and enhance society's capacity to act. Harris and Albury (2009: 16, see also Bason, 2010: 96) argue that social innovations are innovations explicitly focused on the social and public good, addressing important societal challenges such as ageing, pollution or declining election turnout. In general, it is arguable that social innovation in the public sector refers to the following characteristics, which have a *normative* connotation:

1. Social innovation is intended to produce *long-lasting outcomes* that are *need-oriented*. This is in contrast to the dominant thinking in many public organizations, which are supply-driven, based on the implementation of laws and regulations. This adds to the radicalness of the ideas being pursued. Social innovations are intended to meet the needs of society or specific groups in society in a long-lasting way, given the challenges with which societies are grappling, such as ageing or youth unemployment. When discussing the outcomes that are being achieved, the emphasis is on the creation of added public value, which goes beyond sheer economic value captured in values such as efficiency and effectiveness. Public value also refers to political values such as equity, liberty and security and more democratic values such as participation, transparency and accountability.

2. To develop and implement these need-driven innovations, it is import that end-users and other relevant stakeholders *participate in the development, implementation and adoption of the innovations*. This is why social innovation is regarded as the outcome of an open process of co-creation (Chesbrough, 2003). This often takes place in 'collaborative innovation networks' (Gloor, 2005; Bommert, 2010; Sørensen & Torfing, 2011). Relevant stakeholders contribute their knowledge, information, experiences and resources. In social innovation especially, attention is devoted to the co-creating role of citizens as relevant end-users (Voorberg, Bekkers & Tummers, 2015). The radicalness of social innovation concepts refers to breaking up the monopoly in producing new ideas and approaches that are 'good' for society.

3. Social innovation advocates also stress that innovation should fundamentally change the relationships between relevant stakeholders. Social innovation is intended to act as a *'game changer'*, breaking through grown practices and path-dependencies that often challenge the privileged role of government. Again, this element also refers to the proclaimed radicalness of the change that innovation is said to be. Through social innovation, it is argued that the governance capacity of a social order to address new pressing challenges is enhanced because the game is being changed (European Commission, 2011: 33). An example is the emergence in several countries of local solar energy co-cooperatives in which citizens share the solar energy that is produced in their neighborhood, thereby bypassing the traditional energy company, which is frequently a state-owned corporation that operates within a rather protected, non-competitive market. New energy markets develop as a result.

4. Given the importance that social innovation attaches to open process of collaboration with stakeholders, especially citizens, government is forced

to take on another role (Von Hippel, 2007). Instead of being the initiator of innovation processes in the public sector, *government should support and facilitate collaborative, bottom-up initiatives among citizens and other stakeholders.* As a result, the role of government shifts toward a new form of governance that can be defined as meta-governance (Sørensen, 2006).

Having defined some normative characteristics of social innovation, we can illustrate it with a real-life example related to public sector reform: Urban Gardens in Ørestad, Copenhagen.[3] The Urban Gardens are a result of a process whereby several interests collided and made space for a citizen initiative to create a garden where people could come and garden or simply enjoy the new green urban space while sitting on benches. The stakeholders involved included the municipality, the local urban-environmental organizations and a citizen network. The government supported the initiative but did not lead it. As a result of this social innovation, a 'green lung of the city' developed. Furthermore, the relationships between the stakeholders changed fundamentally. In this way, public spheres are being transformed.

Although the social innovation literature offers many examples of social innovation, systematic empirical evidence is weak, which can partly be explained by the normative connotation of the concept. It is often regarded as a 'magic concept' used to stimulate and justify governmental and societal reforms (Pollitt & Hupe, 2011).

Drivers of and Barriers to Public Sector Innovation

The previous section provided a background on innovation in the public sector and social innovation in particular. If we wish to apply an innovation perspective to the reform of the public sector, the next step is to assess the relevant drivers of and barriers to—in terms of influential factors—innovations. In other words, what influences whether citizens and governments will embark on the 'innovation journey' (Van de Ven, 1999)? Three types of factors can be distinguished that can be located at different levels: environmental factors, organizational factors and individual factors.

To scope the research, we must acknowledge that we had to choose from a wide variety of potential drivers and barriers that could influence public sector innovation (for a more elaborate overview, see Bason, 2010; Osborne & Brown, 2011; Bekkers, Tummers, Stuijfzand & Voorberg, 2013). Furthermore, we note that many influential factors are *related*. For instance, effective leadership in an organization can influence the creativity of public employees (Amabile et al., 1996).

Drivers and Barriers Related to the Innovation Environment

Public organizations do not operate in a vacuum. They are working in environments that can be regarded as a reservoir of possible (dis)incentives for innovation. Hence, environmental characteristics can influence the content, course and consequences of innovation processes. The literature notes that the following four aspects of the innovation environment can be important. First, *media and political pressures* can trigger innovation. Politicians have particular agendas (often influenced by the media) that they wish to execute, and this may require public organizations to innovate. Furthermore, incidents widely broadcast on media (consider, for instance, patient mortality in hospitals) can spur innovations. Hence, although high media and political attention can stimulate innovation, it can also stymie it, as failures are often highly publicized (management in a fishbowl, see Borins, 2002).

Second, and related to the first point, innovation can be stimulated by *economic, social, demographic and technological change* to which governments have to respond (Osborne & Brown, 2005). Regarding economic changes, mounting social security and healthcare costs can stimulate innovation, such as novel policies for work disability (Tummers, Bekkers & Steijn, 2009; European Commission, 2013). Concerning demographic changes, the contemporary problem of ageing comes to mind. This stimulated the Dutch central government to decentralize care, meaning that responsibilities will be shifted to municipalities, healthcare organizations and citizens. Technological changes can, for instance, stimulate platforms initiated by governments to crowdsource public sector innovations or open source programming platforms such as 'GitHub' in the US (Mergel, 2014).

Third, *competition* can stimulate innovations in public organizations. Although some argue that competition is absent from public organizations (cf. Bason, 2010), this is not entirely the case. For instance, there is increased competition between regions and cities over being an attractive place to work, live or be a tourist. The technological center of Palo Alto (with Stanford) competes with New York (with New York University) as a place to study, work, live and innovate. This highlights the importance of the presence of so-called 'regional innovation systems' (Asheim & Gertler, 2005). Public organizations, private organizations and citizens collaborate to make their location the most attractive place. This sparks innovations, such as new collaborations between universities and private organizations to develop new traineeships for students. Moreover, there is also competition between individual public organizations. One of the reasons for this is that the increased importance of transparency and high-quality service stimulated public organizations and their professional associations to develop benchmarking and other performance management systems. In many cases, this stimulated product and service innovations (Folz, 2004).

Fourth, the *embeddedness* of a public sector organization in a specific environment can be an important factor that stimulates innovation. The literature on network management (e.g., Koppenjan & Klijn, 2004; this volume) shows that the recognition of *mutual dependency* within networks is vital. Recognition of interdependency implies that the actors involved are able and willing to explore whether they can support one another instead of competing, thereby enhancing collaboration (Van Buuren & Loorbach,

2009). Moreover, the recognition of interdependency supports the sharing of resources, capacities and capabilities across boundaries, thereby going beyond the legal mandates and jurisdictions involved, which often seem to stifle innovation (Kelman, 2008).

Drivers and Barriers Related to the Characteristics of the Public Organizations Involved

Innovation in the public sector normally requires the active involvement of public sector organizations in the form of the latter's willingness and ability to be engaged. What factors, related to the characteristics of these organizations, influence their innovation capacity? Here, we discuss three important organizational factors.

First, it is important to consider the capacities of an organization (e.g., people, money, time, competences, information, knowledge, political support and contacts) in terms of '*slack*' that can be devoted to support innovation activities (Hartley, 2005). Walker (2006) argues that the larger an organization is, the more 'slack' this organization has because it has more opportunities for the cross-fertilization of ideas and a larger variety of relevant skills that can be exploited. In addition to size, other frequently discussed slack factors are organizational wealth and capacity (e.g., Bhatti, Olsen & Pedersen, 2011) and the presence of talented employees in the organization (e.g., Maranto & Wolf, 2012). However, we also fully acknowledge that scarcity can stimulate innovation, as the many reforms instilled by austerity measures illustrate (Kickert, 2011).

The dominant *administrative culture* of the involved organization is a second potential driver of or barrier to innovation. This is primarily related to the client and learning orientation within the organization. Research has shown that an organization with a culture of a strong client orientation will give high priority to continuously findings ways to provide superior client value. In so doing, these organizations seek to be engaged in meeting customers to learn from them (Han, Kim & Srivastava, 1998). Such organizations are more involved in the innovation generating process to develop new service products, services and processes. Moreover, they are also more easily convinced of adopting innovations that have been developed elsewhere, thereby spreading new knowledge (Salge & Vera, 2012). Related to these observations regarding client orientations, the degree of risk aversion within an administrative culture is also important (Voorberg et al., 2015). A learning culture implies 'trial and error', 'bricolage' and experimentation' as necessary conditions for exploring new ideas and ways of working (Pärna & Von Tunzelmann, 2007). However, in the public sector, there seems to be a negative attitude toward risk and risk-taking (Osborne & Brown, 2011). Bureaucratic and political cultures are perceived as risk-avoiding, due to the emphasis placed on accountability and the related 'blame games' (who is responsible and should be blamed?) that are related to this issue (Albury, 2005).

A third important organizational factor is the type of *leadership* that is present in the organization. The literature often notes the importance of having leaders who have a vision, are 'credible', are willing to take risks and can really transform an organization (Gabris, Golembiewski & Ihrke, 2001). Such leaders have 'transformational' leadership styles (Bass & Bass, 2009). Borins (2002) shows that the people who drive innovations (as innovation champions) often act as informal leaders. In so doing, they proactively attempt to solve problems before the problems become crises, by taking opposition seriously and attempting to address it forthrightly through persuasion or accommodation, rather than through power politics. Such leaders develop a clear vision of an innovation and constantly analyze an innovation to determine whether it is working. Furthermore, they are not risk-averse and acknowledge that innovation is by definition a risky endeavor (Osborne & Brown, 2013).

However, we must note that the ability to effectively use such types of leadership is partly dependent on the age of the organization. It seems to disappear when organizations mature, as the main preoccupation becomes making the organization operate like a machine (Bernier & Hafsi, 2007). As a result, innovation is stifled in bureaucratic rigidities, whereas the innovations that are being pursued are of a more incremental nature.

In addition to the importance of transformational-like leadership styles (often focused on processes *inside* the organization), studies show that 'linking leadership' is important (Bekkers et al., 2011). Linking leaders span boundaries: they build relationships, connections and dependences *across organizations*. They involve other stakeholders, such as non-profit organizations, citizens and other actors, to become active participants in an innovation process to promote the quality of life in a neighborhood. Linking leaders bring together people, ideas and resources and thereby develop knowledge, expertise, information and the perspectives of weakly or non-involved actors (Voets & De Rynck, 2008). Moreover, linking leadership also refers to connecting the political realm to the innovation project. This can increase the legitimacy of the project and mobilize the necessary resources, such as the acquisition of new or the protection of already allocated budgets (Considine, Lewis & Alexander, 2009).

Drivers and Barriers Related to the Individuals Involved: Citizens and Employees

People are a very important force in the development and adoption of innovations. We should, therefore, consider the third and last level of innovation processes: the individual level. Two types of actors are often important in relation to innovation in the public sector: governmental actors (policy makers, public professionals) on the one hand and citizens on the other. We will address four important factors that relate to the involvement of both of these types of actors for stimulating innovation.

To implement an innovation, someone (or a group) should gain the support of others who must invest time and energy during the process to potentially develop an innovation. A first important factor here relates to the *expected performance* that people have of such participation, given the limited amount of time they have and the transaction costs involved (Berman, 1997). This 'performance expectancy' has been shown to have a strong influence on behavior (Venkatesh, Morris, Davis & Davis, 2003).

Citizens are often cynical regarding the degree to which they believe that governments are actually prepared to address the needs and wishes that they advance (Berman, 1997). When it is made very clear why participation in the innovation process generates outcomes that are in the interest of citizens, they will be more willing to participate (Alford, 2009). These outcomes need not, by definition, refer to the self-interest of citizens; they can also refer to intrinsic motivations and rewards that refer to social values that motivate people. For instance, Schudson (1998) argues that citizens, who generally have a passive attitude, are actually willing to mobilize themselves to participate if vital interests are being threatened.

Regarding policy makers and professionals, performance expectancy is highly related to the meaningless dimension of 'policy alienation'. Policy alienation can be broadly described as a feeling of psychological disconnection from a new policy (or, here, an innovation) (Tummers et al., 2009). It consists of two main dimensions, powerlessness and meaninglessness. Here, powerlessness relates to the feeling that one is unable to influence an innovation, whereas meaninglessness focuses on the lack of added value of innovations. High meaninglessness occurs when public service employees feel that an innovation it not beneficial for their clients (client meaninglessness) or for society at large (societal meaninglessness). Hence, high meaninglessness (at both a client and societal level) can indicate that policy makers or professionals do not feel that the expected performance of an innovation is high because it is not benefiting their clients or society at large. The meaninglessness dimension of policy alienation is highly relevant in explaining why public professionals resist innovations, for instance, in mental healthcare (Tummers, 2011) or law enforcement (Loyens, 2014).

A second factor on the individual level relates to the effort needed to participate. This is known as the *effort expectancy* (Venkatesh et al., 2003). Policy makers, professionals and citizens need information, knowledge, skills and competences to participate. This is also dependent on the complexity of the innovation and the outcomes that are being pursued (Bovaird & Löffler, 2012). From the citizen perspective, a possible solution is offered on the internet and social-media-driven facilities such as crowdsourcing, open data and open idea banks that help to link dispersed people and ideas in an easy way, such that knowledge can be accessed and shared beyond boundaries (Bekkers, 2004; Mulgan, 2009). From the perspective of policy makers and professionals, it can be valuable when organizations are more compatible with innovations (and social innovation in particular). This can refer to an infrastructure that allows policy makers and professionals to easily communicate with citizens (for instance, to assess new ideas via a citizen panel).

Finally, prior experience can be important. Research shows that citizens and public organizations already participating make use of the additional opportunities that are offered to become further involved (Bekkers, 2004; Holmes & Smart, 2009). Although prior experience can be beneficial for innovations, when it leads to institutionalization, it can also have various deleterious effects. This issue especially arises when citizens and professionals erect organizations to represent them. Internal goals and personal motives may then replace the original representation goals. In this way, goal displacement may take place, whereby the goals of the intermediary organizations (which should be means to voice the concerns of their supporters) become the ultimate goals. Such developments can also occur with local policy makers or public professionals. For instance, the influence of professional associations does not by definition heighten the support of the professionals themselves, as everyday professionals are different and disconnected from the elite representing them in their associations (Tummers, 2011).

Conclusion

This chapter analyzed public sector reform from the perspective of (social) innovation. It defined innovations in the public sector, both as an object and a locally embedded process, and analyzed the increasingly popular notion of social innovation. Furthermore, the chapter noted ten potentially important environmental, organizational and individual factors that can stimulate or hinder innovations. These are shown in table 5.2.

Table 5.2 Potential drivers and barriers for public sector innovation

Dimension	Driver/barrier	Expected influence on public sector innovation
Environmental level	1. Political and media pressure	+
	2. Economic, demographic and technological changes	+
	3. Competition	+
	4. Networks	+
Organizational level	1. Slack (money, time, people) available	+ (or -, as austerity can also simulate innovation)
	2. Administrative culture: client orientation and risk-taking	+
	3. Leadership: transformational and boundary spanning	+
Individual level	1. Performance expectancy	+
	2. Effort expectancy	+
	3. Prior experience	+

We argue that innovation studies help in understanding public management reforms because this approach specializes in studying a specific type of reform, namely a reform that represents a qualitative break from the past, thereby introducing fundamental discontinuity. However, public innovation studies suffer from the fact that innovation itself is a fuzzy, multi-interpretable and normative concept. On the one hand, this 'magic concept' (Pollitt & Hupe, 2011) of social innovation inspires public organizations and citizens to take up the reform challenge. For instance, framing something as a 'social innovation' might generate considerably less resistance than framing it as a 'reform' or a 'change'. On the other hand, its multi-interpretable character and normative connotation can also blur our understanding of what is really happening. One might even say that public sector innovation studies are suffering from this. One of the challenges of public innovation studies is to unravel the assumptions underlying public innovation movements and to critically reflect on the outcomes of these processes. Social innovation is an example of the power of such reform movements that are popular among policy makers, politicians and other opinion leaders. It can also be argued that public innovation studies represent a body of knowledge that can be used, as it is increasingly being rooted in empirical research, to describe, analyze, evaluate and explain the process and outcomes of public sector innovation.

In this chapter, we have discussed factors that could stimulate or hinder public sector innovations. However, we must note that the potential of this body of knowledge could be improved if we were also able to take into account innovations that were not perceived as successful. A handicap when studying reform from an innovation studies perspective is that the cases that are selected suffer from a 'pro-innovation bias' (Rogers, 2003). Innovation scholars predominantly focus on those practices that have proven to be an innovation. Failed innovations are rarely considered, because they are more difficult to find. Hence, there seems to be an understudied 'graveyard of innovations' (Cleff, 2008). Interestingly, when considering the related concepts of reform and change, the opposite seems to be true. Change studies often begin by noting that '70% of change efforts fail' (see, for instance, Beer & Nohria, 2000: 14). Reform in the public sector is often viewed with suspicion, especially under the label of *New Public Management* (see, for instance, Kickert, 1997a; Pollitt & Talbot, 2004). Hence, combining the study of innovation with the change management and reform literatures could be a welcome addition for both sides (compare Van der Voet, Kuipers & Groeneveld, this volume).

Notes

1. This chapter is partly based on the LIPSE working paper no: 1, Social innovation in the public sector: an integrative framework. LIPSE (Learning from Innovation in Public Sector Environments) is a research program under the European Commission's 7th Framework Programme as a Small or Medium-Scale Focused

Research Project (2011–14). The project focuses on studying social innovations in the public sector (www.lipse.org).
2. http://www.whitehouse.gov/administration/eop/sicp/initiatives/social-innovation-fund, last accessed 19 February 2016
3. http://www.dac.dk/en/dac-cities/sustainable-cities/all-cases/green-city/copenhagen-urban-gardens-liven-up-oerestad/ accessed October 7, 2014.

References

Albury, D. (2005). Fostering innovation in public services. *Public Money & Management, 25*(1), 51–56.

Alford, J. (2009). Public value from co-production by clients. *Public Sector, 32*(4), 11–12.

Amabile, T.M., Conti, R., Coon, H., Lazenby, J., & Herron, M. (1996). Assessing the work environment for creativity. *Academy of Management Journal, 39*(5), 1154–1184.

Asheim, B., & Gertler, M. (2005) [2006]. The geography of innovation. In J. Fagerberg, D.C. Mowery and R.R. Nelson (Eds.), *Oxford handbook of innovation* (pp. 291–318). Oxford: Oxford University Press.

Bason, C. (2010). *Leading public sector innovation*. Bristol: Policy Press.

Bass, B.M., & Bass, R. (2009). *The Bass handbook of leadership: Theory, research and managerial applications*. New York: Free Press.

Beer, M., & Nohria, N. (2000). Cracking the code of change. *Harvard Business Review, May–June,* 14–22.

Bekkers, V. (2004). Virtual policy communities and responsive governance: Redesigning on-line debates. *Information Polity, 9*(3–4), 118–129.

Bekkers, V., Edelenbos, J., & Steijn, B. (Eds.). (2011). *Innovation in the public sector: Linking capacity and leadership*. Houndsmills: Palgrave McMillan.

Bekkers, V., Tummers, L., Stuijfzand, B. G., & Voorberg, W. (2013). *Social innovation in the public sector: An integrative framework (No. 1)*. LIPSE Working papers. Rotterdam: Erasmus University Rotterdam.

Berman, E. M. (1997). Dealing with cynical citizens. *Public Administration Review,* 105–112.

Bernier, L., & Hafsi, T. (2007). The changing nature of public entrepreneurship. *Public Administration Review, 67*(3), 488–503.

Bhatti, Y., Olsen, A., & Pedersen, L. (2011). Administrative professionals and the diffusion of innovations: The case of citizen service centers. *Public Administration, 89*(2), 577–594.

Bommert, B. (2010). Collaborative innovation in the public sector. *International Public Management Review, 11,* 15–33.

Borins, S. (2002). Leadership and innovation in the public sector. *Leadership & Organization Development Journal, 23*(8), 467–476.

Bovaird, T., & Löffler, E. (2012). From engagement to co-production: The contribution of users and communities to outcomes and public value. *Voluntas, 23*(4), 1119–1138.

Castells, M. (1996). *The rise of the network society*. Cambridge: Blackwell.

Chesbrough, H. (2003). *Open innovation: The new imperative for creating and profiting from technology*. Harvard: Harvard Business School Press.

Cleff, T. (2008). French oysters and German cabbage demand and country-specific drivers and barriers for innovation in the European (EU-25) food & drink industry. In D. Barkovic and B. Runzheimer (Eds.), *Interdisciplinary management research IV, Osijek* (pp. 389–426). Osijek: Josip Juraj Strossmayer University of Osijek

Considine, M., Lewis, J., & Alexander, D. (2009). *Networks, innovation and public policy: Politicians, bureaucrats and the pathways to change inside government.* Basingstoke, UK: Palgrave Macmillan.

Damanpour, F., & Schneider, M. (2009). Characteristics of innovation and innovation adoption in public organizations: Assessing the role of managers. *Journal of Public Administration Theory and Practice, 19,* 495–522.

European Commission. (2011). *Empowering people, driving change: Social innovation in the European Union.* Luxemburg: Publications of the European Union.

European Commission, expert group on public sector innovation. (2013). *Powering European public sector innovation.* Brussels: European Commission (Directorate General for Research and Innovation).

Folz, D. (2004). Service quality and benchmarking the performance of municipal services. *Public Administration Review, 64*(2), 209–220.

Gabris, G.T., Golembiewski, R.T., & Ihrke, D.M. (2001). Leadership credibility, board relations, and administrative innovation at the local government level. *Journal of Public Administration Research and Theory, 11*(1), 89–108.

Ghoshal, S., & Bartlett, C.A. (1988). Creation, adoption, and diffusion of innovations by subsidiaries of multinational corporations. *Journal of International Business Studies, 19*(3), 365–388.

Gloor, P.A. (2005). *Swarm creativity: Competitive advantage through collaborative innovation networks.* Oxford: Oxford University Press.

Greenhalgh, T., Robert, G., Macfarlane, F., Bate, P., & Kyriakidou, O. (2004). Diffusion of innovations in service organizations: Systematic review and recommendations. *Milbank Quarterly, 82*(4), 581–629.

Han, J.K., Kim, N., & Srivastava, R. K. (1998). Market orientation and organizational performance: Is innovation a missing link? *The Journal of Marketing, 62*(4), 30–45.

Hansen, M.B. (2011). Antecedents of organizational innovation: The diffusion of new public management into Danish local government. *Public Administration, 89*(2), 285–306.

Harris, M., & Albury, D. (2009). *The innovation imperative: Why radical innovation is needed to reinvent public services for the recession and beyond.* London: NESTA.

Hartley, J. (2005). Innovation in governance and public services: Past and present. *Public Money and Management, 25*(1), 27–34.

Holmes, S., & Smart, P. (2009). Exploring open innovation practice in firm-nonprofit engagements: A corporate social responsibility perspective. *R&D Management, 39*(4), 394–409.

Kelman, S. (2008). The 'Kennedy School School' of research on innovation in government. In S. Borins (Ed.), *Innovations in government: Research recognition and replication* (pp. 28–52). Washington: Brookings Institute.

Kickert, W.J. (1997a). Public governance in the Netherlands: An alternative to Anglo-American 'managerialism'. *Public Administration, 75*(4), 731–752.

Kickert, W.J. (1997b). *Public management in the United States and Europe: Public management and administrative reform in Western Europe.* Cheltenham: Edward Elgar.

Kickert, W.J. (2011). Distinctiveness of administrative reform in Greece, Italy, Portugal and Spain: Common characteristics of context, administrations and reforms. *Public Administration, 89*(3), 801–818.

Koppenjan, J.F.M., & Klijn, E.H. (2004). *Managing uncertainties in networks: A network approach to problem solving and decision making.* London: Routledge.

Loughlin, J., & Peters, B.G. (1997). State traditions, administrative reform and regionalization. In M. Keating and J. Loughlin (Eds.), *The political economy of regionalism* (pp. 41–62). London: Frank Cass.

Loyens, K. (2014). Coping with policy alienation in law enforcement. In P. Hupe, M. Hill and A. Buffat (Eds.), *Understanding street-level bureaucracy* (pp. 99–114). London: Routledge.

Maranto, R., & Wolf, P. (2013). Cops, teachers and the art of the impossible, explaining the lack of diffusion of innovations that make impossible jobs possible. *Public Administration Review, 73*(2), 230–240.

Mergel, I.A. (2014). *Introducing open collaboration in the public sector: The case of social coding on github*. Speyer: IRSPM.

Mulgan, G., & Albury, D. (2003). *Innovation in the public sector*. London: Strategy Unit Cabinet Office.

Mulgan. J. (2006). *Social innovation: What it is, why it matters and how it can be accelerated*. Oxford: Oxford Said Business School.

Mulgan, J. (2009). *The art of public strategy*. Oxford: Oxford University Press.

Murray, R., Caulier-Grice, J., & Mulgan, G. (2010). *The open book of social innovation*. London: National Endowment for Science, Technology and the Art.

Osborne, D., & Gaebler, T. (1992). *Reinventing government: How the entrepreneurial spirit is transforming the public sector*. Reading, MA: Addison-Welsey.

Osborne, S.P., & Brown, L. (2005). *Managing change and innovation in public service organizations*. London: Routledge.

Osborne, S.P., & Brown, L. (2011). Innovation, public policy and public services delivery in the UK: The word that would be king? *Public Administration, 89*(4), 1335–1350.

Osborne, S.P., & Brown, L. (Eds.). (2013). *Handbook of innovation in public services*. Cheltenham: Edward Elgar Publishing.

Pärna, O., & Von Tunzelmann, N. (2007). Innovation in the public sector: Key features influencing the development and implementation of technologically innovative public sector services in the UK, Denmark, Finland and Estonia. *Information Polity, 12*(3), 109–125.

Pierson, P. (Ed.) (2001). *The new politics of the welfare state*. Oxford, UK: Oxford University Press.

Pollitt, C., & Bouckaert, G. (2011). *Public management reform: A comparative analysis-new public management governance, and the Neo-Weberian state*. Oxford: Oxford University Press.

Pollitt, C., & Hupe, P. (2011). Talking about government: The role of magic concepts. *Public Management Review, 13*(5), 641–658.

Pollitt, C., & Talbot, C. (Eds.). (2004). *Unbundled government: A critical analysis of the global trend to agencies, quangos and contractualisation*. London: Routledge.

Rogers, E. (2003). *Diffusion of innovations*. 5th edition. New York: Free Press.

Salge, T., & Vera, A. (2012). Benefiting from public sector innovation: The moderating role of customer and learning orientation. *Public Administration Review, 72*(4), 550–560.

Schudson, M. (1998). *The good citizen: A history of American civic life* (p. 192). New York: Martin Kessler Books.

Schumpeter, J.A. (1934). *The theory of economic development*. Boston: Harvard University Press.

Schumpeter, J.A. (1942). *Capitalism, socialism and democracy*. New York: Harper.

Shalley, C.E., Zhou, J., & Oldham, G.R. (2004). The effects of personal and contextual characteristics on creativity: Where should we go from here? *Journal of Management, 30*(6), 933–958.

Simmons, R., & Shiffman, J. (2007). *Scaling up health service innovations: A framework for action*. Scaling up health service delivery, World Health Organization.

Sørensen, E. (2006). Metagovernance the changing role of politicians in processes of democratic governance. *The American Review of Public Administration, 36*(1), 98–114.

Sørensen, E., & Torfing, J. (2011). Enhancing collaborative innovation in the public sector. *Administration & Society, 43*(8), 842–868.

Tummers, L. (2011). Explaining the willingness of public professionals to implement new policies: A policy alienation framework. *International Review of Administrative Sciences, 77*(3), 555–581.

Tummers, L., Bekkers, V., & Steijn, B. (2009). Policy alienation of public professionals: Application in a new public management context. *Public Management Review, 11*(5), 685–706.

Van Buuren, A., & Loorbach, D. (2009). Policy innovation in isolation. *Public Management Review, 11*(3), 375–392.

Van de Ven, A. (1999). *The innovation journey.* Oxford: Oxford University Press.

Venkatesh, V., Morris, M., Davis, G., & Davis, F. (2003). User acceptance of information technology: Toward a unified view. *MIS quarterly, 27*(3), 425–478.

Voets, J., & De Rynck, P. (2008). Exploring the innovative capacity of intergovernmental network managers: The art of boundary scanning and boundary spanning.

Von Hippel, E. (2007). Horizontal innovation networks—by and for users. *Industrial and Corporate Change, 16*(2), 1–23.

Voorberg, W., Bekkers, V.J.J.M., & Tummers, L.G. (2015). A systematic review of co-creation and co-production: Embarking on the social innovation journey. *Public Management Review, 19*(9), 1333–1357.

Walker, R.M. (2006). Innovation type and diffusion: An empirical analysis of local government. *Public Administration, 84*(2), 311–335.

Walker, R.M. (2014). Internal and external antecedents of process innovation: A review and extension. *Public Management Review, 16*(1), 21–44.

Windrum, P., & Koch, P. (Eds.). (2008). *Innovation in public services: Entrepreneurship, creativity and management.* Cheltenham: Edgar Elgar.

6 A Change Management Perspective

*Joris van der Voet, Ben S. Kuipers
and Sandra Groeneveld*

Introduction

Public sector reform can be defined as 'deliberate changes to the structures and processes of public sector organizations with the objective of getting them (in some sense) to run better' (Pollitt & Bouckaert, 2004: 8). This definition, widely used by students of public sector reform, makes clear that, in essence, public sector reform is concerned with intentional organizational change on the level of public organizations. To have any effect, reform programs and initiatives must ultimately result in changes in the work processes of public organizations and in the attitudes and behavior of employees who work in these organizations. However, research has unequivocally shown that public sector reform does not always result in the anticipated effects (Pollitt & Dan, 2013). We argue in this chapter that this discrepancy between anticipated and actual effects can be understood if the implementation of reform within organizations is examined more closely. Despite the above definition, research on public sector reform has largely overlooked the implementation processes it invokes on the organizational and individual level. Instead, most studies on public sector reform have focused on the macro-level of sectors and civil service systems. We believe this to be a consequence of the theoretical approaches that have been dominant in the study of public sector reform.

Institutionalism—which we conceive of as the dominant approach within the literature on public sector reform—comprises a set of several neo-institutionalist approaches (see, for instance, the chapters by Christensen, Lægreid and Olsen in this volume). Institutional approaches emphasize how organizations comply with environmental pressures in their respective organizational fields to achieve legitimate outcomes. Although some institutional approaches devote attention to the role of agency within processes of change, in the study of public sector reform, this has primarily been limited to political actors and decision-making processes at the system level. What we take from an institutional approach to the study of public sector reform is the attention on the role of the public sector context. Our aim is to add a focus on the micro-foundations of organizational change considering the

rational-adaptive behavior of managers and employees within public organizations by introducing a change management perspective on public sector
reform.

It is important to note that the change management literature is extensive and internally incoherent. Rather than a coherent framework, theory
on change management is informed by distinct academic disciplines and is
often studied based on different epistemological and ontological traditions.
For example, some approaches conceptualize organizational change as a
temporary episode of organizational upheaval (e.g., Grundy, 1993; Kotter,
1996), whereas other approaches depart from the notion that organizations
are a product of social construction and instead contend that they are in a
continuous state of flux (Weick & Quinn, 1999). Moreover, some authors
focus on large-scale organizational turnarounds and highlight the planned
nature of organizational change (Burke, 2002; By, 2005), whereas others
focus on the incremental notion of change and its emergent characteristics
(Kelman, 2005; Plowman et al., 2007). In addition, the change management
literature also consists of (quasi) practitioner-oriented works that both build
on and feed back to the academic literature on change management
(cf. Brunsson, 2000; Boyne, 2006).

Despite the conceptual complexity inherent to the literature on change
management, this literature offers much to enrich our understanding of public sector reform. We address the following question: how can change management perspectives complement dominant (institutionalist) approaches to
the study of public sector reform? We identify distinct building blocks that
comprise the implementation of organizational change, such as the process,
content, context and actors of change. In the following sections, we elaborate on these building blocks through five questions for change management. We will discuss how these questions are addressed in the literature on
change management. In so doing, we reveal how this literature can be combined with insights from the public management literature to create a better
understanding of change in public sector organizations. Subsequently, we
provide an empirical illustration of the application of change management
perspectives, which we develop by presenting a case study of the implementation of reform in a public organization. We conclude this chapter by identifying three contributions of integrating the change management literature
and public sector reform literature as complementary fields of study.

Questions for Change Management: What, Why, How, Who and Where

In the introduction, we noted that there is not a single change management
literature. As in many fields, there is a variety of views and angles and a
diverse methodological and theoretical background. The reader will find
interpretive and positivist methodologies, along with backgrounds in managerial, public administrative, organizational, institutional, psychological,

leadership, network, complexity and chaos literature. What the field of change management (or often referred to as organizational change) combines is the study of the processes of change within and between organizations and the role of actors in these processes. Whether the field always manages to address these issues well is a continuous matter of debate. Various scholars, such as Pettigrew (1985, 1990) and Armenakis and Bedeian (1999), note the flaws and gaps in this field of study. Based on the issues they address, and the outcomes of a literature review by Kuipers et al. (2014) on change management in public organizations, we formulate a number of questions that help to clarify where organizational change may contribute to understanding public sector reform. These questions refer to the context of change (where and when?), the content of change (what and why?), the process of change (how?), and the actors of change (who?). Based on Kuipers et al. (2014), we observe that the main contributions of the change management literature relate to the questions concerning how and who, whereas the reform literature contributes primarily to the questions regarding 'what' and 'why' as well as 'when' and 'where'. Below, we elaborate on these questions and how the literature addresses them.

Where and When? The Context of Change

By answering the question of where and when the change takes place, we obtain important information on the context of organizational change. This helps us to understand what is triggering and driving the change, or hampering it, and at what instance. By answering these questions, it becomes clear that every change is embedded in an environment of actors and factors and in a history, all of which help to understand what type and scale of change is taking place and the reference frames that can be applied (Kickert & Van der Meer, 2011; Kuipers et al., 2014). Hartley, Butler and Benington (2002) show how change simultaneously has different contexts at the societal level, governmental level, organizational level and actor level. The literature on organizational change in public contexts shows how the role of complex stakeholder networks and their competing values (e.g., Grimshaw, Vincent & Willmott, 2002) and political involvement (e.g., Weissert & Goggin, 2002) may affect not only the shape and occurrence of change but also, directly, the process of implementation. Some studies have suggested that research on organizational change in the public sector should devote particular attention to the aspects of public organizations that encompass the differences between public and private organizations (e.g., Boyne, 2002; Rainey, 2012). For example, some studies assess how the particular motivational bases of public sector workers—often conceptualized as public service motivation (Perry & Wise, 1990)—affect their attitudes toward organizational change (e.g., Naff & Crum, 1999; Wright, Christensen & Isett, 2013; Van der Voet, Steijn & Kuipers, 2015). Other studies investigate the extent to which the complex political environment and bureaucratic organizational structures that often characterize public organizations affect the implementation of organizational change (Robertson & Seneviratne, 1995; Coram & Burnes, 2001; Van der Voet, 2015; Van der Voet, Kuipers & Groeneveld, 2015a).

What and Why? The Content of Change

Closely interacting with 'where' and 'when' are the questions of 'what' and 'why' in relation to change. The 'what' question relates to the content of the change, e.g., the new direction, policy, procedure or structure (Kuipers et al., 2014). The content of the change is one of the main issues in the reform literature but also receives considerable attention in the change management literature. Typical themes for change and reform in the public sector are sector reforms and the introduction of new or changed policies. Health service reforms (e.g., Pope, Robert, Bate, Le May & Gabbay, 2006), welfare reforms (e.g., Askim, Christensen, Fimreite & Lægreid, 2009), EU reforms (e.g., Bauer, 2008), education sector reforms (e.g., De Boer, Enders & Leisyte, 2007), and the introduction of e-governance (e.g., O'Neill, 2009) are some of the themes that determine the content of change. The literature review by Kuipers et al. (2014) reveals that many of these changes are New Public Management (NPM) related. Partly, this is a context issue, as governments are focusing on improved efficiency (which may also be urged by an economic crisis), effectiveness and service quality. This often specifies the content of the change (or reform) because new systems, policies, procedures and laws may be especially designed to achieve these goals.

In the literature on change management, several authors offer conceptual tools to classify the content or magnitude of change. For example, Greenwood and Hinings (1993) discuss radical and incremental change, and Van de Ven and Poole (1995) refer to frame-breaking change versus frame-bending change. These conceptualizations can be helpful to distinguish large-scale transformations from changes that are aimed at small-scale improvement rather than organizational turnarounds. Apart from the magnitude of change, it is also important to consider the reasons for organizational change. In the public sector, it is important to recognize that organizational change is often imposed on individual organizations as a result of policy change or system-wide reform. Brunsson (2000), therefore, makes another relevant distinction between adaptive changes and imposed changes. Adaptive changes arise automatically as a result of environmental pressures and demands, whereas imposed changes are intentional changes that must be implemented through the actions of individuals. This is congruent with Pollitt and Bouckaert's (2004: 8) definition of public management reform as 'deliberate' changes aimed at improvement. Related to this, Kuipers et al. (2014) discuss different orders of change (cf. Bartunek & Moch, 1987), sub-system change (first-order), organization change (second-order), and sector change (third-order).

How? The Process of Change

One of the main contributions of the change management literature is that it highlights the process through which change is implemented. The central assumption in change management is that the implementation of organizational change is dependent not only on what changes—the content of change—but also on the process of change through which organizational change arises. Organizational change, thus, can be managed. The literature on organizational change offers many different theories and approaches regarding how the implementation of organizational change arises. Akin to many theories in the organization sciences, these approaches are often presented as a dichotomy. For example, Russ (2008) discusses differences between programmatic and participatory change, Beer and Nohria (2000) propose theory E and O, Boonstra, Steensma and Demenint (2008) discuss design and development approaches, Burke (2002) uses revolutionary versus evolutionary change and Sminia and Van Nistelrooij (2006) refer to strategic management and organizational development. Although there are conceptual differences between these approaches, the literature on change processes is often summarized by clustering them into two anti-typical traditions. In this chapter, we refer to these traditions with the often-used distinction between planned and emergent change (Burnes, 1996, 2004, 2009; Pettigrew, 2000; Bamford & Forrester, 2003; By, 2005; Kickert, 2010; Kuipers et al., 2014; Van der Voet, Groeneveld & Kuipers, 2014; Van der Voet, 2014a).

The planned approach to organizational change is likely the most applied approach to implement organizational change (By, 2005). Planned processes of change rely heavily on the role of management. The implementation of planned change is top-down and programmatic in the sense that the objectives of change are formulated at the beginning of the change process. Subsequently, managers attempt to implement the organizational change by convincing employees that the proposed change is desirable. Through a process of 'telling and selling', managers communicate the content of change and why employees should be committed to implementing it (Russ, 2008). Popular change management approaches often fit the planned change perspective (e.g., Kanter, Stein & Jick, 1992; Kotter, 1996; Fernandez & Rainey, 2006). In planned processes of change, the role of leadership is that of a prime mover who creates change (Weick & Quinn, 1999). Leaders develop with the vision for change and attempt to build commitment among employees (Beer & Nohria, 2000; Boonstra, 2004).

The emergent approach to change implementation arose as a reaction to the planned approach to change (Bamford & Forrester, 2003; By, 2005). In the research—based on a view of organizations as processes, the term emergent change is often used to refer to ongoing, sporadic and unpredictable changes (e.g., Weick, 2000; Plowman et al., 2007). In this chapter, the emergent approach to change is regarded as a more devolved and bottom-up approach to implementing change. In this sense, the use of the term emergent change is thus comparable to what other authors refer to as organizational development (e.g., Beer & Nohria, 2000; Boonstra, 2004). The content of change is not the starting point as in the planned approach to change but rather the outcome of an emergent change process. The content of emergent change processes comes about through the participation of employees. Employees, thus, are not seen as passive recipients of the organizational change but as active participants in the change process (Russ, 2008). Managers may facilitate emergent change, but they do not formulate detailed change objectives for the organization to implement. Emergent change can be more unpredictable and time-consuming than a planned change process, but it may also result in changed content that is better suited to the situation or the interests of employees.

Although the approaches are often discussed as dichotomous and antitypical, other authors argue that the successful implementation of change requires a combination of the two approaches (e.g., Beer & Nohria, 2000; Pettigrew, 2000; Boonstra, 2004; Burnes, 2004). Planned and emergent change should be seen as a duality: they have properties that may seem contradictory or paradoxical but in fact are complementary (Pettigrew, 2000: 245). However, combining planned and emergent change is difficult to accomplish (Sminia & Van Nistelrooij, 2006). Alternating between both change approaches too frequently may result in confusion among employees. Moreover, a planned change approach may override the results of an emergent change approach and damage employee morale and trust in management (Beer & Nohria, 2000; Sminia & Van Nistelrooij, 2006). The preferred way of combining planned and emergent change may be to have managers provide direction from the top and have employees create the content and meaning of organizational change from the bottom. In such an approach, the combination of planned and emergent change may lead to desirable change outcomes (Van der Voet, 2014a).

Who? Actors in the Change

The actors in the change play a pivotal role in all of these questions. They are part of the context (internal and external), they shape and interpret the content and they act and respond in the implementation process. Various issues concerning actors within and around a public organization can be addressed when examining reform and organizational change. In addition to internal actors such as managers and employees, other studies emphasize external actors such as politicians, unions, citizens and partner organizations on which public organization may be dependent during change (e.g., Fernandez & Rainey, 2006; Van der Voet, Kuipers & Groeneveld, 2015b). In this section, we focus on three general phenomena that relate to the actors in the change and that are often discussed in change management literature. These are the process of sense-making, attitudes and behaviors in change and change leadership. We acknowledge the overlap between them and the various theoretical perspectives that could be further used to study these phenomena.

When examining who is involved in the change, we often use the term sense-making (Weick, 2001). Thereby, we refer to the phenomenon that every actor has his or her own personal perception of the change. In other words, there is not one content and context to the change but as many as there are actors in the change process. Each of them has his or her personal experiences and creates his or her own perceptions of why the change is occurring and what it is about. For example, for one person, a healthcare sector reform may entail the possibility of finally focusing on what healthcare should be about, for another person the profession may change in such a way that all securities built up over a 30-year career are broken down. Sense-making implies that there is no objective interpretation of change but only personal, situational definitions of change. This corresponds to the so-called Thomas theorem: 'if men define situations as real, they are real in their consequences.' The issue is that sense-making always takes place, in every type of change, great or small. Do we disregard it, disqualify different perceptions as resistance, or regard it as a fact of change and attempt to build on it during the change?

How change recipients make sense of organizational change ultimately determines their attitudes and behavior regarding the change and, thereby, ultimately the performance of or outcomes for the organization. In the literature on change management, the term 'success' is often used to account for the effects of organizational change (e.g., Kotter, 1996; Fernandez & Rainey, 2006; Higgs & Rowland, 2010). However, success is a subjective term. Different stakeholders may have different perceptions of the success of a certain change initiative. Especially in the case of an emergent approach to change, in which the objectives of change are not formulated a priori, it may be difficult to assess the degree in which the organizational change was 'successful' (Kuipers et al., 2014). Moreover, studies that refer to the success of change are often not based on empirical evidence (e.g., Miller, 2001; Gill, 2002). Pettigrew (2000) and Pettigrew, Woodman & Cameron (2001), therefore, state that studies should seek to incorporate objective outcome variables such as organizational performance.

Alternatively, studies on organizational change often assess the outcomes of change with affective or behavioral criteria. Because successful change is argued to be dependent on the support of employees, researchers often focus on the attitudes of employees toward change (Self, Armenakis & Schraeder, 2007; Walker, Armenakis & Berneth, 2007; Herold, Fedor, Caldwell & Liu, 2008). Examples of such attitudes are resistance to change (Van Dam, Oreg & Schyns, 2008), cynicism about organizational change (Wanous, Reichers & Austin, 2000; Bommer, Rich & Rubin, 2005), willingness to change (Metselaar, 1997; Tummers, 2011; Tummers, Steijn & Bekkers, 2012; Van der Voet, 2014b) and commitment to change (Herscovitch &

Meyer, 2002; Herold et al., 2008). Such employee attitudes are shown to be an important antecedent of the behavioral intentions of employees to support organizational change. Oreg, Vakola and Armenakis (2011), in their review of 60 years of research into change recipients' reactions to change, distinguish among affective reactions (how change recipients feel), cognitive reactions (what change recipients think) and behavioral reactions (what change recipients (intend to) do in response to change).

The literature on sense-making and attitudes toward change focuses primarily on change recipients. As a consequence, these aspects generally refer to forms of followership, thereby neglecting the important role of leadership in processes of change. Change leadership is commonly conceptualized as a specific form of behavior and activities aimed at initiating or advancing the implementation of change. In some studies, the function of leadership is also associated with sense-giving, the attempts of leadership to influence the sense-making process among actors in the change (Caldwell, 2009). Generally, leadership is regarded as a crucial condition to create support among employees in both the private sector (Kotter, 1996; Higgs & Rowland, 2005, 2010) and the public sector (Fernandez & Rainey, 2006; Karp & Helgø, 2008). Although the influence of leadership on commitment to change is rarely challenged, little empirical evidence exists (Burke, 2002; Herold et al., 2008), especially in the public sector (Fernandez & Pitts, 2007). The central assumption of this change leadership approach (Liu, 2010) is that appropriate change-related behaviors can be prescribed and applied to achieve positive results (Herold et al., 2008). Most models of change leadership refer to formal leaders at the top-management level and concern attention to envisioning a future state, communicating the vision, providing a plan for action and consolidating changes (e.g., Kotter, 1996; Herold et al., 2008). Change leadership is often conceptualized from a 'heroic' perspective: the transformational change leader.

The core of transformational leadership theory is that 'by articulating a vision, fostering the acceptance of group goals, and providing individualized support, effective leaders change the basic values, beliefs, and attitudes of followers so that they are willing to perform beyond the minimum levels specified by the organization' (Podsakoff, MacKenzie & Bommer, 1996: 260). Although some studies directly relate transformational leadership to employee support for change (Oreg & Berson, 2011; Van der Voet, 2014b), transformational leadership is not aimed at the implementation of a specific organizational change (Herold et al., 2008). Rather, transformational leaders seek to transform the values of their followers such that the latter value the interests of the group or organization above their personal interests (Bass, 1985). Nevertheless, there is an overlap between typical change leadership activities and the behaviors that underlie transformational leadership behavior (Eisenbach, Watson & Pillai, 1999; Higgs & Rowland, 2011; Van der Voet, 2015). The literatures on both change leadership and transformational leadership highlight behaviors such as articulating desirable future visions for the organization, leading by example and intellectually stimulating subordinates (Bass, 1985).

An Empirical Application

In this section, we present an empirical application of perspectives based on the change management literature by addressing the previously introduced questions for change management. It draws on a case study of an organizational change within the City Works Department of the Dutch city Rotterdam, based on both a qualitative analysis (Van der Voet, Groeneveld & Kuipers, 2014) and a quantitative analysis (Van der Voet, Kuipers & Groeneveld, 2015a). This case is a relevant and perhaps typical example of public sector reform in contemporary public organizations. The empirical illustration shows that public sector reform may require a large transformation at the organizational level. The purpose of the illustration is to apply some central concepts of the change management literature: the content, process and context of change, as well as behaviors and attitudes of actors toward the change. The empirical illustration shows that an organizational change that is similar in terms of change content can be implemented through different processes by different departments within a single organization. The empirical illustration highlights the central role of leadership in the change process and shows how leadership behavior is contingent on the context in which change takes place. Finally, the separate aspects are connected to the outcomes of organizational change by assessing their relationship with commitment to change.

The Content and Context of the Change: Where, When, Why and What?

Through 23 interviews with managers in the organization, the content and process of change were analyzed. The City Works Department is concerned with the urban planning and spatial upkeep of the City of Rotterdam in The Netherlands. The activities of the organization are captured in its slogan: the City Works Department gives shape to the city, and keeps the city in shape. This slogan is twofold to account for the two units the organization is composed of: the Engineering Bureau and the Public Works Sector. The Engineering Bureau is concerned with shaping the city: directing the realization of infrastructural and spatial planning. The Public Works Sector performs maintenance of the city. It maintains the city's public grounds, parks and roads.

The City Works Department has existed for over 100 years. Over this time, the organization developed a set a dominant values and a distinct way of interacting with its environment. Members of the organization characterize the organization as very hierarchic and bureaucratic. According to them, the City Works Department consisted mainly of highly skilled professionals, many of them engineers, who were intrinsically motivated to achieve the highest quality in their work. Professionals enjoyed a high degree of professional autonomy in their projects, but simultaneously, decision-making in the organization was highly centralized. The dominant management style in the organization was directive and aimed at control. For outsiders, the organization was sometimes perceived as an unresponsive, closed organization. As part of a citywide reform, a change was initiated to address these issues. The logic underlying this reform was based on the New Public Management (NPM). The reform was intended to increase the organization's emphasis on time and cost-effectiveness and making the organization more responsive to the demands and needs of citizens, politicians and other external stakeholders. To achieve this, the organization's directive management style was to be replaced by decentralizing more responsibilities to lower-level managers and employees. The characteristics of the current organization and the objectives of the change are summarized in table 6.1.

Although the reform was intended to improve cost-effectiveness and increase responsiveness, the reform was perceived as a radical transformation. The content of change implied a profound change relative to the organization's dominant values. The City Works Department emphasized rigid structures, hierarchy and control to ensure typical public sector values such as accountability, reliability and equity (e.g., Van der Wal, De Graaf & Lasthuizen, 2008). In contrast, the reform highlighted private sector values such as efficiency, client service and responsiveness. Such values are often secondary or even alien to public sector organizations. Rather than merely improving the operations of public organizations, public sector reform may thus require the radical transformation of public organizations' core values.

Table 6.1 The content of change

	Current organization	*Desired organization*
Sense of self	Civil servant	Public manager / public professional
Central values	Quality Task-oriented Professional autonomy (Being in) control	Time and cost efficiency Environment oriented Transparency and consultation Participation and decentralization
Attitude toward environment	Paternalistic: 'we know what's best for citizens', 'the city is ours'	Responsive: 'we are here for the city'
Dominant management style	Directive, top-down	Delegating responsibilities, participative

(adapted from Van der Voet, Groeneveld & Kuipers, 2014)

The Process of Change: How?

The City Works Department case is interesting to study from a change management perspective, as there are two organizational units that employed very different processes of change to implement the same reform (cf. Van der Voet, Groeneveld & Kuipers, 2014). The Engineering Bureau opted for a change process with many characteristics of planned change, while the Public Works Sector embarked on a change process that had more characteristics of emergent change. This makes the case uniquely appropriate to compare different processes of change, in a context with few differences in the content of the change.

The approach of the management team of the Engineering Bureau was to first develop the content of the desired change to be able to clearly communicate the vision of change to the employees of the organizational unit. The content of the desired change was developed almost entirely by members of the management team. To be able to clearly communicate the change, the management team felt that it was important to develop with a slogan that summarized the content of change. During the change process, multiple slogans were used, such as ´New Engineering´ and ´From Engineering to Advisory´. One of the main challenges for the management team of the Engineering Bureau was to make what the change was about clear to employees. However, the employees of the Engineering Bureau were engaged in a broad array of tasks, which made it difficult to clearly communicate what behavior was expected of them. The content of change was characterized, thus, by a high degree of ambiguity, which was perceived as a problematic issue by members of the management team. In the words of a manager in the Engineering Bureau:

> 'Everybody in the organization says that we have to go ´From Engineering to Advisory', but everybody has a different view on what that means in daily practice. [. . .] We have to make clear what it means for the behavior of employees!'

Managers found it difficult to clearly communicate the content of the change to employees. As can perhaps be expected of engineers, their solution was to further plan out and specify the content of change in the boardroom, rather than openly discussing the change with employees. A manager of the Engineering Bureau explains:

> 'It is absolutely pointless to start informing people when things are still in the idea stage. It will cause people to become insecure and start asking questions I don't have an answer to. [. . .] However, what becomes apparent now, at least in my department, is that too little has been communicated in the past years.'

At a later point in the change process, the management team created a so-called strategy team, consisting of employees with no managerial position, to participate in the change process by elaborating on the objectives that were defined by the board of directors. However, the degree of employee participation was limited in the change process of the Engineering Bureau because few employees were part of this strategy team, it had only limited decision-making authority and it could only elaborate on the strategic direction already determined by the management.

In contrast, employee participation was at the core of the change process of the Public Works Sector. The management team initiated the change process, but the responsibility for the change process was quickly delegated to a project team consisting of lower-level managers and frontline employees. For an organization that was traditionally characterized by hierarchy and a directive management style, this was an unconventional approach. Based on a round of interviews with external stakeholders, the project team then developed four broad themes that together comprised the vision of the change, which was named 'Topshape'. This name was deliberately connected to the former slogan of the organization, which also contained the word 'shape'. Because of this, the reform was framed as an improvement on the organization's current values, rather than radical break from the past. A member of the project team explains this approach:

> 'The idea there is to appreciate what was before. It is a form of respect, so to say. I've seen organizational changes where a new leader barges in out of nowhere saying: "Everything you have been doing is wrong!" I don't think that is much of a motivation for most people.'

The four themes that were formulated by the project team had names such as 'Expertise in Topshape' and 'Connection in Topshape'. Similar to the change process, the vision of change was not particularly operational or detailed and, thus, contained a high degree of ambiguity. Rather than attempting to eliminate this ambiguity, ambiguity was deliberately preserved by inviting employees to discuss what the four themes meant to them in working groups and other sessions. A member of the project team explains:

> 'We could have written an elaborate plan, complete with many examples of what 'Connection in Topshape' means. But it means something different for everyone. So we shortly described it in abstract terms but not what kind of actions or behaviors are attached to it. We decided to leave that open. It is something different for every department and every employee. It allows them to discuss it with each other.'

Behaviors and Attitudes of Actors in the Change: Who?

Despite the similarities in the content of these changes, the Engineering Bureau and the Public Works Sector implemented organizational change through different change processes. In this final section of this empirical

Table 6.2 The process of change

	Engineering Bureau	Public Works Sector
Development of the content of change	- Top-down: Devised by board of directors - A priori planned objectives of change	- Bottom-up: Devised by project team and environmental stakeholders - Emergent objectives of change
Content of change	- Replacement / Frame breaking: content of change is disconnected from former slogans and values	- Modification / Frame bending: Former slogans and values as foundation for the objectives of change
Communication	- Focused on sense of urgency - Focused on content of change - Aimed at decreasing ambiguity	- Focused on sense of urgency - Aimed at stimulating interpretation by employees
Participation	- Relatively late in the change process - Participation by project team - Outcome is advisory	- Delegation to project team from the start - Participation of project team and over 140 employees - Outcome is binding
Role of ambiguity	- Ambiguity as a threat - Eliminate it!	- Ambiguity as an opportunity - Preserve it!

(adapted from Van der Voet, Groeneveld & Kuipers, 2014)

illustration, we assess how these different processes are related to the outcomes of change in terms of the attitudes and behaviors of the various actors. We base this part of the empirical illustration on a study based on quantitative methods (Van der Voet, Kuipers & Groeneveld, 2015a). As an outcome variable, commitment to change was measured among employees of the organization using an online survey to which 515 employees responded (response rate of 35.5 percent). Herscovitch and Meyer (2002: 475) define affective commitment to change as 'a desire to provide support for the change based on a belief in its inherent benefits.' This analysis thus allows us to examine what type of implementation process—planned or emergent change—is more likely to create support for change among employees. To account for different processes of change, a measure developed by Farrell (2000) was used to measure the extent to which employee perceptions of the change process reflected planned or emergent change. In addition, as the qualitative study revealed important differences in terms of change communication and participation between the two change processes, the quality of change communication and the degree of participation were measured.

Apart from the process and outcomes of change, the study also incorporated variables that accounted for the context of change, as well as the leadership behaviors of direct supervisors. The context of change was captured in the study by measuring employee perceptions of environmental complexity and formalization. The rationale for these variables was that some employees of the organization—most notably those in the Engineering Bureau—performed organizational tasks that were highly complex and characterized by a high degree of autonomy, while other employees—mostly located in the Public Works Sector—performed more routine tasks with a higher degree of written rules and regulations. In addition, these variables relate to theoretical assumptions regarding the specific environmental and structural characteristics of public organizations. The transformational leadership behaviors of direct supervisors were included in the analysis because the role of leadership is generally considered essential during the implementation of organizational change. Transformational leadership may contribute to commitment to change because transformational leaders provide employees with appealing visions of changes for the future of the organization. Moreover, transformational leadership encourages employees to accept innovative solutions to organizational problems by intellectually stimulating and challenging employees (Oreg and Berson, 2011). By doing so, transformational leadership behaviors shape the process of change through which change is implemented, thereby indirectly affecting employee commitment to change.

A theoretical model involving these variables was constructed and fitted to the data using the statistical technique of Structural Equation Modeling (SEM). The results are presented in figure 6.1 below. For the purposes of this chapter, a few results are particularly worth noting. First, both planned change and emergent change processes are positively related to commitment to change among employees. However, the relationship between both change approaches and commitment to change is indirect. The analysis indicates that high degrees of both change communication and employee participation are positively related to commitment to change. This result is consistent with the qualitative analysis of the change process presented

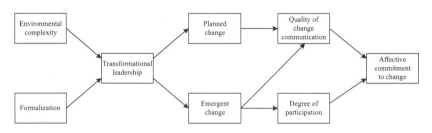

Figure 6.1   Structural model

(adapted from Van der Voet, Kuipers & Groeneveld, 2015a)

above, which also indicates that communication and participation were central aspects of the process of change. The analysis indicates that an emergent change process is likely to result in high-quality change communication and a high degree of employee participation, but that a planned change process is only positively related to the quality of communication. Second, our analysis confirms that transformational leadership may play a central role in the implementation of change. Transformational leadership indirectly influences affective commitment to change by shaping planned and emergent change processes. Some dimensions of transformational leadership, such as envisioning and role modeling, can be assumed to be a core aspect of planned change processes. Moreover, other transformational leadership behaviors such as intellectual stimulation and individual consideration may be expected to be important in emergent change processes. A third result of our analysis is that transformational leadership behavior during change is influenced by the context of change. Environmental complexity is positively related to transformational leadership, while formalization has a negative effect. These factors reflect the contradictory context in which public managers operate: their complex environment encourages transformational leadership behaviors to adapt to environmental shifts and developments, whereas the rules and procedures that characterize the organizational structure simultaneously discourage transformational leadership.

Conclusion

In this chapter, we combined perspectives from the change management literature and the public sector reform literature. We argued that the reform literature primarily emphasizes questions concerning 'what', 'where', 'when' and 'why'. Such questions provide thorough insights into the context and content of the reform and help to compare types of reforms (e.g., in different subsectors or countries) and issues related to policies and politics that determine the content, scope and nature of reform. Change management as a field of study—albeit rather multidisciplinary and diverse—also supports questions regarding the 'how' and 'who' of change. In other words, the implementation processes of reform and the attitudes and behavior of especially actors within the targeted public organizations receive a central role in the change management literature. Both this literature and our empirical illustration of the City Works Department of Rotterdam reveal how these questions play a crucial role in understanding how reform initiatives are actually implemented and the extent to which they become successful.

In conclusion, change management perspectives may contribute to existing research on public sector reform in at least three ways. The first contribution concerns the multi-level nature of public management reform. Reform involves transitions at the national or societal level. However, such transitions often require transformation at the (intra-) organizational level. For example, a current reform in The Netherlands is intended to decentralize youth care from the national to the municipal level. A large part of the success of this reform will depend on how it is implemented by municipal organizations and youth care organizations and to what extent the reform objectives are incorporated into the work of the professionals on the front line (Van der Voet, Steijn & Kuipers, 2015). Perspectives adopted from the change management literature can be applied to examine the implementation of reform at these micro (individuals and teams) and meso levels (the organization) (Higgs, Kuipers, Steijn & Tummers, 2015). To put it boldly, the dominant approach to public sector reform in the public management literature addresses primarily *change made to organizations*, whereas change management literature focuses on *change made by or within organizations*. Integrating the two viewpoints may deliver a strong conceptual basis for understanding the multi-level dimensions of change taking place in the public sector.

Related to this is what we refer to as the factor-actor issue. We argue that the literature on public management reform focuses primarily on factors: the antecedents and consequences of public management reforms. Change management perspectives, thus, can complement the reform literature in this regard because they are predominantly focused on actors. Change management emphasizes the perceptions, preferences and behaviors of those implementing the change (often managers), as well as the perceptions of the change recipients (often employees) (Oreg, Vakola & Armenakis, 2011). An important aspect in the change management literature is the sense-making process that determines how individual actors perceive and react to change and how this sense-making process affects their behavior during organizational change (Weick, 2000). Regarding the example of the decentralization of youth care in the Netherlands, the change management perspective can provide insights into the attitudes of professionals, as well as the ways in which managers (attempt to) influence these attitudes.

The third issue for which applying change management perspectives can make a contribution concerns the content-process disconnect of public management reform. The literature on reform is focused primarily on the reasons for and content of change and not on the change processes (Kickert, 2014; Van der Voet, Kuipers & Groeneveld, 2015a). The reasons—the 'why'— and the content—the 'what'—of change concern the vision and direction of change, for example, an improved customer focus or the use of a new technology. In contrast, the process—the 'how'—of change is concerned with the strategy and interventions that are used to implement change. The change management literature generally recognizes that the success and outcomes of change are not dependent solely on the content of change but particularly on the implementation processes. For example, resistance to change can be a result of a misalignment between the objectives of the reform and the values of the public professionals involved (the content of change), as well as a lack of consultation and participation between change leaders and change recipients during the implementation of the change (the process of change) (see for an example Van der Voet, Steijn & Kuipers, 2015). As such, the change management literature can make an important contribution to understanding and explaining the effects or outcomes of public sector reform.

To conclude, we believe that combining insights from the change management literature and public sector reform literature is beneficial for our understanding, and ultimately the success, of public sector reform. For public administration scholars and practitioners such as politicians, policy makers, managers and consultants, the integration of perspectives from both bodies of literature allows the conceptualization and application of more powerful frameworks to study the phenomena of public sector reform. In particular, the dominant institutionalist perspective on public sector reform can benefit from the attention to the meso and micro levels of individual public organizations, departments, managers and employees that is central to the change management literature. In addition, change management's emphasis on the subjective, personal interpretation of reform initiatives may complement the institutionalist functional interpretation of reform. Finally, change management perspectives highlight the dynamics and agency that is inherent to the implementation of public sector reform, which often stands in stark contrast to the deterministic, structural explanations offered by the institutionalist perspective. Inversely, the use of change management perspectives for the study of public sector reform should also incorporate the strengths of the institutional tradition. In particular, change management research in public sector organizations can benefit from the institutionalist attention to the context and content of reform. Failing to consider the institutional characteristics of public organizations, for instance, their environmental dependencies, history, power relations and the norms and values inherent to the public sector, may lead to an oversimplified and possibly overly optimistic view on public sector reform. We therefore end this chapter by stressing the double-sided complementarity of change management and institutional perspectives on public sector reform.

References

Armenakis, A.A., & Bedeian, A.G. (1999). Organizational change: A review of theory and research in the 1990s. *Journal of Management, 25*(3), 293–315.

Askim, J., Christensen, T., Fimreite, A.L., & Lægreid. P. (2009). How to carry out joined-up government reforms: Lessons from the 2001–2006 Norwegian welfare reform. *International Journal of Public Administration, 32*(12), 1006–1025.

Bamford, D.R., & Forrester, P.L. (2003). Managing planned and emergent change within an operations management environment. *International Journal of Operations & Production Management, 23*(5), 546–564.

Bartunek, J.M., & Moch, M.K. (1987). First-order, second-order, and third-order change and organization development interventions: A cognitive approach. *The Journal of Applied Behavioral Science, 23*(4), 483–500.

Bass, B.M. (1985). *Leadership and performance beyond expectations.* New York: Free Press.

Bauer, M.W. (2008). Introduction: Organizational change, management reform and EU policymaking. *Journal of European Public Policy, 15*(5), 627–647.

Beer, M., & Nohria, N. (2000). Cracking the code of change. *Harvard Business Review, May-June,* 14–22.

Bommer, W.H., Rich, G.A., & Rubin, R.S. (2005). Changing attitudes about change: Longitudinal effects of transformational leader behavior on employee cynicism about organizational change. *Journal of Organizational Behavior, 26*(7), 733–753.

Boonstra, J.J. (2004). (Ed.). *Dynamics of organizational change and learning.* Chichester: Wiley Publishers.

Boonstra, J.J., Steensma, H.O., & Demenint, M.I. (2008). *Ontwerpen en ontwikkelen van organisaties: Theorie en praktijk van complexe veranderingsprocessen.* Den Haag: Reed Business.

Boyne, G.A. (2002). Public and private management: What's the difference? *Journal of Management Studies, 39*(1), 97–122.

Boyne, G.A. (2006). Strategies for public service turnaround: Lessons from the private sector? *Administration & Society, 38*(3), 365–388.

Brunsson, N. (2000). *The irrational organization: Irrationality as a basis for organizational action and change.* Copenhagen: Copenhagen Business School Press.

Burke, W.W. (2002). *Organization change: Theory and practice.* Thousand Oaks: Sage Publications.

Burnes, B. (1996). No such thing as . . . a 'one best way' to manage organizational change. *Management Decision, 34*(10), 11–18.

Burnes, B. (2004). Emergent change and planned change—competitors or allies? The case of XYZ construction. *International Journal of Operations and Production Management, 24*(9), 886–902.

Burnes, B. (2009). Organizational change in the public sector: The case for planned change. In R.T. By and C. Macleod (Eds.), *Managing organizational change in public services: International issues, challenges and cases* (pp. 111–132). London and New York: Routledge.

By, R.T. (2005). Organisational change management: A critical review. *Journal of Change Management, 5*(4), 369–380.

Caldwell, R. (2009). Change from the middle? Exploring middle manager strategic and sense-making agency in public services. In R.T. By and T. Macleod (Eds.), *Managing organizational change in public services* (pp. 74–96). London: Routledge.

Coram, R., & Burnes, B. (2001). Managing organizational change in the public sector: Lessons from the privatization of the Property Service Agency. *The International Journal of Public Sector Management, 14*(2), 94–110.

De Boer, H.F., Enders, J., & Leisyte, L. (2007). Public sector reform in Dutch higher education: The organizational transformation of the university. *Public Administration, 85*(1), 27–46.

Eisenbach, R., Watson, K., & Pillai, R. (1999). Transformational leadership in the context of organizational change. *Journal of Organizational Change Management, 12*(2), 80–88.

Farrell, M.A. (2000). Developing a market-oriented learning organization. *Australian Journal of Management, 25*(2), 201–222.

Fernandez, S., & Pitts, D.W. (2007). Under what conditions do public managers favor and pursue organizational change? *The American Review of Public Administration, 37*(3), 324–341.

Fernandez, S., & Rainey, H.G. (2006). Managing successful organizational change in the public sector: An agenda for research and practice. *Public Administration Review, 66*(2), 168–176.

Gill, R. (2002). Change management—or change leadership? *Journal of Change Management, 3*(4), 307–318.

Greenwood, R., & Hinings, C.R. (1993). Understanding strategic change: The contribution of archetypes. *Academy of Management Journal, 36*(5), 1052–1081.

Grimshaw, D., Vincent, S., & Willmott, H. (2002). Going privately: Partnership and outsourcing in UK public services. *Public Administration, 80*(3), 475–502.

Grundy, T. (1993). *Managing strategic change*. London: Kogan Page.

Hartley, J., Butler, M.J.R., & Benington, J. (2002). Local government modernization: UK and comparative analysis from an organizational perspective. *Public Management Review, 4*(3), 387–404.

Herold, D.M., Fedor, D.B., Caldwell, S.D., & Liu, Y. (2008). The effects of change and transformational leadership on employees' commitment to change: A multilevel study. *Journal of Applied Psychology, 93*(2), 346–357.

Herscovitch, L., & Meyer, J.P. (2002). Commitment to organizational change: Extension of a three-component model. *Journal of Applied Psychology, 87*(3), 474–487.

Higgs, M.J., Kuipers, B.S., Steijn, A.J., & Tummers, L.G. (2015). *Change experiences and leadership in government reform: How bureaucracy threatens commitment to change*. Presented at International Research Society for Public Management Conference: Birmingham, United Kingdom, March 30, 2015, April 1, 2015.

Higgs, M.J., & Rowland, D. (2005). All changes great and small: Exploring approaches to change and its leadership. *Change Management Journal, 5*(2), 121–151.

Higgs, M.J., & Rowland, D. (2010). Emperors with clothes on: The role of self-awareness in developing effective change leadership. *Journal of Change Management, 10*(4), 369–385.

Higgs, M.J., & Rowland, D. (2011). What does it take to implement change successfully? A study of the behaviors of successful change leaders. *Journal of Applied Behavioral Science, 47*(3), 309–335.

Kanter, R.M., Stein, B.A., & Jick, T.D. (1992). *The challenge of organizational change*. New York: The Free Press.

Karp, T., & Helgø, T.I.T. (2008). From change management to change leadership: Embracing chaotic change in public service organizations. *Journal of Change Management, 8*(1), 85–96.

Kelman, S. (2005). *Unleashing change: A study of organizational renewal in government*. Washington, DC: Brookings Institution Press.

Kickert, W.J.M. (2010). Managing emergent and complex change: The case of Dutch agencification. *International Review of Administrative Sciences, 76*(3), 489–515.

Kickert, W.J.M. (2014). The specificity of change management in public organizations: Conditions for successful organizational change in Dutch ministerial departments. *The American Review of Administrative Sciences, 44*(6), 692–717.

Kickert, W.J.M., & Van der Meer, F.B.L. (2011). Small, slow and gradual reform: What can historical institutionalism tell us? *International Journal of Public Administration, 34*(8), 475–485.

Kotter, J.P. (1996). *Leading change*. Boston, MA: Harvard Business School Press.

Kuipers, B.S., Higgs, M., Kickert, W.J.M., Tummers, L., Grandia, J., & Van der Voet, J. (2014). The management of change in public organizations: A literature review. *Public Administration, 92*(1), 1–20.

Liu, Y. (2010). *When change leadership impacts commitment to change and when it doesn't. A multi-level multi-dimensional investigation*. Atlanta: Doctoral dissertation Georgia Institute of Technology.

Metselaar, E.E. (1997). *Assessing the willingness to change: Construction and validation of the DINAMO*. Doctoral dissertation, Amsterdam: Free University of Amsterdam.

Miller, D. (2001). Successful change leaders: What makes them? What do they do that is different? *Journal of Change Management, 2*(4), 359–368.

Naff, K.C., & Crum, J. (1999). Working for America does public service motivation make a difference? *Review of Public Personnel Administration, 19*(4), 5–16.

O'Neill, R. (2009). The transformative impact of e-government on public governance in New Zealand. *Public Management Review, 11*(6), 751–770.

Oreg, S., & Berson, Y. (2011). Leadership and employees' reactions to change: The role of leaders' personal attributes and transformational leadership style. *Personnel Psychology, 64*(3), 627–659.

Oreg, S., Vakola, M., & Armenakis, A. (2011). Change recipients' reactions to organizational change: A 60-year review of quantitative studies. *The Journal of Applied Behavioral Science, 47*(4), 461–524.

Perry, J.L., & Wise, L.R. (1990). The motivational bases of public service. *Public Administration Review, 50*(3), 367–673.

Pettigrew, A.M. (1985). *The awakening giant*. Oxford: Blackwell.

Pettigrew, A.M. (1990). Longitudinal field research on change: Theory and practice. *Organization Science, 1*(3), 267–292.

Pettigrew, A.M. (2000). Linking change processes to outcomes: A commentary on Ghoshal, Bartlett, and Weick. In M. Beer and N. Nohria (Eds.), *Breaking the code of change* (pp. 243–265). Boston: Harvard Business School Press.

Pettigrew, A.M., Woodman, R.W., & Cameron, K.S. (2001). Studying organizational change and development: Challenges for future research. *Academy of Management Journal, 44*(4), 697–713.

Plowman, D.A., Baker, L.T., Beck, T.E., Kulkarni, M., Solansky, S.T., & Travis, D.V. (2007). Radical change accidentally: The emergence and amplification of small change. *Academy of Management Journal, 50*(3), 515–543.

Podsakoff, P.M., MacKenzie, S.B., & Bommer, W.H. (1996). Transformational leader behaviors and substitutes for leadership as determinants of employee satisfaction, commitment, trust, and organizational citizenship behaviors. *Journal of Management, 22*(2), 259–298.

Pollitt, C., & Bouckaert, G. (2004). *Public management reform: A comparative analysis*. Oxford: Oxford University Press.

Pollitt, C., & Dan, S. (2013). Searching for impacts in performance-oriented management reform: A review of the European literature. *Public Performance & Management Review, 37*(1), 7–32.

Pope, C., Robert, G., Bate, P., Le May, A., & Gabbay, J. (2006). Lost in translation: A multi-level case study of the metamorphosis of meanings and action in public sector organizational innovation. *Public Administration, 84*(1), 59–79.

Rainey, H.G. (2012). *Understanding and managing public organizations*. San Francisco: Jossey-Bass.

Robertson, P.J., & Seneviratne, S.J. (1995). Outcomes of planned organizational change in the public sector: A meta-analytic comparison to the private sector. *Public Administration Review, 55*(6), 547–557.

Russ, T.L. (2008). Communicating change: A review and critical analysis of programmatic and participatory implementation approaches. *Journal of Change Management, 8*(3–4), 199–211.

Self, D.R., Armenakis, A.A., & Schraeder, M. (2007). Organizational change content, process and context: A simultaneous analysis of employee reactions. *Journal of Change Management, 7*(2), 211–229.

Sminia, H., & Van Nistelrooij, A. (2006). Strategic management and organization development: Planned change in a public sector organization. *Journal of Change Management, 6*(1), 99–113.

Tummers, L.G. (2011). Explaining the willingness of public professionals to implement new policies: A policy alienation framework. *International Review of Administrative Sciences, 77*(3), 555–581.

Tummers, L.G., Steijn, A.J., & Bekkers, V.J.J.M. (2012). Explaining the willingness of public professionals to implement public policies: Content, context and personality characteristics. *Public Administration, 90*(3), 716–736.

Van Dam, K., Oreg, S., & Schyns, B. (2008). Daily work contexts and resistance to organizational change: The role of leaders-member exchange, development climate, and change process characteristics. *Applied Psychology, 57*(2), 313–334.

Van de Ven, A.H., & Poole, M.S. (1995). Explaining development and change in organizations. *The Academy of Management Review, 20*(3), 510–540.

Van der Voet, J. (2014a). *Leading change in public organizations: A study about the role of leadership in the implementation of change in a public sector context.* Doctoral dissertation, Rotterdam: Erasmus University Rotterdam.

Van der Voet, J. (2014b). The effectiveness and specificity of change management in a public organization: Transformational leadership and a bureaucratic organizational structure. *European Management Journal, 32*(3), 373–382.

Van der Voet, J. (2015). Change leadership and public sector organizational change examining the interactions of transformational leadership style and red tape. *The American Review of Public Administration*, online first.

Van der Voet, J., Groeneveld, S.M., & Kuipers, B.S. (2014). Talking the talk or walking the walk? The leadership of planned and emergent change in a public organization. *Journal of Change Management, 14*(2), 171–191.

Van der Voet, J., Kuipers, B.S., & Groeneveld, S.M. (2015a). Implementing change in public organizations: The relationship between leadership and affective commitment to change in a public sector context. *Public Management Review*, online first.

Van der Voet, J., Kuipers, B.S., & Groeneveld, S.M. (2015b). Held back and pushed forward: Leading change in a complex public environment. *Journal of Organizational Change Management, 28*(2), 290–300.

Van der Voet, J., Steijn, A.J., & Kuipers, B.S. (2015). *What's in it for others? The relationship between pro-social motivation and commitment to change among health care professionals.* Presented at International Research Society for Public Management Conference: Birmingham, United Kingdom (2015, March 30–2015, April 1).

Van der Wal, Z., De Graaf, G., & Lasthuizen, K. (2008). What's valued most? Similarities and differences between the organizational values of the public and private sector. *Public Administration, 86*(2), 465–482.

Walker, H.C., Armenakis, A.A., & Berneth, J.B. (2007). Factors influencing organizational change efforts: An integrative investigation of change content, context, process and individual differences. *Journal of Organizational Change Management, 20*(6), 761–773.

Wanous, J.P., Reichers, A.E., & Austin, J.T. (2000). Cynicism about organizational change: Measurement, antecedents and correlates. *Group & Organization Management, 25*(2), 132–153.

Weick, K.E. (2000). Emergent change as a universal in organizations. In M. Beer and N. Nohria (Eds.), *Breaking the code of change* (pp. 223–242). Boston: Harvard Business School Press.

Weick, K.E. (2001). *Making sense of the organization.* Oxford: Blackwell.

Weick, K.E., & Quinn, R.E. (1999). Organizational change and development. *Annual Review Psychology, 30*, 361–386.

Weissert, C.S., & Goggin, M.L. (2002). Nonincremental policy change: Lessons from Michigan's medicaid managed care initiative. *Public Administration Review, 62*(2), 206–216.

Wright, B.E., Christensen, R.K., & Isett, K.R. (2013). Motivated to adapt? The role of public service motivation as employees face organizational change. *Public Administration Review, 73*(5), 738–747.

7   A Cultural Theory Perspective

Christopher Hood

Introduction

There is a beguiling and apparently culture-free view of how to improve the provision and organization of public services as an issue to be solved by a process of assembling more, technically better and precise evidence about 'what works' to deliver effective remedies. From this viewpoint, the main obstacle to the effective reform of public services is a lack of sufficiently convincing evidence on the beneficial effects or of alternative instruments, strategies or forms of organization. The answer is to make public sector reform resemble more closely the development of medicine, with a well-established research industry continuously engaged in rigorous clinical trials, analogous to those applying to the development of new drugs, to identify and spread best practice.

The development of the policy analysis and evaluation industry over the past four decades in part reflects such a view (although most academic policy evaluators, such as Taylor and Balloch (2005), would argue for a far more nuanced view). The growth of that evaluation industry has itself figured in the reform of government organization, through the embedding of units concerned with analysis and evidence within and around the executive government machine, largely led by the US but also evident in some other countries. In the UK, Tony Blair (1998: 4) once famously said that 'what matters is what works' (although he added, significantly, 'in pursuit of our values') and presided over a notable increase in evaluation research in UK central government during the 'high noon' of New Labour. Although spending cutbacks later bit into such activity, the 2010–2015 Conservative-Liberal Democrat coalition government in the UK endorsed a development of the same sort of approach, with the creation of a set of so-called 'What Works' centers concerning key areas of policy, explicitly endorsing random control trials approach used in drug evaluation as the 'gold standard' of evidence that can improve the delivery and design of effective policy.

So how exactly does 'culture' fit into this rationalistic view of how public sector reform should be conducted? Is it 'a fly in the ointment,' an embarrassing x-factor often to be found at the heart of the failure of apparently rational efforts to improve the instruments and organization of public policy? Is it a feature of public sector reform that is in fact eminently tractable to proper scientific analysis? Is it something else? Part of the problem of fitting culture into a 'normal science' view of institutional design is the admitted ambiguity of a nebulous term (Lane & Wagschal, 2012: 3) that is commonly but confusingly used in two ways in political science. One is to denote characteristic national ways of doing things, which are embedded in formal institutions and customs. The other is to denote any set of shared attitudes, assumptions and ways of living within all types of social groups, including the clashing subcultures that invariably lie behind any characterization of overall national cultures.

Nor is there a single, accepted way of conceiving of or categorizing cultural types in traditional and modern writing. There are several alternative frameworks on offer, including Émile Durkheim's (1912) classic account of the fundamental types of religious life, Gabriel Almond and Sidney Verba's (1963) famous distinction between 'civic' and other political cultures, Geert Hofstede's (1980) elaborate and well-known framework for cross-national comparison of organizations, and the neo-Durkheimian work of Mary Douglas (1982) and her followers expounding 'way of life theory' around a quartet of fundamental cultural types (Thompson, Ellis & Wildavsky, 1990). All accounts of culture focus on how groups interact with individuals to shape shared meanings, assumptions and accepted practices or beliefs, and all lead to the conclusion that cultures are multiple and can come into conflict. However, there is less agreement on how to characterize (let alone measure) basic cultural traits or what prompts cultural change or stability. Compared to, say, microeconomics, where basic concepts and methods of analysis are broadly agreed upon, even amongst economists with different political preferences, cultural analysis looks much less like 'normal science,' with an agreed analytic ABC.

This essay briefly considers four contrasting approaches to considering the relationship between culture and public sector reform, namely:

- Culture as a *problem* to be overcome in the process of reforming public sector organizations and practices, either in the destruction of what are seen as dysfunctional attitudes or practices or in the removal of obstacles to modern rationality to make way for more scientifically grounded and experimental approaches to organization and policy design.
- Culture as a vital *diagnostic tool* for formulating and designing effective reforms—a way of identifying options or understanding differences in assumptive worlds—that can help both to sharpen the analysis of the problems to be addressed by reforms and to widen the range of options considered.
- Culture as a *condition or intervening variable*, something that cannot readily be designed but has to be circumvented in designing reformed structures and processes that are tailored to their social context.

- Culture as the only real *solution* to effective public sector reform (rather than just a condition that has to be recognized and accepted), as part of transformational leadership or other ways of engineering radical changes in values, assumptions or forms of social interaction.

These four perspectives on the relationship between culture and public sector reform are not necessarily jointly exhaustive, and they are certainly not mutually exclusive. Indeed, the first and the fourth ways overlap so considerably that they are in effect mirror images of one another, and the second two are also closely related. However, at a minimum, these approaches can be said to represent differences in emphasis and capture slightly different angles on culture and public sector reform. Each is, therefore, discussed separately in the following sections.

Cultural Demolition Work: Culture as a Problem or Obstacle to be Overcome in Reform

Culture can be argued to be the central problem or obstacle to be overcome in public sector reform from at least two rather different viewpoints. One applies to how culture can play into policy formulation or analysis, and the other concerns how it features in policy application. Relating to the process of policy formulation or analysis, culture can be understood as a problem to be overcome from the perspective that the proper direction of travel in reform (as noted at the outset) should be to somehow make policy a more rationalistic process, guided by systematic evidence, professional expertise and careful argument rather than raw assertion or visceral assumption. From this perspective, departures from that ideal should be minimized even if they cannot be eliminated altogether.

Such a view on how to reform policymaking institutions and processes can be expressed in several ways. For example in the 1950s and 1960s, much was made by critics of the British civil service of that time of the need to destroy a culture of so-called 'amateurism' in the conduct of economic policy (in the sense of civil servants trained in subjects other than economics) and for policy formulation and advice to instead be dominated by professionally trained economists with appropriate skills in macro- and microeconomic analysis. Such criticisms figured prominently in the Fulton Committee Report on the Civil Service of 1968 and in a famous attack on the traditional civil service culture of 'dilettantism' by the economist Nicholas Kaldor (1959). A generation later, in the New Labour era (as noted earlier), stress was placed on the need to replace intuitive or impressionistic assessments of policy by systematic social science evaluations of policy initiatives. Common to both of those developments was the idea that the chief obstacle to better policy was an outdated culture that overvalued intuition and impressionistic judgment against professional academic training and systematic social-science methodology.

The other way of seeing cultural demolition as the route to effective reform is at the level of policy application, by targeting unhelpful or unwanted beliefs, attitudes and modes of behavior among those at the delivery level (such as teachers or police) or at the receiving end of policy (such as the population in general or key subsets). Indeed, the key problem to be addressed by reform is often identified as a dysfunctional set of shared attitudes and forms of behavior at such levels, and the object of reform is to sweep such cultures away or at least radically modify them. For example, perceived cultures of corruption, cronyism, amateurism, racism, sexual abuse, patriarchy, factionalism and blame (to mention only a few) often feature prominently in diagnoses of what needs to change in public institutions. That understanding often figures prominently in ideas about how to address 'failing organizations' in policing, healthcare or education or instilling a new culture of responsibility in the general population (or key subsets of it) for managing their own health.

Indeed such problems are not far to seek. Entrenched assumptions and how to destroy them often constitute the central problem for reforms to address. The aim of many reform initiatives is precisely to change 'hearts and minds' within public organizations or in society more generally on issues as diverse (but fundamental to human life) as drink, diet, treatment of children, social discrimination in its various forms and even aspects of religious belief considered to be 'extreme'.

There are limits to both of these approaches, and certainly neither is incontestable. Regarding the first, there are well-known limitations to the idea of turning politics or policy making into a purely pragmatic, trial-and-error process in which strong value assertions can be set aside—and as mentioned earlier, even Tony Blair's famous 'what works' dictum contained the significant rider 'in pursuit of our values.' As for the sweeping away of cultures that stand in the way of reform objectives desired by governments (such as the religious beliefs or scruples of public officials), there will always be legitimate debates on how far states with any pretensions to liberalism should take 'cultural cleansing' in the name of some greater good. At some point, such a course begins to approximate to Berthold Brecht's (2006: 118) ironic suggestion, in his famous poem *Die Lösung* (The Solution), originally written after the East Berlin rising against the German Democratic Republic in 1953, that the government should dismiss the people and elect a new one.

Further, if cultural demolition is often important in reforms directed both at the formulation and implementation of public policy, this means that the proper place of cultural analysis is at the heart of public sector reform, not at the periphery. While cultural demolition is often central to such reform, the result is never going to be the social equivalent of a vacant lot—a culture-free space. In social as opposed to civil engineering, cultural vacant lots are not really possible. It is not possible to demolish one culture without replacing it with another. Thus, if culture is a problem in the process of reform, it is necessarily also a solution.

The scope and limits of reform through cultural demolition are raised sharply by the expansive claims made recently for the power of 'nudge' approaches to shift the behavior of individuals and groups in directions desired by reformers. In areas such as tax compliance and charitable donations, the claim is that careful attention should be devoted to 'choice architecture,' particularly but not only in digital transactions in which the setting of default options can make a substantial difference to everyday human behavior without resort to more draconian state action such as compulsion or prohibition (Thaler & Sunstein, 2008; Sunstein, 2013). However, the examples usually given of successful nudges in public policy tend to be in areas (such as online form-filling or installing insulation to improve the efficiency of heating systems) that approximate lower-stakes consumer behavior. Much less has been said or claimed about the power of the nudge approach as a tool for reforming institutional workings or altering dysfunctional behavior by elites, and the same is true for the power of 'nudges' in contexts (such as police corruption) where shared attitudes and beliefs are more deep-seated and subject to 'counter-nudges' from the community in question. Further, at some point, the 'nudge' approach to changing human behavior reaches its limits—even at what Robert Baldwin (2014) sees as high levels of intrusion on individual autonomy through presentation of the issues that clearly biases the decision in one direction rather than another instead of simply provoking more deliberation without introducing bias. Those limits illustrate the difference between aspects of culture that can be readily destroyed by measures that fall short of physical coercion and those more deep-seated shared attitudes and assumptions out of which individuals cannot be so readily 'nudged'.

Culture as a Diagnostic Tool for Formulating or Designing Effective Reforms

In contrast to the idea that culture is primarily a problem to be overcome in the process of eliminating dysfunctional attitudes and behavior and extending the reach of scientific rationality in the sense of an experimental and evidence-driven approach to the framing and conduct of public policy, the analysis of culture per se can be regarded as a valuable and necessary forensic or diagnostic tool for public sector reforms. Such analysis can in principle provide lenses that can be used both for explanatory purposes—better identification and understanding of why events developed as they did in particular instances of reform—and even for crafting or designing reforms by surveying a fuller range of possible approaches.

A classic example of the diagnostic use of culture in understanding the outcomes of reforms is Don Moynihan's (1969) study of the effort to design highly participatory structures and processes in anti-poverty and community development initiatives as part of the US 'War on Poverty' Program under the Kennedy and Johnson administrations in the 1960s. Moynihan's analysis brought out the dramatic mismatch between the attitudes and assumptions of key activists on the ground and those of the high-powered economists and lawyers in the Washington 'bubble' who crafted the legislation and institutional frameworks. The result was that eminently well-intentioned efforts to increase community engagement and local participation unintendedly became a route for mobilizing devastating challenges to democratically elected officeholders, confounding the reformers' assumptions and leading Congress into swift and embarrassing action to cut off the funding. That cultural mismatch is at the heart of Moynihan's famous 'maximum feasible misunderstanding' analysis of what went wrong in the Office of Economic Opportunity.

Going beyond that sort of analysis of outcomes, it can be argued that culture can play a central part in more prospective analysis of approaches to public sector reform, as a way of mapping possible approaches to policy or institutional design in any setting. Grid-group or neo-Durkheimian cultural theorists in particular have made much of the possibilities of using their categorization of ways of life in that way. (The terms 'grid' and 'group' refer to Mary Douglas' seminal account of four fundamental worldviews or ways of life, namely hierarchism, individualism, egalitarianism or sectarianism and fatalism, which are rooted in her account on two dimensions, namely the extent to which transactions are governed by rules ('grid') and the extent to which individuals are subjected to the influence of groups ('group'). The term neo-Durkheimian is used in particular by Perri 6 (2011) to refer to Émile Durkheim's (1912) early-twentieth century work, which was the source from which Douglas originally developed her theory; there are some analysts, notably Michael Pepperday (2009), who have argued that the four worldviews that Douglas identifies can be derived from factors other than 'grid' and 'group' and must necessarily involve three rather than two social dimensions.)

For example, Aaron Wildavsky applied grid-group analysis of cultural variation in a range of institutional settings to explore approaches to leadership, accountability and the design of institutional frameworks for taxing and spending (see, for example, Webber & Wildavsky, 1986; Wildavsky, 1989). In analyzing reforms for the transition to market economies in former communist states, Michael Intriligator and his colleagues (2006) have argued that the different outcomes of the Chinese and Russian transitions away from a command economy system reflect the incorporation of hierarchist and egalitarian threads into the transition process in the former case but not in the latter. The current author has also applied the framework to approaches to public management reform in general (Hood, 1998), control over bureaucracy in particular (Hood, 1996) and ways of maintaining control of state institutions more broadly (Hood, James, Peters & Scott, 2004), using the approach to highlight approaches that are normally concealed by focusing on a simple dichotomy between markets and hierarchies, in particular the use of more or less contrived randomness as an instrument of control.

Similarly, in the context of debates on regulatory reform, Martin Lodge and colleagues have applied the approach to analyze different approaches to regulation in general and, more particularly, have shown how particular debates on the performance and shortcomings of regulatory institutions (such as over the heavily publicized failure of the German bureaucracy's meat inspection regime in 2006) corresponded (or otherwise) to the predictions of grid-group cultural theory (Lodge, Wegrich & McElroy, 2008). Indeed, Gerald Mars (1982: 38) has argued that the discriminatory power of cultural theory can be steadily increased by continuous sub-division, using an optometric analogy: 'It is always possible [. . .] to slip a more powerful lens into any quadrant [of cultural theory analysis] by [. . .] dividing it into a further 2 x 2 matrix and to continue to do so until the analysis applies at the level of the individual'.

The potential (and powerful) advantage of using cultural analysis as a diagnostic tool in understanding public sector reform is that, in principle, it permits the identification of possible styles or approaches to institutional reform, grounded in foundational analysis of a very limited number of fundamental forms of social organization that are both mutually exclusive and jointly exhaustive (which Verweij et al. [2006: 2] boldly compare to the six basic particles from which all material objects on earth are formed). What is disputed or unclear includes whether or to what extent there are viable approaches to public sector reform that correspond to the fatalist worldview (excluded as not 'active' in many cultural theory analyses) and precisely what sort of methodology is to be used for attributing which policy positions to which cultural worldview.

Culture as a Condition or Intervening Variable for Public Sector Reform

A third possible place for culture in the analysis of public sector reform, closely related to the 'diagnostic tool' role, is as an intermediate variable or background condition that has to be taken into account when making interventions in the social context in which they operate. 'Contingency theory' is an approach to institutional analysis that has classical roots, notably in Aristotle's (1984) famous argument (in his *Politics*) that there is no single best form of governance. Aristotle claimed that each of what he saw as the three basic types (rule by a single person, by a small group, or by a mass of people) could take both positive and negative forms, dependent on circumstances. A similar idea of contingency loomed large in management science and organization theory in the middle of the last century, when scholars attempted to depart from the all-purpose reform recipes for 'best practice' or good performance that had been advanced by 'classical management theorists' toward more contingent propositions that related effective organizational structures to contextual variables such as size, task, technology and 'environment' (Burns & Stalker, 1961; Woodward, 1965; Lawrence & Lorsch, 1967).

Contingency theory of that type met with mixed research results and was intellectually sidelined to some extent by the rational choice boom that came to dominate ideas about institutional design and reform in political science in the 1980s/1990s. However, a contingency theory approach (whether or not using that specific term) remains important in management and organization theory. Examples include the well-known 'structure in fives' ideas of the Canadian management guru Henry Mintzberg (1993), which identifies key factors that account for variations in 'best practice' organizational engineering; the various challenges to 'best practice' theory in more recent times (for example, Wagner & Newell, 2004); and Julian Le Grand's (2003) well-known idea that the appropriate recipe for reforming public services depends on whether the key actors are predominantly altruistic 'knights' or self-regarding 'knaves' in how they behave. Indeed, Jeremy Hardie and Nancy Cartwright (2012) (re)introduced the idea of contingency into policy analysis more generally by arguing that the standard methodology for evaluating social interventions (and particularly the view of random control trials, often claimed to be the 'gold standard' of such evaluation) is geared to answering the question, 'did a given policy or intervention work *somewhere?*' but not the more important issue of 'will that intervention work *here?*'

Cultural variation can be viewed in the same way as the decisive factor that shapes how that public sector reforms ultimately perform. It has often been observed that any given way of running public institutions can produce very different results in different times and places; attempts to transplant institutional practices or reform approaches from one cultural setting to another can produce unintended or problematic outcomes. Examples include Bill Mackenzie's (1957) classic paper on the export of electoral systems and Serguey Braguinsky and Grigory Yablonksi's (2000) study of the effects of the production target system that was at the heart of the reforms to the management of the USSR's economy introduced by Josef Stalin in the early 1930s and which persisted until the collapse of that state sixty years later. The puzzle for Braguinsky and Yablonski is to explain how and why such a reform initiative could apparently have produced positive results in the 1930s (when the Soviet Union successfully industrialized while the Western countries were mired in unemployment and stagnation) but led to economic collapse a generation later. What changed was not the technical system of target management—which was virtually unaltered over six decades, despite attempts by some Soviet economists to modify it—but rather (according to Braguinsky and Yablonski) changing expectations of managerial tenure after Stalin's death in 1953 (when arbitrary rule by terror and purges gave way to a more ordered and predictable bureaucratic existence for managers). When that vital random element in their career environment was removed, ratchet-effect gaming (that is, restriction of present output to facilitate the achievement of future targets) by managers expecting to be in their posts for a longer period is argued to have had dire consequences for productivity, thereby seriously damaging the whole Soviet economy to the extent that the viability of the entire state was undermined. A changing political environment combined with the unchanging technicalities of the planning system led to a change in managerial culture and, thereby, to very different economic outcomes.

Building on such observations, the current author (Hood, 2012) has argued that differences in operating culture can account for varying outcomes from the use of three different types of management metrics often associated with attempts to improve and reform public services, namely targets (floor standards), rankings (benchmarks) and 'intelligence' (the use of metrics as a basis for deliberation, as with 'quality circles'). The argument is that none of these recipes for reform through performance measurement is a go-anywhere, fix-everything approach because each has potentially performance-obstructing effects, as well as performance-enhancing ones. None of the three forms is likely to work equally well as a 'performance enhancing drug' in all cultural settings, although all are likely to perform poorly in a wholly fatalist setting. Moreover, the use of management metrics in the form of performance targets requires the sort of culture that is capable of fixing on a few key priorities and sustaining collective effort to achieve them. The use of such metrics in the form of rankings or league tables requires the sort of culture that lends itself to rivalry and competition but is not so hypercompetitive that rankings lead to sabotage or other dysfunctional ways of eliminating rivals. The use of management metrics as 'intelligence' requires the sort of culture that lends itself both to a willingness to pool performance information and to use the power of groups to interpret it. The implication of such analysis is that conditions for effective reform through such metrics are far more contingent than is implied by catch-all ideas of 'best practice' that tend to focus on the technicalities of the metrics rather than on the operating culture that determines the outcome of such reforms.

Culture as a Solution to Problems of Reforming the Public Sector

Finally, in the context of public sector reform, culture can be regarded not so much as a fixed constraint or unalterable condition that has to be circumvented or compensated for but rather as something that can be used as a central feature of effective reform.

The idea of culture as engineerable and manageable is a traditional theme in writing on corporate leadership and management styles (for example, in James McGregor Burns's (1978) much-cited—and criticized—idea of 'transformational leadership' as that which raises followers to some higher plane of attitudes and beliefs). A similar view is often embraced by those who consider organizational culture the key to the effective reform of bureaucracies and organizations. That was the central theme of a six-million-copy best-selling book by management gurus Tom Peters and Bob Waterman (1982) three decades ago, in a study based on their work with major corporate clients of the consulting group McKinsey and Company. Peters and Waterman sought to identify the leading corporations in the US at that time and the practices and attitudes they embodied (such as 'sticking to the knitting'). Their account portrayed corporate 'excellence' as largely a product of a culture that reflected management ethos and influence.

Upbeat and vividly written, Peters and Waterman's culture-focused account of corporate excellence attracted massive attention from both public and private managers in the 1980s as the 'New Public Management' era began to dawn. Later, their approach came to be heavily criticized as both methodologically flawed and misleading (many of the large companies Peters and Waterman identified as 'excellent' later came to grief). However, even if many of Peters and Waterman's assumptions can be questioned (such as the implication that there is an all-purpose recipe for 'excellence' or that culture is something largely owned and readily alterable by managers), the idea that culture is the solution to better performance in public services has not disappeared.

For example, that idea dominated debates on how to develop more resilient and reliable organizations, especially in safety-critical fields, in the late 1980s and 1990s, as in the development of 'high-reliability' organization theory and its stress on 'safety culture' (see, for instance, Sagan, 1993: 21–28). Similarly, culture often took center stage in accounts of what needed to be changed in dysfunctional or dramatically failing companies or organizations in the 2000s. Examples include the fatal mixture of unbridled greed and byzantine accounting that led to the spectacular collapse of the US energy trader Enron in 2001 (Swartz & Watkins, 2003) and the extraordinary culture of autocracy and hubris that led to the Royal Bank of Scotland's near-collapse in 2008 after briefly becoming the world's largest bank through its ill-advised takeover of the Dutch bank ABN Amro on the initiative of Sir Fred ('the Shred') Goodwin the previous year (Martin, 2013).

Another strain of analysis that considers culture the key to effective institutional capacity is the so-called 'clumsy solutions' approach arising out of grid-group cultural theory, as mentioned above, which argues that cultural combinations offer richer approaches to institutional design than monocultures can. The germ of the idea appears in Michiel Schwarz and Michael Thompson's (1990) account of how a 'meeting of opposites' encounter between the hierarchist corporate orthodoxy of a major multinational firm and ultra-egalitarian green activists who were challenging the corporation's plans to market a new lavatory rim-block product in the 1980s eventually served to produce a technically better chemical product. The idea also appears in the account of cultural theory by Michael Thompson, Richard Ellis and Aaron Wildavsky (1990) and was developed further in the following decade by Marco Verweij and Michael Thompson (2006) and numerous other cultural theorists, arguing for cultural variety and mix rather than monocultures as a recipe for institutional efficacy and better problem-solving. In some respects, the idea of the power of 'clumsiness' resembles Charles Lindblom's classic (1965) 'intelligence of democracy' argument that political processes that rely on serial disjointed bargaining among different groups can produce technically better policy solutions than decision-making by more orderly or hierarchist procedures because the former are more likely to take a wider range of values into account.

Indeed, there are numerous similar attacks on excessive hierarchism in the design of governing institutions. Cases in point include James Scott's (1998) well-known account of the dysfunctional effects of 'modernism' in the conduct of institutions (in domains such as economic planning, town planning and development) and Frank Hendriks's (1999) comparison of city government in the cities of Munich and Birmingham since World War II, which concluded that the more culturally pluriform approach of Munich led to superior policy outcomes, albeit also producing more complex and time-consuming decision processes. However, the question remains as to whether cultural pluralism is invariably a recipe for effective public sector reform and monocultures are always negative. Ultimately, some reform issues (for example, over outsourcing or the breaking of previous public service bargains (Hood & Lodge, 2006)) are unavoidably reduced to visceral, zero-sum contests between sharply opposed interests and attitudes. Indeed, Charles Lindblom's related 'intelligence of democracy' argument for the technical superiority of pluralism has been hotly contested in political science for fifty years, with even its originator famously turning to a sharp critique of democratic capitalism and polyarchy and even apparent admiration for Tito's Yugoslavia in subsequent work (Lindblom, 1977).

Conclusion

From any of the four perspectives briefly discussed here—whether the aim is to destroy it, learn from it, work around it, or deploy it as a solution—culture cannot be avoided as a central issue in the design and operation of public sector reform. The view of culture as problem and culture as solution are opposite sides of the same coin, as the public sector can never become a culture-free zone. It is a question of what—or whose—culture predominates and who considers what type of culture to be 'problem' or 'solution,' for example, as between those who regard markets and competition as an all-purpose approach to reforming the public services against those who with equal firmness advocate cooperation and solidarity, leadership and coordination or, indeed, against those who express more agnostic views.

The view of culture as a diagnostic tool and of culture as a key contingency in public sector reform also have matching features and can be understood as variations on the same idea. Both involve some subtlety in assessing the positive and negative aspects of culture. Both lead us away from simple dichotomies into a broader range of possible designs, and for that reason, both may be considered somewhat rarefied by those in the front line of left-right ideological battles (for example, over public sector reform recipes linked to 'austerity'). These two approaches also have the common feature that both begin from some conception of cultural variety or multiple cultural biases to enable a range of alternatives to be identified and solutions tailored to fit any given cultural type or mix. Both in principle offer rich possibilities for identifying alternative approaches to reform and tailoring reform to specific contexts but encounter against entrenched 'best practice' ideas, especially where reform debates are framed and developed within intellectual monocultures.

It remains to be seen whether the idea of cultural contingency theory in the analysis of public sector reform proves to have an equivalent or greater impact than its once-powerful counterpart in organizational analysis in the decades after World War II. However, it is difficult to conceive of an alternative means of addressing such apparently fundamental (but still unanswered) questions as when to use to performance metrics in the form of targets, rankings and intelligence, as discussed earlier.

Going beyond the strict contingency approach, the notion that mixing and matching cultures is a route to better institutional design and operation (as noted earlier) has been advanced by cultural theorists such as Michael Thompson and Marco Verweij for over a quarter of a century. Indeed, that mixing-and-matching idea for institutions seems to resonate with related ideas of multiculturalism in social policy and workplace diversity policies, and, hence, it could be argued to go with the grain of those other strongly entrenched ideas and policies in modern Western states. However, the idea clashes with the view advanced by some cultural theorists that hybrids of different worldviews will tend to be short-lived and unstable.

As yet, the evidence for the superiority of cultural 'clumsiness' remains anecdotal and suggestive, mostly based on qualitative case studies involving selection on the dependent variable, and the key to understanding which cultural combinations are positive and which negative is also elusive. As Martin Lodge, Kai Wegrich and Gail McElroy (2008: 7) judiciously observed some years ago, 'Cultural theory seems very good at putting a different perspective [. . .] on past events, making competing rationalities explicit and pointing to broad mechanisms of change, but there has been too little methodological effort in terms of developing causal mechanisms and observable implications as well as evidence selection that goes beyond the casual and the typological.' That position is beginning to change (partly due to the work of Lodge and his colleagues, as well as other scholars). However, if culture is indeed the answer to important questions of public sector reform, much remains to be done to demonstrate exactly what that answer is and how it works.

References

6, Perri. (2011). *Explaining political judgment.* Cambridge: Cambridge University Press.

Almond, G., & Verba, S. (1963). *The civic culture: Political attitudes and democracy in five nations.* Princeton, NJ: Princeton University Press.

Aristotle. (1984). *The complete works of Aristotle*. Princeton, NJ: Princeton University Press

Baldwin, R. (2014). From regulation to behaviour change: Giving nudge the third degree. *Modern Law Review, 77*(6), 831–857.

Blair, T. (1998). *The third way: New politics for the new century*. London: Fabian Society.

Braguinsky, S., & Yablonksi, G. (2000). *Incentives and institutions: The transition to a market economy in Russia*. Princeton: Princeton University Press.

Brecht, B. (2006). *Poetry and prose*. New York: Continuum.

Burns, J.M. (1978). *Leadership*. New York: Harper and Row.

Burns, T., & Stalker, G.M. (1961). *The management of innovation*. London: Tavistock.

Douglas, M. (1982). Cultural bias. In M. Douglas (Ed.), *In the active voice* (pp. 183–254). London: Routledge.

Durkheim, É. (1912). *Les formes elementaires de la vie religieuse: le système totemique en Australie*. Paris: Felix Alcan.

Hardie, J., & Cartwright, N. (2012). *Evidence-based policy: A practical guide to doing it better*. New York: Oxford University Press.

Hendriks, F. (1999). *Public policy and political institutions: The role of culture in traffic policy*. Cheltenham: Edward Elgar.

Hofstede, G. (1980). *Culture's consequences: International differences in work-related values*. Beverly Hills: Sage.

Hood, C. (1996). Control over bureaucracy: Cultural theory and institutional variety. *Journal of Public Policy, 15*(3), 207–230.

Hood, C. (1998). *The art of the state: Culture, rhetoric and public management*. Oxford: Clarendon.

Hood, C. (2012). Public management by numbers as a performance-enhancing drug: Two hypotheses. *Public Administration Review, 72*(s1), 85–92.

Hood, C., James, O., Peters, B.G., & Scott, C. (Eds.). (2004). *Controlling modern government: Variety, commonality and change*. Cheltenham: Edward Elgar.

Hood, C., & Lodge, M. (2006). *The politics of public service bargains: Reward, competency, loyalty—and blame*. Oxford: Oxford University Press.

Intriligator, M., Wedel, J., & Lee, C. (2006). What Russia can learn from China in its transition to a market economy. In M. Verweij and M. Thompson (Eds.), *Clumsy solutions for a complex world: Governance, politics and plural perceptions* (pp. 105–131). Basingstoke, Palgrave Macmillan.

Kaldor, N. (1959). The apotheosis of the dilettante: The Establishment of Mandarins. In H.S. Thomas (Ed.), *The establishment: A symposium* (pp. 11–53). London: Blond.

Lane, J.-E., & Wagschal, U. (2012). *Culture and politics*. Abingdon: Routledge.

Lawrence, P.R., & Lorsch, J.W. (1967). *Organization and environment*. Boston, MA: Harvard University Press.

Le Grand, J. (2003). *Motivation, agency and public policy: Of knights and knaves, pawns and queens*. Oxford: Oxford University Press.

Lindblom, C.E. (1965). *The intelligence of democracy: Decision making through mutual adjustment*. New York: Free Press.

Lindblom, C.E. (1977). *Politics and markets: The world's political-economic systems*. New York: Basic Books.

Lodge, M., Wegrich, K., & McElroy, G. (2008). *Gammelfleisch everywhere? Public debate, variety of worldviews and regulatory change*. Discussion Paper No. 49. London: LSE Centre for the Analysis of Risk and Regulation.

Mackenzie, W.J.M. (1957). The export of electoral systems. *Political Studies, 5*(3), 240–257.

Mars, G. (1982). *Cheats at work*. London: Allen and Unwin.

Martin, I. (2013). *Making it happen: Fred Goodwin, RBS and the men who blew up the British economy*. London: Simon and Schuster.

Mintzberg, H. (1993). *Structure in fives*. Englewood Cliffs, NJ: Prentice-Hall.

Moynihan, D.P. (1969). *Maximum feasible misunderstanding*. New York: Free Press.

Pepperday, M.E. (2009). Way of life theory: The underlying structure of world-views, social relations and lifestyles, PhD thesis. Canberra: Australian National University.

Peters, T., & Waterman, R. (1982). *In search of excellence*. New York: Harper and Row.

Sagan, S.D. (1993). *The limits of safety: Organizations, accidents and nuclear weapons*. Princeton, NJ: Princeton University Press.

Schwarz, M., & Thompson, M. (1990). *Divided we stand: Redefining politics, technology and social choice*. Hemel Hempstead: Harvester Wheatsheaf.

Scott, J.C. (1998). *Seeing like a state: How certain schemes to improve the human condition have failed*. New Haven: Yale University Press.

Sunstein, C. (2013). *Simpler: The future of government*. New York: Simon and Schuster.

Swartz, M., & Watkins, S. (2003). *Power failure: The inside story of the collapse of Enron*. New York: Doubleday.

Taylor, D., & Balloch, S. (2005). The politics of evaluation: An overview. In D. Taylor and S. Balloch (Eds.), *The politics of evaluation: Participation and policy evaluation* (pp. 1–17). Bristol: Policy Press.

Thaler, R.H., & Sunstein, C. (2008). *Nudge: Improving decisions about health, wealth and happiness*. New Haven: Yale University Press.

Thompson, M., Ellis, R., & Wildavsky, A. (1990). *Cultural theory*. Boulder, CO: Westview Press.

Verweij, M., Douglas, M., Ellis, R., Engel, C., Hendriks, F., Lohmann, S., Ney, S., Steve Rayner, & Thompson, M. (2006). The case for clumsiness. In M. Verweij and M. Thompson (Eds.), *Clumsy solutions for a complex world: Governance, politics and plural perceptions* (pp. 1–27). Basingstoke: Palgrave Macmillan.

Wagner, E.L., & Newell, S. (2004). 'Best' for whom? The tension between 'best practice' ERP packages and diverse epistemic cultures in a university context. *The Journal of Strategic Information Systems, 13*(4), 305–328.

Webber, C., & Wildavsky, A. (1986). *A history of taxation and expenditure in the western world*. New York: Simon and Schuster.

Wildavsky, A. (1989). A cultural theory of leadership. In Bryan Jones (Ed.), *Leadership and politics: New perspectives in political science* (pp. 87–113). Lawrence: University of Kansas Press.

Woodward, J. (1965). *Industrial organization: Theory and practice*. London: Oxford University Press.

8 An Interpretative Perspective

Rod Rhodes[1]

Introduction

As this volume testifies, Walter Kickert is well known for his contribution to the study of administrative reform, especially his critique of the New Public Management (see, for example, Kickert, 1997, 2011). Thus, I limit myself to two observations. My topic is central to his research interests, and British reforms are not unique. Britain is one member of the 'core' NPM states that also includes Australia, New Zealand, and the US. Reform is not limited to them. As Pollitt and Bouckaert (2011: 9) conclude, '[NPM] has become a key element in many [. . .] countries. It has internationalised.' My British story speaks to larger issues.

This chapter briefly outlines the story of administrative reform in Britain, covering evidence-based policy making, managerialism, and service delivery and choice. I outline an interpretive approach to studying administrative reform, especially the use of ethnography to give voice to groups that are all too often ignored, to understanding 'the black box' of government and, distinctively, to recovering the beliefs and practices of actors. Drawing on the fieldwork in Rhodes (2011), I discuss five axioms under the following headings: coping, institutional memory, storytelling, traditions, and implementation. Finally, I explore the pros and cons of an interpretive, ethnographic approach, concluding that in place of 'the civil service reform syndrome', with its overlapping, short-lived initiatives, we need to reform the constitutional and political role of public administration in the polity.

The Reforms

This section suggests that the reforms of the civil service proposed by both think tanks and the government over the past decade are pervaded by beliefs in the instrumental rationality of evidence-based policymaking, managerialism, and economic choice. These ideas are the shared, almost tacit, knowledge of contributors to the continuing debate on public sector reform. I will be brief because my remarks verge on the obvious.

Evidence-Based Policy Making

At the heart of the Cabinet Office's (1999) professional policy making model is a belief in evidence-based policy making. For example, their model 'uses the best available evidence from a wide range of sources' and 'learns from experience of what works and what doesn't' through systematic evaluation (Cabinet Office, 1999: para. 2.11). A change of government led to no change in essentials. In July 2011, the Coalition government launched its *Open Public Services White Paper* (Cm 8145, 2011). It claimed that 'something very big and different is happening with this White Paper' (Cameron, 2011). Most observers saw only more of the same. The emphasis fell on 'building on evidence of what works.' Phrases such as 'sound evidence base', 'what works', and 'robust evidence' abound. Departments would need a 'clearer understanding of what their priorities are' and need 'to ensure administrative resources match Government policy priorities' so the Government can get 'value for taxpayers' money in delivering its objectives (Cabinet Office, 2012: 14, 16, 20).

Evidence-based policy making displays a marked liking for randomized control trials (RCT), which are prominent in the work of the government's Behavioural Insights Team and the What Works centers.[2] For example, the Behavioural Insights Team claims to be 'global leaders in experiment design' and to have 'run more randomised controlled trials than the rest of the UK government combined in its history.'[3]

Since 2013, six 'What Works Centres' have been launched for England, with one each for Scotland and Wales. The initiative combined existing and new centers with the shared aim of improving 'the way government and other organisations create, share and use (or 'generate, transmit and adopt') high quality evidence for decision-making.'[4] They include the National Institute for Health and Care Excellence, the Centre for Ageing Better, and the What Works Centre for Wellbeing.

In sum, the instrumental rationality of evidence-based policy making is alive and well and at the heart of the Coalition's reform agenda. Moreover, this view of the policy making process is widely shared inside and outside government.[5]

Managerialism

Managerialism has a long history that cannot be retold here (see: Pollitt, 1993). In brief, it is a set of inherited beliefs regarding how private sector management techniques would increase the economy, efficiency and effectiveness—the 3Es—of the public sector. Initially, the beliefs focused on managerialism or hands-on, professional management, on explicit standards and measures of performance, on managing by results and on value for money. Later, it also embraced marketization or neoliberal beliefs concerning competition and markets. It introduced ideas about restructuring the incentive structures of public service provision through contracting-out, quasi-markets, and consumer choice. New Labour introduced a third strand to managerialism with its service delivery agenda.

For my purpose, I need to show only that such reform persists (and for a review of the 2000s, see Public Administration Select Committee (PASC, 2009)). The core concern for decades has been better performance management, whether it is called accountable management or management-by-objectives. Only the labeling has changed. Thus, even today, 'effective performance assessment within government helps to identify how well public organizations are meeting their objectives, as well as highlighting where improvements could be made' (PASC, 2009: 3).[6]

Service Delivery and Choice

The general principles informing the delivery agenda were outlined by Michael Barber, the Prime Minister's former Chief Adviser on Delivery, in his comments about education:

> 'Essentially it's about creating different forms of a quasi-market in public services, exploiting the power of choice, competition, transparency and incentives.'
>
> (Interview with Michael Barber 13 January 2006;
> see also Barber, 2007, chapter 3; and PASC, 2005).

Despite the commotion over its novelty, the Coalition government also focused on service delivery and customers. Although evidence-based policy making and managerialism remain prominent strands in the Coalition's reform proposals, choice is the first principle of the reforms; 'wherever possible we are increasing choice by giving people direct control over the services they use' (Cameron, 2011). The White Paper claims that 'the old centralized approach to public service delivery is broken', and, thus, 'wherever possible we will increase choice' and 'power will be decentralized to the lowest appropriate level.' Such choice will only happen if service delivery is 'opened up to a range of providers of different sizes and different sectors' (Cm 8145, 2011: 8–9). Choice, decentralization and diversity of providers are three core tenets of the proposed reforms.

All the ideas about evidence-based policy making, managerialism and choice are part of the vocabulary of senior civil servants. For example, O'Donnell (2012), former Head of the Home Civil Service, includes clear objectives, objective evaluation and honoring the evidence among his ten commandments of good policy making. As the Regulatory Policy Institute (2009, para 31) observes, 'every suggestion' in the 'numberless' reports on civil service reform are 'a version of the same, how better to manage an ever more centralized state.' In sum, instrumental rationality, managerialism and choice rule, and this is not acceptable. As Brunsson (2009: 15) observes,

> 'Reforms are [. . .] self-referential; they tend to cause new reforms. Thus reforms can be considered as routines: they are likely to be repeated over and over again.'

It adds up to the 'Civil Service reform syndrome', which comprises

> 'ideas like total quality management, red tape bonfires, better consultation, risk management, competency, evidence-based policy, joined-up government, delivery leadership, and now better policymaking. Such initiatives come and go, overlap and ignore each other, leaving behind residues of varying size and style.'
>
> (Hood & Lodge, 2007: 59).

The syndrome persists because the assumptions underlying reforms are not suitable for public sector purposes.

An Interpretive Approach

The 'Interpretive Turn'

Interpretive political studies draw on anti-naturalist philosophical thinking and stress the importance of meanings in the study of human life (see Bevir & Rhodes, 2003, 2015). This approach shifts analysis away from institutions, functions and roles to the beliefs, actions and practices of interdependent actors. We need to grasp the relevant meanings, the webs of beliefs and preferences of the people involved and understand the webs of significance that people spin for themselves. It provides 'thick description' in which the researcher writes his or her construction of the subject's constructions of what the subject is doing (adapted from Geertz, 1973: 9). Thus, the task is to unpack the disparate and contingent beliefs and practices of individuals through which they construct their worlds, to identify the recurrent patterns of actions and related beliefs. The aim of interpretive research is to recover complex specificity in context. It concentrates not only on the construction of practices as people act on beliefs but also on the narratives and traditions that provide the context and historical background to people's beliefs and actions. It focuses on 'situated agents', on individuals using local reasoning consciously and subconsciously to reflect on and modify their contingent heritage (Bevir & Rhodes, 2006: 4–5/7–9). The resulting narrative is not merely a chronological story. Rather, narrative refers to the form of explanation that disentangles beliefs and actions to explain human life. Narratives are the form theories take in the human sciences, and they explain actions with reference to the beliefs and desires of actors. People act for reasons, conscious and unconscious (Bevir, 1999, chapters 4 and 7).

An interpretive approach does not necessarily favor particular methods. It does not prescribe a particular toolkit for producing data but prescribes a particular way of treating data of any type. It should treat data as evidence of the meanings or beliefs embedded in actions. Thus, it is wrong to exclude survey research and quantitative studies from the reach of interpretive analysis. However, the interpretive approach's emphasis on recovering meaning does have implications for how we collect data. It leads to a much greater emphasis on qualitative methods than is common among naturalist political scientists. In short, 'being there' or 'deep hanging out' is an obvious tool for grappling with complex specificity.

Ethnographic Methods or 'being there'

Any account of ethnography begins with the puzzle of what ethnographers do. For Hammersley and Atkinson (2007: 2), 'ethnography does not have a standard, well-defined meaning.' Nonetheless, some words and phrases recur. The ethnographer studies people's everyday lives. Such fieldwork is unstructured. The aim is to recover the meaning of people's actions by deep immersion, whether studying a Congressional district, a government department, or a tribe in Africa. Historically, it meant going to another country, learning the language and studying the everyday lives of the inhabitants of a village, tribe or whatever unit of social organization had been selected. For the novice, it was the only way to become a cultural anthropologist; 'you can't teach fieldwork, you have to do it.' For Wood (2007: 123), it is 'research based on personal interaction with research subjects in their own setting', not in the laboratory, the library or one's office. It is deep hanging out or intensive immersion in the everyday lives of other people in their local environment, normally for a substantial period of time. The task is to 'shake the bag', and the aim is edification: to find 'new, better, more interesting, more fruitful ways of speaking about' everyday life (Rorty, 1980: 360). Thus, fieldwork provides detailed studies of social and political dramas. As Burawoy (1998: 5) suggests, it 'extracts the general from the unique, to move from the "micro" to the "macro".

Fieldwork has several advantages over other methods in political science. As Wood (2007: 124 and 132) notes, it is a source of data not available elsewhere and is often the only way to identify key individuals and core processes. It is well-suited to giving voice to groups all too often ignored, to disaggregating organizations, to understanding 'the black box' of government and, distinctively, to recovering the beliefs and practices of actors. It leads us into the office, the engine room of public administration, where the state is continuously enacted and reshaped. It enables us to explore the contending beliefs and practices of elites. It seeks out the silent voices in the bureaucracy.

In addition, Rhodes, 't Hart and Noordegraaf (2007: chapter 9) argue that 'being there' gets below and behind the surface of official accounts by providing texture, depth and nuance, and in so doing, our stories have richness and context. It allows interviewees to explain the meaning of their actions, providing an authenticity that can only come from the main characters involved in the story. Crucially, the ethnographic approach admits of surprises, of moments of epiphany, which can open new research agendas. It accepts serendipity and happenstance.

Five Axioms

How do we incorporate interpretive ethnography into the study of reform? Although Aronoff and Kubik (2013: 274) are discussing post-communist transformations, their injunction to 'avoid excessive conceptual aggregation (focus on micro-, mezzo-, and, in particular, local mechanisms)' applies with equal force. Local knowledge is conspicuous for its absence in administrative reform (see Rhodes, 2016b). In his survey of public sector reforms, Brunsson (2009: 70) observes the following:

> 'a discrepancy between how the people observed define their own situation and the researcher's definition of the same situation. People's definitions may vary considerably; they may change either quickly or slowly; and they may not be very predictable [. . .]. Nonetheless, the concepts used by people to construct and make sense of their own reality do have important consequences.'

We need to accept that 'people are agents who are capable of fixing themselves and who, in fact, are always doing so' (Aronoff & Kubik, 2013: 273). Many of the problems of reform are 'located in the faulty institutional designs, often hastily implemented by clueless reformers working in social and cultural contexts they misunderstand' (Aronoff & Kubik, 2013: 273).

In Rhodes (2011), I reported my fieldwork, observing ministers and permanent secretaries in three British central government departments. I asked the simple question, 'how do things work around here?' I studied the everyday beliefs and practices of civil servants and their ministers. From this ethnography, I distilled the following five axioms about public service reform. They may oversimplify, but they do dramatize the difference between the reformers' proposals and the everyday world of life at the top.

Coping and the Appearance of Rule, not Strategic Planning

At the top of government departments, we find a class of political administrators, not politicians or administrators. They live in a shared world. Their priorities and skills concern running a government and surviving in a world of rude surprises. The goal is willed ordinariness. They do not need more risk. They are adrift in an ocean of storms. Only reformers have the luxury of choosing the challenge to which they will respond. Ministers and permanent secretaries have to juggle the contradictory demands posed by recurring dilemmas while still appearing to be in control. Policy emerges from routine and develops akin to a coral reef. It is not a matter of solving specific problems but of managing unfolding dilemmas and their inevitable unintended consequences. There is no solution but a succession of solutions to problems that are contested and redefined as they are 'solved'. This view of the minister's and the permanent secretary's world is anathema to the would-be reformers, but it characterizes what happens to their reforms. Strategic planning is a clumsy add-on to this world. Its timescale is too long. Its concerns are too far removed from the everyday life concerns of its short-stay incumbents. The demands of political accountability and the media spotlight are indifferent to strategic priorities. Relatively trivial problems of implementation can threaten a minister's career. Much of government is not a matter of strategy and priorities but the appearance of rule. The job is 'about stability. Keeping things going, preventing anarchy, stopping society falling to bits. Still being here tomorrow.' I do not seek, as the authors of *Yes Prime Minister* did, to make people laugh. I see much wisdom in their irony.

Institutional Memory, not Internal Structures

Reform all too often involves splitting up existing units, creating new units, redeploying staff, bringing in outsiders and revamping IT systems. A key unintended consequence is the loss of institutional memory. All three departments that I studied reformed their internal structure. It was a tacit policy of running down a proven asset for unproven gains. Institutional memory is the source of the department's folk psychology, providing the everyday theories and shared languages for making sense of the world. It explains past practice and events and justifies recommendations for the future. Ministers see the gaps. Permanent secretaries say there has been a serious weakening of corporate memory. However, nothing is done, and I am tempted to suggest that the priority in reform is to repair institutional memory.

Storytelling, not Evidence-Based Policy

Speaking of storytelling might imply that I trivialize the art of briefing ministers. However, ministers and civil servants regularly tell one another stories about what happened yesterday. They talk of getting the story straight. They ask what the story is. Such stories can include an evidence-based policy analysis. It is simply another way of telling a story alongside all the other stories in a department. Each story is one set of glasses for interpreting the world. Thus, civil servants ask whether a story is defensible, accurate and believable. They test 'facts' in committee meetings and rehearse story lines or explanations to see what they sound like and whether there is agreement. They judge how a story will play publicly by the reactions of their colleagues and ministers.

Contending Traditions and Stories, not Just Management

Even today, ministers and civil servants act as if the nineteenth century liberal constitution sets the rules of the political game. They continue to believe in ministerial accountability to parliament as if ministers can be forced to resign. The British constitution reminds me of geological strata, a metaphor that captures the longevity of the beliefs and practices. I do not wish to suggest that nothing has changed. Obviously, much has changed, but much remains. Thus, for example, managerial reforms coexist with the inherited generalist tradition. As a result, there is no agreed standard for comparing stories. Even within a government department, let alone across central government, there is no shared story of how British government works. Yesterday's story remains an important guide to today's practice. Therefore, the managerial story (in its various forms) has not replaced the Westminster tradition. Indeed, managerial reform is all too often a secondary concern for Ministers and their civil servants, and I can see why. When I imagine myself in a minister's or a permanent secretary's shoes, management does not matter; it is useful but not where the real action is. Ministers are not managers. It is not why they went into politics. A minority of Secretaries of State take an interest, even fewer Ministers of State. These brute facts undermine reform. The civil service exists to give ministers what they want, and most do not want anything to do with management reform. At best, it is not a priority. At worst, it is not even on the radar.

The Politics of Implementation, not Top-Down Innovation and Control

One strand in the British political tradition asserts that 'leaders know best', yet the track record of much top-down policy making does not inspire confidence. We know that street-level bureaucrats shape service delivery in crucial ways. They use local knowledge to determine policy for clients. Understandings of how 'things work around here' are embedded in the taken-for-granted routines and rituals of the department. However, the beliefs and practices of actors at lower levels of the hierarchy are equally important. Not only is such knowledge rarely part of the policy process, it is not valued. However, the success of policies, especially in their implementation, depends on such knowledge. Moreover, when implementation is part of government thinking, it is strangely divorced from everyday knowledge. Thus, the *Civil Service Reform Plan* (2012) adopts the top-down, rational model of implementation, with its imperatives for clear objectives, robust management information, and project management. If social science research ever teaches us anything, it tells us that the top-down model is plagued with implementation failures (see Van der Voet, Kuipers & Groeneveld, this volume). Everyday knowledge would inform policy makers of the limits to implementation, but no one is listening (for a more detailed discussion, see Rhodes, 2016b).

The Challenges

There are several challenges in conducting observational fieldwork in public administration, and they concern roles, relevance, time, evidence and fieldwork relationships.

Roles

There is no agreement on the role of the ethnographer, let alone on whether ethnography should be 'relevant' and how that could be achieved. Van Maanen (1978: 345–346) describes his relationship with the police he was observing as: 'a cop buff, a writer of books, an intruder, a student, a survey researcher, a management specialist, a friend, an ally, an asshole, a historian, a recruit and so on.' He was 'part spy, part voyeur, part fan and part member.' Similarly, Kedia and Van Willigen (2005: 11) distinguish between 'policy researcher or research analyst; evaluator; impact assessor, or needs assessor; cultural broker; public participation specialist; and administrator or manager.' Applied ethnography can serve many masters, and a key question is for whom the research is being done.

Relevance

For Van Willigen (2002: 150 and chapter 10), applied anthropology is a matter of providing information for decision-makers to allow them to can make rational decisions. It is a 'complex of related, research-based, instrumental methods which produce change or stability in specific cultural systems through the provision of data, initiation of direct action, and/or the formulation of policy.' Not everyone would agree that the task is to help decision-makers. For Agar (1980: 27), 'no understanding of a world is valid without representation of those members' voices'. For him, 'ethnography is *populist* to the core', and hence, the task in studying administrative reform would be to seek out the silent voices in the bureaucracy. Managers are scarcely sympathetic to such aims. They perceive ethnographers as 'coming forward with awkward observations' and 'as wishing to preserve "traditional" ways' (Sillitoe, 2006: 10). Managers criticize ethnographers because 'their findings often failed to conform to expectations held by employers about the causes of problems and their solutions.' They were dismissed as 'irrelevant or disruptive' (Sillitoe, 2006: 14).

Time

The claim to relevance is further compounded by the problem of time. Observation in the field takes time and fits uncomfortably with the demands of politicians and administrators alike. The brutal fact is that if one wishes to understand everyday life one needs to stick around, go where one is led, and take what one is given. The Minister or Departmental Secretary will not wait on the results of such unstructured soaking. Of course, fieldwork does not have to be a decade-long immersion of a lone researcher. There are other tools and shortcuts (see below). Nonetheless, getting below and behind the surface of official accounts to provide texture, depth and nuance cannot be done overnight.

Evidence

There is the problem of what counts as evidence. It might seem obvious that 'not everything that counts can be counted, and not everything that can be counted counts' (a sign hanging in Albert Einstein's office at Princeton). It is not obvious in the world of public administration with its given facts, positive theory and hypothesis testing. The popularity of evidence-based policy making with its preference for randomized control trials simply makes matters worse. Qualitative data simply does not meet such expectations and does not count as generalizable evidence.

Fieldwork Relationships

As Shore and Nugent (2002: 11) observe, 'Anthropology, by definition, is the study of the powerless "Others".' Public administration studies administrative elites. When discussing administrative reform, we are 'studying-up', and there are some obvious difficulties in 'being there'. The most obvious 'game changer' is that 'the research participants are more powerful than the researchers' (Shore & Nugent, 2002: 11). They control access and exit. They conclude interviews, refuse permission to quote interviews, and deny us documents. They can control what we see and hear. The researcher's role varies, at times with bewildering speed. One day, one is the professional stranger walking the tightrope between insider and outsider. The next day, one is the complete bystander, left behind in the office to twiddle one's thumbs. They not only enforce the laws on secrecy but also decide what is secret (see Rhodes et al., 2007). The powerful are different. They can shape one's research and change everyday life even before one's eyes.

Observation may have its problems, but all can be managed. To do so, we must accept that ethnographic practice is diverse and no longer limited to participant observation at a single site for a year or more. Instead, we have hit-and-run ethnography. Fieldwork can be done in teams that conduct research across multiple sites, taking snapshots across these locations.

It will be 'Yo-Yo research' with regular movement in and out of the field and participant observation in many local sites (Wulff, 2002). Ethnography can be conducted in collaboration with a client. If we cannot generalize, we can aspire to 'plausible conjectures', that is, to making general statements that are plausible because they rest on good reasons, and the reasons are good because they are inferred from relevant information (paraphrased from Bourdon, 1993). Ethnographers seek edification rather than generalization. I incline toward Fox's (2004: 4) practical and pragmatic assessment of fieldwork; it is a 'rather uneasy combination of involvement and detachment', but it 'is still the best method we have for exploring the complexities of human cultures, so it will have to do.' Thus, for all its limits, the classic intensive fieldwork study remains a key tool, but it now coexists with hit-and-run ethnography.

There is also a more varied toolkit encompassing focus groups (Rhodes & Tiernan, 2015), visual ethnography (Pink, 2013) and storytelling (Gabriel, 2000). A more flexible approach to fieldwork coupled with a more varied toolkit adds up to a distinctive twist in our understanding of ethnography; it is more baroque. However, it remains rooted in recovering and interrogating the stories of those we study and recounting them to find a shared understanding, an understanding that can be a source of lessons for practitioners.

Conclusion

My fieldwork provides little or no sustenance for conventional reform proposals. Rather, my axioms are the antithesis of evidence-based policy making, business management, and user choice. Attempts to impose private sector management beliefs and techniques to increase economy, efficiency and effectiveness resulted in the civil service reform syndrome. If private sector techniques offer such obvious and available approaches to management, then why is the track record so patchy? It is not because public managers are ill-trained, stupid or venal but because private sector techniques do not fit the context. Such techniques can be neutered by both bureaucratic and political games and are subjected to public accountability. Public sector officials do not share the same risks and rewards as private sector managers. Politics, value clashes, interests, cultures, symbolic imperatives and accountability all make the business model untenable in public policy decision-making. As Brunsson (2009: 133) concludes

> 'The aim of many reforms is to turn organizations into obedient instruments for their leaders. But reforms are difficult to realize, simply because even in reform processes, this is not the way organizations work.'

Ethnography is the ideal tool for exploring the way organizations work, for peering into the workings of the black box. It explores the beliefs and practices of situated agents. Walter Kickert has often stressed the differences between American and European practice stemming from their different national, historical, institutional traditions (Kickert, 2011). An interpretive approach produces accounts of reform that concentrate on complex specificity in context, on beliefs and practices and the traditions in which they are embedded. We may have different starting points, but we have the same destination. I go one step further. I move beyond differences in administrative traditions to arguing for the importance of local knowledge in designing administrative reforms.

Reform in Britain must begin with the relationship between ministers and the top civil servants because that is the fulcrum of the system. Ministers and civil servants have overlapping roles and responsibilities in which the old idea of a Civil Service 'generalist' is not dead. Ministers need political administrators with the political antennae that detect any holes before they fall in. Civil servants need the political skills to pull ministers out of the hole afterwards, and argue that their minister never fell in. Have would-be reformers persuaded ministers to desert the cocoon of willed ordinariness at the top of departments that exists to protect them? Private offices exist to domesticate trouble, to defuse problems and to take the emotion out of a crisis. Protocols are key to managing this pressurized existence. Everyday routines are unquestioned and unrecognized. When critics of the civil service attack it for the slow pace of change, they attack the wrong target. They should look instead to ministers as the main wellspring of change in British government. As long as ministers are in the spotlight for civil servants, they will give priority to preserving the cocoon and willed ordinariness.

Would-be reformers must be aware of the likely pitfalls, that is, to understand what they are seeking to reform. The reformers have had the field to themselves for decades with, at best, modest success. They forget, perhaps conveniently, the failures of previous reforms. Thus, they create little beyond civil service reform syndrome. I use observations of everyday life to explain why that success is modest. Reformers who recommend evidence-based policy making need to draw on observational evidence in designing change. It is conspicuous for its absence. Ministers bleat for reforms that they then do little to support. A key part of the inertia is not the civil service but the politicians, and reformers will continue to see their reforms fail because they continue to target the civil service. We must never forget that civil service reform concerns the constitutional and political role of public administration in the polity; it is not a matter of better management.

Notes

1. Walter Kickert and I worked together as members of the editorial team of Public Administration. It was a happy collaboration, but for me, it is not his major contribution. That honor goes to a trip to the Scheveningen and Simonis fish shop, where he introduced me to raw herring straight from the trawler with a shot of jenever . . . for breakfast! He started me on a rocky road that led to my addiction to the many varieties of raw and pickled herrings in Denmark and the

devastating mix of schnapps followed by a Baltic porter chaser . . . but never again for breakfast. So, I contribute to his Festschrift if only to tell the world of his role as a trafficker . . . in herrings.

2. On evidence-based policy making and RCTs, see Davies, Nutley and Smith, 2000; Sanderson, 2002; Pawson, 2006; Cartwright and Hardie, 2012; Haynes, Service, Goldacre and Torgerson, 2012. On behavioral economics, see Thaler and Sunstein, 2009; and Lunn, 2014.
3. See: http://www.behaviouralinsights.co.uk/ Last accessed 2 July 2015.
4. See: https://www.gov.uk/what-works-network. Last accessed 2 July 2015. See also Cabinet Office, 2013; and What Works Network, 2014.
5. See, for example: Davies et al., 2000; Bullock, Mountford and Stanley, 2001; National Audit Office, 2001; Sanderson, 2002; Lodge and Rogers, 2006; Mulgan, 2009; Regulatory Policy Institute, 2009; Better Government Institute, 2010; and Institute for Government, 2010.
6. See also Cabinet Office 2012: 28–29; PASC, 2003; Better Government Institute (BGI), 2010: 33.

References

Agar, M. (1980). *The professional stranger.* 2nd edition. San Diego: Academic Press.

Aronoff, M.J., & Kubik, J. (2013). *Anthropology and political science: A convergent approach.* New York: Berghahn Books.

Barber, M. (2007). *Instruction to deliver: Tony Blair, public services and the challenge of targets.* London: Politico's.

Better Government Institute. (2010). *Good government: Reforming parliament and the executive. Recommendations from the executive committee of the better government initiative.* London: BGI.

Bevir, M. (1999). *The logic of the history of ideas.* Cambridge: Cambridge University Press.

Bevir, M., & Rhodes, R.A.W. (2003). *Interpreting British governance.* London: Routledge.

Bevir, M., & Rhodes, R.A.W. (2006). *Governance stories.* Abingdon, Oxon: Routledge.

Bevir, M., & Rhodes, R.A.W. (2015). Interpretive political science: Mapping the field. In M. Bevir and R.A.W. Rhodes (Eds.), *The Routledge handbook of interpretive political science* (pp. 3–27). Abingdon, Oxon: Routledge.

Bourdon, R. (1993). Towards a synthetic theory of rationality. *International Studies in the Philosophy of Science, 7,* 5–19.

Brunsson, N. (2009). *Reform as routine: Organizational change in the modern world.* Oxford: Oxford University Press.

Bullock, H., Mountford, J., & Stanley, R. (2001). *Better policy making.* London: Centre for Management and Policy Studies (CMPS).

Burawoy, A. (1998). The extended case method. *Sociological Theory, 16,* 4–33.

Cabinet Office. (1999). *Professional policy making for the twenty-first century.* London: Cabinet Office.

Cabinet Office. (2012). *The civil service reform plan.* London: Cabinet Office 2012.

Cabinet Office (2013). Government Guidance. What Works Network. Cabinet Office, 28 June 2013. Retrieved from: https://www.gov.uk/guidance/what-works-network

Cameron, D. (2011). Speech on open public services, 11th July. Available on: http://www.number10.gov.uk/news/speech-on-open-public-services/ Last accessed 2 July 2015.

Cartwright, N., & Hardie, J. (2012). *Evidence-based policy making. A practical guide.* Oxford: Oxford University Press.

Cm 8145. (2011). *Open public services white paper*. London: Stationary Office.

Davies, H.T.O., Nutley, S.M., & Smith, P.C. (Eds.). (2000). *What works? Evidence-based policy and practice in public services*. Bristol: The Policy Press.

Fox, K. (2004). *Watching the English: The hidden rules of English behaviour*. London: Hodder and Stoughton.

Gabriel, Y. (2000). *Storytelling in organisations: Facts, fictions, and fantasies*. London: Oxford University Press.

Geertz, C. (1973). Thick description: Toward an interpretive theory of culture. *The interpretation of cultures: Selected essays by Clifford Geertz* (pp. 3–30). London: Fontana.

Hammersley, M., & Atkinson, P. (2007). *Ethnography: Principles in practice*. 3rd edition. London: Routledge.

Haynes, L., Service, O., Goldacre, B., & Torgerson, D. (2012). *Test, learn, adapt: Developing public policy with randomised controlled trials*. London: Cabinet Office.

Hood, C., & Lodge, M. (2007). Endpiece: Civil service reform syndrome—are we heading for a cure? *Transformation*, 58–59.

Institute for Government. (2010). *Shaping-up: A Whitehall for the future*. London: Institute for Government.

Kedia, S., & Van Willigen, J. (2005). Applied anthropology: Context for domains of application. In S. Kedia and J. Van Willigen (Eds.), *Applied anthropology: Domains of application* (pp. 1–32). Westport, CT: Praeger.

Kickert, W.J.M. (Ed.). (1997). *Public management and administrative reform in Western Europe*. Aldershot: Edward Elgar.

Kickert, W.J.M. (Ed.). (2011). *The study of public management in Europe and the US: A comparative analysis of national distinctiveness*. Abingdon, Oxon: Routledge.

Lodge, G., & Rogers, B. (2006). *Whitehall's black box: Accountability and performance in the senior civil service*. London: Institute for Public Policy Research.

Lunn, P. (2014). *Regulatory policy and behavioural economics*. Paris: OECD Publishing.

Mulgan, G. (2009). *The art of public strategy: Mobilizing power and knowledge for the common good*. Oxford: Oxford University Press.

National Audit Office (NAO). (2001). *Modern policy-making: Ensuring policies deliver value for money, report by the comptroller and auditor general*. HC 289 Session 2001–02 November 2001. London: National Audit Office.

O'Donnell, L. (2012). *Ten commandments of good policy making: A retrospective*. Available on: http://eprints.lse.ac.uk/48283/1/blogs.lse.ac.uk-Ten_Commandments_of_good_policy_making_a_retrospective_by_Sir_Gus_ODonnell.pdf. Last Accessed on 2nd July 2015.

Pawson, N. (2006). *Evidence-based policy: A realist perspective*. London: Sage.

Pink, S. (2013). *Doing visual ethnography*. 3rd edition. London: Sage.

Pollitt, C. (1993). *Managerialism and the public services*. 2nd edition. Oxford: Blackwell.

Pollitt, C., & Bouckaert, G. (2011). *Public management reform: A comparative analysis: New public management, governance and the Neo-Weberian state*. 3rd edition. Oxford: Oxford University Press.

Public Administration Select Committee. (2003). *On target? Government by measurement. Volume 1. Report together with formal minutes*. Fifth report, Session 2002–03, HC 62–1. London: Stationary Office.

Public Administration Select Committee. (2005). *Choice, voice and public services*. Fourth report, Session 2003–04, HC 49-I. London: Stationery Office.

Public Administration Select Committee. (2009). *Good government*. Eighth Report, Session 2008–09, HC 97–1. London: Stationary Office.

Regulatory Policy Institute. (2009). *Trust in the system: Restoring trust in our system of government and regulation*. Oxford: Regulatory Policy Institute.

Rhodes, R.A.W. (2011). *Everyday life in British government*. Oxford: Oxford University Press, paperback edition 2015.

Rhodes, R.A.W. (2016a). Ethnography. In M. Bevir and R.A.W. Rhodes (Eds.), *The Routledge handbook of interpretive political science* (pp. 171–185). Abingdon, Oxon: Routledge.

Rhodes, R.A.W. (2016b). Local knowledge. In M. Bevir and R.A.W. Rhodes (Eds.), *Rethinking governance: Ruling, rationalities and resistance* (pp. 198–215). Abingdon, Oxon: Routledge: forthcoming.

Rhodes, R.A.W., 't Hart, P., & Noordegraaf, M. (2007). So what? The prospects and pitfalls of being there. In R.A.W. Rhodes, P. 't Hart and M. Noordegraaf (Eds.), *Observing government elites: Up close and personal* (pp. 206–233). Houndmills, Basingstoke: Palgrave-Macmillan.

Rhodes, R.A.W., & Tiernan, A. (2015). Focus groups as ethnography: The case of prime ministers' chiefs of staff. *Journal of Organizational Ethnography, 4*(2), 208–222.

Rorty, R. (1980). *Philosophy and the mirror of nature*. Oxford: Blackwell.

Sanderson, I. (2002). Evaluation, policy learning and evidence based policy making. *Public Administration, 80*(1), 1–22.

Shore, C., & Nugent, S. (Eds.). (2002). *Elite cultures: Anthropological perspectives; ASA monographs 38*. London: Routledge.

Sillitoe, P. (2006). The search for relevance: A brief history of applied anthropology. *History and Anthropology, 17*(1), 1–19.

Thaler, R.H., & Sunstein, C.R. (2009). *Nudge: Improving decisions about health, wealth, and happiness*. Revised & Expanded edition. London and New York: Penguin Books.

Van Maanen, J. (1978). Epilogue: On watching the watchers. In P.K. Manning and J. Van Maanen (Eds.), *Policing: A view from the street* (pp. 309–349). Santa Monica, CA: Goodyear.

Van Willigen, J. (2002). *Applied anthropology: An introduction*. 3rd Edition. Westport, CT: Bergin & Garvey.

What Works Network (2014). What Works? Evidence for Decision Makers. Cabinet Office, 25 November 2014. Retrieved from: https://www.gov.uk/government/publications/what-works-evidence-for-decision-makers

Wood, E.J. (2007). Field research. In C. Boix and S.C. Stokes (Eds.), *The Oxford handbook of comparative politics* (pp. 123–146). Oxford: Oxford University Press.

Wulff, H. (2002). Yo-Yo fieldwork: Mobility and time in multi-local study of dance in Ireland. *Anthropological Journal of European Cultures, 11*, 117–136.

Part II
Objects of Reform

9 Reforming Organizational Structures

Steven Van de Walle

Introduction

Structural and organizational reform is the most visible aspect of public sector reform. Government reform plans, in general, contain a substantial section devoted to structural reorganization, with attention to establishing and abolishing organizations or parts thereof, centralizing and decentralizing organizations (both administratively and geographically) and merging and splitting organizations. More often than not, structural reforms are accompanied by an explicit desire to downsize, to reduce complexity or to align structures with new policy priorities or new perspectives on social and administrative issues. When we discuss structural reforms in this chapter, we mainly address reforms to the structure of government—or the structure of the administrative apparatus as a whole—and only to a lesser extent the reform of structures within public organizations.

Government structures have traditionally been some of the most frequently studied topics within public administration research (see also the work of Walter Kickert, e.g., Kickert, 2001). This was especially the case in the early days of the discipline, when the 'science of administration' sought a 'one best way' of organizing and did so by studying organizational structures, the division of work and coordination within organizations. Classic names such as Fayol, or Gulick and Urwick, with their 'Papers on the Science of Administration' (1937) laid the foundation for this line of work. The strong focus on organizations' structures was challenged in different ways. Herbert Simon's 'The proverbs of administration' (1946) challenged the scientific nature of the 'science of administration', by arguing that it was not particularly scientific and that many of its law-like conclusions concerning organizational structures were in fact inherently contradictory. Dwight Waldo's 'The administrative state' (1948) challenged the science of administration's presumed value-free approach to public administration. These criticisms also marked the beginning of a shift in the discipline of public administration away from a pure focus on structures and institutions to a study of actual behaviors within government organizations (Fry & Raadschelders, 2014). Contingency theorists challenged the idea of a 'one best way of organizing' and also demonstrated the field's further move away from prescriptive approaches to government structures. Finally, scholars shifted from a focus on structures *within* organizations to a wider focus on structures *of* organization (structure of government).

New Public Management (NPM) ideas, with their focus on structural disaggregation, placed organizational structures firmly back on the research agenda. More recently, challenges of both downsizing and a desire to achieve better government coordination led to renewed interest in amalgamation and reaggregation. This pendulum swing from disaggregation to reaggregation can be considered the main trend in recent structural administrative reforms (Norman & Gregory, 2003). It reflects an inherent contradiction in public sector reforms intended to establish single-purpose agencies yet, simultaneously, improve horizontal coordination (Pollitt & Bouckaert, 2004). This chapter first describes the principles and ideas behind such disaggregation and reaggregation. It then discusses a number of disaggregation trends, such as agencification, outsourcing and privatization. We continue by discussing more recent trends of reaggregation, with a particular focus on centralization, mergers and renationalization.

Main Transformation: Disaggregation and Reaggregation

Christopher Hood lists the disaggregation of units in the public sector as one of the doctrinal components of NPM. This means breaking up large government monoliths and decentralization, as well as a separation of functions therein, to make government units manageable. Additionally, it suited a wider desire for subsidiarity in service delivery (Hood, 1991: 3). In other words, centralized, monolithic government bodies should not deliver services if these services can be delivered at lower levels of government, or by nongovernmental bodies. Internally, autonomy and liberating managers from rules and restrictions was seen as an added benefit of such disaggregation. Moving to such smaller, single-purpose bodies would make government simpler and more transparent and facilitate government management of these bodies. NPM thereby followed the core Taylorist principle of task specialization, but at the higher level of the public sector as a whole. Within organizations, however, NPM would attempt to break with the bureaucratic principle of organization through a focus on output rather than on detailed processes.

Disaggregation as means of improving the public sector was very well-suited to the new institutional economics and public choice analysis of what was wrong with the public sector (Lane, 1997; see also the chapter by Van Thiel in this volume), in a situation with both an information deficit and information asymmetry, where principals' and agents' interests did not align, monolithic organizations were notoriously difficult to control and steer. However, when organizations have simple and clear purposes, steering and control become easier, and managers can be held to account for the performance of their organization.

Such disaggregation went further than the mere structural change of creating smaller, single-purpose bodies. Simultaneously, a series of 'decouplings' occurred, whereby different functions were decoupled or disentangled (Christensen, Lægreid, Roness & Røvik, 2007). The best-known example is the decoupling of policy from operation, or of steering from rowing, as Osborne and Gaebler (1992) have called it. This means that policy making functions and service delivery functions were to be placed in separate organizational entities. Such decoupling also meant that in most cases there was little reason to assume that government had to deliver services itself. This opened up opportunities for outsourcing and privatization. Regulatory functions were also to be placed into disaggregated units. Other types of decoupling also occurred (Christensen et al., 2007). Examples are a decoupling of commercial from non-commercial functions of government, rather than having these jointly included in a single organizational unit or even a single budget or decoupling of the ownership, funding, purchasing and provision of public services and infrastructures. With these decouplings also came a decoupling of ministerial responsibility from managerial accountability, whereby managers could more easily be held to account for their performance, based on quantifiable targets for their units. These processes of decoupling meant that the public sector was moving from a situation with strongly integrated departments to one in which functions had been decoupled horizontally, with a vertical decoupling between ministers and chief executives, or between parent ministries and agencies.

Disaggregation, however, quickly became fragmentation, where each body pursued its own narrow objective (Terry, 1995; Norman, 2003: 200). Disaggregation created a new need for coordination across the disaggregated units, not only within government but also beyond. New Zealand, one of the forerunners in NPM–style reforms, also became one of the first countries to formally recognize this problem of fragmentation and the resulting absence of joint work or the pursuit of a common long-term strategy (Schick, 1996: 8). Horizontally, delivery bodies competed with one another or worked totally alongside one another. This became especially visible in areas in which policy issues cut across organizational borders. A good example is youth crime, where education, policing, housing, employment and youth work departments each have a role to play. Disaggregation risked creating organizational silos and made collaboration difficult. Vertical fragmentation meant that principals found it difficult to control activities and interactions among agents, and frequent turnovers and outsourcing meant strategic capacity at the center of government was being lost (Painter, 2005). In many cases, agents drifted away from government and began to pursue their own interest, generally away from democratic bodies' curious eyes. These centrifugal movements created a new need for coordination, resulting in patterns of reaggregation across Western countries' public sectors (Verhoest, Bouckaert & Peters, 2007).

Disaggregation: Breaking up Monoliths

The disaggregation of large public sector units, often called public sector monoliths, has been the key structural trend in Western public sectors and began in the 1980s. It was thought that these monoliths were impossible to steer and control because of the opaqueness of internal developments. This opaqueness was not just due to the size and of these organizations but also, it was thought, due to the self-serving character of those working within them, who obviously did not enjoy transparency and accountability, and who wanted to protect their perks and policy preferences. Indeed, large government organizations, such as large local governments, or ministries employing thousands of people, had little insight into cost structures or the efficiency of their operations. They were shielded from disruptive market forces and did not compare themselves to private sector actors. Often, comparable private actors did not even exist. A process of disaggregation was to insert market pressures into the public sector and to reduce information deficits and asymmetries. Such processes of disaggregation are visible at different levels. We discuss four trends. At the level of the structure of government, NPM favored the creation of (quasi-)autonomous agencies. Disaggregation processes are also visible in a trend toward outsourcing and privatization, whereby government tasks are disaggregated from government and placed within the private sector. Within government organizations, NPM promoted decentralization and autonomization.

Agencification

Probably the most visible structural reform in Western public sectors since the advent of NPM has been the establishment of executive agencies or autonomous agencies (Kickert, 2001). Such agencies are structurally disaggregated from government departments. They are governed through a contractual relation with the parent department. Some agencies, often former ministerial directorates, remain part of the wider department but have received internal autonomy. Other agencies are the result of external autonomization and are located at some distance from (ministerial) departments. Thus, the concept of 'non-departmental public body' is a good description of their status. Such has been the popularity of agencies that substantial numbers, and in many cases even over half of the civil servants in Western countries, work for such agencies (OECD, 2002). Pollitt et al. in 2001 even discussed an international agency fever (Pollitt, Bathgate, Caulfield, Smullen & Talbot, 2001). Agencies are a typical expression of reinventing government's 'steering, not rowing' mantra: policy and delivery are strictly separated, and delivery, if not outsourced, is then achieved through autonomous agencies that can be run like a company. In this way, the managers have the freedom and duty to manage, and political interference in delivery and operations is minimized. A potential implication of this freedom is also a proliferation of the organizational structures these managers choose for their organizations.

While agencies come in many forms and shapes, they share a number of characteristics (Pollitt & Talbot, 2004). They are structurally disaggregated organizations that are task-specific. In other words, they are responsible for single, specific tasks. Tasks are 'unbundled'. There is also some type of performance contracting relationship with a principal or a parent organization. Finally, they enjoy a certain degree of deregulation with respect to personnel, finance, and other management matters.

Outsourcing and Privatization

A related structural transformation has been a move to outsourcing delivery functions. As is the case with agencification, outsourcing means that certain functions are placed at a distance in a separate structural unit. In the case of outsourcing, this is a unit outside the public sector. Although not a structural change in itself, a change from in-house production to delivery via a private actor entails considerable changes to the public sector organization. On the one hand, it means staff and departments become redundant and government is downsized; on the other hand, a need for contract management and procurement means new functions and units had to be established within government.

A more extreme expression of public sector disaggregation can be found in the privatization of public organizations (Clifton, Comín & Díaz Fuentes, 2006). Through privatization, parts of government are transferred to the market. The new private organizations continue to deliver services, sometimes even using public money, but they are formally entirely disaggregated from government. Privatization meant a considerable change in the structure of Western public sectors because these sectors tended to employ large numbers of people, especially in areas such as utilities, manufacturing and transport.

Decentralization and Autonomization

A final general trend towards decentralization and autonomization during the early days of NPM-style reforms is a structural change *within* public sector organizations. Decisions that had hitherto been made at central levels were decentralized to lower levels of the organization. Examples are the decentralization of HR and finance functions to the line, as well as a decentralization of procurement. This allowed lower-level bodies and managers to make their own hiring, firing, buying and financial decisions, whereas such functions had previously been centralized (for a discussion on trends in HR, see the chapter by Groeneveld and Steijn, as well as Farnham & Horton, 2000). Autonomy for managers increased, and organizations were managed through a chain of contractual relations from the top to the bottom, rather than through traditional hierarchical steering. Such decentralization, it was thought, would do away with typical bureaucratic phenomena such as centralized civil service entrance exams or the need to contact a central body to obtain new desks or pencils. Such decentralization brought flexibility but also duplication, new types of inefficiencies, and a loss of buying power (and skills) for public sector organizations. For this reason, public sectors have recently again been moving toward a stronger centralization of support functions (housing, cleaning, ICT, etc.), whereas these had previously been decentralized. This often takes the form of shared service centers.

Reaggregation: Stitching Government back together

The trend toward structural disaggregation discussed in the previous section continues to a certain extent: agencies are still established, and outsourcing and privatization continue. Moreover, in response to perceived and real fragmentation, the desire for more and better coordination led to a move toward reaggregation (Bouckaert, Peters & Verhoest, 2010). In other words, a public sector that was once deliberately broken up is now being stitched back together, with the aim of strengthening both policy cohesion across policy domains and the delivery capacity of a public sector that had decoupled delivery from policy (and often placed these functions in different structural entities). The Report of the Ministerial Advisory Group on the Review of the Centre in New Zealand (2001, pg. 4) stated this as follows: 'Fragmentation makes coordinated service delivery more complicated, adds to the costs of doing business, and blurs accountability for some issues. Structural fragmentation means many small agencies, spreading leadership talent and other skills more thinly and increasing the risk of weak capability. Fragmentation means Ministers need to build relationships with multiple agencies, and at times reconcile conflicting agency positions at an excessively detailed level. Fragmentation can make alignment more difficult.'

Many distinct phenomena can be interpreted as expressions of such a trend toward reaggregation. Whereas different reforms trends are discernible, the coherence of terminology and the strength of arguments are not yet as solid as in the case of the disaggregation trend. Concepts such as joined-up government, whole-of-government, integrated governance and coordination all reflect similar tendencies. In this section, we discuss the emergence of crosscutting arrangements, the strengthening of central agency, mergers and amalgamations, departmentalization, remunicipalization and nationalization and, finally, regulation.

Crosscutting Arrangements

One way of combatting fragmentation in the public sector is by collaboration across borders. Rather than establishing special-purpose bodies to administer a certain policy area, organizations can also choose to establish various crosscutting collaboration structures, with a more or less permanent status. Such structures allow public organizations (and, indeed, public and private ones) to collaborate and share and exchange resources (see also the chapter by Klijn & Koppenjan in this volume). Examples are interdepartmental committees, task forces, interorganizational networks and other types of collaborations and collaborative networks. Such collaborations can be complemented by targeted crossdepartmental bodies or even the appointment of more permanent staff. This means the dividing line between a mere crosscutting collaborative arrangement and the establishment of a new organizational structure becomes very thin.

Strengthening Central Agency

Organizational structures can be used to facilitate collaboration across domains, and non-permanent collaboration is a common way in which organizations work together. Coordination can also be organized more hierarchically, with a 'coordinator' or a coordinating body responsible for steering collaboration. This is, for instance, the case when new or existing bodies are placed in charge of managing a network of public organizations in which they participate (the lead organization approach—Provan & Kenis, 2008). Such a body can also be placed above the other bodies and take on a formal coordination role within the public sector system. Chancelleries and Cabinet Office-like structures are a particularly good example of such bodies that are formally in charge of the coordination of a system. Coordination can also be centralized by placing an individual in charge. This can be, among other possibilities, a network manager, a coordinator, or a task force leader. The appointment of policy czars or special advisors is another popular approach, whereby one person is placed in charge of coordinating a number of bodies to address a social or policy problem on which collaborations among organizations is desirable (The LSE GV314 Group, 2012; Vaughn & Villalobos, 2015). Such czar positions have proliferated in recent years, at both the central and local levels. Their strength generally comes from the fact that they have a direct line to political executives and can thus exert pressure on public sector organizations. Political executives themselves can play a similar role. The appointment of political executives with cross-departmental portfolios to stimulate collaboration between departments is one example. The appointment of a superminister in charge of several major departments or policy domains is another. Even within political executive bodies, scholars have observed a tendency toward the presidentialization of prime ministerial posts, with prime ministers increasingly playing the role of a coordinator of the entire public sector (Borrás & Peters, 2011; see also the chapter by Peters in this volume). Mayors play a similar role at the local level (Steyvers et al., 2008).

Mergers and Amalgamations

A more drastic way of making organizations work together across domains (horizontal), or to strengthen steering by the principal (vertical), is to simply merge or amalgamate them. This is very similar to the process of departmentalization described below. Such amalgamations have been very popular recently, although not always motivated by a desire to better coordinate but presented as a way to improve operational efficiency through scale advantages or to strengthen the administrative and technical capacity in organization, which is thought to be deficient in organizations that are too small. Horizontal amalgamation mainly occurs for policy-related and territorial reasons. An example of the former is merging two organizations performing tasks that are closely related to reduce transaction costs or minimize the likelihood of the two organizations pursuing conflicting goals. An example of this is the merger of regulatory bodies and inspection services to avoid companies having to cope with high burdens of repeated visits by different inspection bodies. It can also result from the emergence of new views on a policy domain. For instance, social issues such as juvenile delinquency can be addressed within stand-alone organizations, but such a unit can also be part of a criminal justice-related organization instead of an education-focused organization. Mergers, therefore, often reveal how policy makers' views on social problems change. A good example is the merger of the Ministry of Economic Affairs with that of Agriculture, Nature and Food Quality in the Netherlands in 2010, which reflected the new government's view that environmental issues should not excessively hinder businesses; a second example is the merger of the Ministry of Justice with a directorate general of security into a new Ministry of Security and Justice, reflecting a more repressive approach to justice issues, whereas justice- and policing-related policy domains have previously been held meticulously separate.

Other attempts at achieving horizontal coordination can be seen in territorial amalgamations, notably municipal amalgamations (Kaiser, 2015). One of the ideas behind such amalgamations is that policy issues and social problems often cut across territorial lines: urban planning, crime or public transport-related issues do not stop at territorial borders. Through upscaling territorial units, policy makers attempt to better align organizational scale with the territorial scale of social issues—the old story of equivalence advanced by Oates (1972). The result has been a substantial wave of municipal amalgamations throughout Europe. Similar trends can be seen in other public services such as fire services or police forces, many of which have been merged into ever-larger organizational units.

Departmentalization

Mergers and amalgamations can in particular be observed in the process of departmentalization, or the reversal of agencification, in many countries. This meant that many agencies lost their autonomous status and were returned to the direct control of a ministry or a local government department. Examples are so-called departmentalization in Australia, part of Australia's move toward integrated governance, the UK government abolishing some agencies following David Cameron's announcement of a 'bonfire of the quangos', and similar trends in New Zealand, Ireland, and many Central European countries (Halligan, 2007; Talbot & Johnson, 2007; Flinders & Skelcher, 2012; Van Thiel, 2012). The arguments for departmentalization have mainly been linked to a desire to be better able to coordinate and to directly steer what is happening in the agencies. Political arguments for reaggregation have also been advanced. The main argument is that disaggregation has created a lack of political control and oversight. In the case of agencies, this has meant, for example, that elected bodies could not easily control agencies because these had received autonomy, and steering occurred through long-term agreements and contracts. The same goes for various QUANGOs, where a veritable quangocracy had developed that essentially controlled itself (Skelcher, 1998). Executive politicians in turn found it difficult to work with agencies with which steering contracts had been signed by their predecessors, especially when things were going wrong, without having an easy way of intervening.

Nationalization and Remunicipalization

A further aggregation or reaggregation trend is related to the desire to strengthen vertical coordination for organizations that had been given very high levels of autonomy or that have recently been hived off. This is visible primarily in a trend toward strengthening regulation in sectors that had previously been liberalized and in trends toward moving organizations back into government after being granted high levels of autonomy or even privatized. Likely the best example is the nationalization of financial institutions as a way for governments not only to save these institutions but also to be able to better steer and control them (Monnet, Pagliari & Shahin, 2014). Some of these financial institutions were government controlled or government owned in the past and had been privatized. A similar trend is visible in the renewed strengthening of governments' control over central banks, whereas the idea before the fiscal crisis had been to grant these as much autonomy as possible and to shield them from government intervention (Roberts, 2011). Another expression of this trend is visible in processes of remunicipalization, whereby local authorities retake control over utilities that had previously been given autonomy or privatized (Hall, Lobina & Terhorst, 2013). Such direct control strengthens governments' capacity to steer these organizations and helps governments to directly protect social and political imperatives. This can be achieved through a local version of nationalization, by taking financial positions or by delegating heavyweights to the boards of such companies when the municipality still owns shares. At national levels, we observe such desires for coordination in privatized sectors, in increasing concerns with the national interest dimension of utilities or in political desires to shield national economic champions from market pressures. In a way, Western countries appear to be moving to systems of national economic coordination, in line with what is already common in many Asian emerging (and now established) economies and in line with what was common in pre-NPM times. Processes of insourcing following a decades-long focus on outsourcing appear to reflect similar concerns.

Regulation and Reregulation

A less extreme, but not less common, phenomenon is the strong growth of regulatory institutions in past couple of decades. The sharp increase in the number of regulatory bodies is simultaneously a logical consequence of disaggregation trends and an expression of a willingness to reaggregate. NPM-inspired liberalization and privatization of public services, especially in the utility and health sectors, have created a need to control these sectors to ensure that they continue to work with the public interest in mind or in accordance with the government's policy. Especially because customers have increasingly been paying directly for service delivery, the steering capacity of governments has been undermined. Through establishing regulatory bodies, governments can still attempt to coordinate an otherwise fragmented field and to ensure that the public interest dimension in these sectors is not undermined (Majone, 1994).

Conclusion: Pendulum Swings in Structural Reform

When examining reforms of organizational structures in the public sector, one can clearly observe strong pendulum swings. NPM-inspired disaggregation is now followed by a new wave of reaggregation intended to address crosscutting policy issues and strengthen central control. Some of these changes appear to be a return to pre-NPM structures, but others can be interpreted as a further perfection of NPM reforms or as the emergence of new ways of organizing. Processes of centralization and decentralization also alternated in the public sector in the past, both within the central government and in central-local relations. One can observe similar swings in processes of outsourcing and privatization, especially with respect to long-term changes. Coordination has in recent years moved to the core of public management research as one of the main trends in public sector reform. Such coordination often comes in the form of new coordinating entities and reflects a desire to stitch the public sector back together. Whereas disaggregation was considered a solution to perceived problems of efficiency, effectiveness and control in the NPM era, aggregation and reaggregation have now taken over as preferred solutions for exactly the same types of perceived problems. In addition, these structural aggregations are regarded as essential solutions for legitimacy and accountability problems that emerged following disaggregation.

Studying changing structures remains one of the best ways to study how governments reform (MacCarthaigh, Roness & Sarapuu, 2012): organizations are established and abolished; they grow and they shrink; they are amalgamated and split up again; they receive autonomy, or it is taken away from them; and they are placed at a distance, or they are brought back under central control. One can track changing political priorities through structural changes in government organizations (see, e.g., Sarapuu, 2012).

Public sector reforms are generally, or even mainly, structural reforms. For students of reform, structural reforms are some of the best-documented reforms, as they tend to leave highly visible traces, even in the long term. However, we know little about the effect of such structural reforms. This is problematic because structural reforms are some of the most popular ways of reforming the public sector, as they allow policy makers to demonstrate leadership and reform zeal, precisely because they are so visible.

References

Borrás, S., & Guy Peters, B. (2011). The Lisbon strategy's empowerment of core executives: Centralizing and politicizing EU national co-ordination. *Journal of European Public Policy, 18*(4), 525–545.

Bouckaert, G., Peters, B.G., & Verhoest, K. (2010). *The coordination of public sector organizations: Shifting patterns of public management.* London: Palgrave Macmillan.

Christensen, T., Lægreid, P., Roness, P.G., & Røvik, K.A. (2007). *Organization theory and the public sector: Instrument, culture, and myth.* London: Routledge.

Clifton, J., Comín, F., & Díaz Fuentes, D. (2006). Privatizing public enterprises in the European Union 1960–2002: Ideological, pragmatic, inevitable? *Journal of European Public Policy, 13*(5), 736–756.

Farnham, D., & Horton, S. (Eds.). (2000). *Human resources flexibilities in the public services.* London: Palgrave Macmillan.

Flinders, M., & Skelcher, C. (2012). Shrinking the quango state: Five challenges in reforming quangos. *Public Money & Management, 32*(5), 327–334.

Fry, B.R., & Raadschelders, J.C.N. (2014). *Mastering public administration: From max weber to dwight waldo.* 3rd edition. Thousand Oaks: CQ Press.

Gulick, L., & Urwick, L. (Eds.). (2004) [1937]. *Papers on the science of administration.* London: Routledge.

Hall, D., Lobina, E., & Terhorst, P. (2013). Re-municipalisation in the early twenty-first century: Water in France and energy in Germany. *International Review of Applied Economics, 27*(2), 193–214.

Halligan, J. (2007). Reintegrating government in third generation reforms of Australia and New Zealand. *Public Policy and Administration, 22*(2), 217–238.

Hood, C. (1991). A public management for all seasons. *Public Administration, 69*(1), 3–19.

Kaiser, C. (2015). Top-down versus bottom-up: Comparing strategies of municipal mergers in Western European countries. *Der moderne staat, Zeitschrift für Public Policy, Recht und Management, 8*(1), 113–127.

Kickert, W.J.M. (2001a). Public management of hybrid organizations: Governance of quasi-autonomous executive agencies. *International Public Management Journal, 4*(2), 135–150.

Kickert, W.J.M. (Ed.). (2001b). *Public management and administrative reform in Western Europe.* Cheltenham: Edward Elgar.

Lane, J.-E. (Ed.). (1997). *Public sector reform: Rationale, trends and problems*. London: Sage.

The LSE GV314 Group. (2012). New life at the top: Special advisers in British government. *Parliamentary Affairs, 65*(4), 715–732.

MacCarthaigh, M., Roness, P.G., & Sarapuu, K. (2012). Mapping public sector organizations: An agenda for future research. *International Journal of Public Administration, 35*(12), 844–851.

Majone, G. (1994). The rise of the regulatory state in Europe. *West European Politics, 17*(3), 77–101.

Monnet, E., Pagliari, S., & Shahin, V. (2014). *Europe between financial repression and regulatory capture*. Bruegel Working Paper 2014/08, July 2014.

Norman, R. (2003). *Obedient servants? Management freedoms and accountabilities in the New Zealand public sector*. Wellington: Victoria University Press.

Norman, R., & Gregory, R. (2003). Paradoxes and pendulum swings: Performance management in New Zealand's public sector. *Australian Journal of Public Administration, 62*(4), 35–49.

Oates, W.E. (1972). *Fiscal federalism*. New York: Harcourt Brace Jovanovich.

OECD. (2002). *Distributed public governance: Agencies, authorities and other government bodies*. Paris: OECD Publishing.

Osborne, D., & Gaebler, T. (1992). *Reinventing government: How the entrepreneurial spirit is transforming the public sector*. Reading: Addison Wesley.

Painter, C. (2005). Managing criminal justice: public service reform writ small? *Public Money and Management, 25*(5), 306–314.

Pollitt, C., Bathgate, K., Caulfield, J., Smullen, A., & Talbot, C. (2001). Agency fever? Analysis of an international policy fashion. *Journal of Comparative Policy Analysis, 33*(3), 271–290.

Pollitt, C., & Bouckaert, G. (2004). *Public management reform: A comparative analysis*. Oxford: Oxford University Press.

Pollitt, C., & Talbot, C. (Eds.). (2004). *Unbundled government: A critical analysis of the global trend to agencies, quangos and contractualisation*. London: Routledge.

Provan, K.G., & Kenis, P. (2008). Modes of network governance: Structure, management and effectiveness. *Journal of Public Administration Research and Theory, 18*(2), 229–252.

Roberts, A. (2011). *The logic of discipline: Global capitalism and the architecture of government*. Oxford: Oxford University Press.

Sarapuu, K. (2012). Administrative structure in times of changes: The development of Estonian ministries and government agencies 1990–2010. *International Journal of Public Administration, 35*(12), 808–819.

Schick, A. (1996). *The spirit of reform: Managing the New Zealand state sector in a time of change*. Wellington: State Services Commission.

Simon, H.A. (1946). The proverbs of administration. *Public Administration Review, 6*(1), 53–67.

Skelcher, C. (1998). *The appointed state: Quasi-governmental organizations and democracy*. Buckingham: Open University Press.

Steyvers, K., Bergström, T., Bäck, H., Boogers, M., Ruano De La Fuente, J.M., & Schaap, L. (2008). Introduction: From princeps to president? Comparing local political leadership transformation. *Local Government Studies, 34*(2), 131–146.

Talbot, C., & Johnson, C. (2007). Seasonal cycles in public management: Disaggregation and re-aggregation. *Public Money & Management, 27*(1), 53–60.

Terry, L.D. (1995). The thinning of administrative institutions in the hollow state. *Administration and Society, 37*(4), 426–444.

Van Thiel, S. (2012). Debate: From trendsetter to laggard? Quango reform in the UK. *Public Money & Management, 32*(6), 399–400.

Vaughn, J.S., & Villalobos, J.D. (2015). The policy czar debate. In R.P. Watson, J. Covarrubias, T. Lansford and D.M. Brattebo (Eds.), *The Obama presidency: A preliminary assessment* (pp. 315–342). Abany: Suny Press.

Verhoest, K., Bouckaert, G., & Peters, B.G. (2007). Janus-faced reorganization: Specialization and coordination in four OECD countries in the period 1980–2005. *International Review of Administrative Sciences, 73*(3), 325–348.

Waldo, D. (1948). *The administrative state: A study of the political theory of American public administration.* New York: Ronald Press Co.

10 Bureaucrats and Politicians
Reform Begets Reform

B. Guy Peters

Introduction

The spate of reform in the public sector in recent decades has touched all areas of governing and has had a significant impact on the roles of politicians and public servants. Whereas the initial rounds of reform described as New Public Management tended to denigrate the role of political leaders, subsequent reforms have involved those leaders attempting to reassert control through a variety of forms of politicization. The pendulum of power between bureaucrats and politicians has swung many times before and continues to move back and forth with continuing change in the public sector.

The relationship between senior public servants and their political *masters* is one of the most crucial factors affecting the quality of governance. For political leaders, this linkage can be important for advice on public policy and for their capacity to steer government. The linkage is also important politically because the lower echelons of public organizations are generally in closer contact with the clients of the organization than are the politicians. This connection between the lower echelons of organizations is important in part because the political leadership of organizations depends upon the civil service, and the senior public servants, for the effective implementation of policies and, therefore, for at least some part of their (real or perceived) success as leaders within the organization. Particularly important for political leaders is the capacity to use administrative performance to mobilize political support among the clients of programs.

The senior public service, and the remainder of the public service within the organization, also depends upon their political leadership. At a very basic level, the organization depends upon the capacity of the minister to influence the remainder of government for budgets, political power and policies. A minister who cannot 'fight his/her corner' weakens the capacity of the organization to perform its tasks and, therefore, will not be well-regarded within the organization or without. Political leaders must also provide direction to the organization and its employees and legitimate the activities of the organization. The minister also must be willing to be responsible for the activities of his or her organization in front of parliament, other public sector organizations, and the public, thus protecting the anonymity of public servants.

This potentially symbiotic, and potentially contentious, relationship between political and administrative leaders varies to some extent across types of political systems. Presidential and parliamentary systems, for example, may have marked differences in how the political leadership can appoint members of the administration and impose their will over the bureaucracy (see Hammond & Butler, 2003). Even in authoritarian political systems, the interactions between political leaders and the bureaucracy are important for governance and for the performance of the bureaucracy (Greene, 2010). Authoritarian leaders may have more forceful means of resolving conflicts with their bureaucrats than do democratic leaders, but they must still be concerned about their capacity to control.

This relationship also has substantial importance for ideas of democratic governance. The development of the idea of a public bureaucracy with 'neutral competence' has been one of the major struggles in reform movements in industrial democracies (see Ingraham, 1995). That struggle is far from over in many transitional and developing systems, as eliminating clientelism continues to be necessary and patronage remains deeply entrenched (Panizza, Peters, Ramos & Schleris, 2014). Moreover, there are also pressures for 'responsive competence' for public servants, with political leaders (and to some extent the public) demanding that civil servants be more open to political demands, rather than maintaining a strictly neutral stance. The Wilsonian dichotomy between politicians and administrators has been subject to many footnotes and amendments but remains a central tenet in many administrative systems (Svara, 2001)

Given the continuing distinction between these two forms of competence for civil servants, the continuing processes of 'reform' of the public bureaucracy, and of the executive branch of government more generally, is hardly surprising. As with many fundamental issues in public administration, reform often resembles a pendulum going back and forth between two poles of a continuum, with each pole having some virtues (Aucoin, 1990). In this case, there has been a continuing swing between more neutral and more politicized approaches to administration. As both forms of competence for public administrators have some virtues, finding some golden mean between the two has proven elusive.

Models of the Relationship between Civil Servants and Politicians

Given the importance of this relationship between civil servants and politicians for effective governance, there have been a number of attempts to describe and explain the relationship. In the traditional conceptualization of this relationship, the civil service was charged with the 'mere implementation' of the laws and directives coming from the political leadership.[1] That was a useful normative model, perhaps, but was not very useful for explaining the actual interactions among these actors, as they were necessarily working together in the processes of governing.[2] Therefore, alternative models of the relationship were developed in political science and public administration.

Although the four models to be discussed here utilize different variables to explain and describe the relationship, all contain at their core an assumption about competition and conflict as the fundamental nature of this relationship. In the best of all worlds, these two sets of actors would work together smoothly to govern. For example, Heclo and Wildavsky (1974) argued that there was a 'village' within the UK Treasury occupied by civil servants and politicians. These officials had common social backgrounds and were all committed to effectively managing the affairs of the nation. That level of integration does not appear as clearly in the other models of governing, and in most there is a strong assumption that the two sets of actors compete for power and resources.

Although there is a strong assumption of self-interest in some of these models of the relationship between politicians and bureaucrats, the conflict may also arise from more benign causes. Most important, the conflict between politicians and bureaucrats may arise because they have different policy commitments or different policy ideas. Political leaders may believe that they have the legitimate right to alter programs, while career administrators may have a commitment to the status quo or have different ideas about change. Further, career administrators may have more direct connections with their clientele and be more committed to service (the public service motivation) than are political leaders.

Economic Models: Rational Choice and Utility Maximization

The earliest of these models of interaction was based on rational choice economics and assumed that civil servants were motivated to maximize their own utility. That utility was defined in terms of increasing the budget and personnel allocations of their organizations (Niskanen, 1971) or maximizing their leisure through shirking (Hanusch, 1980). Whatever the maximand, the assumption was that bureaucrats were able to shape their own working lives through information asymmetry, trading information for whatever values they preferred (see Miller, 2005). Thus, rather than being a collaborative relationship directed toward governance, these models were clearly based on competition over resources and power.

Although these models of bureaucratic behavior were well-argued, relatively little empirical support has been found for the assumptions of maximization (see Blais & Dion, 1991). Rather than pursuing a rather simple maximizing strategy, public bureaucrats, as well as politicians, were engaged in much more complex interactions with multiple goals. Thus, in addition to perhaps desiring greater power and resources, they also wanted to govern effectively, they had a public service motivation (Perry, 2011) and they may have been committed to particular public policies (Goodsell, 2011). Thus, there was a complex political game balancing a number of objectives and utilizing a variety of resources for bargaining. Even when the pursuit of utility is abandoned as an assumption, there remains some sense that the two sets of actors involved in the executive branch may well be pursuing different goals in public policy.

Roles

Another important approach to understanding relationships between politicians and bureaucrats (Aberbach, Putnam & Rockman, 1981) is based on attitudes and roles, contrasting the role conceptions of classical and political bureaucrats (see also Selden, Brewer & Brudney, 1999). Civil servants in the first category adhered rather strictly to the formal, depoliticized model associated with Weber or Wilson, whereas those in the second category were willing, or even anxious, to become involved in policy making. These political bureaucrats were generally not political in the partisan sense, but they were interested in shaping policy. In addition to this rather sharp dichotomy in role conceptions, there were hybrids who played both roles, perhaps at different times or in relationship to different issues.

Although this approach to the relationship does not depend upon an assumption of conflict between politicians and bureaucrats, the research in this tradition certainly reveals considerable tension if not overt conflict. For example, Aberbach & Rockman's (2000) study of the American bureaucracy and its political masters demonstrates the intense politics associated with the attempts of politicians to control that bureaucracy. The understanding of the roles of the actors involved assists in understanding and explaining these conflicts over governance within the American system.

Hansen and Ejersbo (2002) provide an explanation for the emergence of different roles for actors in the political process, as well as the potential conflict between politicians and bureaucrats. They argue that these differences in these actors arise in part from different epistemologies embedded in the minds and activities of the various actors. Politicians are argued to have a more inductive style of addressing public problems, attempting to solve the problem in front of them, while career civil servants tend to consider decisions more in terms of general legal or policy principles. Those different conceptions of how to make policy then constitute a natural basis for conflict.

Structural Patterns

The relationship between political and administrative actors in government can also be conceptualized in more structural terms, although attitudes concerning the roles of the actors involved may undergird them. For example,

Peters (1987) discussed five possible patterns of relationship, ranging from domination by political leaders through to bureaucratic domination based on the control of information and processes. These five versions of the relationship could be considered Ideal Types against which one can compare actual patterns of interaction. Further, these models contain cooperation as well as conflict, especially in the 'Village Life' model derived from Heclo and Wildavsky (1974).

While conflict between politicians and bureaucrats represents the primary factor defining these relationships, other factors such as conflicts among public organizations over policy also influence the interactions. Most notably, the vertical integration of politicians and bureaucrats in 'functional villages', or epistemic communities (Zito, 2001), may minimize conflicts between politicians and bureaucrats within an organization but create conflicts with other organizations and make governance understood more generally more difficult.

As was true for the economic models above, these Ideal Types tend to oversimplify complex realities in governing. For example, the 'Village Life' model assuming that both sets of actors worked together in a small elite community dedicated to governance may underestimate the extent of conflict and competition that exists even in tightly constrained elite communities. At what level of conflict is the village set on fire (Peters, 1986)? That said, these Ideal Types do provide a useful point for beginning the analysis and a means of understanding the complexities that actually exist.

Bargains

A fourth approach to understanding the relationships between politicians and bureaucrats is based on the explicit or implicit bargains that exist between the two sets of actors (see Hood & Lodge, 2006). Both sets of actors have something to give, and something to gain, in such relationships, and they interact to produce a bargain. In some cases, that bargain is well-established and largely accepted, but in others there may be continuing negotiations–explicit or implicit–over the proper nature of the bargain. The actors involved have different interests, although there is not as strong a sense of manifest or potential conflict between the groups as found in the other approaches. This model of the relationship can easily be expressed in more game-theoretic terms, with the actors attempting to reach a bargain that can satisfy both sets of actors, with the expectation of creating 'serial loyalists' among the civil servants.

The presentation of the 'Schafferian' bargain by Hood and Lodge (2006) contains two apparent equilibrium outcomes of that game. First, the trustee bargain assumes that civil servants should be given substantial latitude to act in the public interest, and to define that public interest, without excessive intervention from political actors. The trustee model is to some extent vestigial, reflecting a relatively traditional pattern of delegation to career civil servants, especially within well-established democratic systems.

In the Hood and Lodge analysis, the agency bargain is the alternative to the trustee model. This bargain is analogous to the familiar principal-agent model in economics in which the principal delegates to an agent but is more active in monitoring the activities of that agent (Lane, 2005). In this version of the bargain, the civil servant is an agent who the politician must monitor to ensure compliance. There is not the trust implied in the trustee model, and, hence, there is an underlying sense of conflict, even if the bargain may limit the amount of overt conflict.

Summary

These models of interactions between politicians and bureaucrats all provide some insights into the manner in which these two sets of actors function together, and apart, to govern. That said, they all tend to emphasize patterns of difference more than they do mechanisms for producing cooperation. It appears that there is a need to build those models of cooperation, using perhaps general models of coordination in government (Peters, 2015) or the literature on building governing coalitions in parliament (Bergman et al., 2008).

Politicians and Bureaucrats in Reform

Setting aside for the moment the theoretical models of relationships between politicians and bureaucrats, the real world of these actors has been shifting very rapidly under their feet. Whereas civil servants in particular may hold their own conceptions of their role in governing, that role may not be available to them, as cycles of reform continue to alter the structures and processes of governing. In particular, reforms beginning with the New Public Management in the early 1980s and continuing to the present have attempted to strike a balance between the power of political and administrative leaders that would be acceptable according to both democratic and governance criteria.

These cycles of reform also reflect the underlying assumption of much of the theoretical literature that these actors are in competition for power. That competitive, or conflictual, view appears to be held most clearly by the politicians, who feel that their capacity to control government is undermined by a permanent and unelected bureaucracy. Even if the bureaucracy attempts to be compliant with the wishes of their political masters, there is a lingering perception that the career public service is somehow lurking, waiting for opportunities to impose their own views on government policy.[3] The somewhat negative views of the actors involved in government help fuel the continuing saga of reform.

Increasing the Autonomy and Power of Managers

In the contemporary period, the first wave of the reforms, following the dictates of the New Public Management, was based in part upon the classic Wilsonian notion of the separation of politics and administration. This separation was to be achieved through the formal separation of policy making and implementation, with implementation being assigned to quasi-autonomous agencies or, perhaps, to contractors from the public and private sector. This separation was also brought about by de-emphasizing the policy advice role of civil servants in favor of more politicized sources of policy advice.

Somewhat paradoxically, the attempt to separate management and policy making has tended to enhance the power of civil servants, rather than diminish it. Some of this empowerment of the upper-level civil service, or its equivalents hired from outside government, was a function of the ideology of New Public Management that emphasized the importance of management.[4] That ideology was reinforced by the structural separation of policy implementation into agencies and analogous organizations, providing the managers of those agencies substantial autonomy. Whereas some of this autonomy for agencies was intended, having the capacity to make more decisions rather obviously enhances the power of these managers. As a consequence, the capacity of political leaders to control those organizations and their decisions declined.

The increased openness of the public sector to recruitment of its senior managers from outside the career public service has also enhanced the relative power of the 'bureaucracy', although that effect may not have been intended. As many senior public managers were being recruited, they did not appear to have as much commitment to the traditional public service values such as anonymity–the classical bureaucratic model of Aberbach, Putnam and Rockman (1981). As they are generally working on personal contracts and, therefore, must demonstrate good performance in their positions, they may be more aggressive in pursuing their own goals, and their organizational goals, than might traditional civil servants.

This behavior by public managers, and their organizations, placed in an autonomous and somewhat exposed position should have been expected. The independent regulatory commissions in the US also emerged from the Wilsonian tradition of separating policy and administration. These organizations found, however, that they still required political support and consequently tended to develop their own political connections, primarily coming from the groups they were designed to regulate. That regulatory capture has not been as much of a problem for the agencies created as a component of the New Public Management, but the loss of political control does appear to have been.

Politicians Strike Back

The story of the New Public Management above may have glossed over some nuances and differences among cases, but it is a reasonable description of the enhanced power of the bureaucracy during that time. The paradox, perhaps, is that these reforms were to a great extent designed by political leaders attempting to exert greater control over a bureaucracy that they may have considered out of control (Savoie, 1994). The assumption that separating administration and politics would mean that policy could be made without reference to its implementation was perhaps understandable but also seemed to be disproven by events. This was true despite that the model of agencies developed in the United Kingdom and in many other cases provided more political direction over agencies than was found in the original Swedish version of this organizational form.[5]

For political leaders, and especially ministers responsible for particular policy areas, the agency model created responsibility without power. That is, the minister of agriculture, for example, appeared responsible for what happens in agricultural programs, even if he or she had little or no direct control over the implementation of those policies. Reforms designed to free ministers from quotidian concerns with administration were not able to achieve this, but they did reduce or eliminate the capacity of the ministers to directly influence programs. That, along with the general denigration of political leaders by many managers and the ideology of NPM, placed those political leaders in a very poor position.

At the same time that ministers appeared to be losing some influence over the implementation of programs in their policy areas, they were also losing some of their powers to prime ministers. Parliamentary governments have been transforming into cabinet governments, and cabinet governments have been transforming into prime ministerial governments. This process of 'presidentialization' (Poguntke & Webb, 2007) has transferred powers into the hands of prime ministers in parliamentary systems, arguably making them appear more like presidents than the *primus inter pares* status usually associated with a prime minister.[6]

The presidentialization of parliamentary systems has manifested in several ways. One has been the development of support structures for the prime minister in interacting with both the bureaucracy and the remainder of the political executive. Organizations such as the *Bundeskanzlersamt* in Germany (Busse & Hofmann, 2010) and the Prime Minister's Office in Canada have expanded their staffing and their capacity to supervise the actions of individual ministries (see Savoie, 2011). Whereas still not of the magnitude of the Executive Office of the President in the US, these organizations are now substantially more capable policy actors.

As well as strengthening their offices quantitatively, prime ministers have also increased their qualitative controls over ministries, ministers, and especially, civil servants. This expansion of control has been seen, for example, in the control of communications coming from government (see Thomas, 2013), limiting the autonomy of politicians and civil servants to exercise their own judgment in interacting with the press. Prime ministers also appear more willing to use their personnel powers to exert control over the rest of the executive. In short, they definitely have exceeded the role of first among equals in their attempts to shape the actions of government.

These increased powers in the hands of chief executives in government were designed to address not only the problems of accountability created by the separation of policy making and implementation but also a range of other issues. Perhaps most notably, the fragmentation of government into a large number of autonomous or quasi-autonomous organizations exacerbated the underlying problems of coordination and coherence in government (see Dahlström, Peters & Pierre, 2011; but see Hansen, Steen & De Jong, 2013). This familiar coordination issue and the empowerment of political executives can be closely linked. Part of the complaint of political leaders was that they were incapable of imposing their priorities on government. Having been elected to govern, or so they thought, prime ministers, and to a lesser extent other ministers, had found that the 'priority of politics' in selecting policy goals was not as clear as they believed it should be. The empowerment of bureaucratic organizations and senior administrators made enforcing those priorities more difficult, with each of the numerous organizations within the public sector pursuing its own goals with little regard to the goals of other organizations or of the political leadership (see Peters, 2015).

Politicization and Patronage

The development of capacity in organizations directly serving the prime minister or president and the development of coordination mechanisms may be considered positive reactions to the apparent loss of control by political leaders. There have been, however, a number of less positive reactions to that loss of control. One of the more common of these has been the increased politicization of the public service in the industrialized democracies (Peters & Pierre, 2004; Neuhold, Vanhoonacker & Verhey, 2013).

The now common politicization of the public service resulted from several changes within the public sector. Some of these changes have been more political and some have been administrative. First, beginning at about the same time as the general shift to the New Public Management, many political leaders expressed their discontent with the policy advice they were receiving from their career public servants. This concern about policy advice was especially true for political leaders from the political right, who assumed that incumbent public servants were generally committed to a large and active state. These leaders, therefore, wanted their own advisors and–consistent with the ideology of NPM–emphasized management for the careerists.

In addition, the presidentialization of governments has also led to increased politicization of the public sector, especially policy advice. As these 'presidentialized' executives wish to impose their personal marks on government, they also want to exercise as much control over public employment as possible. In general, politicians are especially concerned with controlling the upper echelons of government, but there are also some advantages to placing appointees throughout government. Those appointments are important for control and for collecting intelligence regarding whether the organizations are performing their tasks in conformity with the goals of the leadership.[7]

In addition to the directly political reasons, the governance challenges presented to political leaders through the reform of the administrative system have generated other reasons for attempting to gain tighter control over the public bureaucracy. The autonomy of public organizations has driven political leaders to attempt to control the individuals working with government. Further, tendencies toward decentralization and the empowerment of all levels of the public service (see Peters & Pierre, 2000) have reduced the capacity of political leaders to control policy delivery and, hence, exacerbated their problems of accountability without responsibility for policy.

Varieties of Politicization and Conflict

Most discussions of politicization and patronage in the public sector tend to assume that all deviations from the formal merit system are equally undesirable. That may not be the case, however, and some forms of political appointment may in fact enhance the governance and even democratic capacities of political systems. Thus, understanding the relationships in many political systems depends at least in part in understanding how political appointments are made and managed (see Peters, 2013).

There is not sufficient space in this chapter to analyze all the forms of patronage, but a brief description of four types can help make sense of some of the political dynamics involved. The simplest and most egregious form occurs in cases in which political leaders have the capacity to appoint large numbers of employees at all levels of government, based simply on their political affiliations. This form of patronage may reduce bureaucratic resistance to policy initiatives coming from the elected leaders, but it may also significantly reduce the policy capacity of those governments.

Two other forms of politicization may be especially prone to generating conflict between career and political officials. One, called here duplicative politicization, involves appointing political loyalists to duplicate the career structure at the top of public organizations. This attempt at imposing oversight over the career administrators by appointees was almost certain to engender conflict (on Canada see Bourgault & Nugent, 1995). Similarly, personalized politicization, in which the appointees are loyal more to an individual political leader rather than to a party or the government of the day, may also provoke conflict. In this case, the conflict may be even among political leaders as well as with the career service.

Finally, professionalized politicization, as found in Germany, may permit more responsive competence without engendering conflict (Schröter, 2004). In this model, senior civil servants are professionals, but they are also affiliated with political parties. Thus, they have all the competences required to be effective public servants, but they are also committed to the program of the current government. If there is a change in government, there will also be a new group of professional, but partisan, civil servants installed to assist in governing. In this version of politicization, conflict can be minimized but at the cost of having two or more teams of civil servants prepared to participate in governing.

The point here is that careful institutional design can be employed to attempt to balance the virtues of responsive and neutral competence. An appropriate design may be able to reduce the real or potential conflicts between politicians and bureaucrats, but that is but only one of several goals that can be components of administrative reform. The tendency to assume a stark dichotomy between politicians and bureaucrats, and between neutral and responsive competence, without considering more subtle ways of linking politicians and bureaucrats for cooperative actions to solve public problems can be mitigated by more careful designs.

Summary and Conclusions

The discussion in this chapter thus far has proceeded as if these two sets of actors were functioning in a vacuum, playing their games and producing benefits and losses for themselves. That isolation is true only in part, and more important, it undervalues the importance of these interactions in governing. The capacity of the actors to collaborate and minimize overt conflict plays a major role in governance capacity. Some of the models of these relationships allow for cooperative behaviors, but the general pattern of thinking conceptualizes these relationships as, if not overtly conflictual, at a minimum being between actors with rather different goals and incentives. To some extent, that conflict may be functional, allowing for different ideas about policy to emerge and to be debated, but it can also inhibit effective governance.

The important question then becomes how to move these relationships forward toward a more cooperative relationship. At the academic level, this is the issue of developing models that consider the relationship along a dimension of cooperation and conflict and considers mechanisms for explaining cooperation. At a more practical level, continuing reforms should be directed toward identifying and implementing those mechanisms in the world of governing. Overcoming the mutual suspicion, and the stereotypes, that have often colored these relationships is no simple task, but doing so would improve the governance capacity of the actors and the political systems involved.

Notes

1. This conception of the relationship is stated most explicitly by Woodrow Wilson in the US but is also present in the Weberian model of bureaucracy central to European thinking about public administration.
2. As Rose (1987) argued, civil servants and politicians both have their hands on the tiller, attempting to steer the metaphorical ship of state.
3. This conception of a clever public bureaucracy biding its time and waiting to exert control over policy is in sharp contrast to other stereotypes of indolence and shirking (see Brehm & Gates, 1997).
4. Although the often repeated *mantra* of "Let the managers manage" was actually a part of the Old Public Management, having been used first in the 1950s with respect to managers in the public sector, it was utilized to justify granting greater autonomy to managers during the 1980s and after. That enhanced autonomy was accepted, especially by the managers who were being empowered.
5. In particular, there was no lay board responsible for the organization but rather a direct link with the ministry.
6. In many ways the term presidentialization is a misnomer. Prime ministers in the "reformed" systems described as presidential have considerably more power than do most presidents, as they can be assured of the support of the legislature, whereas presidents are often engaged in competition or conflict with their legislatures. See Cheibub, Elkins and Ginsburg (2014).
7. Before the contemporary period of politicization, President Franklin Roosevelt placed numerous appointees at the lowest echelons of his New Deal organizations to be able to monitor the actual performance of the organizations. Paul Light (1995, 2004) has noted the 'thickening' of political appointments in American governments as the appointments go ever deeper into the administrative apparatus.

References

Aberbach, J.D., Putnam, R.D., & Rockman, B.A. (1981). *Bureaucrats and politicians in Western democracies.* Cambridge, MA and London: Harvard University Press.

Aberbach, J.D., & Rockman, B.A. (2000). *In the web of politics: Three decades of the U.S. federal executive.* Washington, DC: The Brookings Institution.

Aucoin, P. (1990). Administrative reform in public management: Paradigms, principles, paradoxes and pendulums. *Governance, 3,* 115–137.

Bergman, T., Gerber, E.R., Kastner, S., & Nyblade, B. (2008). The empirical study of cabinet government. In K. Strom, W. Mueller and T. Berman (Eds.), *Cabinets and coalition bargaining* (pp. 85–122). Oxford: Oxford University Press.

Blais, A., & Dion, S. (1991). *The budget-maximizing bureaucrat: Appraisals and evidence.* Pittsburgh: University of Pittsburgh Press.

Bourgault, J., & Nugent, P. (1995). Les transitions de gouvernement et la théorie des conflits: Le cas de la transition de 1984 au gouvernement du Canada. *Revue Canadienne Des Sciences De L'administration, 12,* 15–26.

Brehm, J., & Gates, S. (1997). *Working, shirking and sabotage: Bureaucratic responses to a democratic public.* Ann Arbor: University of Michigan Press.

Busse, V., & Hofmann, H. (2010). *Bundeskanzlersamt und Bundesregierung.* Munich: C.F. Müller.

Cheibub, J.A., Elkins, Z., & Ginsburg, T. (2014). Beyond presidentialism and parliamentarism. *British Journal of Political Science, 44,* 515–544.

Dahlström, C., Peters, D.G., & Pierre, J. (2011). *Steering from the centre: Strengthening political control in western democracies.* Toronto: University of Toronto Press.

Goodsell, C.T. (2011). *Mission mystique: Belief systems in public agencies.* Washington, DC: CQ Press.

Greene, K.F. (2010). The political economy of authoritarian single party dominance. *Comparative Political Studies, 43,* 807–824.

Hammond, T.H., & Butler, C.K. (2003). Some complex answers to the simple question 'do institutions matter?': Policy choice and policy change in presidential and parliamentary systems. *Journal of Theoretical Politics, 15,* 145–200.

Hansen, K.M., & Ejersbo, M. (2002). The relationship between politicians and administrators–a logic of disharmony. *Public Administration, 80,* 733–750.

Hansen, M.B., Steen, T., & De Jong, M. (2013). New public management, public service bargains and the challenge of interdepartmental coordination. *International Review of Administrative Sciences, 79,* 29–48.

Hanusch, H. (1980). *An anatomy of government deficiencies.* Berlin: Springer Verlag.

Heclo, H., & Wildavsky, A. (1974). *The private government of public money.* Berkeley: University of California Press.

Hood, C., & Lodge, M. (2006). *The politics of public service bargains: Reward, competency, loyalty–and blame.* Oxford: Oxford University Press.

Ingraham, P.W. (1995). *Foundation of merit: Public service in American democracy.* Baltimore, MD: Johns Hopkins University Press.

Lane, J.E. (2005). *Public administration and public management: The principal-agent perspective.* London: Routledge.

Light, P.C. (1995). *Thickening government: Federal hierarchy and the diffusion of accountability.* Washington, DC: The Brookings Institution.

Light, P.C. (2004). *Fact sheet on the continued thickening of government.* Washington, DC: The Brookings Institution.

Miller, J.G. (2005). The political evolution of principal-agent models. *Annual Review of Political Science, 8,* 203–225.

Neuhold, C., Vanhoonacker, S., & Verhey, L. (2013). *Civil servants and politicians: A delicate balance.* Basingstoke: Palgrave.

Niskanen, W. (1971). *Bureaucracy and representative democracy.* Chicago: Aldine and Atherton.

Panizza, F., Peters, B.G., Ramos, C., & Schleris, F. (2014). *Counselors, political operators and clients: Towards a typology of patronage.* Paper presented at annual NISPACEE Conference, Budapest, 22–24 April.

Perry, J.L. (2011). The growth of public service motivation research. *Korean Journal of Policy Studies, 26,* 1–12.

Peters, B.G. (1986). Burning the village: The civil service under Reagan and Thatcher. *Parliamentary Affairs, 39,* 79–97.

Peters, B.G. (1987). Politicians and bureaucrats in the politics of policymaking. In J.E. Lane (Ed.), *Bureaucracy and public choice* (pp. 256–282). London: Sage.

Peters, B.G. (2013). Politicisation: What is it and why should we care? In C. Neuhold, S. Vanhoonacker and L. Verhey (Eds.), *Civil servants and politicians: A delicate balance* (pp. 12–24). Basingstoke: Palgrave.

Peters, B.G. (2015). *Pursuing horizontal management: The politics of public sector coordination.* Lawrence: University Press of Kansas.

Peters, B.G., & Pierre, J. (2000). Citizens versus the new public manager: The problem of mutual empowerment. *Administration and Society, 32,* 8–28.

Peters, B.G., & Pierre, J. (2004). *Politicization of the civil service in comparative perspective: The quest for control.* London: Routledge.

Poguntke, T., & Webb, P. (Eds.). (2007). *The presidentialization of politics: A comparative study of modern democracies.* Oxford: Oxford University Press.

Rose, R. (1987). Steering the ship of state: One tiller but two pairs of hands. *British Journal of Political Science, 17,* 409–433.

Savoie, D.J. (1994). *Reagan, Thatcher, Mulroney: In search of a new bureaucracy.* Pittsburgh: University of Pittsburgh Press.

Savoie, D.J. (2011). Steering from the centre: the Canadian way. In C. Dahlström, B.G. Peters & J. Pierre. (Eds.), *Steering from the centre: strengthening political control in western democracies.* Toronto: University of Toronto Press.

Schröter, E. (2004). The politicisation of the German civil service: A three-dimensional portrait of the federal ministerial bureaucracy. In B.G. Peters and J. Pierre (Eds.), *Politicisation of the civil service in comparative perspective: The quest for control* (pp. 55–80). London: Routledge.

Selden, S.C., Brewer, G.A., & Brudney, J.L. (1999). Reconciling competing values in public administration: Understanding the administrative role concept. *Administration and Society, 31,* 171–204.

Svara, J.H. (2001). The myth of the dichotomy: Complementarity of politics and administration in the past and future of public administration. *Public Administration Review, 61,* 176–183.

Thomas, P.C. (2013). Communications and prime ministerial power. In J. Bickerton and B.G. Peters (Eds.), *Governing: Essays in honour of Donald J. Savoie* (pp. 53–84). Montreal: McGill and Queens University Press.

Zito, A. (2001). Epistemic communities, collective entrepreneurship and European integration. *Journal of European Public Policy, 8,* 585–603.

11 The Shift toward Network Governance

Drivers, Characteristics and Manifestations

Erik-Hans Klijn and Joop Koppenjan

Introduction

Many authors have proclaimed a shift from government to governance (Kickert, Klijn & Koppenjan, 1997; Rhodes, 1997; Pierre, 2000). Worldwide, government, business and civil society in our contemporary network society increasingly face complex societal problems. As a reaction to this challenge, governments throughout the world are turning to new forms of governance that have a more horizontal character and attempting to include other actors that have important resources necessary for solving social problems. The shift from government to governance is a reform not necessarily always deliberately intended and one that, according to the voluminous literature on governance, networks and collaborative policymaking, takes place gradually (see Kickert et al., 1997; Rhodes, 1997; Pierre, 2000; Sørensen & Torfing, 2007).

The Emergence of Network Governance: The Increasing Wickedness of Policy Problems

As observed in one of our earlier publications with Walter Kickert et al. (1997), attempts to address these complex social problems may result in enduring processes of policy making, policy implementation, and public service delivery that are difficult to manage. Many examples can be given of complex network governance processes:

- Complex decision-making processes in relation to realizing, operating and maintaining public infrastructural works (such as railways, roads, airports, water projects, waste incinerators, power plants and wind turbine parks) in which governments are confronted with a wide variety of stakeholders (such as private firms, citizens' groups, other public actors and environmental interest groups).
- Organizing integrated healthcare and social services for older people, which requires close cooperation among various health, welfare, social

and housing organizations that may be public, private or non-profit, financed by, for instance, government or insurance companies.

- Restructuration processes of inner cities in which municipalities need to collaborate with non-profit organizations (such as housing associations), private actors (developers) and citizens' groups.
- Attempts at developing policies and achieving outcomes in fighting crime and improving social security that require coordinated efforts by various governmental organizations such as the police, justice departments, emergency services and information bureaus, the involvement of private sector organizations and citizens and collaboration between various layers of government and among nation states.
- Processes of policy implementation or law enforcement, for instance in the food industry, where governments attempt to regulate complex food production chains, in which various parties under conditions of competition may trade off food safety against other values.
- Processes intended to prevent and manage large-scale accidents, crises, natural disasters or social disturbances and their aftermaths, such as the Hurricane Katrina disaster in New Orleans, the BP oil spill in the Gulf of Mexico, large-scale power blackouts or outbreaks of epidemics such as Ebola, that require coordination to create resilient networks.

These examples have in common the involvement of difficult issues that require in-depth knowledge of their nature and possible solutions; they also, however, involve many actors, and this may result in a chaotic process with unexpected and unwanted outcomes, or the process may become stuck in enduring and intense debates and conflicts that are not easily resolved. In other words, these problems are characterized by a high degree of wickedness (Rittel & Webber, 1973; Radford, 1977; Mason & Mitroff, 1981). The wicked nature of these problems is not only or even primarily caused by the lack of information or knowledge or the technologically advanced nature of the issue but by the presence of various actors with diverging or even conflicting interests and perceptions on the problem and its solutions.

Moreover, the solutions to these problems are also mostly dependent on a large set of actors because they possess the resources necessary for the solutions or veto possibilities to obstruct solutions. Thus, these so-called 'wicked problems' are addressed in networks of interdependent actors. Addressing problems requires interacting with governance networks and network governance (Klijn & Koppenjan, 2016)

Governance Networks and Network Governance

Network governance is then, in our opinion, the process that takes place within governance networks. Although governance networks are conceptualized in a variety of ways, most definitions have certain common characteristics (see Klijn & Koppenjan, 2016),

- Networks are characterized by complex policy problems that cannot be solved by one actor alone. Actors within networks are highly dependent upon one another because different actors own the resources necessary to solve problems. Therefore, problem solving requires the collective actions of several actors (Hanf & Scharpf, 1978; Mandell, 2001; Agranoff & McGuire, 2003; Koppenjan & Klijn, 2004).
- Networks are composed of actors that are autonomous and have their own specific perceptions of problems, solutions and strategies (Hanf & Scharpf, 1978; Agranoff & McGuire, 2003; McGuire & Agranoff, 2011). Within network processes, this leads to substantial differences in perceptions, value conflicts and disagreement over the policies to be implemented and services to be delivered.
- Interdependencies among actors combined with their diverging and sometimes conflicting perceptions and strategies cause a high degree of strategic complexity and an unpredictable course of interactions within networks, as the actions of one actor affect the interests and strategies of other actors. (Hanf & Scharpf, 1978; Gage & Mandell, 1990; Sørensen & Torfing, 2007)
- Network interactions exhibit some durability over time (Laumann & Knoke, 1987; Agranoff & McGuire, 2003).

Thus, the term governance network is used to describe public policy making, implementation and service delivery through a web of relationships among autonomous yet interdependent government, business and civil society actors. We define governance networks *as more or less stable patterns of social relations among mutually dependent actors, which cluster around a policy problem, a policy program and/or a set of resources and which emerge, are sustained and are changed through a series of interactions* (compare Koppenjan & Klijn, 2004). Network governance then comprises all governance strategies and interactions that take place within these governance networks: the set of conscious steering attempts or strategies of actors within governance networks intended to influence interaction processes and/or the characteristics of these networks. What makes network governance so complicated is that these strategies of all these actors are changing and can interact in unexpected ways, generating unforeseen results.

In this chapter, we highlight this trend toward network governance by focusing on its drivers (section 2) and by elaborating on its main characteristics (section 3) and its manifestations and differences among countries (section 4). We end with some reflections.

Drivers behind the Shift to Network Governance

What are the main drivers behind this shift toward network governance? The literature on governance mostly mentions two broad global trends that are important for the relationship between state and society and the emergence of governance networks. These are 1) the trend toward individualization, resulting in diminishing social bonds and trust in society (e.g., Inglehart, 1977; Putnam, 1995, 2000), and 2) the trend toward the network society (Castells, 1996, 1997). Both trends, authors claim, in certain ways reinforce one another (Castells, 1996). The trends are necessarily sketched here in 'broad strokes', omitting the various nuances and in-depth analyses of the two.

Individualization

Various authors have identified individualization as the major trend of the twentieth century (Bauman, 2000; Sociaal Cultureel Planbureau, 2000). Individualization is the societal process by which individual citizens become less closely tied to societal and religious groups and more inclined to hold individualized norms and values. The result is a more plural society in which citizens are inclined to articulate their interests and do this more themselves than rely on classical 'representatives' such as political parties and leaders of societal organizations. Various authors also argue that there is a strongly related trend whereby social capital is diminishing and citizens are less tied to other citizens (compare Putnam's famous book, *Bowling Alone* (2000)).

However, many authors argue, this has direct consequences for modern decision-making and public service delivery processes. One: citizens have more diverse values and tend to promote their interests more strongly. Two: citizens tend to have a more critical view of public authorities (and public service delivery) and less faith in classical political institutions. These consequences are discussed in the governance literature and generally lead authors to conclude the following (Rhodes, 1997; Pierre, 2000; Sørensen & Torfing, 2007):

1. Decision-making and service delivery have become more complex because there are more value differences that have to be bridged. It is possible that we will witness a more varied range of policy problem definitions that will enhance the 'wicked' character (Rittel & Webber, 1973) of decision-making in governance (Koppenjan & Klijn, 2004).
2. Decision-making processes become more complex because we will encounter more different interest groups present in decision-making processes and service delivery has to be tuned more specifically to the variation across citizens. The demands for tailor-made and integrated solutions will increase. This will increase pressure on public managers and politicians to cope with this complexity (Sørensen & Torfing, 2007).

The Rise of the Network Society

The other major trend is the rise of the network society (Castells, 1996). Drivers of the rise of the network society are the rapid development of technology, especially in the fields of transportation and ICT, leading to the strengthening of global flows of products and production means, including information and humans over the world, resulting in processes such as deterritorialization (spaces of flows and their nodes replacing the old space of places), the penetration of the 24/7 economy, mass individualization and social fragmentation. As a result, a dichotomy between 'the net and the self' has developed: the process of globalization results in the disintegration of local, regional and national communities and their identities. Moreover, in reaction to globalization, people and local communities self-organize around old and new identities using mechanisms and technologies of the network society and by building new global alliances (compare Habermas, 1984; Giddens, 2002). An interesting development in this respect is the emergence of all types of cooperations among citizens, for instance, energy cooperations that jointly buy and exploit solar cells. If this phenomenon is increasing, and this appears to be the case, it will have substantial consequences for energy provision and the role of both public and private actors in these processes.

The implications for government are radical. Hierarchical and territorial forms of politics and governmental steering become obsolete or at least less suited to solve problems. Authoritative decisions are no longer made by elected politicians and government but in fluid networks of civil servants, business representatives, professionals, knowledge producers and stakeholders, cutting across the horizontal and vertical boundaries of traditional jurisdictions (see also Koppenjan & Klijn, 2004; Ansell & Gash, 2008).

Government Responses: The Shift toward Network Governance

Thus, governance networks arise from societal changes and government responses to these changes. Because governments face demands from more diverse actors while simultaneously being more dependent on the resources of various actors to address societal problems, networks emerge and new forms of governing are needed. However, the shift to networks is also a reaction to the New Public Management reforms in the 1980s and 1990s. New Public Management, with its emphasis on market-like mechanisms, specialization and agentification (see Pollitt, 2003), has stimulated special-purpose vehicles and units that focus on specialized tasks but are a problem when more integrated services and policies are needed (Christensen & Lægreid, 2007). If we need more integration, the fragmentation caused by NPM policies will have to be countered by more network-like cooperation.

In response to the rise of governance networks and the fragmentation of NPM policies, governments in nearly all countries are searching for new governance forms that can be identified as forms of network governance. Examples of these are entering into partnerships with private and societal parties and the embracement of concepts such as the joined-up government and whole-of-government approaches (Pollitt, 2003; Christensen & Lægreid, 2007; Koppenjan, 2012). They also seek new ways to communicate with voters and citizens to address the impacts of individualization, e.g., by engaging in interactive policy making and experimenting with all types of new forms of participation (see, for instance, Lowndes, Pratchett & Stoker, 2001). The literature on network governance mentions three main arguments for why the shift to network governance would produce better policy results (or is simply unavoidable whether we want it or not).

The first is veto power. This is a classical argument from the political science literature on interest intermediation and emphasizes the necessary resources and veto power stakeholders have. Thus, it is necessary to involve stakeholders because doing so reduces opposition and mobilizes necessary resources (Williamson, 1989; Jordan, 1990; Kickert et al., 1997).

The second argument is improvement of content. This argument is very different from the previous argument. It rests on the observation that knowledge is spread among various actors and that top-down initiated processes create poor policy problem definitions and solutions (Fischer, 2003). Involving stakeholders that are in the network will enable the inclusion of more value perspectives on the problem, more information, knowledge and ideas and more creativity in designing solutions. Of course, this is an ideal that may be difficult to achieve in practice due to the complexity of the decision-making process and the value and interest differences between the actors (Klijn & Koppenjan, 2016).

A third argument concern democracy and differs from the first two. This argument stresses the fact that including more actors in the decision-making concerning wicked problems and service delivery processes enhances the democratic quality of these processes and accords with individualization and changes in society. Thus, network governance is regarded as a new way to include citizens and bridge the gap between politicians and citizens (see Berry, Portney & Thomson, 1993; Sørensen & Torfing, 2007; Torfing & Triantafillou, 2011; see also the ideas about deliberate democracy: Dryzek, 2002).

Characteristics of Network Governance

What are the main characteristics of this shift toward network governance? To phrase this question differently: if we observe a trend toward network governance and these processes take place in governance networks, the following questions arise:

- What are the relational characteristics of these networks? Here, we consider how the relationships between actors in the networks are presented in the literature and the empirical research on networks.

- What are the characteristics of the governance processes that take place in it? Here, we examine how complex governance processes in networks unfold.
- How are these complex networks and network governance processes governed? Here, we survey the extensive literature and research on network management.

We elaborate on each of these three questions below.

Governance Networks: Changing Social Relations between Governmental and Societal Organizations

Compared to classical government, governance networks are more characterized by horizontal relations. The main reason for this is the interdependencies between actors in networks. Interdependency occurs because governmental actors are dependent on the resources of other actors. These can be all kind of resources including the lack of legitimacy and support needed to realize policy outcomes (see Hanf & Scharpf, 1978; Klijn & Koppenjan, 2016). As result of these dependencies, patterns of interactions emerge that are sustained over a longer period of time (Agranoff & McGuire, 2003; Meier & O'Toole, 2007; Provan, Huang & Milward, 2009). This, of course, does not mean that all actors are equal in networks. There may exist significant power differences due to the importance of the resources actors can contribute and the unilateral or mutual character of the dependency relations (Hanf & Scharpf, 1978; Pfeffer, 1981).

In general, networks are characterized by the following characteristics, according to the available research and publications on the phenomenon (see, for instance, Milward & Provan, 2000; Meier & O'Toole, 2007; Rethemeyer & Hatmaker, 2008; Considine, Lewis & Alexander, 2009; Provan et al., 2009; Klijn, Edelenbos & Edelenbos, 2010).

Patterns of interdependencies. Dependency is the core of the entire argument concerning network governance. Because of the increased dependency of governmental organizations for the formulation and implementation of public policy and service delivery, they are now more interdependent with other organizations. Thus, interdependence seems to be the initial condition for the emergence of networks (Agranoff & McGuire, 2003, Koppenjan & Klijn, 2004). Although, in general, networks are thus characterized by (resource) interdependencies, there will be differences in the nature and tightness of these interdependencies across different types of networks. In some cases, the possibilities of obtaining resources from other actors are very limited and interdependencies have a strong and reciprocal character. Thus, one can consider the differences between a situation in which governments tender a service delivery to a lead organization that organizes the network (Provan & Kenis, 2008) or a situation in which governments are dependent on other actors to form and implement spatial or environmental policy (Klijn, Steijn & Edelenbos, 2010). There is interdependency in both cases, but in the second case this interdependency is more mutual than in the first case (Hanf & Scharpf, 1978), provided, of course, that government has other possible service providers and coordinators. However, in the first case, the interdependency is more task-bound and leads to closer ties and more dense interactions (Isett, Mergel, LeRoux, Mischen & Rethemeyer, 2011). Thus, interdependencies can vary from network to network, and this is assumed to affect processes and outcomes.

Patterns of interactions. Because of resource dependency, actors need to interact with one another to achieve resource exchange. Thus, governance networks can be characterized by the density of their interactions (see also Lewis, 2011). Again, the density of networks can vary substantially across networks. In general, service delivery networks will exhibit a higher density because they involve daily activities related to the service they provide. However, the density will likely also be influenced by the time that the network has existed. The longer networks exist, the more possibilities there have been to form interaction patterns and, usually, more dense interactions have emerged (see Provan et al., 2009).

Patterns of dynamics. Networks can be characterized by more or fewer dynamics. Dynamics can result from unexpected events and strong strategic turbulence in networks. Again, different networks can exhibit various dynamics. In general, one can assume that service delivery networks, which are more characterized by protocols and fixed routines and tight interdependencies, exhibit fewer dynamics than do networks in which policy making takes place and actors struggle over value conflicts. These networks are likely more susceptible to changes in the external environments (political tides, etc.) than are service delivery networks. A higher level of dynamics in networks creates more complexity, and, thus, it would generally be more difficult to manage. One would expect the presence of substantial dynamics to have a negative influence on network performance.

Patterns of conflict between actors. As many authors argue, networks are not 'cozy' places where harmony and cooperation flourish (Scharpf, 1997; Koppenjan & Klijn, 2004, O' Toole & Meier, 2004). Because actors have different interests in and perceptions of (policy) problems and desirable solutions, there is considerable conflict and struggle in governance networks. This is precisely what makes coordination so difficult. Networks can be characterized by intensive or less-intensive patterns of conflict. Generally, there seems to be a tendency in the literature to relate the size of the network to patterns of conflict. Thus, larger networks are believed to be more conflictual than smaller ones (see past typologies of networks in terms of larger, more conflictual issue networks or smaller, more 'cozy' policy communities or subsystems; see Rhodes, 1988, Jordan, 1990). However, the level of conflict can, of course, also be related to the type of policy and or service that is being 'processed' in the network. Service delivery networks generally appear to be less conflictual than, for instance, urban planning decision-making in which there are more intense value conflicts (see Klijn et al., 2010).

Patterns of trust. If decision-making and service delivery in networks is complex and the various actors are interdependent but also have different interests, then it is difficult to achieve collective decisions and realize outcomes. In both the literature on collaborative leadership (Ansell & Gash, 2008; O'Leary & Bingham, 2009) and the network literature (Provan et al., 2009; Klijn, Edelenbos & Steijn, 2010), trust is cited as a vital characteristic in the relationship between actors that facilitates decision-making and service delivery. According to this argument, trust reduces transaction costs, stimulates the exchange of information and innovation and solidifies cooperation between actors, all generally resulting in better performance (see Klijn et al., 2010). Especially in newly emergent networks, trust relations between actors have to develop because trust is not typically present by itself (see Huxham & Vangen, 2005).

Patterns of rules (institutionalization). When networks exist for a longer period, institutionalization processes can and generally will take place. New rules are formed (either formally created rules or informal rules) that guide actors' behavior in the network (Ostrom, 1986; Koppenjan & Klijn, 2004). Thus, networks can be characterized by different levels of institutionalization. Typically, networks that are in place for a longer period will have more stable and explicit rules than networks that have recently emerged.

Thus, governance networks are interaction systems that emerge from interdependency but are then characterized by various patterns of relationships, which will in turn influence the interaction and decision-making that takes place within a network. Networks differ significantly, ranging from the more vertical classical government mode of steering to the classical image of New Public Management, in which governments outsource policy implementation and service delivery and the emphasis is on monitoring and performance indicators. Relational patterns in governance networks between public organizations and (semi-) private and societal organizations are considerably more complex, as demonstrated by most of the research on network governance (see Agranoff & McGuire, 2003; Marcussen & Torfing, 2007; Meier & O'Toole, 2007; Provan et al., 2009; Klijn et al., 2010).

Interaction Processes within Governance Networks

Within governance networks, the 'daily' interactions aimed at problem solving, policy making and implementation and service delivery processes are taking place. If there is one characteristic that stands out in the literature and empirical research on governance networks, it is that decision-making processes surrounding policy formation, implementation and service delivery are highly complex. This complexity is generated by the following factors:

1. The separate strategies of autonomous actors who are dependent but do not share the same perceptions of the (policy) problem, possible solutions and ways to achieve these solutions. This will be enhanced by the interference of more external factors (political events, media attention, economic changes, etc.) that will stimulate actors to change or adapt their strategies.

2. The various places (arenas) where decisions that are relevant for achieving a solution are being made. Addressing wicked problems involves many actors, and many of the decisions that are being made by all of these actors take place in various arenas. Arenas can be situated both in and outside the existing network (Agranoff & McGuire, 2003) (see Klijn & Koppenjan, 2016).

As a result, governance processes within governance networks are complex and can be erratic. Satisfactory results are difficult to achieve. Unsurprisingly, both theory and research on network governance have emphasized that the management of networks is essential.

The Trend toward Network Governance and the Need for Network Management

Crucial for the shift toward network governance is the observation that the emerging governance networks in which these network governance processes occur require a substantially different form of governing from the classical public administration approach to governing social problems. Governance networks and the network governance processes that occur within them require network management to able to produce satisfactory outcomes (Gage & Mandell, 1990; Kickert et al., 1997; Agranoff & McGuire, 2003). Network management is defined as all of the deliberate strategies intended to facilitate and guide the interactions and/or change the features of the network with the intent of furthering collaboration within the network processes (Klijn & Koppenjan, 2016).

The literature mentions a wide variety of network management strategies to guide interaction processes, and, hence, an exhaustive list cannot be provided here (see O'Toole, 1988; Gage & Mandell, 1990; Agranoff & McGuire, 2003). Table 11.1 provides a summary (albeit a non-exhaustive one) of the types of strategies that have been identified in the literature and network governance research. We briefly discuss the various types of network management strategies (see table 11.1).

Connecting strategies such as the activation of actors or resources are required to begin the game. The network management literature stresses that the network manager has to identify the actors required for an initiative and create a situation in which they become interested in investing their resources (see Hanf & Scharpf, 1978). The interactions within the game itself also have to be managed. This can be achieved by appointing a process

Table 11.1 Overview of network management strategies

Types of strategies	Main strategies mentioned in the literature
Process agreements	Rules for entrance into or exit from the process, conflict regulating rules, rules that specify the interests of actors or veto possibilities, rules that inform actors about the availability of information about decision-making moments, etc.
Exploring content	Searching for goal congruency, creating variation in solutions, influencing (and explicating) perceptions, managing and collecting information and research, creating variation through creative competition
Arranging	Creating new ad hoc organizational arrangements (boards, project organizations, etc.).
Connecting	Selective (de)activation of actors, resource mobilizing, initiating new series of interactions, coalition building, mediation, appointment of process managers, removing obstacles to cooperation, creating incentives for co-operation.

(Adapted from Klijn et al., 2010)

manager, who invests time and energy in connecting the actions and strategies of actors to one another during interaction. Once the game has begun, strategies for exploring content are necessary to clarify the goals and perceptions of actors (Fischer, 2003) and to attempt to invest time and money in developing solutions that create opportunities for the actors' participation. However, the process is occasionally short of creative solutions to satisfy the various actors involved. In such cases, greater variation is required, for instance, by using different teams of experts who compete against one another to create solutions. Such managerial strategy arrangement means setting (temporary) structures for consultation, interaction and deliberation, such as project organization and lines of communication (Rogers & Whetten, 1982). The transaction costs of these arrangements must be kept as low as possible (Williamson, 1996), but simultaneously, the arrangements have to be acceptable to the actors involved. Another important type of strategy mentioned in the literature are strategies of process agreements that draft temporary sets of rules for interaction that structure the interactions and protect each actor's core values (Koppenjan & Klijn, 2004). The rules can be regarded as ground rules for behavior and interaction in the network to which that the actors in the network (explicitly) agree.

Gage and Mandell were the first to coin the concept of network management in 1990. Surveying the results of 25 years of research on network management, we observe that the first 15 years were spent primarily on more conceptual research and case study research (Kickert et al., 1997; Agranoff & McGuire, 2001; Mandell, 2001). Only over the past 10 years do we find systematic, large-scale survey research on the impact of network management and the strategies employed. These research findings appear to confirm the theoretical argument that network management is crucial in achieving good results in networks (see Agranoff & McGuire, 2003; Meier & O'Toole, 2007; Klijn et al., 2010; Klijn & Koppenjan, 2016).

These findings also demonstrate that the government's role in network governance is not only very different from, for instance, the role of government in New Public Management but also requires a very active role. Governments are actively attempting to facilitate processes in networks and, thus, are intensively involved in network interactions (see also Meier & O'Toole, 2007).

The Rise of Network Governance: A Uniform Global Trend?

Thus far, we have treated the shift toward governance as a generic phenomenon. The literature appears to emphasize general trends (such as individualizing and the emergence of the network society) and the more or less implicit assumption is that this fuels the emergence of similar governance responses worldwide (Pierre, 2000; Osborne, 2010; Koppenjan & Koliba, 2013). However, we already know from the research on, e.g., New Public Management that these types of concepts may refer to very different and sometimes contradictory developments. Moreover, the evolution of NPM in various countries has taken specific, different pathways (see Pollitt, Van Thiel & Homberg, 2007; Pollitt & Bouckaert, 2010). Thus, we may expect that network governance will also exhibit markedly different manifestations in specific circumstances. Governance in China will not be identical to governance in North European countries. In this section, we explore some of the key factors that may influence how governance is manifested in local circumstances.

Literature on National Differences

Acknowledging that it is very difficult to define precisely what local contexts are, following the literature, we will begin by addressing a significant contextual element driving the shape of governance arrangements, namely that of national context. The role of national context in determining particular responses to public management has been debated in terms of understanding the nation-specific effects of reform, the costs and benefits of change and the emergence and impact of new paradigms for designing new governance arrangements (see, for example, Pollitt & Bouckaert, 2004; Osborne & Brown, 2005).

The literature holds that national differences matter and, specifically, that, e.g., network governance modes are better suited to some countries than others. Various typologies of national differences are available. The volume of literature on national attributes and frameworks demonstrates the prevalence of research focusing on differences: the difference between Anglo-Saxon and Rijnland economies (Albert, 1991), Hofstede's cultural dimensions (Hofstede, 1983), historical traditions such as neo-corporatism in Western Europe (Schmitter & Lehmbruch, 1979) or 'polder politics' in the Netherlands (Hendriks & Toonen, 2001), diverging policy styles (Richardson, 1982) and specific political system characteristics such as a unitary state versus federalism (Hanf & Scharpf, 1978). In this literature, various contextual features are cited as being supportive or hindering to network governance. Table 11.2 provides an overview of the most important characteristics mentioned in this literature.

The literature suggests that these national, contextual factors hindered or enhanced and, thereby, shaped those network governance practices.

National Cultures as 'Local Context' for Governance: An Example

One way to examine the differences across cultures is to employ Hofstede's measurement of culture (Hofstede, 1983). Hofstede developed items to measure cultural differences between countries (see www.geert-hofstede.com for further information on cultural items). In Hofstede's dimensions, five different measurements are used: power distance (PDI), individualism

Table 11.2 Context characteristics supporting or hindering network governance

Unfavorable conditions	Favorable conditions
Policy tradition of planning and control (France)	Policy tradition of negotiation and bargaining (The Netherlands)
Two party system; winner takes all (US, UK)	Multiparty system resulting in coalition governments (Scandinavian countries)
Unitary state (UK)	Federalism; decentralization (US; Germany)
Weak civil society (China)	Strong civil society (US; Europe)
Highly politicized culture; sharp conflicts of interest (UK; US)	Consensus culture (Continental Europe)
Institutional and legal environment that enhances short term relationships, a focus on efficiency and contractual relationships (US; UK)	Institutional and legal environment that enhances long-term relationships, a focus on quality and trust (Continental Europe)
Competitive, individualistic culture in which citizens solve their own problems, do not rely on government and go to court to get their rights (Australia; US)	Egalitarian culture in which citizens are relatively passive and loyal and dependent on government or representation by interest groups (Continental Europe)
Weak implementation culture, in which parties do not have much binding power towards their constituencies (South European countries)	Strong implementation culture, in which parties have binding power towards their constituencies (North European Countries)

(Source: Koppenjan, Mandell & Keast, 2010)

(IDV), masculinity (MAS), uncertainty avoidance (UAI) and long-term orientation (LTO). Below, the dimensions are explained (for references, see: www.geert-hofstede.com).

- Power distance is 'the degree to which the less powerful members of a society accept and expect that power is distributed unequally.' This dimension concerns how a society addresses inequality. A low degree of power distance means that a society strives for equality, whereas a society with high power distance accepts hierarchy. Individualism refers to 'a preference for a loosely-knit social framework in which individuals are expected to take care of themselves and their immediate families only. Its opposite, Collectivism, represents a preference for a tightly-knit framework in society in which individuals can expect their relatives or members of a particular in-group to look after them in exchange for unquestioning loyalty' (www.geert-hofstede.com). According to Hofstede, masculinity represents 'a preference in society for achievement, heroism, assertiveness and material reward for success. Society at large is more competitive. Its opposite, femininity, stands for a preference for cooperation, modesty, caring for the weak and quality of life. Society at large is more consensus-oriented.'
- The uncertainty avoidance dimension in the Hofstede scale expresses the degree to which the members of a society feel uncomfortable with uncertainty and ambiguity. Countries exhibiting strong UAI maintain rigid codes of belief and behavior and are intolerant of unorthodox behavior and ideas. Weak UAI societies maintain a more relaxed attitude in which practice matters more than principles.
- The long-term orientation dimension is related to society's search for virtue. Societies with a short-term orientation generally have a strong concern with establishing the absolute truth. They are normative in their thinking. They exhibit great respect for traditions, a relatively limited propensity to save for the future and a focus on achieving rapid results. In societies with a long-term orientation, people believe that truth depends very much on situation, context and time. They exhibit an ability to adapt traditions to changed conditions, a strong propensity to save and invest, thriftiness and perseverance in achieving results.

There is, for instance, a broad consensus that there are differences between Northern European and Southern European countries and Asian countries. If we consider as examples three countries representative of this distinction, Taiwan, Spain and The Netherlands, we see the following scores (figure 11.1).

To summarize the figure very briefly, one could place Taiwan and The Netherlands on the extreme ends in regard to individualism and masculinity and Spain in between (The Netherlands is very individualistic and not masculine, Taiwan is highly collectivistic and masculine, although on the

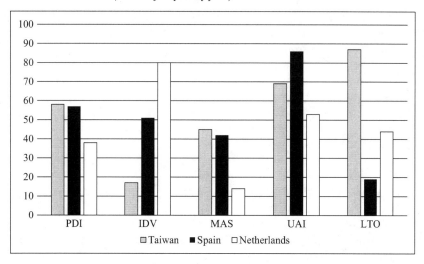

Figure 11.1   Hofstede's national cultural dimensions for Taiwan, Spain and The Netherlands

last characteristic only slightly higher than Spain). The Netherlands also has a clearly lower power distance. Regarding long-term orientation, as expected, Taiwan has by far the highest score and Spain has a very low score.

One can expect that governance networks differ in the various countries and that decision-making processes within those networks are affected by cultural differences between countries. Thus, countries with a higher score on individualism would be expected to have slightly higher levels of conflict and/or differences in perceptions. This will likely result in different processes at the micro level. However, power differences will also be for the process in networks. Countries with lower power differences will exhibit more horizontal processes. However, for instance, we might also expect the use of more network management strategies because people are more accustomed to horizontal interaction. Thus, we might expect a greater use of network management strategies in a country such as The Netherlands, with its very low power distance.

Klijn et al. (2015) conduct survey research on networks and network performance in Taiwan, Spain and The Netherlands and note both similarities and dissimilarities. They consider the number of employed network management strategies and two network characteristics: differences in perceptions in the network and the level of unexpected events as experienced by respondents. They conclude as follows:

'We did see some expected and not expected differences between the countries. The relative high figure for conflict for Taiwan was not expected, the relative large number of employed network management strategies in The Netherlands was [. . .] But the fact that we also find pretty high level of employed network management strategies in other countries points at the fact that network management seems to have become the 'standard equipment' of today's manager whether he/she comes from a North European, a South European or an Asian country and that is an interesting conclusion. And the fact that we find the least explained variance for Taiwan, matches the fact that we also find the least employed network management strategies there, since these explain most variance in network performance.'

(Klijn et al., 2015)

They also provide an explanation for the fact that they do not observe the expected lower levels of conflict in Taiwan:

'Hofstede's depiction of Taiwan's culture being less prone to conflict applies only to within-group unexpected events; between-group unexpected events can be quite harsh and competitive in East Asia when not kept in check by a common hierarchical leader; when such is lacking, conflicts are commonly seen to require interventions from top elected officials such as mayors. Moreover, interview comments suggest that managers commonly engage in horizontal collaboration, anticipating that hierarchy can and will be invoked as the preferred way of dealing with future conflicts, rather than direct negotiation. In this regard, the East Asian concept of 'harmony' does not mean agreement, but rather a lack of manifest conflict among parties where disagreement exists.'

(Klijn & Koppenjan, 2016)

This also means that is not always easy to draw clear, simple conclusions from national cultural scores for governance practices and that local identities matter.

Toward a Global Trend?

Although the survey only covers three countries, it appears to indicate both global characteristics of governance processes and local/national characteristics, local/national characteristics in the sense that we clearly observe cultural differences that appear to affect governance network processes. Examples include the use of a larger number of network management strategies in The Netherlands, which accords with its consensual culture and the characteristics of the Hofstede scores (more individualistic, less power distance). However, we also observe general trends that appear to indicate a unified global trend. An example is that network management and trust are important in all three countries. However, we certainly need more international comparative research on network governance to reach final conclusions on the relationship between (national) cultures and network governance.

Conclusions

In this chapter, we discussed the trend toward network governance. Network governance is related to changes in societies that are emerging worldwide. These societal changes are part of wider global developments, such as the growing complexity of social problems and the emerging self-organization of groups of citizens. Network governance (and governance networks) emerges from these developments and the government's reactions to them.

This leaves us with the question of what we might expect from the further development of this trend toward network governance. First, note that this reform is not uncontested. Often, governments will regard governance networks not so much as a solution but as the problem. Repeated attempts will be made to repulse the influence of governance networks by reinforcing hierarchical approaches to problem solving or organizing policy making and service delivery according to the principles of New Public Management (Klijn & Koppenjan, 2012).

Given the societal trends that underlie the shift toward governance, we regard these relapses as refought battles that nevertheless may have severe consequences: leading to deadlocks, low trust relationships and poor solutions that will only be achieved by overcoming considerable societal resistance and that will not do justice to the variety of perceptions and interests within current complex societies or to its potential. However, we do not believe that network governance is a panacea. Various governmental task and societal problems are not so complex that they require network governance. We believe that network government will not replace government or New Public Management but will co-evolve with these other ways of steering (see Frederickson, 2005; Koppenjan, 2012).

Finally, governance networks and network management are not without problems. Accounts exist of governance networks as forms of closed interaction, intended to realize policies and services that are favorable to the represented parties, producing high interaction costs, excluding non- or weakly represented parties, blocking innovations and lacking democratic control and legitimacy (Jordan, 1990; Koppenjan & Klijn, 2004; O'Toole & Meier, 2004). One of the inspiring ideas that underpinned the book *Managing Complex Networks* that the authors of this contribution co-edited with Walter Kickert in 1997, and that proved to be the breakthrough of our thinking on networks to an international audience, was that networks were here to stay, and that we had better learn to govern them properly. We still consider this idea relevant. Often, the reality of network governance will not meet expectations. This is a reason to engage in further research to increase our understanding of who network governance is practiced and how governance networks function.

References

Agranoff, R., & McGuire, M. (2001). Big questions in public network management research. *Journal of Public Administration Research and Theory, 11*(3), 295–326.

Agranoff, R., & McGuire, M. (2003). *Collaborative public management: New strategies for local governments.* Washington: Georgetown University Press.

Albert, M. (1991). *Capitalisme contre capitalisme.* Paris: Edition du Sseuil.

Ansell, C., & Gash, A. (2008). Collaborative governance in theory and practice. *Journal of Public Administration Research and Theory, 18*(4), 543–571.

Bauman, Z. (2000). *The individualized society.* Cambridge: Polity Press.

Berry, J.M., Portney, K.E., & Thomson, K. (1993). *The rebirth of urban democracy.* Washington, DC: Brookings Institution.

Castells, M. (1996). *The rise of the network society: Economy, society and culture.* Cambridge: Blackwell Publishers.

Castells, M. (1997). *The power of identity.* Cambridge: Blackwell Publishers.

Christensen, T., & Lægreid, P. (2007). The whole-of-government approach to public sector reform. *Public Administration Review, 67*(6), 1059–1066.

Considine, M., Lewis, J., & Alexander, D. (2009). *Networks, innovation and public policy.* Basingstoke: Palgrave-Macmillan.

Dryzek, J.S. (2002). *Deliberative democracy and beyond: Liberals, critics, contestations.* Oxford: Oxford University Press.

Fischer, F. (2003). *Reframing public policy: Discursive politics and deliberative practices.* Oxford: Oxford University Press.

Frederickson, H.G. (2005). What happened to public administration? Governance, governance everywhere. In E. Ferlie, L. Lynn and C. Pollittt (Eds.), *The Oxford handbook of public management* (pp. 282–304). Oxford: Oxford University Press.

Gage, R.W., & Mandell, M.P. (Eds.). (1990). *Strategies for managing intergovernmental policies and networks.* New York: Praeger.

Giddens, A. (2002). *Runaway world: How globalisation is reshaping our lives.* London: Profile Books.

Habermas, J. (1984). *The theory of communicative action.* Cambridge: Polity.

Hanf, K., & Scharpf, F.W. (1978). *Inter-organizational policy making: Limits to coordination and central control.* London: Sage.

Hendriks, F., & Toonen, T. (2001). *Polder politics in the Netherlands: Viscous state or model polity.* Aldershot: Ashgate.

Hofstede, F. (1983). National cultures in four dimensions: A research-based theory of cultural differences among nations. *International Studies of Management & Organization, 13*(1–2), 46–74.

Huxham, C., & Vangen, S. (2005). *Managing to collaborate: The theory and practice of collaborative advantage.* London: Routledge.

Inglehart, R. (1977). *The silent revolution: Changing values and political styles among Western publics.* Princeton: Princeton University Press.

Isett, K., Mergel, I., LeRoux, K., Mischen, P., & Rethemeyer, K. (2011). Networks in public administration scholarship: Understanding where we are and where we need to go. *Journal of Public Administration Research and Theory, 21*, i157–i173.

Jordan, G. (1990). Sub-governments, policy communities and networks: Refilling the old bottles? *Journal of Theoretical Politics, 2*(3), 319–338.

Kickert, W.J.M., Klijn, E.H., & Koppenjan, J.F.M. (Eds.). (1997). *Managing complex networks.* London: Sage.

Klijn, E.H., Edelenbos, J., & Steijn, B. (2010). Trust in governance networks: Its impacts on outcomes. *Administration & Society, 42*(2), 193–221.

Klijn, E.H., & Koppenjan, J.F.M. (2012). Governance network theory: Past, present and future. *Policy and Politics, 40*(4), 187–206.

Klijn, E.H., & Koppenjan, J.F.M. (2016). *Governance networks in the public sector.* Milton: Routledge.

Klijn, E.H., Steijn, B., & Edelenbos, J. (2010). The impact of network management strategies on the outcomes in governance networks. *Public Administration, 88*(4), 1063–1082.

Klijn, E.H., Ysa, T., Sierra, V., Berman, E., Edelenbos, J., & Chen, D. (2015). The influence of network management and complexity on network performance in Taiwan, Spain and the Netherlands. *Public Management Review, 17*(5), 736–764.

Koppenjan, J.F.M. (2012). *The new public governance in public service delivery.* The Hague: Eleven and Boom-Lemma.

Koppenjan, J.F.M., & Klijn, E.H. (2004). *Managing uncertainties in networks: A network approach to problem solving and decision making.* London: Routledge.

Koppenjan, J.F.M., & Koliba, C. (2013). Symposium: Transformation towards new public governance. *International Review of Public Administration, 18*(2), 1–84.

Koppenjan, J.F.M., Mandell, M., Keast, R., & Brown, K. (2010). Contexts, hybrids and network governance: A comparison of three case-studies in infrastructure governance. In T. Bransen and M. Holzer (Eds.), *The future of governance* (pp. 301–325), Newark, NJ: NCPP.

Laumann, E.O., & Knoke, D. (1987). *The organizational state: Social choice in national policy domains.* Madison: University of Wisconsin Press.

Lewis, J. (2011). The future of network governance: Strength in diversity and synthesis. *Public Administration, 89*(4), 1221–1234.

Lowndes, V., Pratchett, L., & Stoker, G. (2001). Trends in public participation: Part 1—local government perspectives. *Public Administration, 79*(1), 205–222.

Mandell, M.P. (2001). *Getting results through collaboration: Networks and network structures for public policy and management.* Westport: Quarom Books.

Marcussen, M., & Torfing, J. (Eds.). (2007). *Democratic network governance in Europe.* Cheltenham: Edward Elgar.

Mason, R.O., & Mitroff, I.I. (1981). *Challenging strategic planning assumptions: Theory, cases and techniques.* New York: Wiley.

McGuire, M., & Agranoff, R. (2011). The limitations of public management networks. *Public Administration, 89*(2), 265–284.

Meier, K., & O'Toole, L.J. (2007). Modelling public management: Empirical analysis of the management-performance nexus. *Public Administration Review, 9*(4), 503–527.

Milward, H.B., & Provan, K.G. (2000). Governing the hollow state. *Journal of Public Administration Research and Theory, 10*(2), 359–379.

O'Leary, R., & Bingham, L. (2009). *The collaborative public manager.* Washington, DC: Georgetown University Press.

Osborne, S.P. (2010). *The new public governance: Emerging perspectives on the theory and practice of public governance.* London: Routledge.

Osborne, S.P., & Brown, K. (2005). *Managing change and innovation in public service organizations.* New York: Routledge.

Ostrom, E. (1986). A method for institutional analysis. In F.X. Kaufmann, G. Majone and V. Ostrom (Eds.), *Guidance, control and evaluation in the public sector: The Bielefeld interdisciplinary project* (pp. 459–479). Berlin: Walter de Gruyter.

O'Toole, L.J. (1988). Strategies for intergovernmental management: Implementing programs in interorganizational networks. *Journal of Public Administration, 11*(4), 417–441.

O'Toole, L.J., & Meier, K.J. (2004). Desperately seeking Selznick: Cooptation and the dark side of public management in networks. *Public Administration Review, 64*(6), 681–693.

Pfeffer, J. (1981). *Power in organizations.* Boston: Pitman.

Pierre, J. (Ed.). (2000). *Debating governance: Authority, steering, and democracy.* Oxford: Oxford University Press.

Pollitt, C. (2003). Joined-up government: A survey. *Political Studies Review, 1*(1), 34–49.

Pollitt, C., & Bouckaert, G. (2004). *Public management reform: A comparative analysis.* Oxford: Oxford University Press.

Pollitt, C., Van Thiel, S., & Homberg, V. (Eds.). (2007). *New public management in Europe.* Basinkstoke: Palgrave.

Provan, K.G., Huang, K., & Milward, B.H. (2009). The evolution of structural embeddedness and organizational social outcomes in a centrally governed health and human service network. *Journal of Public Administration Research and Theory, 19*(4), 873–893.

Provan, K.G., & Kenis, P. (2008). Modes of network governance: Structure, management, and effectiveness. *Journal of Public Administration Research and Theory, 18*(2), 229–257.

Putnam, R.D. (1995). Tuning in, tuning out: The strange disappearance of social capital in America. *Political Science and Politics, 28*(4), 664–683.

Putnam, R.D. (2000). *Bowling alone.* New York: Simon and Schuster.

Radford, K.J. (1977). *Complex decision problems: An integrated strategy for resolution.* Virginia: Reston Publishers.

Rethemeyer, K., & Hatmaker, D. (2008). Network management reconsidered: An inquiry into management of network structures in public sector service provision. *Journal of Public Administration and Theory, 18*(4), 617–646.

Rhodes, R.A.W. (1988). *Beyond Westminster and Whitehall: The sub-central governments of Britain.* London: Unwin Hyman.

Rhodes, R.A.W. (1997). *Understanding governance.* Buckingham: Open University Press.

Richardson, J.J. (Ed.). (1982). *Policy styles in Western Europe.* London: Allen & Unwin.

Rittel, H., & Webber, M. (1973). Dilemma's in a general theory of planning. *Policy Sciences 4*(2), 155–169.

Rogers, D.L., & Whetten, D.A. (Eds.). (1982). *Interorganizational coordination: Theory, re-search, and implementation.* Ames: Iowa State University Press.

Scharpf, F.W. (1997). *Games real actors play: Actor-centred institutionalism in policy research.* Boulder: Westview Press.

Schmitter, P.C., & Lehmbruch, G. (Eds.). (1979). *Trends toward corporatist intermediation.* Sage: London.

Sociaal Cultureel Planbureau. (2000). *Sociaal Cultureel Rapport: Nederland in Europa.* 's-Gravenhage: Sociaal Cultureel Planbureau.

Sørensen, E., & Torfing, J. (Eds.). (2007). *Theories of democratic network governance.* London: Palgrave Macmillan.

Torfing, J., & Triantafillou, P. (Eds.). (2011). *Interactive policy making, metagovernance and democracy.* Colchester: ECPR Press.

Williamson, O.E. (1996). *The mechanisms of governance.* Oxford: Oxford University Press.

Williamson, P.J. (1989). *Corporatism in perspective.* Sage: London.

12 Management of Human Resources

Trends and Variation

Sandra Groeneveld and Bram Steijn

Introduction

A cornerstone of Human Resource Management (HRM) is the belief that putting people first is vital for organizational success (Pfeffer, 1995). Indeed, many studies have shown that HRM is an important determinant of organizational performance (Paauwe, Guest & Wright, 2013), a finding that has been corroborated by several studies within the public sector (Knies, Boselie, Gould-Williams & Vandenabeele, 2015; Vermeeren, 2014). Managing human resources is likely an even more important task in the public sector than in the private sector because many public organizations are 'people organizations': their performance is not so much dependent on technology but primarily on people implementing policies or delivering services. This also implies that human resources represent an obvious object of reform, not only because reducing the number of public employees impacts the overall cost of government, but also because managing people better will improve organizational performance.

Thus, it is no wonder that by the 1990s, the OECD already considered 'Human Resource Management' as a trend common to all countries adopting New Public Management-style reforms intended to improve the effectiveness and efficiency of public sector organizations (Kickert & Jørgensen, 1995a,b). Traditional bureaucratic models of personnel management were gradually abandoned and replaced by HRM. HRM differs from the more traditional models of personnel management by perceiving employees as resources that should be developed in accordance with the organization's goals. HRM models and instruments, mostly developed in the mid-1980s in a private sector context, were introduced into public sector organizations (Boyne, Jenkins & Poole, 1999). The introduction of HRM was soon followed by adding the adjective 'strategic', at least in rhetoric, to further emphasize the importance of the contribution of HRM to organizational performance.

In our view, the introduction and further development of HRM can be considered the main transformation that occurred in recent decades with regard to public personnel policies. As with many reforms, it can be observed in public organizations across sectors and countries, albeit to varying degrees and in diverse appearances. HRM, as part of broader NPM reforms, has been interpreted and implemented differently depending on national and sector-specific institutional arrangements, historical traditions and national styles of public management (Pollitt & Bouckaert, 2011: 90; compare also Christensen & Lægreid, this volume; Olsen, this volume). The observation that there has been some convergence between countries, but only to a limited degree (see also Bach & Bordogna, 2011), fits with a historical institutionalist perspective on reform that emphasizes the path dependency of reform adoption and implementation processes.

This chapter offers a brief overview of several key trends and highlights some important sources of variation with regard to HR-related objects of reform across countries. We will, on the one hand, illustrate the extensiveness of reforms regarding public personnel policies but, on the other hand, show the path dependency. Previous studies have shown that although countries remain different, there are similarities in the directions of the main changes. Although sources differ on the exact nature of these changes (compare Brown, 2004; OECD, 2005; Bach & Bordogna, 2011; Pollitt & Bouckaert, 2011), concepts such as downsizing, decentralization (toward organizations at a lower level), devolution (of HRM tasks toward line managers), flexibilization (of rules and of the employment conditions of public sector employees), individualization and normalization (public and private employees growing alike with respect to employment rights and conditions) are often used to describe the main 'overall' trends. Based on these trends previously described by other authors, in this chapter, the following four key trends are discussed: 1) changes in career systems; 2) the end of government as a model employer; 3) individualization and commoditization; and 4) downsizing. This is preceded by a discussion of the main transformation toward HRM in public organizations.

We needed to limit this chapter both in size and scope. For that reason, we do not discuss other HRM-related trends that can also be observed, especially those related to the employment relationship, such as the position of the trade unions (Bach & Bordogna, 2011) or changes with respect to the remuneration of public sector workers (Giordano et al., 2011). This implies that this chapter discusses neither labor relations nor work practices but instead centers on *employment practices applied in organizations*. In addition, we focus our discussion of key trends on the *national civil service* organizations and workforces in *European countries*.

Main Transformation: HRM Replaces Personnel Administration

The introduction of HRM as such can be seen as a major public sector reform in itself, as it gradually replaced the traditional model of personnel administration (Brown, 2004). According to Brown (2004), HRM implies the application of NPM principles within personnel management, which 'allows a more flexible and responsive approach to questions of recruitment, selection, retention, training and development of public sector employees' (2004: 305). A more effective use of human resources is an important objective of HRM and its public sector application thus fits well within the NPM objective to incorporate private sector management practices in the public sector.

The contemporary HRM literature goes a step further and stresses the importance of *strategic* HRM (SHRM), defined by Wright and McMahan (1992: 298) as 'the pattern of planned human resource deployments and activities intended to enable the firm to achieve its goals.' A major assumption of SHRM is that 'one size does not fit all.' Organizations have to face the particular challenges that emanate from their environment and choose a strategy to cope with these (Boxall & Purcell, 2011). The OECD (2011) acknowledges the importance of SHRM as is illustrated by their development of a composite indicator of Strategic Human Resources to benchmark OECD countries regarding their application of SHRM. Their data show that countries differ in their use of SHRM practices: Australia, Canada and the United Kingdom are leaders in its application, whereas Greece and Hungary are lagging behind.

Whether public organizations fully apply *strategic* HRM or only loosely coupled HRM practices (see Teo, 2000; Teo & Rodwell, 2007) is not that relevant for the purpose of this chapter. The key issue here is that both types of HRM challenge the traditional Weberian model of personnel administration, which is built on standardization as a core principle and is governed by a bureaucratic set of rules and procedures (Brown, 2004). In the Weberian system, decisions and actions with respect to personnel have to be consistent, systematic and formalized across various governmental organizations regardless of their specific environments and goals. To achieve this, central agencies are made responsible for all decisions related to personnel (hiring, firing, assessment, career decisions, etc.). Obviously, this centralization of personnel decisions is at odds with the premises of (strategic) HRM that organizations themselves have to define a HR strategy and the implementation of corresponding activities to cope with the particular challenges they face. It is, thus, no surprise that the OECD (2005: 167) concludes that 'most OECD member countries have moved towards decentralizing control of HRM responsibility in order to increase managerial flexibility and to improve performance and responsiveness.' This decentralization of HR responsibilities fits with what Kickert (2000) has described as typical for 1990s reforms in the Netherlands: they are characterized by 'autonomization'.

The recent HRM literature stresses that the introduction of HRM alone will not automatically result in improved organizational performance. In this respect, the crucial role of the line manager is emphasized (Purcell & Hutchinson, 2007; Nishii & Wright, 2008; Vermeeren, 2014). Line managers influence hiring and firing decisions and conduct assessment interviews with their employees. Therefore, Nishii and Wright (2008) stress the importance of the distinction between *intended* and *actual* HRM. Central or decentralized public organizations can formulate ambitious (intended) HR policies on paper; their actual implementation by line managers may vary and is at least as important.

Meyer and Hammerschmid (2010), in a study on HR decision-making in 27 EU countries, found that the decentralization of HR decision-making is indeed taking place but to varying degrees across countries. Although lower management levels are involved in HR policies and practices in almost all countries, final decisions on HR policies are generally still made at a relatively high level in the managerial hierarchy. Ultimately, decentralization is relatively further advanced in countries such as Sweden, the UK, the Netherlands, Estonia and Malta, whereas countries such as Greece, Spain, Luxembourg and Romania remain highly centralized with respect to HR decisions. Interestingly, according to their analysis, the national administrative tradition has an important effect on the actual degree of centralization, which stresses the importance of national context and path dependency.

It is also is difficult to identify a uniform development within countries. Meyer and Hammerschmid (2010) demonstrate that decentralization sometimes entails renewed centralization, for instance, by the establishment of new central agencies. An illustrative example of the coincidence of decentralization and centralization can be seen in the Netherlands (Steijn & Groeneveld, 2013). Although the Netherlands is an example of a country with a relatively high degree of HRM decentralization, a new shared service organization is responsible for the more basic operational HR tasks, such as the payment of salaries (Weerakkody & Reddick, 2012).

In addition to decentralization, whether or not accompanied by re-centralization trends, a devolution of HR responsibilities to line managers has taken place as, for instance, is illustrated by studies of Harris, Doughty and Kirk (2002), Harris (2008) and Truss (2008). Again, however, substantial differences across countries can be observed. In this respect, Demmke, Hammerschmid and Meyer (2007) conclude that especially in Belgium, Denmark, France, Italy, and Sweden, the amount of discretion given to line managers has increased.

As a consequence of devolution, differences in implementation between organizations or even between managers within organizations may appear (Harris, Doughty & Kirk, 2002; Truss, 2008). Moreover, according to Harris, Doughty and Kirk (2002), devolution is a more complex process than is often assumed. Line managers are reluctant to use their increased responsibility because they feel ill-prepared or insufficiently supported. Furthermore, organizations develop highly structured bureaucratic procedures to prevent personnel policy implementation being affected by the individual biases of line managers (for instance, with respect to selection). As a consequence, line managers are less empowered than one would expect and often 'caught in a bureaucratic web, where not only the policy is monitored, but also their own implementation of the procedures' (Harris, Doughty & Kirk, 2002: 224). Harris (2008) reports similar findings and notes that the growth of employment legislation has in fact reduced line managers' discretion to agree on individual solutions.

In a similar vein, Jakobsen and Mortensen (2015) analyze how performance management intended to reduce rules, make managers attentive to and accountable for results and provide them with greater autonomy requires new rules. They conclude, in their study of primary education in Denmark from 1989 to 2010, that instead of reducing the number of rules, performance management is likely to increase the 'total population of rules' within an organization. These observations suggest that Weberian principles are safeguarded by the introduction of new systems of rules that accompany the introduction of HRM as part of the performance management doctrine of NPM.

Key Trends

With the diffusion of HRM, a different view on the civil service workforce and its management has been adopted. According to this view, civil servants should be perceived as resources and be developed in accordance with the organization's goals. To improve the efficient and effective use of resources, HR policies were decentralized and their implementation was made a responsibility of line managers. These changes set in motion several other changes, and we will address four of these that, in our opinion, are most notable: changes in career systems, de-privilegization of civil service employment positions, individualization, and downsizing.

From Career-Based to Position-Based Civil Service Career Systems

Countries differ in how they have organized public service employment. The distinction between career- and position-based systems has been widely used to describe the key difference (OECD, 2005: 166). In a career-based system, possibilities to enter public employment are limited to an initial entry based on qualification and/or a civil service entry examination. In this system, it is difficult to enter public service at a later moment in one's career. Employees are expected to remain in public service for their entire working life, and career-development is largely dependent on decisions made by the organization. In contrast, within position-based systems, the best-suited candidate is recruited to fill a vacancy and external recruitment is relatively common. Such a system provides less security for public sector employees, as they have to compete with others to make a career advance.

Clearly, both systems are ideal types, as in real life the distinction is less clear. Nevertheless, countries can be discerned based on how they organize entry into the civil service and manage career development. Combining several sources (Van de Walle, Steijn & Jilke, 2015), we conclude that some countries, such as Brazil, Germany, France, Greece, Italy, Japan, Spain, and Portugal, are characterized by a career-based system, whereas other countries, such as Australia, the United Kingdom, the US, Norway, Sweden, the Netherlands, Poland, and Estonia, incline toward the position-based model. Countries such as Austria, Belgium, Denmark, the Czech Republic, Ireland and Korea can be described as having hybrid systems. In general, countries tend to introduce elements of the position-based systems to an increasing extent, although the career-based system is certainly not disappearing (OECD, 2005: 165).

Both systems have advantages and disadvantages. Greater flexibility is an advantage of position-based systems, which suggests that this model fits better with HRM. However, career-based systems are better equipped to ensure that collective public values are upheld, as within such a system public organizations are better able to socialize their employees. The OECD (2005: 205) concludes that although the career-based system is under pressure, as it is less able to deliver specialized skills and flexibility than is the position-based system, many countries that have traditionally relied on a career-based system have still not abolished essential elements of their system. This might explain why recent research continues to employ a classification of countries according to these career systems to explain organizational behavior in the public sectors of several countries (see for instance Demmke et al., 2007; Van de Walle et al., 2015). Furthermore, Hammerschmid, Meyer and Demmke (2007) note a relationship between the nature of the civil service system and the (de-)centralization of HRM. According to their findings, countries characterized by a career-based system still use a more centralized model and rely on a central government-wide unit for personnel issues, whereas countries with a position-based system tend to delegate HR issues. Again, this stresses the relevance of a historical institutionalist perspective and path dependency as a concept for the study of reform. It appears that it is difficult for countries to deviate from the path (either career- or position-based) that has been taken in the past. However, changes do occur, as it also appears that the number of countries in the 'hybrid' category is on the increase, as already noted by the OECD in 2005 (2005: 205). The main drivers of these changes can be both institutional and managerial.

The End of Government as a Model Employer?

Traditionally, the employment status of civil servants has been distinctive and perceived to be privileged (OECD, 2005; Van der Meer, Van den Berg & Dijkstra, 2013). In many countries, this distinctiveness has resulted in a special legal position for civil servants. As a consequence, public sector workers—at least in the recent past—often had substantially higher job security than private sector workers with guaranteed lifelong employment being the norm (OECD, 2005: 171; see also Bossaert, 2005). This distinctiveness has been justified by the need to safeguard broader governance values, for instance, the value that public servants should not operate in a politically partisan manner (OECD, 2005: 160).

Hood (2001) describes distinctiveness as part of the public sector bargain. Politicians and civil servants are dependent on one another: politicians prefer loyal and competent civil servants, whereas civil servants prefer a position with responsibility, employment security and sufficient rewards. In the public sector bargain, these preferences are 'traded' off, one of the results being the distinctive position of civil servants. However, it should be noted that 'the' distinctive position of civil servants does not exist and countries differ considerably in the way it has been filled (OECD, 2005; Van der Meer et al., 2013).

Related to the notion that the employment position of civil servants is a distinctive one as a consequence of the public sector bargain is the idea that the government should act as a model employer (Farnham & Horton, 1996). According to this view, the government sets best practices for the private sector 'in terms of fair treatment of employees and providing good conditions of service including high levels of job security, superior leave entitlements and generous pensions' (Brown, 2004: 305). Furthermore, it has also been argued that equal opportunity policies will be more strongly valued by public sector organizations than by private organizations (Farnham & Horton, 1996; Boyne et al., 1999).

Many authors have noted that due to NPM reforms, the employment relationship of public sector workers has changed. As NPM has induced the incorporation of private sector management practices in the public sector (Hood, 1991), the distinctiveness of the employment relationship of public sector workers has come under pressure. These changes in public management practices spurred several authors to examine the question of whether government is still acting as a model employer. In the late 1990s, Boyne et al. (1999: 416) argued that governments still play this role, as they concluded that 'public organizations have retained a commitment to their traditional role as model employers.' However, in more recent studies, several authors have argued otherwise. For instance, with respect to the UK, Morgan and Allington (2002) believe that the traditional model of good employment practice is under transformation. In this respect, they especially note growing job insecurity within the public sector. They show that in Britain, a permanent job only exists for a minority of public sector workers. Such a trend toward greater flexibility of the employment relationship for public sector workers—with an increasing number of public sector workers on temporary contracts—has been noted in more studies, for instance, by the OECD (2005) and more recently by Bach and Bordogna (2013).

Similarly, Hood (2001) notes that the content of the public sector bargain is changing toward a 'managerial' bargain. The content of this latter bargain is related to the NPM-inspired changes described above and is, among other factors, characterized by a system of rewards based on *individual* competition. Van der Meer et al. (2013), however, in their contribution to this subject, show that not all countries have made a similar change. In fact, many differences with respect to orientation and speed can be noted. Van der Meer et al. (2013: 93) adopt a historical-institutionalist perspective to explain this variation: 'our study demonstrates that each country's political culture and experience over the past 25 years influenced the direction that country ultimately chose.' Some countries (the Netherlands, Sweden, Denmark, Italy, Switzerland) have made what they call 'a turn to the right.' In these countries, the legal position of civil servants and private sector workers has—at least to a large degree—converged. In some other countries (Germany, Belgium, France), the changes are not so substantial, and here the overall distinctiveness of the employment position of civil service employees has remained. In Central Europe (the former communist countries), a different trajectory is visible. These countries have made 'a turn to the left', as the distinct nature of the public sector 'has been emphasized more in the past 15 years than ever before' (Van der Meer et al., 2013: 102). Britain is considered a special case. Although it is an exemplary NPM country, it recently legally formalized the position of several groups of civil servants. In fact, the so-called Governance Act makes the civil service in Britain more distinct by 'formally establishing the core values of the civil service—i.e., impartiality, integrity, honesty and neutrality—and the principle of merit-based appointment' (Van der Meer et al., 2013).

In addition to this nuanced view on the question of whether convergence or divergence is the dominant trend, Van der Meer et al. (2013) note contrasting trends in different aspects of employment status. On the one hand, with respect to labor conditions and social security issues, in many countries the convergence of the employment positions of public and private sector employees is in one way or another taking place. However, on the other hand, in most countries this does not cover the Weberian civil service *values*. In fact, with respect to issues surrounding ethical and professional norms (such as integrity and political neutrality), the distinctiveness of the public sector remains important and is sometimes emphasized more strongly and made more explicit.

Another manifestation of the fact that government still acts as a model employer relates to its adherence to equality of opportunities as one of the core public values. Considerations of equity and fairness have traditionally been intrinsically valued by government organizations, including in the last three decades when the performance logic of New Public Management was dominant. Although efficiency remains a guiding principle of public service delivery at present, the OECD (2015) observes that equity and inclusiveness are increasingly emphasized as performance dimensions of effective public service delivery. To ensure that the needs and preferences of diverse social groups are reflected in administrative decision-making, governments are increasingly devoting attention to the diversity of their workforce with respect to, among other categories, gender, ethnicity, age and sexual orientation. In sum, a business case for diversity is added to the social justice case as a motivation for government efforts to achieve and maintain a diverse workforce (Groeneveld & Van de Walle, 2010).

In conclusion, de-privilegization appears to be the overarching trend, which, however, takes a different shape in different countries. Civil servants have lost certain rights, especially with respect to job security and social security rights. This does not mean that by definition the public sector is no longer a model employer. In many countries, the importance of Weberian civil service values is stressed, which suggests that in the view of most governments, the public sector should still be seen as a *special* employer where certain values need to be upheld. This public distinctiveness is further highlighted when performance goals meet public values, as is the case with policies to increase the representation of diverse social groups such as women or ethnical groups. However, the corresponding trade-off with material advantages for public sector employees is disappearing. The content of the public sector bargain thus appears to be changing.

Individualization

From an HRM perspective, employees are considered resources amounting to the organization's capital that, if adequately managed, contribute to organizational performance. Hence, management should induce the efficient and effective use of the human resources present in the organization and adequately assess their contribution to overall organizational performance. In line with NPM management practices in other domains, performance management has been introduced in the public HRM portfolio. Performance management assumes that the employment relationship is primarily founded on the transaction of costs and benefits of employer and employee. This assumption is at odds with the long-term, rule-based relationship underlying the traditional bureaucratic employment relationship. The view of employees as 'human capital' reveals a commodification of labor that implies that management seeks to assess the monetary value of its use and outcomes. As the productivity of human resources may vary across organizations, work units and individual employees, the employment bargain tends to be individualized. In a similar vein, the OECD (2005: 170) finds that the 'individualization of HR practices is at the heart of the reforms aiming at increasing the responsiveness of the public service.'

An important element in this respect is the use of individual performance management and performance-related pay. According to the OECD (2005), most countries have, in one way or another, introduced individual performance appraisal systems for civil servants (compare also Lah & Perry, 2008). This means that instead of generalized criteria for a job, the employee and the manager agree on job objectives. Initially, countries attempted to use a scientific approach using detailed rating systems. However, in the early 2000s, this approach was replaced by an assessment in a dialogue between employee and line manager (OECD, 2005). Line managers use pre-identified objectives for the assessment of an employee's performance, which is in accordance with the more general trend toward the devolution of HR responsibilities to line managers.

Many countries have also attempted to link performance to (individual) pay (OECD, 2005). The OECD (2005: 175) concludes that although performance-related pay (PRP) is considered an appealing idea, its implementation is difficult and complex. This likely explains why the performance-related component of the salary of public sector employees remains very modest, as recent studies illustrate. For instance, Bordogna and Neri (2014) conclude in their study on Italian local government that although PRP exists in theory, it is often not used. In fact, the economic crisis has made its application in Italian municipalities almost impossible, as there are no resources available to finance it. With respect to France (Rouban, 2008), Spain (Parrado, 2008) and Germany (Keller, 2014), it is also concluded that within public sector organizations, the use of PRP is very limited and that 'high expectations [. . .] were only partially fulfilled' (Keller, 2014: 395–396).

Variation across countries in the extent to which performance management was implemented in civil service organizations can partly be explained by countries' career systems. For instance, Hammerschmid et al. (2007: 163) conclude:

> 'With regard to HR systems, as expected, in position-based systems, performance accountability is more important than in career-based systems, the opposite being true for compliance and judicial accountability. [. . .] As regards the actual choice of tools and instruments, we find evidence that career-based countries tend to focus on supervision or regulation, while position-based countries focus on managerial and performance instruments, such as performance agreements, targets, and indicators.'

Austerity and Downsizing

NPM-style reforms were intended to reduce public sector spending by making public organizations operate in a more efficient way and, as a consequence, minimize the size of government. Cutback and downsizing strategies, therefore, have been part of public sector reform since the 1980s. If governments are forced to reduce spending, including spending on their own administrative apparatus, they also tend to reduce the workforce in addition to other workforce cost-cutting strategies, such as pay freezes and cutting fringe benefits. Downsizing is an obvious strategy, as in principle, a smaller civil service will be less costly. Not only because less funding is needed to pay salaries but also because related costs with respect to, for example, training, ICT and housing will also decrease. It is, therefore, unsurprising that especially during economic downturns, governments have made deliberate efforts to reduce civil service employment and public sector employment in general. This is true for the recession periods in the 1980s and 1990s (OECD, 2005) as well as in the aftermath of the financial crisis of 2008 (OECD, 2015: 110).

However, little is known about the effects of NPM-style reforms on public sector size. To our knowledge, the only study that actually empirically examines the association between NPM reforms and the size of public sector employment is Alonso, Clifton and Diaz-Fuentes (2015), which is based on a panel dataset composed of data from Eurostat, the OECD, and the World Bank on 15 EU countries over the period from 1983 to 2011. They examine two NPM policies, outsourcing and decentralization, and find that these policies generally did not have an impact on the size of public sector employment.

The OECD reports on the main trends in public sector management on a regular basis and attempts to substantiate the link between reform initiatives and public sector size by comparing statistical trends. In a 2005 report, the OECD concludes that despite downsizing efforts, the end result is not entirely clear. Furthermore, an uneven picture emerges when countries are compared. With respect to the 1991–2001 period, public employment has significantly increased in some countries (Ireland, Korea, Luxembourg, the Netherlands, Spain, Turkey), slightly increased in Poland, slightly changed in some other countries (Austria, Belgium, Japan), slightly decreased in Canada and Hungary, and finally, significantly decreased in several other countries (Australia, Finland, Germany, New Zealand, Sweden). These differences between countries can partly be attributed to the fact that in some countries the civil service had to grow because of growth in the working population (OECD, 2005: 161). Nevertheless, in nearly all countries, civil service employment *relative to the labor force* decreased—with Ireland and Luxembourg being important outliers (OECD, 2005: 161).

According to the OECD (2005), workforce reductions are often, but not always, the result of an active strategy. This strategy can include privatization, but it can also be the result of public management re-engineering programs. Dismissals are seldom part of the strategy; reductions are more often achieved by recruitment freezing or non-replacement of retiring staff (OECD, 2015: 111). Moreover, the OECD (2005: 163) also concludes that cutback measures tend to occur in response to a fiscal problem, resulting in some political crisis. This argument is in accordance with the observation that external shocks are primarily responsible for triggering major reforms (Kickert, 2011).

Thus, one would expect that the fiscal crisis that began in the late 2000s has had a substantial impact on public sector employment. However, recent OECD data (2013) do not reveal a clear picture. With respect to 38 OECD countries, the OECD (2013) concludes that *relative to the total workforce*, public sector employment has remained stable at approximately 16%. This stability is visible in most countries, with only four countries (the Slovak Republic, Sweden, Mexico and Portugal) exhibiting a clear decrease. Nevertheless, when we consider the data in greater detail, it is clear that austerity measures have taken their toll on the size of public sector employment in the period since 2008. For instance, recent EU data show that 19 EU member states have experienced job losses in public administration since 2008 (Eurofound, 2015). Bach and Bordogna (2013) also show that austerity measures have led to a decrease in (absolute) public sector employment in several countries in Europe. In contrast, but in accordance with the thesis of historical institutionalism, French public sector employment declined only marginally between 2008 and 2011 (Jeannot, 2014). With respect to municipalities, Leisink and Bach (2014) show that in four out of seven European countries, municipal employment decreased during the recent fiscal crisis. Bach and Stroleny (2014) show that in England and Wales, local government employment decreased by over 19% in the 2008–13 period. If we focus again on employment in central government, the OECD (2015), in its most recent study, observes that from 2008 to 2013, the size of the central government employment declined in two-thirds of OECD countries. OECD countries that decide to reduce central government employment do so through a wide array of strategies: recruitment freezes, across-the-board cuts, outsourcing and attrition. Dismissals are seldom used. Active strategies of public organizations to downsize their workforce affect not only the sheer numbers but also impact the composition of the workforce. In general, less-educated employees, women and minorities are more likely to lose their jobs (Raudla, Savi & Randma-Liiv, 2013).

In summary, it appears that public sector employment in OECD countries has remained essentially stable in recent decades—at least *relative* to the total labor force. Furthermore, it seems that austerity measures primarily affected employment in local government, whereas the national government workforces have been less of a target. It is also clear that most governments have attempted to employ various reform instruments (such as privatization or re-engineering) to reduce—or at least stabilize—public sector employment. The exact measures taken, and their effect, however, differ across countries. A further interesting development is that reduction measures appear to have been most successful during periods of an acute crisis, such as surrounding the financial crisis. It remains to be seen what will happen in the future. Will public sector employment remain at a relatively low level compared with previous years, or will it recover? Will there be differences in this development across countries based on historical patterns?

Conclusion

The HR-related reform that is most evident in most countries is the introduction and diffusion of HRM itself. HRM has replaced traditional bureaucratic personnel administration, not only rhetorically but also to a considerable extent in reality. In this chapter, we identified four key trends that can be understood in the context of the rise of HRM in public organizations: a greater reliance on position-based career systems, a de-privilegization of civil servants' employment status, individualization and downsizing. However, despite these common trends, variation in HRM implementation across countries remains substantial. For instance, relative to countries that had historically been characterized by a career-based system, countries with a position-based system exhibit higher levels of decentralization in HR decision-making and more strongly rely on performance management. It is also relevant to note that although initiatives to downsize are common to nearly all countries, the content of these initiatives and their impact on public sector employment differ widely. Finally, it can be observed that although public sector employment has become de-privilegized, in many countries it remains distinctive. A common trend in many—but not all—countries seems to be that civil service values are re-emphasized as a defining characteristic of public sector employment.

One reason for cross-country variation in HRM-related trends is to be found in distinct points of departure, including with respect to the nature of national civil service systems and cultural beliefs regarding the role and status of civil servants (Pollitt & Bouckaert, 2011). Pollitt (2015), in a recent keynote on European civil services and their workforces, adds that this diversity is also the result of countries travelling 'in somewhat different directions and even, sometimes, do their best to turn back.' This has much to do with international differences in attitudes toward NPM and the salience of nation-specific problems. These explanations concur with a historic-institutionalist perspective on reform, according to which variation is attributed to organizations' responsiveness to institutional pressures.

The trends described in this chapter also suggest that change is largely fueled by major external shocks, such as the recent financial crisis and, earlier, the economic crisis in the 1980s. The exact nature of the accompanying trends, however, is replete with trade-offs, contradictions and paradoxes (compare Pollitt & Bouckaert, 2011). As a result, there is less convergence among countries with respect to the implementation of HRM than one would expect based on the widespread embrace of the HRM *concept*. From a managerial perspective, variation in HRM implementation across organizations and sectors, as well as across countries, should be understood as an outcome of strategic decisions made by management in response to diverse challenges in the organizational environment.

References

Alonso, J.M., Clifton, J., & Diaz-Fuentes, D. (2015). Did new public management matter? An empirical analysis of the outsourcing and decentralization effects on public sector size. *Public Management Review, 17*(5), 643–660.

Bach, S., & Bordogna, L. (2011). Varieties of new public management or alternative models? The reform of public service employment relations in industrialized democracies. *The International Journal of Human Resource Management, 22*(11), 2281–2294.

Bach, S., & Bordogna, L. (2013). Reframing public service employment relations: The impact of economic crisis and the new EU economic governance. *European Journal of Industrial Relations, 19*(4), 279–294.

Bach, S., & Stroleny, A. (2014). Restructuring UK local government employment relations: Pay determination and employee participation in tough times. *Transfer: European Review of Labour and Research, 20*(3), 343–356.

Bordogna, L., & Neri, S. (2014). Austerity policies, social dialogue and public services in Italian local government. *Transfer: European Review of Labour and Research, 20*(3), 357–371.

Bossaert, D. (2005). *The flexibilisation of the employment status of civil servants: From life tenure to more flexible employment relations?* Luxembourg: European Institute of Public Administration.

Boxall, P., & Purcell, J. (2011). *Strategy and human resource management*. 2nd edition. Basingstoke: Palgrave Macmillan.

Boyne, G., Jenkins, G., & Poole, M. (1999). Human resource management in the public and private sectors: An empirical comparison. *Public Administration, 77*(2), 407–420.

Brown, K. (2004). Human resource management in the public sector. *Public Management Review, 6*(3), 303–309.

Demmke, C., Hammerschmid, G., & Meyer, R.E. (2007). *The impact of individual assessments on organisational performance in the public services of EU member states: Survey commissioned by the Portuguese EU-presidency*. Vienna and Maastricht: EIPA and Wirtschaftsuniversität Wien.

Eurofound. (2015). *ERM annual report: Restructuring in the public sector*. Luxembourg: Publications office of the European Union.

Farnham, D., & Horton, S. (1996). *Managing the new public services*. Basingstoke: Macmillan.

Giordano, R., Depalo, D., Pereira, M.C., Eugène, B., Papapetrou, E., Perez, J.J., Reiss, L., & Roter, M. (2011). *The public sector pay gap in a selection of Euro area countries no. 1406*. European Central Bank: Frankfurt am Main.

Groeneveld, S., & Van de Walle, S. (2010). A contingency approach to representative bureaucracy: Power, equal opportunities and diversity. *International Review of Administrative Sciences, 76*(2), 239–258.

Hammerschmid, G., Meyer, R.E., & Demmke, C. (2007). Public administration modernization: Common reform trends or different paths and national understandings in the EU countries. In K. Schedler and I. Proeller (Eds.), *Cultural aspects of public management reform* (pp. 145–169). Amsterdam: Elsevier: JAI Press.

Harris, L. (2008). The changing nature of the HR function in UK local government and its role as "employee champion", *Employee Relations, 30*(1), 34–47.

Harris, L., Doughty, D., & Kirk, S. (2002). The devolution of HR responsibilities—perspectives from the UK's public sector. *Journal of European Industrial Training, 26*(5), 218–229.

Hood, C. (1991). A public management for all seasons. *Public administration, 69*(1), 3–19.

Hood, C. (2001). Public service bargains and public service reform. In B.G. Peters and J. Pierre (Eds.), *Politicians, bureaucrats and administrative reform* (pp. 13–23). London: Routledge.

Jakobsen, M.L.F., & Mortensen, P.B. (2015). Rules and the doctrine of performance management. *Public Administration Review*, online advance access.

Jeannot, G. (2014). Austerity and social dialogue in French local government. *Transfer: European Review of Labour and Research, 20*(3), 373–386.

Keller, B. (2014). The continuation of early austerity measures: The special case of Germany. *Transfer: European Review of Labour and Research, 20*(3), 387–402.

Kickert, W.J. (2000). *Public management reform in the Netherlands: Social reconstruction of reform ideas and underlying frames of reference.* Delft: Eburon.

Kickert, W.J. (2011). Distinctiveness of administrative reform in Greece, Italy, Portugal and Spain: Common characteristics of context, administrations and reforms. *Public Administration, 89*(3), 801–818.

Kickert, W.J., & Jørgensen, T.B. (1995a). Introduction: Managerial reform trends in Western Europe. *International Review of Administrative Sciences, 61*(4), 499–510.

Kickert, W.J., & Jørgensen, T.B. (1995b). Conclusion and discussion: Management, policy, politics and public values. *International Review of Administrative Sciences, 61*(4), 577–586.

Knies, E., Boselie, P., Gould-Williams, J., & Vandenabeele, W. (2015). Special issue of international journal of human resource management: Strategic human resource management and public sector performance. *The International Journal of Human Resource Management, 26*(3), 421–424.

Lah, T.J., & Perry, J.L. (2008). The diffusion of the civil service reform act of 1978 in OECD countries: A tale of two paths to reform. *Review of Public Personnel Administration, 28*(3), 282–299.

Leisink, P., & Bach, S. (2014). Economic crisis and municipal public service employment: Comparing developments in seven EU member states. *Transfer: European Review of Labour and Research, 20*(3), 327–342.

Meyer, R.E., & Hammerschmid, G. (2010). The degree of decentralization and individual decision making in central government human resource management: A European comparative perspective. *Public Administration, 88*(2), 455–478.

Morgan, P., & Allington, N. (2002). Has the public sector retained its 'model employer' status? *Public Money and Management, 22*(1), 35–42.

Nishii, L.H., & Wright, P.M. (2008). Variability within organizations: Implications for strategic human resource management. In D.B. Smith (Ed.), *The people make the place: Dynamic linkages between individuals and organizations* (pp. 225–248). New York, Sussex: Taylor & Francis Group.

OECD. (2005). *Modernising government: The way forward.* Paris: OECD Publishing.

OECD. (2011). *Government at a glance 2011.* Paris: OECD Publishing.

OECD. (2013). *Government at a glance 2013.* Paris: OECD Publishing.

OECD. (2015). *Government at a glance 2015.* Paris: OECD Publishing.

Paauwe, J., Guest, D., & Wright, P.M. (2013). *HRM and performance—achievements and challenges.* Chichester: Wiley.

Parrado, S. (2008). Failed policies but institutional innovation through 'layering' and 'diffusion' in Spanish central administration. *International Journal of Public Sector Management, 21*(2), 230–252.

Pfeffer, J. (1995). Producing sustainable competitive advantage through the effective management of people. *The Academy of Management Executive, 9*(1), 55–69.

Pollitt, C. (2015). *Public servants to public managers: The European story: Transformation or torture?* Paper supporting a keynote address to 11th Transatlantic Dialogue (TAD) Boston, 3–5 June 2015.

Pollitt, C., & Bouckaert, G. (2011). *Public management reform: A comparative analysis-new public management, governance, and the Neo-Weberian state.* Oxford: Oxford University Press.

Purcell, J., & Hutchinson, S. (2007). Front-line managers as agents in the HRM-performance causal chain: Theory, analysis and evidence. *Human Resource Management Journal, 17*(1), 3–20.

Raudla, R., Savi, R., & Randma-Liiv, T. (2013). *Literature review on cutback management.* COCOPS Work package 7, Deliverable 1.

Rouban, L. (2008). Reform without doctrine: Public management in France. *International Journal of Public Sector Management, 21*(2), 133–149.

Steijn, B., & Groeneveld, S. (Eds.). (2013). *Strategisch HRM in de publieke sector (2de ed.).* Assen: Koninklijke Van Gorcum.

Teo, S. (2000). Evidence of strategic HRM linkages in eleven Australian corporatized public sector organizations. *Public Personnel Management, 29*(4), 557–574.

Teo, S.T., & Rodwell, J.J. (2007). To be strategic in the new public sector, HR must remember its operational activities. *Human Resource Management, 46*(2), 265–284.

Truss, C. (2008). Continuity and change: the role of the HR function in the modern public sector. *Public Administration, 86*(4), 1071–1088.

Van der Meer, F.M., Van den Berg, C.F., & Dijkstra, G.S.A. (2013). Rethinking the 'public service bargain': The changing (legal) position of civil servants in Europe. *International Review of Administrative Sciences, 79*(1), 91–110.

Van de Walle, S., Steijn, B., & Jilke, S. (2015). Extrinsic motivation, PSM and labour market characteristics: A multilevel model of public sector preference in 26 countries. *International Review of Administrative Sciences, 81*(4), 833–855.

Vermeeren, B. (2014). *HRM implementation and performance in the public sector.* Faculty of Social Sciences (FSS). Doctoral dissertation. Rotterdam: Erasmus University Rotterdam.

Weerakkody, V., & Reddick, C.G. (Eds.). (2012). *Public sector transformation through E-government: Experiences from Europe and North America.* London: Routledge.

Wright, P.M., & McMahan, G.C. (1992). Theoretical perspectives for strategic human resource management. *Journal of management, 18*(2), 295–320.

13 Public Management Reform and Public Professionalism

Mirko Noordegraaf[1]

Introduction

There are obvious links between public management reform and public professionalism. Reforms are initiated to improve public services and public organizations, which in many ways depend upon *professionals* who treat cases and clients, implement public policies, and serve political programs. Professional workers such as judges, policemen, public persecutors, teachers, professors, medical doctors, nurses, social workers, inspectors, and air traffic controllers are important for reducing crime, improving safety, maintaining social order, strengthening knowledge economies, implementing welfare programs, reducing poverty and overseeing markets.

In mainstream public management reform, which has attracted considerable attention from scholars of political science and public administration, some aspects of these links have been discussed. Mainstream public management reform is often portrayed as businesslike reform, which is supported by political ideologies (*managerialism*) and offers tools for 'running government as a business' (*New Public Management*) (e.g., Hood, 1991; Kickert, 1995, 1997; Pollitt & Bouckaert, 2004). This generates a *performance logic* that—at first sight—contradicts the *professionalism* logic that pervades professional services (for oversight, e.g., Noordegraaf, 2011; 2015a). Whereas better performance requires targets, outputs, measurement and transparency, professionalism requires subjectivity, sociability, knowledge and experience. Whereas better performance is a matter of improving managerial *control*, strengthening professionalism is a matter of enlarging professional *autonomy*.

Although well-known public management scholars (such as Kickert, 2001; Hood, 2002; Pollitt & Bouckaert, 2004) have focused on reforms as performance optimization and been critical of their highly problematic effects, these scholars have hardly explicitly emphasized professionalism and professional work. Although these and other authors (such as Walker & Boyne, 2006; Christensen & Lægreid, 2007; Pollitt, Van Thiel & Homburg, 2007; Diefenbach, 2009; Goldfinch & Wallis, 2009; Ongaro, 2009) have emphasized important themes such as performance systems, red tape, public service motivation, quality, trust and public value, they have hardly dived into the specifics and specificities of professional work, including elements such as professional routines, socialization, education, expertise, methods, identity, power and status. These elements will affect what reforms are initiated, how reforms are implemented, how reform actually happens and which reform effects will occur.

Consequently, explicit links between public management reform and professionalism remain ambiguous in reform studies. First and foremost, the *nature of professionalism* is frequently left unexplored. Terms such as professionalism and professionals are used quite loosely, and different types of professionalism and professional work are not always clearly distinguished (with exceptions being, among others, Ferlie, Ashburner, Fitzgerald & Pettigrew, 1996; Kirkpatrick, Ackroyd & Walker, 2005).

Second, public management reform is more than mere 'New Public Management', that is, more than strict performance optimization. Improving public sector performance might go beyond simple businesslike or managerial interventions (e.g., O'Reilly & Reed, 2011). Moreover, performance improvements do not have immediate effects in professional domains. Reforms themselves are *manufactured,* and their effects are *mediated,* not in the least by professionals and professional groups (e.g., Waring & Currie, 2009). The nature of professionalism affects whether and how reforms are actually implemented.

Third, we tend to focus on the effects of reform for professional work, but we might also study how reforms themselves are shaped by professionalization and how professionalism and professional expertise affect reform. Increasingly, there seem to be multiple forms of *reform professionalism*, whereby so-called organizational professionals (e.g., Larson, 1977; Reed, 1996), such as consultants, controllers, auditors and project managers, are professionalized to make public organizations more professional.

Fourth, there is little systematic attention on changing forms of public professionalism, which do not so much flow from reform projects or programs but from broader social and societal transitions. Instead of merely focusing on reformed professionalism, we might study the *reconfiguration of professionalism* (cf. Noordegraaf, 2013), i.e., the rise of new forms of professionalism with new identities, routines and methods, outside the realm of conscious management reform, but nevertheless altering public services and welfare programs. This chapter explores these various implicit and/or ignored but crucial aspects of the links between public management reform and professionalism:

1. What is (public) professionalism?
2. How does public management reform affect professionalism and professional work?
3. How does professionalism affect reform?
4. What new forms of public professionalism are emerging?

Below, we will provide answers to each of these questions, primarily by relying on insights from strands of research that focus on changing professional services, professionalism and professional work. Although they are rather superficial in regard to public sector reform, they show how new *performance*-based models clash or merge with *professional* practices. These strands of literature are related to broader public management theory (e.g., Skelcher & Smith, 2015), organizational sociology (e.g., Ackroyd, Kirkpatrick & Walker, 2007), social theory (e.g., Clarke & Newman, 1997), implementation studies (e.g., Hill & Hupe, 2008) and institutional theory (e.g., Reay & Hinings, 2009). We conclude this chapter with reflections on the rich (and often simplified) nature of public professionalism and sketch ways forward for obtaining better academic and practical understandings of *reformed professionalism* and *professional reform*.

Public Professionalism as Process

Conceptual clarity is important when we attempt to understand complex processes such as reform processes. However, because these processes are far from neutral and contested, it proves difficult to be clear and precise. This is especially the case when terms such as 'professionalism' are used and linked to reform projects. Terms such as 'professionalism' can be seen as 'discursive resources' (cf. Watson, 2002) used in larger struggles over the meaning and ownership of public policies and services. In the case of public services, for example, professionalism traditionally represents certain service ideals, including quality and humanity, and it relates these ideals to key actors, most particularly professionals at street-levels. More important, professionalism is used to express desires, most specifically the desire to guard (professional) *autonomy* and to minimize (managerial) *control*. This does not only occur in service practices, it also happens when academics study these practices. In fact, many academics defend professionalism against external 'intrusions', such as the rise of managerial and consumer logics (e.g., Freidson, 2001), to 'rescue' a distinctive logic and certain core values in fields such as healthcare. This is used by other academics to define many other street-level workers as 'professionals' and to defend their 'autonomies' and service ideals when social or educational services are reformed.

Professionalism as Self-Regulation

To acknowledge these struggles but create conceptual clarity while simultaneously remaining critical, public professionalism can be defined as follows (e.g., Noordegraaf, 2015a). We see professionalism as a distinctive work logic, which comprises specific ideals and values, as well as specific forms of work, i.e., work performed by professionals. Their work is not necessarily characterized by substantive features, such as certain values and ideals (e.g., 'quality'), a certain work content, a certain amount of autonomy or a specific form of expertise but by its *regulative* features. Professional work can be seen as a matter of well-regulated occupational control or, specifically, *'occupational self-control'* (e.g., Noordegraaf, 2013, 2015b, on the basis of, e.g., Larson, 1977). Workers who belong to a certain occupation jointly control and regulate their own work. This means it is relevant to focus on the mechanisms, including changing mechanisms, for regulating work, as well as how these mechanisms are (de)institutionalized.

Traditionally, typical forms of professional work such as medical work or—outside the public domain—law and accountancy, were controlled by medical doctors, lawyers and accountants themselves by installing and maintaining various sets of regulatory mechanisms during processes of professionalization.

a. *Selection*: members are selected and accepted, or they are kept outside.
b. *Schooling*: members are trained and educated through well-defined educational programs.
c. *Socialization*: members learn how they ought to think and behave.
d. *Supervision*: members are supervised when they begin to practice and when they practice.
e. *Sanctioning*: members are punished or expelled when they make mistakes.

These forms of professional work are understood as classic, 'real' or *pure professionalism*. Occupational fields such as the medical field became strong fields, with strong associations, education, supervision and so forth, in short, into strong 'professions' (e.g., Krause, 1996). To a large extent, these fields manage to determine what their members know, how they feel and behave and their goals.

This is clearly distinguished from non-members, who are excluded from professional practice. The existence of 'real' professions implies that that are fewer 'real' or weaker professions. In the case of 'semi-professions' (e.g., Etzioni, 1969), such as policemen or nurses, regulative mechanisms have been established, but these mechanisms are weaker and less authoritative, and these professionals are more dependent upon other professionals, as well as on policy and organizational contexts.

Establishing Self-Regulation

Professionalization as regulation, including regulated knowledge, is the outcome of so-called 'professionalization projects' (e.g., Larson, 1977). Only when certain knowledge, expert bases and quality ambitions are *jointly regulated* is an occupational field built and professional authority formed. When this does not really or forcefully occur, occupational domains remain fragmented. Consider social work and observe the longing for professionalism but the inability to 'really' become a profession (e.g., Heite, 2012).

In addition, to jointly regulate domains, develop professional authority and make legitimate exchanges, professional fields must be governed and *enabled to govern*. They need other actors to do so, most specifically the state and universities (esp. Burrage & Torstendahl, 1990). These actors grant authority and secure a stable knowledge base. In other words, professional fields such as medicine need government regulation to exert self-control and academic training to reproduce (disciplinary) knowledge, experience and values.

Finally, it is important that outside worlds and others acknowledge professional authority. In other words, professional domains must establish exchanges with outside worlds (cf. Larson, 1977) that are considered *legitimate*. In the case of the medical or judicial fields, these exchanges have become less stable, and professional workers now face legitimacy problems, for instance, when medical errors are made transparent. It is difficult to measure professional effects, including effects of reforms, as different stakeholders will make different evaluations *and* because certain stakeholders cannot make reasonable judgments because they are unaware of the fact that they are or might be stakeholders at all. The more this is 'controlled', the stronger a professional domain can become.

These regulative conditions are especially relevant in the case of *public* professionalism, which is a matter of *specific*, situated interactions, in *generic* societal contexts. When a professional treats a case, he or she addresses a specific assignment, namely a specific client or patient, but he or she does so to serve some larger or higher objective. He or she treats a client or patient to improve employability and employment or to prevent diseases from spreading. This means that it is difficult to judge professionalism and professional effects, as evaluations by those who are directly involved, such as a patient, might deviate from evaluations by those who are more indirectly involved, such as employers or other citizens. What 'effective' and 'legitimate' mean is not determined by clear or absolute yardsticks.

All of this is not to say that knowledge and expertise are unimportant—on the contrary. As indicated above, most public professions need knowledge to act and treat cases. According to Brint (1994), professionalism has become 'expert-based professionalism'. This means that we must not merely analyze how occupational regulation takes place, including the various mechanisms identified above. We must also analyze how knowledge is regulated. This is influenced by the processes we described, especially the ways in which universities contribute to the formation of professionalism, but in addition, it is influenced by how knowledge itself is regulated.

In case of 'real' professions and 'real' *professionals*, strong occupational regulation is accompanied by *regulated knowledge*, supported by books, theories and models, such as biomedical theories and models. A medical doctor studies biomedical sciences and specializes in certain disciplinary subfields, such as surgery or gynecology. When there is strong occupational regulation, but the disciplinary knowledge base is less well-regulated, we speak of *semi-professions*. In the case of teachers, policemen and social workers, there are occupational domains, with selection, education and supervision, but these domains are dependent upon organizational and policy contexts, *and* their knowledge base is less well-defined and formalized.

Understanding Reform

An understanding of (public) professionalism as a highly regulated phenomenon is relevant for understanding public management reform, irrespective of the nature of reform and how reform processes are governed. First and foremost, professionalism and professional work and logic are *not* a matter of 'free' and 'autonomous' professional workers. They concern well-regulated professional fields that establish all sorts of occupational *standards* that constitute professional action and guide professional workers. Professional authority does not depend upon autonomies and absent standards but upon jointly set, self-controlled standards that are applied *in situ* when cases are treated. When public organizations are reformed, professionalism will be under pressure, as there will be struggles over *who sets what standards and why*. When standard setting is drawn away from professional fields and tied to both policy and organizational surroundings, there is a (perceived) weakening of professionalism.

Furthermore, both states and universities contribute to standard setting, and they will only increase these efforts to address changing circumstances. They will not only focus on policy, service and organizational reform to discipline professional work (see below). They will also reform professional fields as such to redirect professionalization processes, make professionals less 'untouchable' and respond to new societal challenges. Governments, for example, might change the selection of new professional workers to reorganize professional labor markets. They might call for educational changes, either in terms of content (such as greater attention to communication skills in medical education) or in terms of length, duration and costs to save money and build new competencies. Inspectorates and other actors such as patient associations and insurance companies might call for the 'resocialization' of professional workers, such as medical doctors who are then forced to change attitudes and behaviors, for example, to combine quality and efficiency. Inspectorates might also closely monitor occupational practices and intervene, especially when there are mistakes, errors and failures, to improve safety such as medical safety. Finally, professional members might be punished and persecuted by outsiders, e.g., through 'naming and shaming', to break through 'blame-free' cultures.

Finally, changing standards and/or setting new standards need not come from outside worlds, either directly (through the state and policy measures) or indirectly (through managers inside service organizations). This might also originate *within* professional fields and spread throughout fields and toward other fields. There might be endogenous demands, coming from professional workers and fields themselves, influenced by new tasks and challenges. Medical doctors, for example, might adopt new protocols and directives for reforming clinical practices, based upon 'evidence based medicine' (EBM), which has become an attractive scientific base for improving biomedical sciences and medical practices. In addition, they might adopt new standards for structuring professional work, for example, concerning safety improvement inside the hospital (e.g., Leistikow, Kalkman & De Bruijn, 2011). In addition, standards—often, stricter standards—are also adopted to address (restricted) working hours and changing career paths of professional workers. Whereas medical doctors were always (24/7) doctors, younger generations opt for work-life balance. It is not only managerialism that objectifies professional work—professional fields themselves also work toward objectification.

Public Management Reforms and their Effects

These various observations clarify links between public management reform and public professionalism. Professionalism implies self-regulated occupational practices, which comes under pressure when reform projects set new occupational standards. These new standards are not directly owned by professional members, and they might not directly be meaningful and workable. This means that there will be potential for conflict.

Reform and Rationalization of Professional Services

Due to reform, new standards are often rational standards that—indeed—seem to fuel conflict. Businesslike organizational, accountability and financing mechanisms have made professional service organizations dependent upon political and policy logics *and* transformed them into well-run performance systems. In higher education (e.g., Kickert, 1995), medical services (Harrison & Pollitt, 1994), policing, public prosecution and the judiciary, strict and systematic organizational and financial tools have altered the workings of these services. Since the 1980s and 1990s, these public organizations have been *rationalized*. Backed by New Public Management (e.g., Kickert, 1997; Pollitt & Bouckaert, 2004; Ackroyd et al., 2007; Evetts, 2009; Leicht, Walter, Sainsaulieu & Davies, 2009; Noordegraaf, 2015a), services had to be rendered in more efficient, transparent and accountable ways. There had to be clearer goals and objectives, better planning and monitoring, more measurability, more customer-orientation and more continuous improvement. When education or healthcare is provided, reform projects intended to modernize service provision by installing new organizational and cultural rules and standards that made services less dependent upon professional insight or professional routines and more dependent upon planning and control and continuous 'plan, do, check, act' (PDCA). This was driven by ambitions to control costs, to reduce errors and failure and to satisfy public (customer) preferences. Policies also had to be formed in more rational ways, not only to make them efficient, transparent and accountable but also to have the right policies with the best 'value for money'. Policies had to be formulated to solve problems.

There have been many studies on the links between management reform and public organizations, although professional services and the roles of professionalism and professional work have not always been highlighted. Although there are exceptions (such as Shain & Gleeson, 1999; Kirkpatrick et al., 2005; De Bruijn, 2007; Leicht et al., 2009; Jarl, Frederiksson & Persson, 2012; Noordegraaf & De Wit, 2012; Numerato, Salvatore & Fattore, 2012; Blomgren & Waks, 2015; Noordegraaf, 2015b), the nature of professionalism has not always been explored to understand the effects of reform. However, when New Public Management is perceived to be privileging a *performance logic*, leading to measurement, objectivity and control, it is easy to assume or believe that this is at odds with a *professional logic*, which embodies meaning, knowledge, subjectivity and trust (Noordegraaf, 2015b). Such conflict is highlighted in various academic strands of research and bodies of knowledge, which do not always explicitly focuses on public management reform but are relevant for understanding the effects of reforms in organizational surroundings that replete with experts and professionals. Although they do not fully understand the complexities and dynamics of reform, they *do* understand clashes between performance and professionalism.

The most basic version of this conflict is discussed under the heading of '*deprofessionalization*': rationalized services and systems eliminate professional *autonomy* (e.g., Ritzer & Walczak, 1988; Broadbent, Dietrich & Roberts, 2005; Clarke, 2005). Professional workers are disciplined and subjected to managerial and consumer control (cf. Freidson, 2001) that negatively affect professional action because their autonomies are taken away. In political and public debates, it is attractive to emphasize such effects and to resist the transformation of professionals into 'normal workers'. Although this proletarization thesis is criticized (e.g., Lewis, 2002; Lewis, Marjoribanks & Pirotta, 2003), it continues to attract considerable attention. This basic line of thought is summarized in figure 13.1

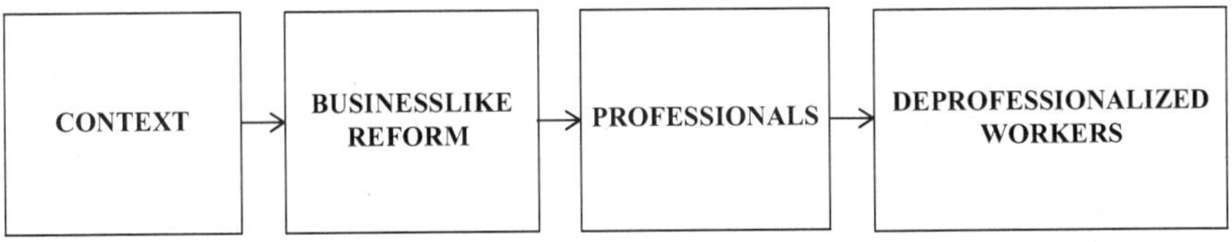

Figure 13.1   Basic effects of reform (de-professionalization)

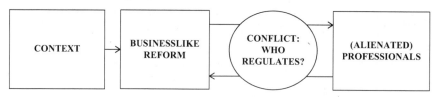

Figure 13.2   Reform effects as conflict

Perspectives on Reform Effects

To go beyond such basic insights (or assumptions), we need to rely upon more refined understandings of potential links between reform and professionalism. There are studies demonstrating that professionalism is no passive recipient of public sector reform and that links between businesslike reforms and professional action are contested. This is not so much because autonomy is at stake but because *self-regulation* is at stake. Reforms fuel conflict over the most fundamental question, *who regulates professional action?* This is visualized in figure 13.2.

First and foremost, clashes between businesslike principles and professionalism have been studied as clashing *institutional logics*, i.e., sets of ideas, values and rules that are strongly embedded in social action. To understand links between reforms and professionalism, there has been considerable emphasis on 'businesslike versus professional logics' (e.g., Reay & Hinings, 2009) and 'corporate versus collegiate logics' (Pache & Santos, 2013). These different logics contain different courses of social action, with conflicts and 'competing logics' as a result.

Second, these clashes are regarded as conflicts between different forms of governance and, especially, different *coordination principles*, particularly 'hierarchical and market coordination versus network coordination' (e.g., Brandsen, Van de Donk & Putters, 2005) and 'hierarchy and consumerism versus communities and collaboration' (Adler, Kwon & Heckscher, 2008). Do managers and consumers regulate professional action, or is this the province of groups and networks of professionals (also Freidson, 2001)?

Third, within organizational sociology, authors have stressed conflicts between managerial and professional action as conflicts in terms of *work forms*. Professional work practices increasingly occur within organizational contexts, and this generates divisions between organizational contexts and occupational practices (e.g., Muzio & Kirkpatrick, 2011). More controlled work settings, it is argued, lead to weakened forms of work.

Fourth, there have been policy studies that primarily focus on clashes between *structure and agency*, for instance, when they juxtapose bureaucratic policy contexts (structure) and street-level bureaucrats or workers (agency) that work within these contexts (e.g., Gleeson & Knights, 2006).

On the one hand, there is policy 'regulation' and 'registration', whereas on the other hand, there is perceived 'leeway', 'space' or 'discretionary space' (e.g., Lipsky, 1980; Hill & Hupe, 2008), and the latter often gives way to the former. This means that workers are burdened and that they might experience 'policy alienation' (e.g., Tummers, 2013).

Effects of Reform and Rationalization

Set against these perspectives, we can go beyond the mere observation of conflict and competing logics; we can analyze how these conflicts play out and, especially, whether professionals are able to cope with reform effects. Kirkpatrick et al. (2005; see also Ackroyd et al., 2007), for example, find that there is an inverse relationship between public sector reform and effects in professional services. In a highly professionalized domain such as healthcare, they demonstrate there were large investments in reform but small effects. In a much less professionalized domain such as public housing, there were small reform investments and large effects. This is understandable because professionalism generates institutional defense mechanisms that can be used to keep organizational 'intrusions' out or to 'drag' intrusions 'in' to neutralize them. The first response occurs when medical doctors *resist* changes and ensure that certain systems are not implemented. The second response emerges when medical doctors appear to comply but with strategic intentions. They *manipulate* reforms. Waring and Currie (2009), for example, demonstrate that medical professionals might embrace safety management systems but do so primarily with an eye on neutralizing management. If they organize safety management themselves, they can keep managers out.

These responses reinforce the professional-managerial dualism (cf. Gleeson & Knights, 2006) and show how professionals and managers are involved in win/lose games. However, professionals have numerous opportunities to be more than passive subjects or victims of reform and 'use' conflicts to further their interests (e.g., Exworthy & Halford, 1999; Noordegraaf & Steijn, 2013). Professionals can resist or manipulate reforms, which prevents them from losing their professional status and stature. These observations are visualized in figure 13.3.

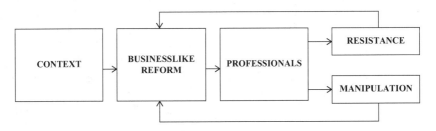

Figure 13.3   Primary responses to reform

This, in turn, leads to additional understandings of other professional (and managerial) responses, which go beyond resistance and/or manipulation. Authors coming from institutional theory have stressed how contradictory logics might be combined in daily practices. Even when there are conflicts between logics, they can be used in pragmatic ways. Reay and Hinings (2009), for example, describe the possibility of *'pragmatic collaboration'* between actors that represent businesslike and professional logics. This might be particularly likely in formalized settings in which multiple logics are consciously combined, such as professional service firms (e.g., Empson, Muzio, Broschak & Hinings, 2015). Various other authors (e.g., Skelcher & Smith, 2015) have shown how conflicting logics and principles can be addressed in multiple ways, based upon earlier insights on 'strategic responses' to complex challenges by, e.g., Oliver (1999; also Modell, 2001). Skelcher and Smith (2015), for instance, demonstrate how businesslike and professional logics can be contrasted, co-existing, combined or even blended.

Whether and how one of these *reform responses* actually occurs will depend on the nature of reform and the context and circumstances. This requires understanding the mechanisms that mediate links between reforms and effects. First, we can assume that reforms are *manufactured* on the basis of multiple reform discourses, including managerialism, entrepreneurialism and leaderism (O'Reilly & Reed, 2011). The effects of reform, moreover, are *mediated* by organizational circumstances. When there is strong leadership, for example, or when there are budgetary incentives, it might be easier to combine logics than when such factors are absent (see, e.g., Noordegraaf, 2015a; Bekkers & Noordegraaf, 2016).

Mediated Effects in Manufactured Reform Contexts

We must take care in opposing performance and professionalism logics or setting businesslike reform and professional action against one another. Although there are 'natural' tensions, there is no simple, let alone one-directional, relationship. Although many people assume—or believe—that managerial reform directly and negatively affects professional actions, we must seriously reconsider such assumptions. The various insights into potential relationships between reforms and professional actions, including those mentioned above (see also Shain & Gleeson, 1999; Leicht et al., 2009; Numerato et al., 2012, on the basis of e.g., Oliver, 1999) have shown (a) there are multiple forms of reform, (b) there are multiple responses of professionals to managerial reform, and (c) these responses and their effects are affected by circumstances.

In terms of reform, there is no single reform model, something that is also discussed elsewhere in this volume. There are multiple models, varying from strict businesslike sets of tools to entrepreneurial outlooks (e.g., Ferlie et al., 1996; Pollitt & Bouckaert, 2004; Noordegraaf, 2015b). In addition, these various models draw upon broader reform discourses, which carry multiple views on organizational and professional realities. O'Reilly and Reed (2011) distinguish among managerialism, entrepreneurialism and leaderism. They represent different reform narratives, which have different effects on professional action. The more reform focuses on businesslike tools, the fewer direct effects on professional work will be identified. However, in addition, these effects also depend on how reform models are used managerially. When they are implemented strictly, assuming that professionals comply, there will be different effects than when the usage of models and tools is seen as a *social* and *interactive process*, in which certain 'alien' tools are meaningfully linked to professional practices (see, e.g., De Bruijn, 2007; Moynihan, 2008; Noordegraaf, 2008).

Furthermore, effects depend upon how professionals react and respond. In terms of multiple responses, various authors (see references above) have explored how professionals and professional groups respond to reform projects, based upon empirical studies. Numerato et al. (2012) provide the most comprehensive overview, on the basis of a systemic literature review. They list the following responses, which have both socio-cultural and task-related dimensions (pp. 629–632):

1. *Managerial hegemony*, or *managerialization*: professional cultures are changed 'under the pressure of managerial hegemony.' Professionals are 'colonized' and their autonomies are reduced. Professional work is standardized.
2. *Co-optation of management culture*: professionals use the 'principles, discourses and logics of management', but they 'maintain their jurisdictions and exercise local control over their tasks.' 'Soft bureaucracy' is installed, for example, when control of professional work is decentralized, and expert teams are established.
3. *Negotiation*, or *hybrid identities* and *adaptive regulation*: professional and managerial cultures are 'merged'. Professionals accept managerial responsibilities and professionals such as medical doctors move into part-time or full-time managerial positions. Technical tools, such as accountancy tools, 'do not infringe on professional judgement.'
4. *Strategic adaptation*, or *reverse managerialization*: professionals 'retain external facets of managerial ideology and discourse while their perspective, identity and culture remain unaffected.' They use the instruments of the 'colonizers' to 'question their authority and build independence.' Professionals control and implement regulatory tools.
5. *Professional opposition*, or *resistance to management*: professionals are 'reluctant to implement management techniques.' The two 'conflicting cultures—professional and management—are struggling to attain power.' Policies and tools 'violate' professional autonomies.

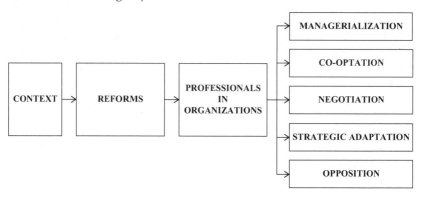

Figure 13.4   Multiple reform responses

This is visualized in figure 13.4. Which reform responses actually occur and which effects are generated, for example, whether real pragmatic or productive collaboration takes place, depends on context. This is not so much a matter of sectoral contexts, such as the healthcare or social work context (as in the Ackroyd et al., 2007, example used above) or national context (e.g., Leicht et al., 2009) but *organizational* and *work contexts*. Whether and how managerial approaches and tools are used, and whether they are used meaningfully, depends on various factors that can vary within a given sector or organization within that organization. On the basis of (empirical) studies, one can think of factors such as leadership, organizational forms, budget and culture. The weaker these factors are, the stronger the conflicts between professional and organizational agendas will be.

Beyond Dualisms

Finally, in addition to these mediated effects of manufactured reform in context, we might go one step further. Instead of regarding performance and professional logics as 'competing' and combinations as 'hybrid' or 'productive', we might challenge dualisms as such (cf. Gleeson & Knights, 2006) and deconstruct distinctions such as 'managerialism versus professionalism.' Instead of presupposing the existence of various logics and, thus, potential clashes or combinations, we might wonder whether these logics are natural and stable phenomena. Logics and principles themselves might also be seen as constructions that are the outcomes of historical processes and that comprise features that 'belong' to them, mainly because we 'believe' they belong to them. These beliefs are societally grounded and reproduced through public debates and professional education. The fact that we link professionalism to cases and quality and the fact that we keep organizing out of professional work is illustrative of such processes. We might also assume that logics can be construed or configured differently; we might assume that realizing performance might be part of professional action and that taking up organizational tasks belongs to effective professional behavior. Below, under 'key themes', we explore the rise of *organizing* professionalism (cf. Noordegraaf, 2015a, and, e.g., Kurunmäki, 2004), which shows how professionals can *co-organize* public actions. This is aimed at better responding to changing contexts, which affect professional work directly, instead of merely addressing businesslike reforms as such (see figure 13.5).

Public Professionalism and Effects on Reform

Public sector reform not only affects professionalism and expertise; professionalism also affects reform. This is the case not only when professionals cope with reform but also when reform itself is professionalized and when 'reform professionals' become active. This especially occurs when so-called 'organizational professionals' (e.g., Larson, 1977; Reed, 1996), including managers, controllers and consultants, begin to professionalize—i.e., form self-regulated professional domains—to become more effective in operating and reforming public organizations. This changes our basic scheme, as indicated in figure 13.6.

Reform Professionals

The professionalization of public managers, for instance, has generated its own research strands, which seek to understand the nature and processes of

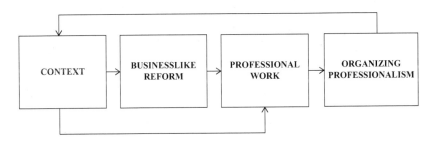

Figure 13.5   (Re)organizing professionalism

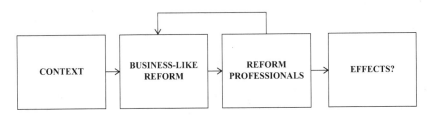

Figure 13.6   The professionalization of reform

managerial professionalization (e.g., Grey, 1997; Noordegraaf, 2006; Van der Meulen, 2009; Jarl et al., 2012; Van der Scheer, 2013; Oldenhof, 2015). Despite pessimistic statements, including statements by Mintzberg, who argued that managers will 'never be real professionals' (1996), we observe a *de facto* professionalization process in various managerial and executive fields. This draws from professionalization in other, more traditional fields such as medicine and accountancy. Executives and managers such as health-care and police managers form associations and become members of these associations; they establish educational programs and formalize certification and accreditation; they present codes of conduct and codes of ethics; they hand out awards and prizes, and they blame and punish bad performers. More specific case studies, such as that by Jarl et al. (2012: 440–442), reveal how this leads to actual professionalization projects that generate managerial forms of professional ethics and develops professional knowledge 'centred on ideas of managerialism' and managerial tools.

All of this does not necessarily create 'good' managers—on the contrary. It can at best create conditions for 'appropriate' management. This is explained by the fact that professionalization mechanisms never directly create 'professional' workers, as well as by the fact that it might be unclear what 'good' work means. This is especially the case in managerial contexts, in which methods, procedures and techniques are difficult to link to more generic prescriptions (e.g., Whitley, 1989). Performing an effective knee operation is relatively unconnected to the context and, thus, easy to standardize, whereas adapting an organizational culture is highly connected to context and, therefore, difficult to standardize. Nevertheless, the right professional conditions might stimulate the rise of more conscious and reflexive managers who are able to address the specificities of organizational challenges and to learn from managerial acts and effects. Even when businesslike reform creates managers, there are multiple ways for managers to respond to and cope with reforms (cf. Modell, 2001).

Professional Reform

Connections between professional practices and organizational contexts do not merely relate to manager/professional interactions and the professionalization of management. They also relate to the professionalization of organizations and organizational actions. The well-known transition from 'organizations of professionals' to 'professional organizations' (e.g., Evetts, 2009; 2011) calls for various organizational transitions that enable administrative and service organizations to install governance and management systems that go beyond mere corporate control. To allow professionals to cope with the specifics of cases and act on the basis of insights and discretionary spaces, while simultaneously establishing organizational parameters and serving more overarching (strategic) objectives, organizations need to find ways to establish meaningful incentive and performance management systems. This also includes experts and officials who work for and in the organization and support organizational processes in 'professional' ways.

Partly, this concerns 'real' professionals, such as HR officials, controllers and accountants who support the personnel and financial dimensions of running an organization. Partly, this concerns professional experts and knowledge workers, such as strategists, project managers, safety officials, risk officers and change agents that support other relevant dimensions (see, e.g., Hodgson, 2002, 2005; Noordegraaf, Van der Steen & Van Twist, 2014). They are members of professional fields, which intend to improve reforms of organizational systems and reform processes.

Together they are part of a *reform industry* that largely goes its own way. This industry ensures that ideas travel and are adopted in such a way that organizational and political agendas are served. Professional groups and groups of experts might form (epistemic) communities busy with sharing ideas and optimizing methods. This is paradoxical, as it inserts the weaknesses of professionalism into the reform of professional services. It tends to isolate professional reform groups from other reform groups, as well as from other (professional) groups, whereas their professional authority and effectiveness lies in *connections* with multiple stakeholders. When HR professionals or controllers become part of occupational domains that are too self-regulated, and, therefore, too self-referential, they disconnect themselves from the work contexts and domains that they are supposed to serve.

Connecting Professional Reform to Professional Action

In short, the professionalization of reform tends to separate reform disciplines and communities that steer reform from other disciplines and communities within and around public organizations. Specifically, two potential *disconnects* are created (see, e.g., Lindemann, 2014). First, these reform disciplines and communities are not automatically linked to professional work. Their actions do not automatically have meaningful effects on professional practices. In fact, professionals might be burdened with reform interventions that they regard as 'intrusive' and 'alien'. Second, these disciplines and communities are not automatically linked to one another. The various reform groups might work independently from one another, while they have an (cumulative) effect on professional work. In that sense, it is not so much reform that is problematic but *disconnected reform* (see figure 13.7).

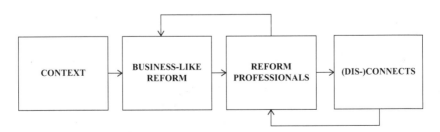

Figure 13.7 The professionalization of reform (II)

The crucial component of professionally mobilizing professional workers and organizational professionals (e.g., Larson, 1977) relates to the question of whether they can maintain *corporate/collegiate* connections that are crucial for viable professional services. Driven by businesslike models and templates, organizational professionals will tend to work toward corporate control. They will set targets, make plans, monitor processes, measure results and control actions. They will contribute to the establishment of PDCA (plan-do-check-act) systems and mentalities, which will be used to optimize professional service delivery. For professional workers, this will be burdensome, as they will not feel that they 'own' service delivery and because PDCA systems as such will have little meaning. Driven by more subtle professional/organizational models, including hybrid professional management, managed professional businesses and professional service firms (e.g., De Bruijn, 2007; Empson et al., 2015), organizational professionals might also opt for respecting the collegiate logic of professional work and work toward more quality-based management systems, dynamic measurement and committed professionals.

Key Trends: Reconfigured Forms of Public Professionalism

The exploration of the previous three crucial aspects of public sector reforms and relations with professional action generates three crucial observations. First, professionalism is a regulative phenomenon, which means that reforms will change how work is regulated in one way or another. Second, reform projects will, in a general sense, cause conflicts between organizations and professionals because businesslike performance standards will be set, which are at odds with the nature of professional work, but this does not mean that professionalism is weakened. There are many possibilities for professional groups to respond: they might resist or manipulate reform projects; they might deploy multiple *reform responses*. Third, public management reform itself is subjected to professionalization processes. So-called reform professionals—such as managers—affect how reforms take place, and there is a reform industry busy with professionalizing reforms. If this generates *disconnects*, however, professional reforms can be said to be problematic. Below, we go beyond these observations by exploring the reconfiguration of public professionalism that flows not so much from reform projects and programs but from social and societal changes. In addition to the research strands that were mentioned when professional services and work were debated, there are strands of research that link professionalism to broader (changing) conditions in new ways (e.g., Adler et al., 2008; Faulconbridge & Muzio, 2008, 2012; Noordegraaf, 2015a). They highlight recent developments that alter professional landscapes and actions in more fundamental ways. We use this, first, to elaborate the notion of 'organizing professionalism' that was discussed above to stress the importance of tendencies to re-define professional capabilities. We discuss *organizing capabilities* that no longer belong to 'the organization' but become part of professional competencies. Next, we go beyond new links between organizations/ organizing and professionalism and discuss the increasing embeddedness of professional action within service networks. We explore *networked professionals* and what this means for professional expertise and specialization. Finally, we discuss increasing connections between professional action and society. Professionalism becomes *participatory* professionalism that is linked to outside worlds and stakeholders. These tendencies are not directly caused by management reform, but they have major consequences for service delivery and the management of welfare programs.

Professional Capabilities

Instead of merely 'blaming' New Public Management for harming professional work or resisting businesslike influences, authors have also begun to adopt wider and more contextual understandings of professionalism, stressing the fragmentation of professional fields and dependencies upon outside worlds (e.g., Noordegraaf, 2015b; also Faulconbridge & Muzio, 2012). Economic, demographic, social, cultural and technological shifts have created new professional challenges, including the necessity to collaborate, detect and address risks, prioritize cases and account for actions. In addition, social, cultural and demographic changes within professions imply that professionals need to better organize their work. When older and younger medical doctors want to have more regular working hours and work/life balance, (younger) doctors are not always available and the division of work (including working hours) needs to be organized. This means that professionalism as 'occupational self-control' is no longer primarily focused on cases and case treatment but on changing and multiple cases in demanding contexts. Professionalism becomes *organizing professionalism* (cf. Noordegraaf, 2015b). Professional workers become co-responsible for organizing service delivery, not only because managers want this but also because work demands and professional interests require this.

Such reform implications shed new light on the much-debated 'dark sides' of New Public Management (cf. Diefenbach, 2009). Reform encompasses more than New Public Management, and reforms call for organizing abilities and might concern new competencies. In healthcare, for example, new models for defining medical competencies are embraced by medical associations throughout the world, such as the CanMEDS model, introduced by the Canadian medical association (see Noordegraaf, 2015a). It enriches medical repertoires by adding new competencies to technical and communicative skills, *inter alia*, collaboration, advocacy and management.

This makes organizing a part of professional action. Similarly, there is an increasing stress on *positive coping* by professionals—instead of negative coping with constraints—and commitment to change instead of resistance to change. Fueled by new combinations of administrative, sociological and psychological insights, scholars increasingly study how professional (street-level) workers cope with difficult circumstances in positive ways (for an overview, see Noordegraaf, Van Loon, Heerema & Weggemans, 2015). By linking insights on street-level bureaucracy (e.g., Lipsky, 1980), the sociology of professions (e.g., Ackroyd et al., 2007) and occupational psychology (e.g., Greenglass & Fiksenbaum, 2009), we can understand how professional workers in the front lines deliver high-quality services, despite policy regimes and administrative burdens, as well as by using bureaucratic and managerial systems. They might ignore certain influences, interpret other influences in productive ways and use registration obligations to trace processes, based upon their personality and motivation, education and expertise, and networks and relations (cf. Noordegraaf et al., 2015).

Networked Professionals

Increasingly, public policies and services are formed in network relations, and increasingly, professionals and experts become part of networks. Due to reforms, they find themselves in 'joined up processes' that are established to 'help manage fragmentation' (Considine & Lewis, 2012: 1). Authors examining this topic distinguish among multiple networking types that they relate to front-line staff: *basic networking, public networking,* and *civic networking.* Other authors have also studied such 'collaborative governance', and although they do not always focus on professionalism, they sometimes analyze the role of professional action within networks (e.g., Ansell & Gash, 2012). Ansell and Gash (2012), for example, summarize the conditions for viable collaborative processes, which they regard as cyclical processes in which trust and commitment must be enhanced—in addition to the proper institutional conditions. This occurs when network partners establish quick wins and consciously work on face-to-face communication. The importance of trust is also emphasized by scholars and is not easy to enact when multiple partners—including professionals—have different agendas, interests and viewpoints. In addition, there are difficulties in sharing information, something that is crucial for establishing trust.

These difficulties can be overcome, according to other authors, by introducing *boundary-spanning* activities, by having both boundary spanners who represent network interests and affect collaboration (Williams, 2002) and boundary objects, such as documents, technologies, rules and projects, which generate inter-professional communication (Kimble, Grenier & Goglio-Primard, 2010). In the case of health networks in which medical professionals work together, there needs to be 'efficient transmission of information and social and professional interaction within and across networks' (Cunningham et al., 2012: 239). Finally, addressing these challenges calls for facilitative leadership (cf. Koppenjan & Klijn, 2004; Ansell & Gash, 2012), which ensures that professionals turn their repertoires into more flexible repertoires and work on improved collaboration, despite all the various barriers.

Participatory Professionalism

Finally, public sector reforms give rise to developments that extend professionalism beyond formal professional and organizational systems. Driven by both financial and societal motives, in domains such as welfare and social work, policy makers and politicians attempt to create a movement that is aimed at either 'co-producing' and 'co-creating' services (e.g., Bovaird & Löffler, 2012; Pestoff, 2012, 2014; Vennik, Van de Bovenkamp, Putters & Grit, 2015) or 'empowering' citizens to solve their own problems (e.g., Newman, 2004; Tonkens, 2010). To address public health issues, or unemployment, youth violence and labor market activation, they attempt to stimulate citizens to take action, supported by other citizens, instead of by specialized professionals who are educated and paid to address these problems. Many welfare reforms in Western countries adopt this more active, citizen-oriented, participatory approach when welfare regimes are restructured. In the UK, the Cameron government began to stress the 'Big Society'. In The Netherlands, politicians and policy-makers speak of the 'Participatory Society'. A few Dutch municipalities are developing 'urban professionals', who are connected to societal challenges, citizens and communities and are able to activate and facilitate societal action.

This has major consequences for public professional action, as it lessens the dependencies on professional insights and expertise, as it breaks through the so-called professional silos of specialized insights and expertise and because it seeks to link societal ambitions to a more active citizenry. At most, existing professionals will act as *back-up professionals* in the event of complex cases, and new professionals appear on the scene, such as activation officials and 'coaches', who facilitate the rise of active citizens. As does New Public Management, this has many dark sides, as it negates the wickedness of social problems and ignores the structural dimensions of empowering citizens—that is, the structural bases of being able to act as empowered citizens. Money and wealth, for example, might be structurally important for this.

With these various key trends, we are far removed from pure professionalism, although it largely affects 'real professionals'. Instead of relying on occupational and disciplinary regulation to isolate professional domains and work from outside environments, regulation is used to *connect* professional action to clients, outsiders and stakeholders.

Conclusion

At first sight, there are clear links between public management reform and professionalism. Public management reform is a matter of businesslike performance, which is at odds with the nature and logic of professional work. Professionals face control and burdens of control, as well as alienation, and their autonomies should be restored. This is too simple, however.

First, there are different forms of professionalism, and there are different paths to reforming professional work and fields. Reforms attempt to *re-regulate* professional action, which is already regulated. The question is not so much whether professionals face new standards but whether there (a) are meaningful (new) standards set by relevant others, and (b) how are (new) standards practically applied? This also concerns endogenous reform movements that originate *within* professional fields. Stricter and more systematic approaches to organizing professional work might also emerge from new professional outlooks, varying from work methods (such as evidence-based medicine) to working hours and careers.

Second, public management reforms have different effects, also depending upon the nature and strength of professional action. There is no unilateral effect in the sense that reform disciplines and de-professionalizes professional work. Depending on the nature of professionalism and the reliance on institutional mechanisms, managerial and professional logics might be related in multiple ways. There might be resistance or manipulation but also combination and hybridization.

Third, professionalization also affects reform, in the sense that reform processes as such demand knowledge and expertise, as well as (professional) workers who know how to design and implement reform. In this regard, one can think of consultants, managers, process managers, controllers and auditors. In addition, experts such as safety officials and occupational psychologists might be hired to address specific reform demands, varying from designing safety systems to improving motivation. All of this has generated a reform industry that is little studied. This industry ensures that reform ideas travel and makes reform trends more massive and monolithic.

Fourth, forms of professionalism and professional work are changing, not so much in terms of reform projects and programs but due to broader social and societal changes. Instead of merely regarding professional action as treating cases and clients, we understand professional work as organizing work, aimed at securing sound professional processes. Furthermore, these processes increasingly occur within network settings, which require new connections between professional and other domains. Finally, these professional work forms are increasingly opened up; services are co-created by professional groups and clients; citizens take active ownership in realizing public action.

Implications

In terms of implications, we might focus on *reformed professionalism*, not so much from a 'dark sides of reform' perspective but from a perspective that highlights *reconfigured professionalism*. Instead of regarding a professional logic as unavoidably and objectively at odds with a businesslike and managerial logic, organizing services might become part of professional action. When professional workers are taught to look beyond mere case treatment and learn how to address multiple cases in demanding contexts, organizational reform becomes a less managerial and more professional endeavor. Priorities need to be established, preferences need to be addressed, and public exposure—for instance of risks and incidents—needs to be anticipated and/or mitigated. This is not only relevant because managerial values, such as efficiency, are at stake but also because multiple values have to be combined to deliver high-quality services. Efficiency and legitimacy might be seen as dimensions of quality. Medical doctors deliver 'good' work when they treat patients well, on time, at low costs and with appropriate patient experiences. Judges work 'successfully' when they deliver good verdicts on time that are understandable and effective in resolving conflicts. Interestingly, this will help public management reform, as organizing is no longer occurring around professionals and outside of professional action but is incorporated into professional practices. Moreover, realizing this is no mere element of reform projects, as it calls for re-educated professionals with re-adjusted routines and standards that are not established by organizations. Professional schooling and education are crucial vehicles for realizing reform.

Second, we might focus on *professional reform*, as addressing reform demands and implementing reform can be practiced in professional ways to a greater or lesser extent. We have particularly emphasized that the professionalization of reform projects is vulnerable to generating disconnects in one way or another. When professional reform actions are disconnected from one another *and* when they are disconnected from professional actions, there will be many negative effects, such as job dis-satisfaction, stress and burnout, and many lost opportunities. This means that the professionalization of reform, in light of improving and, therefore, reconfiguring professional capabilities, is a matter of building sound connections. These connections only acquire new meaning when services are rendered in network settings and when societal stakeholders take an active role in (co-) creating public action.

Professionals with new capabilities become part of networks in which disciplines must be combined, *and* they are linked to societal stakeholders that are increasingly empowered to take matters into their own hands. Public professionalism becomes participatory, which is far removed from the original meanings of professionalism and traditional professionalization trajectories. This calls for new regulatory processes. Instead of building professional domains that regulate themselves, closed off from outside worlds, we need regulatory processes that build domains *in relation to* outside worlds. Instead of merely regulating how such domains can effectively treat cases and clients, we need to regulate how such domains treat difficult cases and clients, in broader contexts that call for accountability, collaboration and financial stringency. This in itself is also a reform project that underlines the need for professional reform. Professionally reforming forms of professionalism is one of the new essences of public sector reform.

Note

1. The author thanks the editors of this volume for their valuable comments on an earlier version of this chapter, as well as Dr Karin Geuijen (USG) for her additional input. He thanks Mirthe de Kok for her editorial support.

References

Ackroyd, S., Kirkpatrick, I., & Walker, R.M. (2007). Public management reform in the UK and its consequences for professional organization: A comparative analysis. *Public Administration, 85*(1), 9–26.

Adler, P.S., Kwon, S.W., & Heckscher, C. (2008). Perspective-professional work: The emergence of collaborative community. *Organization Science, 19*(2), 359–376.

Ansell, C., & Gash, A. (2012). Stewards, mediators, and catalysts: Toward a model of collaborative leadership. *The Innovation Journal, 71*(1).

Bekkers, V., & Noordegraaf, M. (2016). Public managers and professionals in collaborative innovation. In J. Torfing and P. Triantafillou (Eds.), *Enhancing innovation by transforming public governance*. Cambridge: Cambridge University Press.

Blomgren, M., & Waks, C. (2015). Coping with contradictions: Hybrid professionals managing institutional complexity. *Journal of Professions and Organization, 2*(1), 78–102.

Bovaird, T., & Löffler, E. (2012). From engagement to co-production: How users and communities contribute to public services. In V. Pestoff, T. Brandsen and B. Verschuere (Eds.), *New public governance, the third sector and co-production* (pp. 35–60). London: Routledge.

Brandsen, T., Van de Donk, W., & Putters, K. (2005). Griffins or chameleons? Hybridity as a permanent and inevitable characteristic of the third sector. *International Journal of Public Administration, 28*(9–10), 749–765.

Brint, S.G. (1994). *In an age of experts*. New Jersey: Princeton University Press.

Broadbent, J., Dietrich, M., & Roberts, J. (2005). *The end of the professions? The restructuring of professional work*. London: Routledge.

Burrage, M., & Torstendahl, R. (1990). *Professions in theory and history: Rethinking the study of the professions*. London: Sage Publications.

Christensen, T., & Lægreid, P. (2007). *Transcending new public management: The transformation of public sector reforms*. Aldershot: Ashgate.

Clarke, J. (2005). Performing for the public: Doubt, desire, and the evaluation of public services. In P. Du Gay (Ed.), *The Values of Bureaucracy* (pp. 211–232). Oxford: Oxford University Press.

Clarke, J., & Newman, J. (1997). *The managerial state: Power, politics and ideology in the remaking of social welfare*. London: Sage Publications.

Considine, M., & Lewis, J.M. (2012). Networks and interactivity: Ten years of street-level governance in the United Kingdom, the Netherlands and Australia. *Public Management Review, 14*(1), 1–22.

Cunningham, F.C., Ranmuthugala, G., Plumb, J., Georgiou, A., Westbrook, J.I., & Braithwaite, J. (2012). Health professional networks as a vector for improving healthcare quality and safety: A systematic review. *BMJ Quality & Safety, 21*(3), 239–249.

De Bruijn, J.A. (2007). *Managing performance in the public sector.* 2nd edition. London: Routledge.

Diefenbach, T. (2009). New public management in public sector organizations: The dark side of managerialistic 'enlightenment'. *Public Administration, 87*(4), 892–909.

Empson, L., Muzio, D., Broschak, J., & Hinings, B. (2015). *Oxford handbook of professional service firms*. Oxford: Oxford University Press.

Etzioni, A. (1969). *The semi-professions and their organization: Teachers, nurses, social workers.* New York: The Free Press.

Evetts, J. (2009). New professionalism and new public management: Changes, continuities and consequences. *Comparative Sociology, 8,* 247–266.

Evetts, J. (2011). A new professionalism? Challenges and opportunities. *Current Sociology, 59*(4), 406–422.

Exworthy, M., & Halford, S. (Eds.). (1999). *Professionals and the new managerialism in the public sector.* Buckingham: Open University Press.

Faulconbridge, J., & Muzio, D. (2008). Organizational professionalism in globalizing law firms. *Work, Employment & Society, 22*(1), 7–25.

Faulconbridge, J., & Muzio, D. (2012). Professions in a globalizing world: Towards a transnational sociology of the professions. *International Sociology, 27*(1), 136–152.

Ferlie, E., Ashburner, L., Fitzgerald, L., & Pettigrew, A. (1996). *The new public management in action.* Oxford: Oxford University Press.

Freidson, E. (2001). *Professionalism: The third logic.* Cambridge: Polity.

Gleeson, D., & Knights, D. (2006). Challenging dualism: Public professionalism in 'troubled' times. *Sociology, 40*(2), 277–295.

Goldfinch, S., & Wallis, J. (Eds.). (2009). *International handbook of public sector reform.* Cheltenham: Edward Elgar Publishing.

Greenglass, E.R., & Fiksenbaum, L. (2009). Proactive coping, positive affect, and well-being: Testing for mediation using path analysis. *European Psychologist, 14*(1), 29–39.

Grey, C. (1997). Management as a technical practice: Professionalization or responsibilization? *Systemic Practice and Action Research, 10*(6), 703–725.

Harrison, S., & Pollitt, C. (1994). *Controlling health professionals.* Buckingham: Open University Press.

Heite, C. (2012). Setting and crossing boundaries: Professionalization of social work and social work professionalism. *Social Work & Society, 10*(2).

Hill, M., & Hupe, P. (2008). *Implementing public policy: An introduction to the study of operational governance.* London: Sage.

Hodgson, D. (2002). Disciplining the professional: The case of project management. *Journal of Management Studies, 39*(6), 803–821.

Hodgson, D. (2005). Putting on a professional performance: Performativity, subversion and project management. *Organization, 12*(1), 51–68.

Hood, C. (1991). A public management for all seasons? *Public Administration, 69*(1), 3–19.

Hood, C. (2002). The risk game and the blame game. *Government and Opposition, 37*(1), 15–37.

Jarl, M., Fredriksson, A., & Persson, S. (2012). New public management in public education: A catalyst for the professionalization of Swedish school principals. *Public Administration, 90*(2), 429–444.

Kickert, W.J.M. (1995). Steering at a distance: A new paradigm of public governance in Dutch higher education. *Governance, 8*(1), 135–157.

Kickert, W.J.M. (2001). Public management of hybrid organizations: Governance of quasi-autonomous executive agencies. *International Public Management Journal, 4*(2), 135–150.

Kickert, W.J.M. (Ed.). (1997). *Public management and administrative reform in Western Europe.* Cheltenham: Edward Elgar.

Kimble, C., Grenier, C., & Goglio-Primard, K. (2010). Innovation and knowledge sharing across professional boundaries: Political interplay between boundary objects and brokers. *International Journal of Information Management, 30*(5), 437–444.

Kirkpatrick, I., Ackroyd, S., & Walker, R. (2005). *The new managerialism and public service professions.* Basingstoke: Palgrave Macmillan.

Koppenjan, J.F.M., & Klijn, E.H. (2004). *Managing uncertainties in networks: A network approach to problem solving and decision making.* London: Routledge.

Krause, E.A. (1996). *Death of the guilds: Professions, states and the advance of capitalism.* New Haven: Yale University Press.

Kurunmäki, L. (2004). A hybrid profession—the acquisition of management accounting expertise by medical professionals. *Accounting, Organizations and Society, 29*(3), 327–347.

Larson, M.S. (1977). *The rise of professionalism: A sociological analysis.* Berkeley: University of California Press.

Leicht, K.T., Walter, T., Sainsaulieu, I., & Davies, S. (2009). New public management and new professionalism across nations and contexts. *Current Sociology, 57*(4), 581–605.

Leistikow, I.P., Kalkman, C.J., & De Bruijn, H. (2011). Why patient safety is such a tough nut to crack. *BMJ (Clinical Research Ed.), 342,* d3447.

Lewis, J.M. (2002). Policy and profession: Elite perspectives on redefining general practice in Australia and England. *Journal of Health Services Research & Policy,* 7(suppl 1), 8–13.

Lewis, J.M., Marjoribanks, T., & Pirotta, M. (2003). Changing professions general practitioners' perceptions of autonomy on the frontline. *Journal of Sociology, 39*(1), 44–61.

Lindemann, B. (2014). *Lost in translation. How public professional services reconfigure professional practices.* Doctoral dissertation. Utrecht: Utrecht University.

Lipsky, M. (1980). *Street-level bureaucracy.* New York: Russell Sage.

Mintzberg, H. (1996). Managing government, governing management. *Harvard Business Review, 74*(3), 75–83.

Modell, S. (2001). Performance measurement and institutional processes: A study of managerial responses to public sector reform. *Management Accounting Research, 12*(4), 437–464.

Moynihan, D.P. (2008). *The dynamics of performance management: Constructing information and reform.* Washington, DC: Georgetown University Press.

Muzio, D., & Kirkpatrick, I. (2011). Introduction: Professions and organizations-a conceptual framework. *Current Sociology, 59*(4), 389–405.

Newman, J. (2004). Modernizing the state: A new style of governance. In J. Lewis and R. Surender (Ed.), *Welfare State Change: Towards a Third Way* (pp. 69–88). Oxford: Oxford University Press.

Noordegraaf, M. (2006). Professional management of professionals: Hybrid organization and professional management in care and welfare. In J.W. Duyvendak, T. Knijn and M. Kremer (Eds.), *Policy, people, and the new professional: De-professionalisation and re-professionalisation in care and welfare* (pp. 181–193). Amsterdam: Amsterdam University Press.

Noordegraaf, M. (2008). *Professioneel bestuur. De tegenstelling tussen publieke managers en professionals als 'strijd om professionaliteit'.* The Hague: Lemma.

Noordegraaf, M. (2011). Risky business: How professionals and professionals fields (must) deal with organizational issues. *Organization Studies, 32*(10), 1349–1371.

Noordegraaf, M. (2013). Reconfiguring professional work: Changing forms of professionalism in public services. *Administration & Society,* online first.

Noordegraaf, M. (2015a). Hybridity and beyond: (New) forms of professionalism in changing organizational and societal contexts. *Journal of Professions and Organizations, 2*(2), 187–206.

Noordegraaf, M. (2015b). *Public management: Performance, professionalism, politics.* Basingstoke: Palgrave McMillan.

Noordegraaf, M., & De Wit, B. (2012). *Van maakbaar naar betekenisvol bestuur-63,* Den Haag: WRR.

Noordegraaf, M., Schneider, M.M.E., Van Rensen, E.L.J., & Boselie, J.P.P.E.F. (2015). Cultural complementarity: Reshaping professional and organizational logics in developing frontline medical leadership. *Public Management Review*, online first.

Noordegraaf, M., & Steijn, B. (Eds.). (2013). *Professionals under pressure: The reconfiguration of professional work in changing public services*. Amsterdam: Amsterdam University Press.

Noordegraaf, M., Van der Steen, M., & Van Twist, M. (2014). Fragmented or connective professionalism? Strategies for professionalizing the work of strategists and other (organizational) professionals. *Public Administration, 92*(1), 21–38.

Noordegraaf, M., Van Loon, N., Heerema, M., & Weggemans, M. (2015). Proactieve 'coping' door publieke professionals. *Beleid & Maatschappij, 42*(4), 287–309.

Numerato, D., Salvatore, D., & Fattore, G. (2012). The impact of management on medical professionalism: A review. *Sociology of Health & Illness, 34*(4), 626–644.Oldenhof, L. (2015). *The multiple middle: Managing in healthcare*. Doctoral dissertation. Rotterdam: Erasmus University Rotterdam.

Oliver, E.W. (1999). Public and private bureaucracies: A transaction cost economics perspective. *Journal of Law, Economics, and Organization, 15*(1), 306–342.

Ongaro, E. (2009). *Public management reform and modernization: Trajectories of administrative change in Italy, France, Greece, Portugal and Spain*. Cheltenham: Edward Elgar Publishing.

O'Reilly, D., & Reed, M. (2011). The grit in the oyster: Professionalism, managerialism and leaderism as discourses of UK public services modernization. *Organization Studies, 32*(8), 1079–1101.

Pache, A.C., & Santos, F. (2013). Embedded in hybrid contexts: How individuals in organizations respond to competing institutional logics. *Research in the Sociology of Organizations, 39*, 3–35.

Pestoff, V. (2012). Co-production and third sector social services in Europe—some crucial conceptual issues. In V. Pestoff, T. Brandsen and B. Verschuere (Eds.), *New public governance, the third sector and co-production* (pp. 13–34). London: Routledge.

Pestoff, V. (2014). Hybridity, coproduction, and third sector social services in Europe. *American Behavioral Scientist, 58*(11), 1412–1424.

Pollitt, C., & Bouckaert, G. (2004). *Public management reform: A comparative analysis*. Oxford: Oxford University Press.

Pollitt, C., Van Thiel, S., & Homburg, V. (2007). New public management in Europe. *Management Online Review*, 1–6.

Reay, T., & Hinings, C.R. (2009). Managing the rivalry of competing institutional logics. *Organization Studies, 30*(6), 629–652.

Reed, M. (1996). Expert power and control in late modernity: An empirical review and theoretical synthesis. *Organization Studies, 17*(4), 573–597.

Ritzer, G., & Walczak, D. (1988). Rationalization and the deprofessionalization of physicians. *Social Forces, 67*(1), 1–22.

Shain, F., & Gleeson, D. (1999). Under new management: Changing conceptions of teacher professionalism and policy in the further education sector. *Journal of Education Policy, 14*(4), 445–462.

Skelcher, C., & Smith, S.R. (2015). Theorizing hybridity: Intuitional logics, complex organizations, and actor identities: The case of nonprofits. *Public Administration, 93*(2), 433–448.

Tonkens, E. (2010). De kwaliteit van burgerparticipatie in de stad: de casus bewonersbudgetten. *Bestuurskunde, 19*(4), 34–42.

Tummers, L. (2013). *Policy alienation and the power of professionals: Confronting new policies*. Cheltenham: Edward Elgar Publishing.

Van der Meulen, M. (2009). *Achter de schermen: Vakontwikkeling en professionalisering van publieke managers in de zorg en bij de politie.* Delft: Eburon.

Van der Scheer, W. (2013). *Onder Zorgbestuurders: Omgaan met bestuurlijke ambiguïteit in de zorg.* Rotterdam: Instituut Beleid en Management Gezondheidszorg (iBMG).

Vennik, F.D., Van de Bovenkamp, H.M., Putters, K., & Grit, K.J. (2015). Co-production in healthcare: Rhetoric and practice. *International Review of Administrative Sciences, online first.*

Walker, R.M., & Boyne, G.A. (2006). Public management reform and organizational performance: An empirical assessment of the UK Labour government's public service improvement strategy. *Journal of Policy Analysis and Management, 25*(2), 371–393.

Waring, J., & Currie, G. (2009). Managing expert knowledge: Organizational challenges and managerial futures for the UK medical profession. *Organization Studies, 30*(7), 755–778.

Watson, T. (2002). Professions and professionalism: Should we jump off the bandwagon, better to study where it is going? *International Studies of Management and Organization, 32*(2), 93–105.

Whitley, R. (1989). On the nature of managerial tasks and skills: Their distinguishing characteristics and organization. *Journal of Management Studies, 26*(3), 209–224.

Williams, P. (2002). The competent boundary spanner. *Public Administration, 80*(1), 103–124.

14 Recent Shifts in Public Financial Management

Tiina Randma-Liiv and Geert Bouckaert

Introduction

The recent financial crisis has forced public administrations from across the globe to cut budgets, restructure service delivery strategies, rethink priorities and assume enormous new financial responsibilities. This experience reemphasizes the centrality of financial resources to public service delivery and, consequently, of the various functions of public management, brings public financial management to the fore.

Whereas the patterns of reform in financial management that have occurred in recent decades have been relatively well-documented in the academic literature (e.g., Rubin & Kelly, 2007; Pollitt & Bouckaert, 2011), more recent shifts are less well-known. This chapter will first investigate how the financial cycle has been modernized and then address the latest changes in public financial management to determine whether and how the financial crisis has affected existing practices and reform trajectories in public financial management. Three broader shifts—the financial cycle becoming more accrual-based, more linked to performance and more participatory—have laid the ground for more immediate changes in public financial management caused by the crisis.

Countries seeking to relieve the pressure of budgetary imbalances are attempting combinations of prioritization, spending caps, cutbacks and tax reforms, with cutbacks being the most common measure (OECD, 2011; Kickert & Randma-Liiv, 2015). We are interested in whether such actions beyond 'fiscal normalcy' have also affected the existing processes of public financial management. It is now clear that such fiscal stress was not a temporary and/or short-term influence; it will remain an important contextual factor for several years to come, as many governments around the world will continue to struggle with debts and deficits, and the need for cutbacks has not disappeared in the eight years since the start of the 2008 financial crisis. Although the economic figures show signs of recovering economic growth, the influence of fiscal stress on public administration and management is likely to continue for several years (Pollitt, 2010). If Posner and Blöndal are correct in arguing that 'In contrast to previous recessions, the return of strong growth will not end the fiscal gaps facing these nations but will serve as the prelude for even more difficult and wrenching choices' (2012: 11), then the immediate effects of fiscal crisis may signify longer-term and more general changes in public administration and, specifically, in public financial management.

Before examining the shifts caused by the financial crisis in greater detail, we provide an overview on the longer-term trends in public financial management reform.

Managing Finances: Modernizing the Financial Cycle

Recent decades have witnessed various attempts to reform public budgeting and financial management, which have been more broadly affected by New Public Management (NPM) reforms. The more substantial changes include moving from simple line-item budgeting under a centralized government bureaucracy to program and performance budgeting, performance contracts, contracting with the business and nonprofit sectors, more entrepreneurial management, output and outcome measurement and fiscal decentralization (Rubin & Kelly, 2007; Pollitt & Bouckaert, 2011). These reforms drew on an economic, largely public choice, rationale and were intended to reduce the size and cost of the public sector by reshaping the incentive structure underpinning public institutions. This entailed increasing freedom to select inputs, separating out the purchasers and providers of public services, and introducing contracting out and privatization. The main goal of these reforms has been to shift the role of central budget actors—legislators, ministers and central (budget) agencies—from arguably inappropriate micro-management (input control) to the consideration of broader policy goals and implications.

Ultimately, we can identify three major shifts in the management of public sector financial cycles: the financial cycle and its management have become more accrual-based, more linked to performance and more participatory.

Financial Cycles became More Accrual-Based

In accounting, the major shift from cash-based registrations to, first, cash and commitments and, then, to accrual accounting is significant. On the 'in' side, it means that not only are cash flows registered but also that these cash-in amounts are recalculated as 'income', which is linked to the specific accounting period under consideration. On the 'out' side, it means that not only are cash flows registered but also that these cash-out amounts are recalculated to correspond to the specific accounting period under consideration. This shift also means that capital assets are connected to depreciation (appreciation) and that several accounting corrections are added to provide a fair picture of 'costs'. In addition to cash information, which concerns money coming in and going out, there is a registration of income and costs.

Cost accounting is implemented with different degrees of intensity and a range of 'models' (such as 'direct costing' or 'full costing'). Interestingly, some countries have transferred this accrual logic of cost accounting to budgeting. This resulted in accrual budgeting where, in addition to cash budgeting, costs are also budgeted. New Zealand, for a period, had a system of full accrual budgeting. Finally, in addition to accounts and budgets, accrual logics have affected auditing. Auditing is applied to cost information to be able to offer an opinion on the economy and efficiency of services.

Financial Cycles Became More Linked to Performance

Linking financial to non-financial information is a widespread modernization in all stages of the financial cycle. Performance budgeting became a generic term for the general shift from allocating and budgeting inputs to allocating money to activities, to outputs, and even to outcomes. This was also correlated with the development of contracts within the public sector. Performance-based contracts between ministries and agencies were embedded in general performance-based budgets. The use of performance information in public financial management, together with its contractual and entrepreneurial elements, has been intended to increase transparency and accountability of government. The degree to which resources have been connected to outputs has differed across countries and policy fields. Some countries that essentially employed NPM initially followed a strict (p) x (q) logic, whereby a unit price was multiplied by the volume of services to determine the budgeted amount. More pragmatically, most countries varied the levels of 'performance' (activity, output, outcome), and the coverage rate (measuring what makes sense to measure). On the accounting side, the connection of financial and non-financial information resulted in the ability to calculate costs. On the audit side, this made it possible to have value-for-money or performance audits.

Financial Cycles Became More Participatory

The control over the financial cycles was initially technical control by the professionals connected to the financial cycle: budget specialists, accountants and auditors. This has since shifted toward internal participation and external participation. Connecting financial and non-financial information requires connecting financial professionals and those working on content. If, in addition to this connection, there is an enhanced responsibility for line departments to be accountable for performance, it is a logical step to allow the line departments to participate in and even become owners of their financial information. A significant first move has been internal participation: line departments participate in all budgeting, accounting and auditing activities. A second significant move has been to allow citizens/ customers to participate in the budgeting process. Participatory budgeting became a particular movement and an expression of democratically upgrading a political system. Citizens are not particularly involved in accounting, but they are involved in auditing and evaluation. Participatory auditing and evaluation exist, even if these practices are not widespread.

Assessing the Modernization of the Financial Cycle

These reforms—although imposed in a variety of forms in different countries and sometimes only partially implemented—have affected the rules and processes of budget preparation, authorization, implementation and reporting, as well as public financial management more broadly, and ultimately, how public services are delivered. The cost of this financial management information and control system has been a key issue. The cost-benefit analysis was not always clear, and the information necessary to perform such an analysis was often lacking. The necessary political and managerial motivation was not always present. As a result, these three shifts have been implemented with different degrees of intensity and conviction. The critics of such reforms (e.g., Rubin & Kelly, 2007) argue that despite ambitious intentions, the devolution and decentralization of fiscal governance has led to a gradual reduction in the capacity of government to address questions of cross-governmental policy development and coordination. Additionally, loosening input controls and performance monitoring have proved problematic both politically and technically. Such concerns have, in turn, led to broader whole-of-government-type initiatives such as Whole-of-Government Accounting, which is intended to combine all public sector actors under a single financial management framework (Grossi & Newberry, 2009). The 2008 global financial crisis has, however, left its mark on ongoing reforms in public financial management.

Managing Crises: Incremental Muddling through or Making Fundamental Changes

Crises and Language

There seems to be a tension between the direct and unambiguous word 'crisis' and the nearly euphemistic labeling of the response to the crisis as 'consolidation'. Both risks of and responses to catastrophes, revolutions or crises are culturally determined, as Mary Douglas clearly demonstrated (see also Walter, 2008). A culture of determinism is possible, as is one of voluntarism, as expressed in statements such as 'one never should waste a crisis.' There have been various responses to the fiscal crisis and its governance appears to not always have been proportional or equilibrated. Although there were standard and technocratic responses to redesign the 'architecture' of a financial system (Cangiano, Curristine & Lazare, 2013), they also resulted in (ideological) discussions of 'hollow' states (Frederickson & Frederickson,

2006), the rule of a 'state of exception' (Agamben, 2005), significant power shifts to financial institutions (Kickert & Randma-Liiv, 2015), the failure of government, the general loss of trust, the end of authority (Schoen, 2013) or even the crisis of the state itself (Bauman & Bordoni, 2014).

Responses to the crisis have also had a rhetorical dimension. One of the most popular slogans is 'doing more with less'. Van Dooren, Bouckaert & Halligan (2015: 27) develop four additional scenarios to increase efficiency: doing more with the same, doing much more with a bit more, doing the same with less, and doing a bit less with much less resources. Moreover, the concepts of 'savings' or 'economies' appear to have various meanings. There are roughly nine ways to define 'savings', which means that 'claims that savings have been made should therefore always be subject to further questioning and scrutiny' (Pollitt & Bouckaert, 2011: 135–136). The politics of (financial) numbers appears to go beyond pure 'evidence based' policies (Bardet, 2014).

Crises and Learning

There are single-loop crises within a financial system that could be solved within that system by respecting, e.g., standards for deficits or levels of debt. There are also double-loop crises in which the rationality of the system itself is affected. The debates on the volumes of money in a system, stop-go investment policies or failing efficiency in markets (see the controversy surrounding the 2013 Fama, Schiller and Hansen Nobel prizes) are expressions of the failure of the justification for a fiscal system. Finally, there are deutero-crises, in which there is a crisis concerning the very concept of 'crisis'. The concept of crisis itself shifts. If there is a conviction that systems are 'too big to fail', then the concept of 'crisis' shifts. This may become a 'state of exception' (Agamben, 2005), which is unprecedented, where 'exceptions' suddenly become 'normality' and 'standard operating procedures'. It is also a situation in which weak or even 'hollow' states (Frederickson & Frederickson, 2006) emerge and crisis becomes a relative reality.

Addressing single-loop crises assumes that known causes lead to known consequences. Double-loop crises require adjusting the systemic key characteristics and rationality of these systems. The OECD (2009) has emphasized the need to have independent authorities that also can enforce certain logics. Cangiano et al. (2013) demonstrated the need for new macro governance architecture with new logics and rationalities. Deutero-crises exhibit all the characteristics of wickedness and could be unmanageable if there is no time or authority to establish a new system with a new rationality. The level of describing, explaining and even predicting depends on the levels of the crises themselves. Single-loop crises will be easier to address than their double-loop counterparts, which will be less difficult than deutero-crises.

How Has the Fiscal Crisis Affected Public Financial Management?

The existing literature provides sufficient evidence that the need to undertake large-scale cutbacks in response to the fiscal crisis has led to shifts in budgeting practices and public financial management. In response to the fiscal crisis, the following changes have been implemented. The first of these changes is the struggle for the increased use of performance information in budgetary decision-making processes with the potential to contribute to 'more rational' budgetary decision-making techniques such as performance budgeting, results-based budgeting, program budgeting or zero-based budgeting. The second is a shift from decentralized and bottom-up modes of budgeting to centralized and top-down modes. The third is the influence of supranational bodies (such as the Troika of the IMF-ECB-EC) on domestic budgeting and public financial management.

A Shift from Inputs to Outputs/Outcomes: An Increase in the Importance of Performance Information in Decision-Making?

Although it has been argued that the fiscal crisis tested the performance agenda (Hood, 2013), the direction of the effects of such fiscal stress is unclear. During the crisis, there was increased focus on delivering public services, innovation and performance (OECD, 2011). The OECD has asked how to deliver better public services under fiscal pressure and how countries should respond to these challenges:

> 'The crisis has had different consequences for different countries, whose circumstances differ. Several countries have been directly affected, with necessary restraint in the public service as a consequence (Austria, Canada, Denmark, Estonia, Greece, Ireland, Italy, Japan, the United Kingdom . . .). Some have only been indirectly affected through drops in investment or tourism. Others have suffered a milder impact, where the need for fiscal prudence remains compatible with counter-cyclical policies (e.g. Brazil, Chile)'
>
> (OECD, 2011: 8).

Many countries have established explicit priorities to remain focused on their fiscal objectives, and three main fiscal objectives remain in place in most countries. The first is to do more with less: in addition to classical responses (i.e., economic, efficient and effective processes), there are also new solutions that use IT and innovative practices, as well as partnerships with citizens and the private and voluntary sectors. The second is to develop and maintain trust. Communicating results helps to meet expectations. The third is to engage with the public and stakeholders to foster sustainable reform. However, in many countries, the first objective receives the most attention (OECD, 2011: 8–9), leading to increased interest in the use of rational decision-making (including the use of performance information) in government processes.

On the one hand, many studies have shown that the reforms highlighting the need to 'rationalize' budgetary decision-making with the aid of performance measures are likely to attract more attention from policy makers following a fiscal crisis. Earlier studies have referenced the fact that performance budgeting reforms in various countries were inspired by fiscal crises (e.g., Straussman, 1979; Levine, Rubin & Wolohojian, 1981; Schick, 1988; Dunsire & Hood, 1989). Fiscal crises have been argued to motivate governments to adopt budgetary reforms to realize performance budgeting, results-based budgeting, program budgeting or zero-based budgeting (see, e.g., Straussman, 1979; Levine et al., 1981) and to enhance the inclusion of performance information into the budget preparation process (Levine et al., 1981; Schick, 1988). Management consultants, policy makers and academics claim that the use of performance information in the budgetary process could make cutback decisions more 'intelligent' and 'objective'. A fiscal crisis is likely to trigger an increase in the steering and evaluation of an organization's activities and a renewed emphasis on management efficiencies to eliminate waste, enhance cost-consciousness and increase 'value for money' through the use of performance budgeting (Schick, 1988; Dunsire & Hood, 1989). Thus, more 'rational' forms of budgeting are believed to be helpful in coping with reduced finances and enhancing efficiency and effectiveness in the public sector.

The more severe and long-lasting a fiscal crisis is, the more likely governments are to turn to targeted cuts rather than implementing proportional, across-the-board cuts (Kickert, Randma-Liiv & Savi, 2015). This raises the question of what the basis should be for decisions concerning targeted cuts. Performance information can provide valuable analytical input to the decision-making process, help policy makers impose expenditure constraints or undertake cuts on a more rational and transparent basis, and ultimately make cutbacks more selectively. This could involve setting clear political priorities, cutting low-performing programs and implementing cuts in those programs that are considered of lower importance (Straussman, 1979; Levine et al., 1981). This can be an attractive solution for politicians because when budget cuts are made on the basis of priorities and performance indicators, various stakeholders will perceive such cuts to be more 'objective' (MacManus, 1984).

Moreover, it is argued that performance-based budgeting can also be appealing for individual public sector organizations. When central budget actors (parliament, the central government, the Ministry of Finance) relax input controls (less-detailed control over the specific line items and more extensive use of lump sums and aggregate budgets), individual public sector organizations receive increased discretion in the use of budgetary resources and in making more specific cutbacks while managers are made accountable for outcomes and outputs (Raudla, 2013).

On the other hand, several academics are more skeptical of the feasibility of structural reforms (e.g., adopting a new performance budgeting system) during a period of crisis. The argument here is that scarcity may make the implementation of such structural reforms more difficult because they cannot be 'lubricated with new money' (Pollitt, 2010: 18). Schick (1988) maintains that in the midst of a crisis, budgeting becomes more focused on the short- than on the long-term and that policy makers will be more concerned with expenditure control than with the planning or management functions of budgeting, which is why reforms establishing 'rationality-enhancing' budgeting systems could be better suited for environments characterized by growth rather than retrenchment. In another study of OECD countries, Schick (1986) showed that fiscal stress brought about the re-orientation of planning in the budget process: plans were converted into spending controls, and multiyear budgets were used to control spending rather than to plan programs.

In addition, budgeting can be considered a highly time-sensitive process: whereas this limits the use of performance information even in 'normal' times, in the context of a fiscal crisis, the time pressure becomes even more significant because decisions need to be made quickly. During urgent decision-making (and crisis, by definition, entails urgency), the use of performance information may lead to information overload and could be perceived as a hindrance for policy makers (Moynihan, 2006; Van Dooren, 2011). There are limited opportunities for developing discussions of performance information and its implications for resource allocation in the parliament, the Cabinet and between Ministries of Finance and line ministries, as a result of which budget actors may not include performance information in budgetary negotiations. In addition, gathering and interpreting performance information requires analytical, financial, human and technological resources that are likely to become scarce during fiscal crises (Raudla, 2013).

The most recent empirical study shows that during the 2008 global financial crisis, European governments tended to expand their use of performance information in the decision-making process (Kickert & Randma-Liiv, 2015). The senior public service executives from all European countries considered in that study agreed that the use of performance information increased in the budgeting and decision-making processes during the crisis. The increase in the relevance of performance information was considered the highest in Finland and Denmark, followed by Lithuania, Ireland, Sweden, the Netherlands, the UK, France and Italy. The remaining European countries reported slightly smaller increases in the use of performance information. However, none of the European countries considered in that study introduced structural reforms by establishing performance budgeting systems during the fiscal crisis (Kickert & Randma-Liiv, 2015). However, the abolition of the UK Audit Commission, which focused on local governments, is a clear example of decreased focus on performance. Michael O'Higgins, chairman of the Audit Commission, was surprised, stating, 'given the fiscal consolidation, if anything we anticipated there would be a bigger role for a body that focused on value for money and providing comparative examples of how you could do things better' (Timmins, 2012). According to Van Dooren et al. (2015), 'while the story of the Audit Commission is a testimony of the tensions between centralized performance regimes, political accountability and public budgeting, we should not generalize the whereabouts of the UK Audit Commission too easily' (p. 6). As argued by Pollitt (2009), countries are not all in the same boat. We may all be at sea in the same storm, but we are traveling in different types of vessels. Hence, the general impact of the fiscal crisis, if any, remains uncertain, especially with a macro-economic focus on inputs (see also: Office of the Parliamentary Budget Officer, 2014).

A Shift from Decentralized and Bottom-Up Modes of Budgeting to a Centralized, Top-Down Approach

The centralization of decision-making can be considered a necessary precondition for undertaking retrenchment (Boin, Hart, Stern & Sundelius, 2008; Peters, Pierre & Randma-Liiv, 2011; Kickert & Randma-Liiv, 2015). The need to determine cutbacks entails reconsidering government priorities. When scarce resources and expenditure cuts are on the agenda, centralization is often considered the only feasible mechanism to achieve systematic spending cuts and prioritizations in organizational resource allocations (Levine, 1979). As any prioritization assumes a certain degree of centralization, the government's decision to impose targeted cuts based on strategic prioritizations (in contrast to across-the-board cuts) automatically leads to centralized budgeting and decision-making (Raudla, Savi & Randma-Liiv, 2015). Moreover, decisions concerning the general priorities of the government belong to the political realm rather than to routine administrative decision-making. If politicians wish to have greater influence over budgetary matters, they are likely to grant more decision-making power to central budgetary institutions. Governments' seeking to centralize decision-making in this way is expected to facilitate the rapid legitimization of decisions (Peters, 2011). It is also believed that the more centralized the budgetary institutions are, the greater the fiscal discipline of the government will be (Hallerberg, Strauch & Von Hagen, 2009).

Centralization and stronger control over decision-making are materialized through general priority-setting by the government, the standardization of procedures, empowering the central (budgetary) departments, setting limits to organizational spending and activities or setting targets for spending cuts (Pollitt, 2010; Di Mascio, Natalini & Stolfi, 2013; Raudla, 2013). Consequently, the need to reduce budgets reinforces top-down and rule-based budgetary procedures and increases the power of budgetary institutions (Schick, 2009).

In brief, in top-down budgeting, the Ministry of Finance or its equivalent establishes expenditure ceilings that have to be followed by the line ministries and agencies when preparing their budget proposals. In contrast, in the bottom-up process, the line ministries and agencies formulate their requests without a prior ceiling, typically on the basis of the previous year's budget, and budget negotiations then focus on optimizing these requests (Schick, 1986). It has been argued that in countries where bottom-up budget processes dominated before the crisis, the pressure to adopt a more top-down approach to preparing the budget would emerge, whereas in countries where top-down processes had already prevailed, these practices would be strengthened (Raudla, 2013). This is the case because the line ministries and agencies would likely emphasize their 'special characteristics' that make them unsuitable for cuts (Dunsire & Hood, 1989). Hence, appeals for budget-cutting are likely to provoke 'you first, then me' types of responses from individual public sector organizations, necessitating a centralized, top-down imposition of specific cutback targets (Levine, 1979: 181). In other words, it would be difficult to achieve cutbacks through bottom-up modes of budgeting because line ministries and agencies would be unlikely to volunteer to make the cuts. In addition, bottom-up processes are likely to lead to serious conflicts between the line ministries and the central budgeting agency (Ministry of Finance) in the event that the line ministries propose spending that would force the government to spend more than it prefers (Schick, 1986). Consequently, to reduce conflict and make cutbacks feasible, the Ministry of Finance would have to give the line ministries and agencies targets or spending ceilings before the latter begin formulating their budget requests at the beginning of the budget cycle (Raudla, 2013).

In parallel with more centralized, top-down decision-making, cutback budgeting may contribute to greater flexibility at the organizational level, as individual public sector organizations would have to determine exactly where the budget cuts would fall. This is common practice with across-the-board cuts. When targeted cuts are fundamentally central decisions regarding which institutions will face larger cuts than others, across-the-board-cuts imply cuts in the same amount for all institutions, and the government may delegate decisions of what to cut (within pre-established limits) to institutions or even street-level bureaucrats, whose choices are considered better informed (Dunsire & Hood, 1989; Pollitt, 2010; Raudla, Savi & Randma-Liiv, 2015). It has also been argued that tighter central controls and less discretion may demotivate public servants, and, hence, increased managerial flexibility can be a form of compensation for awarding agencies less money, which may also reduce resistance to cuts (Schick, 1988; Dunsire & Hood, 1989).

The shift toward top-down budgeting assumes that greater power is granted to the Ministry of Finance vis-à-vis the line ministries, and the Minister of Finance vis-à-vis the rest of the Cabinet, especially in imposing expenditure ceilings or targets for expenditure cuts (Schick, 1986; Di Mascio et al., 2013; Raudla, 2013). In addition, budgetary units in individual public sector organizations are likely to gain greater power and a more important role in organizational decision-making. This was confirmed in a large-scale survey of European public sector executives (Kickert & Randma-Liiv, 2015), where the extensive increase in the power of Ministries of Finance and, to a slightly lesser extent, in the power of organizational budget planning units was reported in all European countries studied. The study also found a general increase in the centralization of organizational decision-making. Both the control and coordination functions of the Ministry of Finance tended to intensify during periods of fiscal stress. Public executives in Ireland reported a substantial increase in the power of the Ministry of Finance. Interestingly, Norway—a country not severely affected by the crisis – experienced a remarkable increase in the power of the Ministry of Finance vis-à-vis the line ministries. Public sector executives also perceived that the role of budgetary units in public sector organizations increased as a consequence of the crisis. The greatest increase in the power of budgetary units was reported in Sweden, Denmark, Ireland, Italy, France and Spain. Public executives from the other countries reported a fairly similar shift in the power of budgetary units. The increased power of budgetary units relative to their horizontal counterparts reflects the fact that in the presence of cutbacks, the organizational units are regarded as 'budget holders' and planning and implementing cuts receives most of the politicians' and public managers' attention.

The Increased Influence of Supranational Bodies on Domestic Budgeting and Public Financial Management

Typically, budgeting and public financial management are considered solely from the perspective of domestic political and administrative processes. The period of fiscal crisis adds another level to such an approach: the supranational level. A comparative study of European governments' responses to the fiscal crisis shows that supranational influence plays a considerable role in explaining decision-making regarding domestic cutbacks (Kickert, Randma-Liiv & Savi, 2015). First, developments in the global economy clearly affected the domestic economies and public finances of European countries. In addition, the EU's Maastricht Treaty imposes ceilings on budget deficits and state debt. In many European countries, pressure from the EU to remain within the deficit limit was influential in forcing governments to make cuts.

Most important, countries such as Greece, Iceland, Ireland, Italy, Latvia and Spain that received financial assistance (bailouts) from the IMF or the Troika of IMF-ECB-EC had to comply with strict and specified fiscal consolidation conditions. The conditionality of the assistance from the Troika forced governments to impose immediate austerity measures, including targeted cuts and fundamental priority-setting (Kickert, Randma-Liiv & Savi,

2015). It is important to note that the Troika holds an orthodox view on addressing the crisis (Dellepiane-Avellaneda, 2015), fiscal consolidation should begin early and be imposed rapidly in a front-loaded strategy to restore market confidence in governments' ability to manage their public finances (Pisani-Ferry, 2007). It is, therefore, unsurprising that countries following the requirements of the Troika's loan programs were rapidly forced to impose real cutbacks.

One of the basic questions concerning crisis responses is whether governments maintained their existing approaches to governance or the crisis imposed a persistent change in budgeting and public financial management. The expression that one should 'never waste a crisis' is apparent in efforts to combine a shift in policies to realize societies that are resilient and sustainable (Sachs, 2015).

Although the abovementioned changes initially relied on specific short-term conditions (Troupin, Steen & Stroobants, 2015), they may reflect a long-term change. The changes in budgeting and financial management triggered by cutback environment can be *ad hoc,* not become formalized and cease to exist once the immediate fiscal stress is over. Alternatively, the crisis context can also impel formal (legislative) changes that may persist, represent a longer-term effect of the crisis and pave the way to further systemic reforms, although this has yet to be determined.

From the Crisis of Discipline to the Discipline of Crisis: Moving Beyond Accountancy to Governance

If the analysis of government responses to the financial crisis were conducted solely in the field of accounting, perhaps the main conclusion would be at the balance sheet level: 'what is left is right, and what is right has left.' However, robust and reliable monitoring, surveillance, and oversight are indispensable for financial and non-financial information. Historically, public sector budgeting was not merely a matter of accounting but also concerned macro-economic issues, policy allocation and managerial functions. Various academic disciplines (economics, policy studies and political science and management) are involved in the study of public budgeting and fiscal crisis. In addition, governments' crisis responses are also legally framed. In several countries, there were appeals to the highest courts to combat the proposed 'solutions' to the crisis. Common law countries have different legal frameworks and degrees of freedom than do civil law countries. Thus, legal studies have the potential to contribute to understanding the responses to the crisis. Finally, anthropology and cultural theory provide a context to avoid blind copy-pasting of 'solutions'. The field of public administration, as a scientific platform that consolidates various disciplines, should use the financial crisis as an opportunity not only to promote multidisciplinary research but especially to develop serious interdisciplinary research.

The era of fiscal crisis has strengthened public financial management's position relative to other public management functions because scarce financial resources have shaped many of the outcomes important to public administration, including the effectiveness of public service delivery. Research on public financial management can offer interesting opportunities to better understand the role of administrative expertise in democratic institutions, how to manage public organizations to achieve the best outcomes and how public organizations adapt to their changing environments (see also Kioko et al., 2011). Under fiscal stress, more than ever, speaking truth to power means the ability to talk about euros and dollars, which automatically makes an organization's competence in financial management crucially important. Increasing the awareness and responsiveness of political and administrative leaders to public financial management issues, and making these issues more transparent, can in turn improve government accountability.

Upgrading fiscal governance is not an objective in itself. The ultimate purpose is to guarantee a sustainable, transparent and democratic system that governs efficient and effective policies and the management of the related service delivery. This requires a functional combination of macroeconomic designs, policy designs (including choices of policy instruments) and managerial designs that define responsibilities and accountabilities. This entails complex governance that combines technical tools (the monitoring of financial and non-financial information, including accounting systems), clear responsibilities and accountabilities with checks and balances, including independent and transparent decision making capacity, strategic visions that are inspired by forecasting and scenarios and, if ultimately necessary, legitimate enforcement capacity. Creating economic financial systems is part of this governance challenge. This entails massive effort at achieving comparable classifications (IMF, 2009) and the harmonization of financial systems in the public sector (Brusca, Caperchione, Cohen & Rossi, 2015). The results envisioned are not merely the substantial elements of the fiscal crisis but to an even greater extent the level of trust in a system that has the capacity to solve problems and improve realities.

References

Agamben, G. (2005). *State of exception*. (K. Attell, Trans.). Chicago: University of Chicago.

Bardet, F. (2014). *La contre-révolution comptable: Ces chiffres qui nous gouvernent*. Paris: Les Belles Lettres.

Bauman, Z., & Bordoni, C. (2014). *State of crisis*. Cambridge: Polity Press.

Boin, A., Hart, P., Stern, E., & Sundelius, P. (2008). *The politics of crisis management: Public leadership under pressure*. Cambridge: Cambridge University Press.

Brusca, I., Caperchione, E., Cohen, S., & Rossi, F.M. (Eds.). (2015). *Public sector accounting and auditing in Europe: The challenge of harmonization*. Basingstoke: Palgrave.

Cangiano, M., Curristine, T., & Lazare, M. (Ed.). (2013). *Public financial management and its emerging architecture*. Washington, DC: International Monetary Fund.

Dellepiane-Avellaneda, S. (2015). The political power of economic ideas: The case of 'expansionary fiscal contractions'. *The British Journal of Politics & International Relations, 17*(3), 391–418.

Di Mascio, F., Natalini, A., & Stolfi, F. (2013). The ghost of crises past: Analyzing reform sequences to understand Italy's response to the global crisis. *Public Administration, 91*(1), 17–31.

Dunsire, A., & Hood, C. (1989). *Cutback management in public Bureaucracies: Popular theories and observed outcomes in Whitehall*. Cambridge: Cambridge University Press.

Frederickson, D.G., & Frederickson H.G. (2006). *Measuring the performance of the hollow state*. Washington, DC: Georgetown University Press.

Grossi, G., & Newberry, S. (2009). Theme: Whole of government accounting—international trends. *Public Money and Management, 29*(4), 209–213.

Hallerberg, M., Strauch, R., & Von Hagen, J. (2009). *Fiscal governance in Europe*. Cambridge: Cambridge University Press.

Hood, C. (2013). Reflections on public service reform in a cold fiscal climate. In H. Kippin, G. Stoker and S. Griffiths (Eds.), *Public services: A new reform agenda* (pp. 215–229). London: Bloomsbury Academic.

International Monetary Fund. (2009). *Budget classification*. Washington, DC: International Monetary Fund.

Kickert, W., & Randma-Liiv, T. (2015). *Europe managing the crisis: The politics of fscal consolidation*. London: Routledge.

Kickert, W., Randma-Liiv, T., & Savi, R. (2015). Politics of fiscal consolidation in Europe: A comparative analysis. *International Review of Administrative Sciences, 81*(3), 562–584.

Kioko, S., Marlowe, J., Matkin, D., Moody, M., Smith, D., & Zhao, Z. (2011). Why public financial management matters. *Journal of Public Administration Research and Theory, 21*(suppl. 1), i113–i124.

Levine, C.H. (1979). More on cutback management: Hard questions for hard times. *Public Administration Review, 39*(2), 179–183.

Levine, C.H., Rubin, I., & Wolohojian, G.G. (1981). Resource scarcity and the reform model: The management of retrenchment in Cincinnati and Oakland. *Public Administration Review, 41*(6), 619–628.

MacManus, S.A. (1984). Coping with retrenchment: Why local governments need to restructure their budget document formats. *Public Budgeting & Finance, 4*(3), 58–66.

Moynihan, D.P. (2006). What do we talk about when we talk about performance? Dialogue theory and performance budgeting. *Journal of Public Administration Research and Theory, 16*(2), 151–168.

OECD. (2009). *Strategic response to the financial and economic crisis: Contributions to the global effort*. Paris: OECD Publishing.

OECD. (2011). *The call for innovative and open government: An overview of country initiatives*. Paris: OECD Publishing.

Office of the Parliamentary Budget Officer. (2014). *Analysis of performance budgeting during recent fiscal consolidation*. Canada: Ottawa.

Peters, B.G. (2011). Governance responses to the fiscal crisis: Comparative perspectives. *Public Money & Management, 31*(1), 75–80.

Peters, B.G., Pierre, J., & Randma-Liiv, T. (2011). Global financial crisis, public administration and governance: Do new problems require new solutions? *Public Organization Review, 11*(1), 3–27.

Pisani-Ferry, J. (2007). Foreword. In J. Henriksson (Ed.), *Ten lessons about fiscal consolidation* (pp. 3–4). Brussels: Bruegel Lecture and Essay Series.

Pollitt, C. (2009). *Public management reform during financial austerity*. Presentation at the EUPAN Directors General meeting, Stockholm.

Pollitt, C. (2010). Cuts and reforms—public services as we move into a new era. *Society and Economy, 32*(1), 17–31.

Pollitt, C., & Bouckaert, G. (2011). *Public management reform: A comparative analysis-new public management, governance, and the Neo-Weberian state.* Oxford: Oxford University Press.

Posner, P., & Blöndal, J. (2012). Democracies and deficits: Prospects for fiscal responsibility in democratic nations. *Governance, 25*(1), 11–34.

Raudla, R. (2013). Budgeting during austerity: Approaches, instruments and practices. *Budgetary Research Review, 5*(1), 30–39.

Raudla, R., Savi, R., & Randma-Liiv, T. (2015). Cutback management literature in the 1970s and 1980s: Taking stock. *International Review of Administrative Sciences, 81*(3), 433–456

Rubin, I., & Kelly, J. (2007). Budget and accounting reforms. In E. Ferlie, L. Lynn, and C. Pollitt (Eds.), *The Oxford handbook of public management* (pp. 563–590). Oxford: Oxford University Press.

Sachs, J.D. (2015). *The age of sustainable development.* New York: Columbia University Press.

Schick, A. (1986). Macro-budgetary adaptations to fiscal stress in industrialized democracies. *Public Administration Review, 46*(2), 124–134.

Schick, A. (1988). Macro-budgetary adaptations to fiscal stress in industrialized democracies. *Public Administration Review, 48*(1), 523–533.

Schick, A. (2009). Crisis budgeting. *OECD Journal on Budgeting, 2009*(3), 1–14.

Schoen, D.E. (2013). *The end of authority: How a loss of legitimacy and broken trust are endangering our future.* Lanham: Rowman & Littlefield.

Straussman, J.D. (1979). A typology of budgetary environments: Notes on the prospects for reform. *Administration & Society, 11*(2), 216–226.

Timmins, N. (2012, October 9). Audit Commission's ex-head: Its abolition will affect public services. *The Guardian.* Retrieved from http://www.theguardian.com/society/2012/oct/09/audit-commission-chairman-abolition-value.

Troupin, S., Steen, T., & Stroobants, J. (2015). Fiscal consolidation in federal Belgium. *International Review of Administrative Sciences, 81*(3), 457–478.

Van Dooren, W. (2011). Better performance management. *Public Performance & Management Review, 34*(3), 420–433.

Van Dooren, W., Bouckaert, G., & Halligan, J. (2015). *Performance management in the public sector.* Abingdon: Routledge.

Walter, F. (2008). *Catastrophes: Une histoire culturelle XVIe-XXIe siècle.* Paris: Seuil.

Part III

Studying and Practicing Reform

15 Public Sector Reform amidst Societal and Administrative Shifts

Kim Putters

Introduction

In 1986, Walter Kickert had already noted that—after a long period of central government planning—it is rather difficult to approach policy making and implementation as purely rational processes. Insecurity regarding social trends and crises urges government to be an open and adaptive system (Kickert, 1986). In practice, reforming the public sector often entails shifting away from drawing-table plans and centrally planned design and implementation. This is especially the case in a social and political context where various countries appear to be moving away from systems in which the central government is the core actor. Recent policy trends suggest a move toward decentralization, whereby local communities are being put in charge, and toward bottom-up participation in the production of public goods, as evidenced by, for instance, the British focus on 'big society' or the Dutch policy focus on the transition to a 'participation society'. The term 'decentralization' is largely an administrative concept pertaining to a change in the relationships among different layers of government. 'Participation society' refers to the way in which societal stakeholders interact with one another, and to social engagement and to social networks, to provide public goods. It is a model in which government, and especially the central government, takes a back seat.

These trends are especially visible in welfare state services. However, they are all but new. In the Netherlands, their origins can be traced back to the 1970s. Consider the following extract from a letter written by Jo Hendriks, a public health secretary in the Dutch government, in 1976:

> 'However important the benefits of the welfare state may be, there is a danger that they may cause people to become disempowered and dependent. The responsibility for looking after our own and others' welfare has increasingly been taken over by omnipresent care systems. This is forcing us to look for different ways of making people less dependent. The emphasis will have to lie on self-help, volunteering, small-scale organization and decentralization of management'
>
> (author's translation).

These words would fit seamlessly into the Letters to Parliament from the current Dutch State Secretary for Health, Welfare and Sport. Decentralization and the 'participation society' are frequently used concepts in current policy but have long been a subject of debate (De Boer & Van der Lans, 2014). In recent decades, social policies have gradually been changed to enable and enforce individual responsibilities and cooperation in local health, housing and education networks (Kickert, 1991; Kickert & Van Vught, 1995).

Only in 2007 did the Dutch Parliament adopt a legislative framework with full local responsibilities for social security, the re-integration and education of handicapped people in the labor market and youth and elder care. Local authorities, societal organizations and citizens are now responsible for these welfare state provisions (De Boer & De Klerk, 2014). Nevertheless, the national government remains constitutionally responsible and allocates the financial means necessary for these services. This challenges existing relationships, changes the nature of the relationship between citizens and government and requires a different approach to steering.

In this chapter, I illustrate how public sector reform should not be regarded merely as a top-down exercise, practiced in splendid isolation. Major transformations in the public sector reflect major social changes and require a new type of organization and new type of public sector leadership. Reforms in the Dutch public sector and in welfare state services in particular, will be used to illustrate these transformations

New Social Divides and the Need for New Governance Models

What happens in society happens in public administration, although often with a certain time lag. Western societies are characterized by a number of social divides: between ethnic groups, between age groups and between the more and less educated. Whereas quality of life and life expectancy continue to rise, the gap between the general population and those without work, in poor health and with little to no education is widening. These latter groups are also those making the greatest use of social services. Estimates in the Netherlands are that approximately 6% of the population uses the majority of collective provisions (SCP, 2014).

For local government and societal organizations, it is important to have insights into how resources and needs are allocated among citizens, to be adaptive and to tailor specific policies and services. Not all citizens have the economic, cultural and social capital to fully participate in society, and not all are able to rely on social networks. This group also frequently lacks faith in administrative and political institutions (SCP, 2014), and this lack is growing, especially among low-income earners, low-skilled workers and migrants. Whereas the Netherlands is not a polarized, class-based society such as the US or the United Kingdom, differences are growing, and this creates challenges for local organizations, residents and, consequently, local government and policy (SCP, 2014).

First, there is an increasing *ethnic divide* that influences local networks. For example, social networks have become more ethnically uniform, and there has been a decline in mixed marriages (Sterckx, 2014). Societal organizations are increasingly created along ethnic lines. These are signs of segregation in society, which concerns not only local residents but also schoolteachers and care professionals working in neighborhoods (Dekker & Den Ridder, 2015).

Second, there appears to be a growing *age divide*. As the number of people aged over 65 increases, so does uncertainty regarding the availability and affordability of care and pensions. There is an increasing demand for children to deliver informal care to parents and neighbors, as well as to combine paid work with voluntary care. This leads to financial pressure, illness and stress (Josten & De Boer, 2015), which are compounded by uncertainty among younger people regarding whether they will be able to enjoy similar provisions when they are older. Support for intergenerational solidarity remains high, and there is no 'age war', but the age divide is increasing nonetheless (SCP, 2014).

Third, we observe an *educational divide*, with a growing gap between more and less educated people. Children with well-educated parents are more likely to enter higher education (CBS, 2012). This polarization is experienced chiefly in the labor market. Unemployment is structurally higher among the low-skilled. The same applies for the likelihood of being promoted. Low-skilled workers are more frequently employed in temporary jobs and on flexible contracts. Access to retraining funds primarily benefits highly skilled workers. Taken together, this divide entails important challenges for the future of the welfare state.

What do those three societal divides mean for the local community and for governance? Such societal divides create new challenges for delivering public services and governing the welfare state. This challenge is particularly difficult when groups in society have low trust in government. Approximately 85% of the (Dutch) population look for and find their own solutions for care, work or support. The other 15% are not able to do so. This group needs intervention and support from societal organizations, churches, neighbors or local government. A small percentage of this group (3%) has a complex set of problems and permanently needs all types of services. They demand the full attention of local policy makers and politicians. To find solutions, the local community and local authorities have to cooperate and find solutions. Different types of networks are created in which care, work, housing and education are linked together.

New forms of network governance and new modes of public management (Kickert, 2014; see also the chapter by Klijn & Koppenjan, this volume) are needed to be adaptive to changing societal relationships. This is difficult in a time of shrinking budgets. In addition, decentralization means that local choices and solutions lead to different policies, different fees and different resource allocations. Such new governance models may be difficult for local and national politicians to accept when they lead to differences in service delivery and finances because they concern constitutional responsibilities for the accessibility and quality of services. New relationships between national and local government arise, and new perspectives emerge on how social service organizations, local governments, civil society organizations and citizens work together.

Public Sector Reform amidst Societal and Administrative Shifts

Public sector reforms changing welfare state arrangements are intended to simultaneously cope with major social changes, a need for cost containment and political pleas for increasing individual responsibilities. At their core, these reforms concern devolving responsibilities to citizens themselves and social networks (e.g., through informal care arrangements). In practice, this means local governments have to take on new responsibilities, that more private initiatives emerge and that intersectoral collaboration becomes increasingly important. We discuss each of these implications below.

From National to Local Government

In Dutch healthcare, since 2006, local governments have become increasingly responsible for home-, elder- and youth-care. Since 2015, there has been a requirement that care provision be put up for tender and contracted by local government, with national government operating at a distance and supervising these processes. Budget allocation remains controlled by the national government, and given their limited local taxation authority, local governments have limited space to make a difference. Nevertheless, most local communities have taken up their new challenges and fulfilled their legal care obligations, notwithstanding some shortfalls in provisions for the disabled. For local civil servants, the change from central to local organization and provision is made more challenging by a lack of financial means that make it difficult to make real choices. They also struggle with developing a familiarity with these new client groups that had not hitherto been served (people with psychological problems being a good example).

From Government to Private Initiative

Decentralization to local government in itself remains far from exhibiting a shift from government-led service provision to a 'participation society'. First, there have always been numerous private initiatives in Dutch healthcare and social services. One out of four citizens engages in voluntary work, which varies from informal care provision to work with family and neighbors, working with the disabled or elderly in one's spare time and supporting children in after-school teaching activities, to being active in cultural and sport associations. Whereas an increase in voluntary care activities can be observed, as preferred and stimulated by recent government policies, the evidence for a causal link is weak. For private initiative and volunteering in care provision to be effective, support from local governments and healthcare organizations is necessary. People increasingly need to care for both children and elderly parents. The elderly themselves are caring for one another (partners, neighbors or friends). This means that relationships intensify, and the burdens may become too heavy to bear.

From Sectoral to Intersectoral Perspectives

Social change requires intersectoral cooperation at a local level, allowing crossovers among healthcare, labor and educational policy and service delivery. This is a tremendous challenge for public sector reform. Some of these crossovers already exist, such as within networks in which nursing homes, home care, voluntary organizations, schools and businesses cooperate to serve the citizen, patient or client. Different sectors, however, have different rules, expectations and professional codes, which makes change difficult. Changing regulations that block such collaborations, thereby allowing local initiatives to flourish, and financial means can allow intersectoral collaboration to succeed.

Decentralization and Participation: Muddling through

Education is one of the resources necessary to engage in the so called 'participation society' (Putters, 2015). If anywhere, the boundaries between society and the educational system are diffuse. Developments in society are also being reflected in educational programs, discussed in classrooms and, thus, transported into schools. First, education influences peoples' health and their opportunities and capacity to help others. Second, schools—as institutions—are at the center of local social networks. They facilitate participation and connect pupils, parents and social stakeholders, including in healthcare or the labor market. Examples include the development of partnerships with regional labor market stakeholders and local communities, to create internships and practical exchanges, or teaching digital skills. Working with numerous stakeholders and attempting to satisfy all of their needs creates tensions and means that schools have to organize themselves differently.

This is visible in the governance of schools (Commissie Goed Onderwijsbestuur VO, 2014). Supervisory Boards have become better equipped to supervise new collaborations and have been made aware of society's new expectations. To strengthen their legitimacy, the position of relevant stakeholders in schools has been bolstered, through forms of participation, consultation and co-determination by pupils and students, parents and businesses and public authorities. The same is happening in healthcare organizations. Finally, collaboration requires improved transparency. Transparency is a condition for accountability and for demonstrating how the institution improves society. Transparency also shows how public resources are spent.

Balancing and controlling multiple public, private and professional objectives and working across sectoral boundaries is more difficult in reality than it appears on the drawing boards of public sector reform planners. When multiple parties with multiple interests collaborate, the politicians tend to increasingly shift toward uniform and measurable performance targets. The more horizontal and local accountability is required, the greater the extent to which national government employs a hierarchical model of supervision, prohibition and sanctioning. The more important the dialogue with stakeholders becomes, the more that direct supervision makes this dialogue difficult to emerge. Theory and practice of reform are often separated by a broad gulf. Local initiatives are expected to achieve more in terms of service quality, red tape reductions and public engagement with fewer resources, under strict market rules, and burdened by audits and privacy rules. Absent local dialogues between stakeholders, conflicts and tensions are inevitable. Such dialogue appeals to the interpersonal skills of politicians, board members and professionals, as it cannot be achieved merely by checks and controls based on performance indicators. The search for a balance between central steering and control and local participatory arrangements creates dilemmas in governance practices because existing systems make dialogue difficult.

From a Steering Reform Culture to an Adaptive Culture

The above makes clear that reforms toward new governance modes will not succeed through new legal frameworks alone. For boundary crossing among the public, private and professional sectors to succeed, and to foster civic engagement and local partnerships, we need to rethink the organization of the dialogue with and between stakeholders and the language needed.

We still observe a strong focus on formally prescribed responsibilities and top-down decision-making structures. Within that system, however, there is no automatic consensus on what is needed to achieve quality and accessible services. A dialogue is, therefore, necessary. This requires an adaptive culture and engaging in relationships. An example from the care sector can illustrate this. Postma (2015) studied how decisions regarding scale (e.g., in mergers) are made and experienced in the healthcare system and what they mean for the organization and care delivery. He concluded that an optimum scale or structure simply does not exist and cannot be imposed. Small-scale care can be organized within a merged organization if community nurses are able to shape their work in consultation with families and clients. Emergency care professionals must be able to act rapidly while being confident that their administrators will support them. The key is, thus, how professionals (are able to) perform their work in an adaptive way and how they experience this. It requires bonding among professionals, patients and families.

The essence of reforms toward a participation society concerns how to establish these types of links with and between stakeholders. That is difficult in very large organizations with a wide diversity of stakeholders. In an adaptive culture, there must be a well-organized dialogue, with sufficient money, time and other resources, and management that can organize these dialogues across stakeholders, both within public organizations and with other societal organizations (Van der Voet, 2014; Oldenhof, 2015). There is no optimal form for such dialogues, and, therefore, institutions and programs need to be allowed to experiment with different forms of client participation, thereby allowing them to formulate their own performance targets and making them accountable for their choices. Deviating from uniformly formulated laws may be part of such local experimentation and allows for locally inspired choices.

Experimentation with dialogues and coordinated service delivery requires boards to rethink their old and romantic understandings of formal participation. Thinking within those formal structures could, again, prevent new stakeholders from being a partner in decision-making. A board member's seat is always connected to a dominant interest. Openness to (new) stakeholders is a condition for adaptive governance. This can be achieved by creating co-decision making structures and by gathering wide-ranging information, insights, convictions and perceptions from all relevant stakeholders within and outside the organization.

Finally, people in these new types of local collaborations do not automatically begin regarding the world differently. The staff is trained in a certain way, as are board members and inspectors. This requires 'unfreezing' on the part of professionals. They must distance themselves from what they were taught about the right and wrong way of doing things. Experimenting with responsibilities for teaching or nursing teams (or neighborhood care teams) is part of this, with a robust role for peer review. The same applies for board members. Compared with five years ago, boards now have to focus more on outcomes and finances. This may have brought boards closer to the primary process of organizations and requires a different type of board member (Lubberman & Verbeek, 2014). Unfreezing thus means abandoning old (governance) practices to give new role interpretations a chance (Lubberman & Verbeek, 2014). To do things differently, it is necessary to be able to imagine things differently. That requires leaders who can devise a language for this and spread the dialogue within the organization. A public sector based on decentralization and participation requires new leadership. This leadership needs to be able to formulate performance standards in partnership with all stakeholders. It requires a dialogue with the stakeholders to determine the choices they would make, to know how they would raise quality standards and to know what mix of objectives they favor. Trust between stakeholders and trust in one's staff are then important, which is a departure from the mutual distrust that now often exists.

Toward Decentralization and Network Governance: Public Sector Reform Challenges

Moving to an adaptive culture, collaborating between public and private partners, experimenting with new forms of network governance, and engaging interested residents entails major consequences for public sector reforms. First, we need a different reform language, one that allows for a diversity of views and approaches. To make public service delivery at the local level effective, one needs to search for alternative sources of information and to break open the discussion on what constitutes good service delivery. In other words, it means breaking down boundaries between societal organizations, businesses and local government. It means allowing diversity, and this implies ending centrally imposed benchmarks and performance contracts intended to impose uniformity.

It means that the 'finish line' for an organization may lie beyond its own (organizational) boundaries and current performance indicators. For instance, consider a school that thinks beyond performance targets or health organizations that think beyond the treatment. The social significance of a public service, formulated and achieved jointly with stakeholders, lies beyond annual reports, benchmarks and audits.

This entails a variety of performance agreements based on trust and local professionalism replacing uniform, top-down performance agreements. Achieving this may be difficult and requires breaking down established boundaries not only between public organizations but also between public and private organizations. It means setting priorities at the local level, and allowing diversity is a crucial part of doing so. For public leaders, courage is needed, as these are the greatest challenges in local network governance. Public sector reforms will not succeed without some disobedience against top-down reform planners. In that respect, Professor Walter Kickert and his work set a challenging example.

References

Centraal Bureau voor de Statistiek (CBS). (2012). *Statline onderwijsstatistieken.* Den Haag: CBS.

Commissie Goed Onderwijsbestuur VO. (2014). *De letter en de geest. Adviezen voor versterking van de bestuurskracht in het voortgezet onderwijs. Eindrapport.* Den Haag: *Commissie Goed Onderwijsbestuur VO.*

De Boer, A., & De Klerk, M. (2014). *Perspectives of caregivers and non-caregivers on the options to increase informal care.* Presentation at the EUGMS / NVG KNOWS conference. Rotterdam, 19 September.

De Boer, N., & Van der Lans, J. (2014). *Decentraal: De stad als sociaal laboratorium.* Amsterdam: Atlas.

Dekker, P., & Den Ridder, J. (2015). *Burgerperspectieven 2015|1*. Den Haag: Sociaal en Cultureel Planbureau.

Josten, E., & De Boer, A. (2015). *Concurrentie tussen mantelzorg en betaald werk*. Den Haag: Sociaal en Cultureel Planbureau.

Kickert, W.J.M. (1986). *Overheidsplanning: Theorieën, technieken en beperkingen*. Assen: Van Gorcum.

Kickert, W.J.M. (1991). *Complexiteit, zelfsturing en dynamiek: Over management van complexe netwerken bij de Overheid*. Alphen aan den Rijn: Samsom.

Kickert, W.J.M. (2014). Specificity of change management in public organizations: Conditions for successful organizational change in Dutch ministerial departments. *American Review of Public Administration, 44*(6), 693–717.

Kickert, W.J.M., & Van Vught, F.A. (Eds.). (1995). *Public policy & administration sciences in the Netherlands*. London: Prentice Hall.

Lubberman, J., & Verbeek, F. (2014). *Rolopvatting van besturen. Een studie naar de rolopvattingen van bestuurders en de wijze waarop dit door schoolleiders wordt ervaren*. Nijmegen: ITS Radboud Universiteit Nijmegen and Amsterdam: Kohnstamm Instituut.

Oldenhof, L.E. (2015). *The multiple middle: Managing in healthcare*. Doctoral dissertation. Rotterdam: Erasmus University.

Postma, J.P. (2015). *Scaling care: An analysis of the structural, social and symbolic dimensions of scale in healthcare*. Doctoral dissertation. Rotterdam: Erasmus University.

Putters, K. (2015). *Moedig onderwijsbestuur*. Den Haag: Ministerie van Onderwijs, Cultuur en Wetenschap.

Sociaal en Cultureel Planbureau. (2014). *Verschil in Nederland: Sociaal en cultureel rapport*. Den Haag: SCP.

Sterckx, L. (2014). *Trouwen met een vreemdeling: Afstand en nabijheid in de relaties van 'Turken' en 'Marokkanen' in een gemengd huwelijk*. Diemen: AMB-Press.

Van der Voet, J. (2014). *Leading change in public organizations: A study about the role of leadership in the implementation of organizational change in a public sector context*. Doctoral dissertation. Rotterdam: Erasmus University.

16 Two Varieties of Administrative Reform

US vs. Europe

Richard Stillman

Introduction

Morristown, Tennessee, is hardly a hotbed of American radicalism. Nestled in the Smokey Mountains, the village of 30,000 is predominately rural, economically farm-based, and regularly votes Republican. Although the City Fathers recently swore to defy the government through civil disobedience, and jail time if necessary, to shield Uwe Romeike, his wife and seven children from federal-ordered deportation to return them to Germany. The Romeikes were asylum-seekers fleeing Germany because of religious and social persecution. This story is not one of the horrors of 1930s German Nazism but rather one of the present and concerns Americans' and continental Europeans' very different definitions of the fundamental values of community, individual rights and the role of the state. German laws forbid parents from educating their children at home, out of a fear of the dangers of growing parallel communities. Schools, from this German perspective, are the best places for those from diverse backgrounds to learn tolerance and respect for one another. By contrast, all 50 American states have, for more than a generation, permitted parents the option of home-schooling their children. From the Romeikes' perspective, they were forced to flee Germany to shield their children from the wicked godlessness of public schools, where Darwinism, homosexuality and secularism are encouraged and taught. Fortunately, the question of their deportation was resolved by the Supreme Court's refusal to hear the case, thereby upholding a lower court's decision that allowed the federal government to place the case on indefinite hold. The family has been allowed to remain in the US without setting legal precedents that would anger Germany and harm foreign relations with Europe.

As this case underscores, cultural values matter for defining contrasting American and continental European views on how best to advance human freedom, public welfare and the good society. Similarly, administrative reform is defined very differently on the two sides of the Atlantic based upon what is considered culturally appropriate and proper for the state to do, as well as what it cannot or should not do. As an idea, administrative reform takes root, flowers and influences public actions within distinctive normative Europe/US environments. America, unlike any other nation, is a product of an extreme anti-statist tradition. The US Declaration of Independence is largely a laundry list of complaints against King George III for what the colonists regarded as administrative abuses against their God-given English liberties. In Thomas Jefferson's ringing words in the Declaration: 'We hold these truths to be self-evident that all men are created equal and endowed by their Creator with life, liberty, and the pursuit of happiness.' Of course, Jefferson had merely paraphrased Locke's philosophy, but had conveniently switched Locke's 'property rights' to the far more sweeping democratic phrase, 'the pursuit of happiness'. Hence, when the Founders wrote the US Constitution more the a decade later, no mention was made of administration but rather a tangle of limits are placed upon government, e.g., separation of powers, federalism, enumerated powers, to prevent government action from infringing upon individual freedom. Indeed, the first ten amendments, the Bill of Rights, added immediately after the Constitution's ratification to placate the Anti-Federalists, begins, 'Congress shall make no law. . . .' Here was the ultimate protection of what Lord Acton would later refer to as 'negative liberties' to prevent government intrusion into a citizen's rights to free speech, press, religion, bearing arms and so forth. This Jeffersonian/Lockean formulation of a limited government as a 'public trust' erected upon the 'consent of the governed' was further embedded in a strict Calvinism that regarded mankind as corrupt due to Adam's Fall. Thus, no one could be trusted with exercising public power for very long; as stressed by James Madison's famed Federalist 51: 'Ambition must be made to counteract ambition.' This tough-minded realism concerning human nature erected a sort of Newtonian Constitution, or a 'machine that would go of itself' to govern America based upon eternal, universal laws with the aim of continuously smashing public power to secure human liberty. This ingrained distrust of authority was reinforced by waves of immigrants to the New World fleeing oppression abroad. To be sure, there were no stout advocates among the new arrivals for Machiavelli's 'Prince', Bodin's 'Divine Right of Kinds', or Hobbes' 'Leviathan'. The few British Tories left at the outbreak of the Revolution fled back to England or up to Canada. Abundant resources, geographic isolation, a lack of major foreign threats, a largely self-sufficient agricultural economy and a minimal need for extensive public services together further reinforced the 'self-evident rightness' of America's virulent anti-statist beliefs. The result was the birth of a new republican way of thinking about politics, in stark contrast to the centuries old classical theory of politics. As Gordon Wood reminds us, with the ratification of the US Constitution, 'The Americans had reversed in a revolutionary way the traditional conception of politics: the stability of government no longer relied, as it had on for centuries, upon its embodiment of the basic social forces of the state. Indeed, it now depended upon the prevention of various social interests from incorporating themselves too firmly in government. [. . .] Americans placed a new emphasis on the piecemeal and the concrete at the expense of order and completeness.' (Wood, 1969: 606).

If the normative values that define administrative reform in America from the outset are culturally infused with the peculiar amalgam of Jeffersonian/ Lockean/Calvinism to protect the individual from real and imaginary government threats, administrative reform in the European Union grew out of remarkably dissimilar circumstances that also fashioned dissimilar values and outlooks that profoundly shape European countries' approach to administrative reform. The EU was founded upon the rubble of a century of catastrophic warfare. As Tony Judt (2005: 13) put it so aptly, 'Europe in the aftermath of World War II offered the prospect of utter misery and desolation.' The chief villain was the totalitarian state. Here, the world witnessed the culmination of global destruction by powerful states mobilized to wage total war. No conflict in history killed so many in so short a time. An estimated 19 million civilians were slaughtered, accounting for roughly half of the total World War II deaths. Few urban areas were left intact: great cities such as Rotterdam, Dresden, Stalingrad, and Le Havre were either totally destroyed or heavily damaged. Especially destructive was the German retreat. In France alone (largely untouched by war until then), 10,000 railroad engines, or 80% of the country's rail transport, were destroyed, as were two-thirds of its merchant fleet and one-half million homes and apartment complexes. George Kennan, the respected American diplomat, described the Russian advance into Germany as follows: 'The disaster that befell this area with the entry of the Soviet Forces has no parallel in modern European History. There were considerable sections of it where [. . .] scarcely a man, woman, or child of the indigenous population were left alive after the initial passage of Soviet Forces [. . .]. The Russians [. . .] swept the population clear [. . .]' (Judt, 2005: 19).

First, enter Adam Smith via the Marshall Plan to rebuild post-war Europe. Fear of the spread of communism throughout Europe along with the urgent necessity of feeding, housing, employing and caring for millions of refugees who had lost everything, even their homelands, in the aftermath led to the unprecedented and visionary Marshall Plan (named for its author, Secretary of State George Marshall). While the Plan contributed $13 billion (over $100 billion in today's dollars) to European recovery during the critical crisis years 1948–52, its institutional legacy of breaking down trade barriers and promoting European-wide cooperation was far greater. It was no secret that this major motive was behind American largess. As CIA Director Allen Dulles explained at the time, 'The Plan presupposes that we desire to help restore Europe which can and will be able to compete with us in world markets and for that very reason will be able to buy substantial amounts of our products.' (Judt, 2005: 44) In several ways, American practical business self-interest mixed with the Wilsonian desire to 'make the world safe for democracy' forced Europeans to shift from a preoccupation with power politics to the pursuit of laissez-faire policies. Recipients were left to determine their own priorities regarding how to spend funds for their recovery, but they were also expected to meet and confer, not only with the US but also with one another to plan for European recovery as a whole. To facilitate financial transactions, the Marshall Plan established a European Payments Union, a clearinghouse for debits and credits among countries, which facilitated 'multi-laterialized' free trade among participants. Incrementally, free trade ideals grew into the present EU: first, with the creation in 1951 of the European Coal and Steel Community among the Benelux, German, and French nations; then the 1957 Treaty of Rome, expanding the open market commitment to six nations; and accelerating after the fall of the Soviet Union with the 1992 Maastricht Treaty that gave birth to a common currency with open borders among 28 EU countries at present.

What better way to smash the strong state tradition than appeal to individual economic self-interest to promote the general public good? Inspired by Adam Smith's 'The Wealth of Nations', such an approach fundamentally advances an economic doctrine for idealistic political ends: i.e., smash state control to open the unrestricted flow of goods, services, people; through the pursuit of individual self-interest, the general community welfare will be vastly increased, harmonized and prosper in the long run. However, not entirely, because morality, especially that grounded on Catholicism in secular guise, silently framed the normative foundations of present-day Europe. In some ways, Catholicism served to fill the post-war intellectual void that shunned enthusiasm for the total ideologies of the past. Fired by faith in a better tomorrow, built upon moral cohesion, transcending national sovereignty, devoted to advancing community welfare and collective responsibility, post-war leaders and their political parties were almost entirely governed by Christian Democrats who grew up in the traditional Church and embraced its humane doctrines: e.g., Konrad Adenauer of West Germany, General De Gaulle in France, Alcide de Gasperi of Italy, and Paul-Henri Spaak of Belgium. With right wing parties banned and pleas from the pulpit to vote against communists, Catholic voters had little alternative but to cast ballots for Christian Democrats. Often they did so in large numbers because of official Church directives that gave Christian Democrats unprecedented ruling majorities and political clout throughout post-war continental Europe. It did not escape notice that all six foreign ministers who signed the 1951 Coal and Steel Treaty were Catholics, as were all the early EU Fathers—Robert Schuman, George Bidault, and Jean Monnet of France; Adenauer of Germany; Gasperi of Italy; and Spaak of Belgium, all of whom witnessed first-hand the devastation of the Continent, most coming from marginalized regions of their societies, with many suffering direct persecution and jail-time for their opposition during the war. Thus, much of the high-flown rhetoric of EU Founders is laced with Catholicism's belief in adherence to the transcendence of a higher natural law for advancing collective moral betterment. Schuman's words, for example, refer to 'a high authority' in initiating the 'Schuman Plan' to incorporate West Germany into European Affairs: 'The French Government proposes the entire French-Coal and steel production be placed under a joint high authority within the framework of an organization which would also be open to the participation of other countries of Europe.' As with the incremental advancement of Smithian open markets throughout the Continent from six to 28 nations, so too did collective moral enlightenment and responsibility arrive little by little or, perhaps more accurately, by cash redistribution, under the EU's purview. With the establishment of the European Regional Development Fund in 1975, EU funds were automatically transferred from affluent nations to underdeveloped regions. These vast monetary redistributions had grown to 35% of the total EU budget by the dawn of the twenty-first century and were intended to promote structural and cohesive unity by reducing economic inequities in the EU. They also represented a powerful enticement for new nations to join the EU and old ones to remain members, but the funds came with a high price, i.e., membership required adhering to increasingly detailed requirements and strict legal restrictions covering a vast range of business, development, criminal, judicial, environmental, health and safety standards. Ironically, as established Church attendance and adherence to The Faith declined dramatically throughout post-war Europe, Catholicism secured a degree of universal morality in a secular EU guise, no small thanks to Adam Smith's individualistic pursuit of self-interest, a humanistic universalism neither legitimized nor enforced throughout Europe since the Middle Ages.

What an odd philosophical couple. Strange that a protestant product of the eighteenth century Scottish Enlightenment, Adam Smith, foisted upon Europeans by the victorious Yanks, combined with two millennia of Catholic theology, should shape the normative foundations of the European countries' administrative reform. However, one more critical value component required addition, and it came thanks to the French. The entire EU edifice needed structure and talent to operate. Here, Saint Simon, the nineteenth century anti-revolutionary, idealist French philosopher, who decidedly shaped the structure of the modern technocratic state in France, turned out to be just the right answer. Recall that the French, specifically in the 'Schuman Plan', took the initiative to reach out to incorporate Germany into the early 1951 Treaty, and throughout the EU's development, the French considered it in their national interest to tightly bind the Germans to a permanent European Community under French guidance and regime to prevent another catastrophic war. Thus, replicating the Saint Simonian French-style state for the EU became a natural means and method to securely tie German efficiency to French rule via top-down governance by neutral experts, especially economists and lawyers, to enhance Europe's overall performance, efficiency and effectiveness. The EU administrative elite would manage the European economy and industrial development to create the 'good society' for the entire Continent. It would be the ideal positivist technocratic state, free of politics, class conflict and ideology, devoted to problem-solving, and result in the increasing flow of goods and services to promote material blessings for human welfare regardless of class, race or nationality. Here, technocrats would rule, based upon meritocratic selection, and apply unbiased rationality to promote the general welfare. If Adam Smith's *Wealth of Nations* was ultimately a moral treatise that argued for the advancement of mankind via free markets and the traditional theology of Catholicism in sacral form similarly sought to transcend the nation-state to raise mankind to a higher morality, so too was Saint Simon a moralist who optimistically envisioned a new secular religion of humanity, replacing competitive power politics, traditional religion and classical metaphysics with a value-free, applied scientific method that transcended nation-state rivalry to benefit humanity as a whole. Granted, the Smithian-Catholicism-Saint Simon's procedural means and end-goals differed radically, but the normative foundations of institutional enterprises are rarely logical and uniform in practice, and the EU is certainly no exception. However, what this odd fellowship achieved was something no one could quite describe: was 'it' a confederation, federation, union or what? Certainly by the dawn of the twenty-first century, 'it' was more than merely a common market, but 'it' was hardly a traditional nation-state. The EU increasingly encompassed the whole of the Continent and intruded deeply into traditional national sovereignty by enforcing universal 'positive liberties' for citizens via its laws, rules and regulations. Here was a fundamentally different, utopian approach to advance human freedom, in stark contrast to that of uniquely American 'negative liberty', and this would have profound consequences for the substance and practice of administrative reform on both sides of the Atlantic.

The Meaning of Administrative Reform: US vs. Europe

What does this all-too-brief review of the normative bases of US/European governance have to do with administrative reform on both sides of the Atlantic?

Everything!

First, it explains the fundamentally different rationale for administrative reform in the US compared with Europe. The US may be one of the most modern, wealthiest and advanced societies on the planet. However, its government is also the only one that is constantly forced to look backward to a normative eighteenth century great charter to legitimize its twenty-first century public decisions. The charter's inherent values epitomize a tough-minded realism concerning the dangers to individual liberty posed by strong government, and its Newtonian machinery is designed to run in perpetual motion, breaking up public power to safeguard individual freedom and that, in turn, continues to legitimize its popularity and worth. This is why it took so long for the very idea of administrative reform to arrive in the US, precisely a century after the Constitution was drafted. Not until

1887 did Woodrow Wilson's famed essay, 'The Study of Administration,' that merely advocated the concept of public administration to 'run the Constitution' (Wilson, 1887). By the late nineteenth century, the survival of the Constitution was in doubt due to the massive forces of change, the swiftest and most encompassing in American history, thanks, among other factors, to industrialization, urbanization, foreign immigration, labor/management unrest, technological innovation, overseas involvement, the closing of the frontier and the democratic enfranchisement of new citizens. Only when its back was against the wall, so to speak, or its fundamental constitutional legitimacy under siege, did the American people reach for administrative reform as means of sustaining the governing order designed to ensure 'negative liberty'. If America first adopted a republican Constitution, then extended democracy throughout the nation after the Jacksonian Revolution and Civil War, and finally only then accepted the necessity of administrative reform because there was no other choice to sustain its great charter of 1787, the EU was born from a long history of administrative reform ideas rooted in Roman Law and developed more extensively in Machiavelli, Bodin, Hobbes, the Napoleonic Code, and many other sources. Along with free trade ideas, Catholic morality in secular guise, and Saint Simonian technocracy, administrative reform in Europe was refashioned after World War II to break the grip of past strong state rule to create a more open, equitable, free and humane continental society. Its ultimate rationale was utopian and forward-looking to promote a better tomorrow for citizens through turning administrative reform in the opposite direction, from one that had originally fathered the penultimate totalitarian state hell-bent on mass warfare into the reverse, namely, an instrument to promote greater democracy and 'positive liberty'.

Second, strict Jeffersonian/Lockean/Calvinist anti-statism meant that American administrative reform came incrementally, piecemeal, often silently, and without fanfare as a response to specific empirical issues as they arose: a civil service system for a state or city here and there to end corrupt political practices or regulatory commissions to regulate interstate railroad rates and then another commission to oversee a different economic market, such as food and drug regulation. Administrative reform developed without plan or form and only as pragmatic circumstances demanded. The result is that administrative reforms appear neither uniform nor consistent; rather, they are more or less experimental, temporary and haphazardly constructed through trial and error as pragmatic instruments to fix specific problems as they arose. The EU's administrative reforms, by comparison, have been developed and implemented in a far more holistic and uniform manner. Its civil service follows the strict French model with a clear hierarchy, applied bureaucratic neutral expertise, a distinct corporate identity and a strong sense of ethical purpose. Its central bank, the European Central Bank, modeled on the German Bundesbank, is independent, neutral, professional and meritocratic to the core. When the EU inaugurated the euro, on January 1,

1999, the complex endeavor of starting a common Continent-wide currency came off without a hitch. Rules for membership are uniformly enforced across 28 nations over a wide array of social, economic, political, judicial areas. Whereas political controversies are numerous and often serious, threatening the entire EU project's very survival, EU administrative reforms, at least by contrast to America, appear remarkably well-planned, efficiently implemented and consistently organized.

Third, the EU's administrative structure was initiated, led and operated for much of its history thanks to European top-down elite support, especially from a generation who had endured the horrific memories of World War II. Each step forward in creating the present-day EU came from leaders of the major states agreeing, bit by bit, to concede portions of their state sovereignty to the EU. From the 'Schuman Plan' that first created the 1951 Coal and Steel Community to the creation of the euro on January 1, 1999, to sustaining the EU's existence stems from the ongoing commitment by nation-state political elites. Often, administrative advances came through complex, lengthy and difficult negotiations either directly by elites themselves or their representatives. American administrative reform, by contrast, largely 'bubbled up' from the grassroots, imbued with Protestant 'moral uplift' and 'democratic idealism'. Local reform groups such as the National Civil Service League, National Municipal League, League of Women Voters, and Bureaus of Municipal Research spawned numerous administrative reforms across the nation, first in localities, then moving upward to the state and federal levels. Executive budgets, for example, began with experiments by the NYC Bureau of Municipal Research at the turn of the century to improve economy/efficiency and reduce corruption in city government. The budget idea was refined and spread across cities by 'the bureau movement' and was eventually established at the federal level with the passage of The Budget and Accounting Act of 1922. To this day, significant American administrative reform, from welfare reform in 1996 to 'No Child Left Behind' educational reform in 2005, was—and is—mainly a product of 'bubbling up' from grassroots innovation rather than 'trickling down' from national government directives.

Fourth, the positive law tradition, which drove (and still drives) most European development, was missing entirely in America when administrative reform began during the Progressive Era. Rooted in notions of Fundamental Law, the US Constitution, and common law, or law based upon case precedent, public law did not exist until Frank Goodnow literally 'discovered' public law by recognizing its necessity and importance in the first essay he penned on this topic in 1886. The US, therefore, had to look elsewhere for means and methods to build its administrative state by reforms from the ground up, so to speak. It was the field of management to which the reformers turned. The two most important books that administrative reformers looked to as 'Holy Gospels' at the dawn of the twentieth century were Frank Goodnow's 'Politics and Administration' (1900) and Frederick Taylor's 'The Principles of Scientific Management' (1911). The former justified a sharp separation between politics and administration that created room for administrative reform to originate and grow; the later proposed management principles rooted in science and popular business values of economy and efficiency to propel reform throughout government. Without a sense of state, here was a masterful yet sleight-of-hand route to graft onto the Constitution administrative reforms it never mentioned: e.g., budgets, personnel systems, planning methods, executive organizations. Management, not law, became the basis for formulating public administration reform in America, starting with Leonard White's first textbook in 1926, 'An Introduction to the Study of Public Administration', and continuing to the present, where repeated public cries to 'make government run more like a business' are heard, something inconceivable to many continental Europeans because the traditional nation-state has been, for better or worse, front and center throughout their historical tradition and its public laws sanctified to promote uniformity and equity throughout society. Indeed the EU's Document of Fundamental Rights extends positive law to protect and enforce an unprecedented range of citizenship rights to healthcare, education, union membership, strike, limit work hours, require rest periods, free placement services, environmental protection, consumer protection, prevention of discrimination on the basis of age, sex, race, social origin, genetic features, language discrimination and every conceivable human right. While American rights begin with limits on government intrusion, the EU extends positive law to advance human rights to nearly everything and anything, thereby legitimizing an almost unlimited potential for the EU's application of positive law.

Ultimately, American administrative reform does not advance a new ideology that challenges or fundamentally undermines national authority; rather, it intends to restore and sustain the existing constitutional order. Woodrow Wilson's original argument for the field's urgent need in America, 'to run the Constitution' remains true to this day, namely, most major administrative reforms seek to revitalize and ensure that the country's universal values and ideals continue. This is why administrative reform in America becomes such a passionate moral issue, at times because it was—and is—inherently linked to sustaining who we are as an American People, the American Creed as embodied in the US Constitution. Reading about the work of key progressive administrative reformers from Richard Childs, who 'fathered council-manager government' across America, to Louis Brownlow, who chaired the 1937 'Brownlow Report' that fundamentally reorganized the office of the US Presidency for the first time since 1789, the passion for their reforms was clear and unequivocal because the cause was all about sustaining American Democracy and its Constitutional ideals. Granted, administrative reform had to be slipped into the governing apparatus quietly here and there, often adapting and changing the Founders' original design, but reformers' ideas always had be made to conform, at times by court orders, to basic constitutional doctrines. Some such as Don Price have referred to the entire edifice of administrative reforms as 'the unwritten constitution' (1982) because it is currently so essential to make society run, government tick and the American Constitution live in the twenty-first century. The word 'public' in public administration reform is critical to its ongoing legitimization and broad appeal because its aims seek to address problems of all people and ultimately conform to the American Creed embodied in the Constitution. As Herbert Croly once defined it, administrative reform '[. . .] is a moral protest and awaking, which seeks to enforce the violated laws and restore American political and economic tradition to its pristine purity and vigor [. . .] Reform means at the bottom no more than moral and political purification.' (Croly, 1909: 144) By contrast, for the EU, administrative reform is founded upon a uniquely forward-looking utopian ideology designed to break up the monopoly of traditional nation-state power for the continent-wide material-social-political betterment of humankind. It grew from odd mix of moral visions, Adam Smith, Catholicism, and Simonian Technocracy, to escape the politically repressive politics built upon the strong nation-state of the past. Thus, the EU's route and means to smash the state were hardly the same as America's. Americans again were 'born free', lacking any sense of a strong state to smash, whereas continental Europeans were very aware of the total state's profoundly devastating post-war impact everywhere around them. The old European order had to be fundamentally changed and challenged by new ideas or an entirely unique ideology, first by freer trade and open markets, then by the redistribution of funds from the rich to the poor, to forge 'a social model' via administrative enforcement of uniform membership rules and procedures. Hardly cultivating or growing out of the same grassroots, moral reformist enthusiasms as America, or intricately linked to restoring and sustaining the fundamental identity of a people as in America, but nonetheless a genuinely original utopian vision for governing, imposed from the top-down, to forge a new European-wide identity free of its past horrors.

How US/EU Administrative Reform Really Works: Twin Economic Crises

When major crises occur, how do the US and EU administrative systems respond? Do their systemic survival strategies manifest the forgoing five administrative reform characteristics that exhibit more differences than similarities?

Both the US and the EU suffered severe economic crises. During 2007–08, America endured the worse economic downturn since the Great Depression of the 1930s, and in 2010 the Euro Zone faced a financial crisis that tested its very survival as a common currency. The sources of the two crises differed significantly: the US' was rooted in a housing bubble in which the Federal Reserve (Fed) maintained low interest rates for too long, thereby stimulating excessive investment in residential and business mortgages, which were often highly speculative, risky and traded with little transparency. When creditors began demanding their money back, major financial institutions with high leverage and shaky debt, such as Lehman Brothers, which declared bankruptcy on September 15, 2008, failed, triggering panic throughout financial markets. However, while the euro crisis was partially exacerbated by America's deep recession, the former crisis was triggered essentially by the low interest rates of the ECB, prodded by large states such as Germany to maintain industrial productivity and low inflation. However, the one-size-fits-all universal rates imposed by the ECB throughout the entire zone had direr consequences for the poorer EU nations around the periphery. There was the popular misconception that the national bonds of every EU nation carried approximately similar risks of default. When Greece and other countries on the EU's southern borders, after years of excessive public and private spending fostered by the ECB's low rates, faced default, no financial safeguards were in place for either bondholders or bank depositors. Severe panic spread rapidly throughout the EU. Bond interest rates immediately shot upward on high-risk national loans with those countries' banks in serious jeopardy of collapse.

The administrative responses to these unprecedented economic shocks on both sides of the Atlantic underscore the basic differences between administrative reform styles. First, America's leadership felt a deep reluctance for government to intervene in private markets. Alan Greenspan's devout adherence to libertarian free market philosophy had initially helped fuel the market meltdown by keeping interest rates too low for too long, but his successor, Ben Bernanke, as well as senior White House economic officials, were similarly initially reluctant to intervene with public monies to prop up failing firms such as Lehman Brothers. This attitude would change rapidly as all watched with horror the panic that ensued, but nonetheless, they held a conscious belief in the separation of the public and private spheres. Throughout the EU crisis, the public/private separation was not as much a concern as the survival of its member nations and the EU as a whole. Whereas there were critics who considered Greece unfit to belong to the euro zone because of its various rule infractions, no mechanism was in place to allow its departure. When the welfare of the community was threatened by Greece's potential collapse, Jean-Claude Trichet, the ECB President, assembled a team of experts who secretly flew to Greece, examined the fiscal situation, and returned with their recommendations. Whereas Trichet had publicly stated, 'No government, no state can expect special treatment from us', (as quoted in Irwin, 2013: 207), he rapidly reversed his position, allowing banks to post Greek bonds as collateral at the ECB for ready cash and enlisted the IMF for assistance. The survival of the whole could not be jeopardized by the failure of one nation (or as rapidly became the case, several).

Second, the US responded characteristically in an incremental, experimental fashion, in contrast to the EU's system-wide approach. Many critics of America's reaction to the crisis commented on its lack of consistency and even unfairness. Why bail out AIG and GM but not Lehman Brothers or Bear Sterns? Why let the Fed dramatically expand the money supply and keep interest rates excessively low through its innovative bond purchases of (quantitative easing) QE1, QE2, and QE3? Why give the Treasury Secretary nearly a blank check to spend $700 billion in TARP funds that went primarily to prop up large financial institutions such as AIG, Fannie Mae and Freddie Mac but not homeowners who lost their homes due to foreclosures? Was this not over-the-top abuse of its discretionary authority? It certainly appeared so to those skeptical of the government's policies and the constitutionality of its actions, but its statutory authority and fear of sliding into another Great Depression propelled the use of all available methods, no matter how unique or unprecedented. The ECB, by contrast, from the outset of the euro crisis had to view economic matters far more systemically because of its charter and EU rules. If the Fed charter gave it numerous responsibilities such as addressing BOTH inflation and unemployment issues, the ECB had only one mission, namely combatting inflation, which in turn decidedly limited the scope of the ECB President's policy actions. Further, if Greek bonds were allowed to serve as collateral at the ECB, the same opportunity must be open to other European nations. The ECB might encourage better economic management for those such as Greece that had been profligate or EU-wide bank standards and deposit insurance to safeguard deposits, but national sovereignty strictly prevented such expanded and experimental administrative remedies.

Third, the US' bottom-up, often contradictory and confusing administrative approach, as opposed to the ECB's top down, far more coordinated, unified style, was also evident. America's is imposed by the Fed's structure. Its Open Market committee, its chief policy arm, is composed of 19 members, the Fed Chair, six governors (the Treasury Secretary and five presidential appointees), plus the Presidents of 12 Regional Federal Reserve Banks, representing local banks, businesses, and consumers in their respective regions. Moreover, the Regional Banks are hardly representative of the national economy because Missouri has two Regional Banks, in St. Louis and Kansas City, an area that reflects less than 2% of the US economy, vs. only one in San Francisco covering all of California, which has 20% of the national economy. The Fed Chair may be first among equals, but he/she acts based upon committee consensus that is also deeply influenced by local interests. Further, US economic regulatory policy is highly fragmented and decentralized, exhibiting numerous gaps. Each of the 50 states has its own bank and insurance regulators, and within the Federal Government three agencies share bank oversight—the Fed, FDIC, and Controller of the Currency—and this does not even begin to count the number of congressional oversight committees and subcommittees that also have considerable influence over these matters. Regarding gaps, the most notable and one that sparked the recent crisis was transactions that were entirely unsupervised and involved the huge national mortgage market, especially the sub-prime mortgage market that grew to represent 20% of residential/business loans. If America reflects bottom-up, fragmented institutions sharing regulatory authority, often ad hoc and haphazardly, the ECB is clearly structured and designed to be run by elites, top-down. The ECB was modeled on the German Bundesbank and is strictly required to be independent from EU politics. It is headquartered in Frankfort as a condition for its creation in 1997 and for German agreement to participate in the euro. While 28 member states compose the ECB's Governing Council, the five-member Executive Council, made up of the President and, typically, the four largest EU nations, set policy. Deliberations are conducted entirely in English and its minutes are sealed for thirty years, which inhibits national politics and promotes unity (the Fed releases its minutes within weeks). The decisions of the larger Governing Council, which must ratify the Executive Council's decisions, are limited to five minutes from each member. Thus, when the ECB President states his opinion, most others concur and dissent limited because no lengthy debates are allowed (unlike the Fed Chair, who must realize consensus on the Board, the members of which have unlimited time to voice dissent).

Fourth and as a result of their contrasting governing arrangements, Ben Bernanke spent much of his time listening, coordinating, convincing, bargaining, persuading and managing relationships among Fed board members, the administration, congressional leaders, business and other interest groups to cope with and contain the recession. He never ordered because he could simply not do so, but he was a master consensus builder, coordinator and conciliator of diverse interests. Certainly, his stature as a leading academic economist and the urgent need to address the worst financial crisis since the Great Depression helped to immensely boost his influence and leadership relative to other economic players, but the Fed Chair was always one among many and had to remain conscious of his limits to be effective at negotiating solutions. By comparison, Trichet forcefully steered, directed, and at times, dictated policy from above. He was expected to do so given the authority vested in his office, and he readily used it. As a senior French civil servant, he rose to become French Finance Minister and represent France throughout the numerous, complex and long negotiations that created the ECB and Common Currency. Trichet was appointed to head the ECB in 2003 for an eight-year term not only because he knew the internal operations of the ECB well but also because he shared the values of the post-war elites of large nations that the EU had to survive for the sake of Europe's future prosperity. It was said, 'He spoke French with a German accent' (as cited in Irwin, 2013: 115). In short, he closely hewed to the German insistence upon tight monetary policy and would play by the ECB's rules to enforce its single mandate, i.e., combatting inflation. Legal procedure, following established rules and formal procedures, insistence on giving direction based upon what the law allows and giving discretion were his talents, which he had honed as a seasoned French Civil Servant with years of crisis-fighting experience. The centralized, neutral ECB Presidency further discouraged publicity and open negotiation and promoted secrecy, unanimous agreement without dissent, and the application of nonpartisan expertise with dispatch yet within clear guidelines.

Finally, when Congress passed the 2319-page Dodd-Frank Act in 2010 to 'fix' what many regarded as a failed system, for all the sound and fury, the system changed little. The Fed's authority was not reformed substantially, only a review by the Government Accountability Office (GAO) was called for; the same fragmented, decentralized regulatory structure remained in place, except that the Office of Thrift Supervision, which had somehow neglected oversight of the massive derivatives market, a major cause of the recession, was abolished and its responsibilities moved elsewhere. Consumer protection, which had been a responsibility of several government agencies, now was consolidated into one, an independent Consumer Financial Protection Agency, headed by a presidential appointee. Securitization or requiring banks to have '5%' skin in the game was defeated as was rating agency reform, and the Volcker Rule that would end bank involvement in proprietary trading remains under discussion over its implementation, as does the meaning of 'too big to fail' and banning the trading of derivatives. In short, the American constitutional system in regards to economic regulation operates essentially as it had before the crisis began, which again underscores how the system copes and adapts while fundamental reform of the status quo is rare because of the unshaken American faith in the great charter, free markets and individual freedom. By contrast, the EU also weathered the crisis, but here future survival turns on whether individual member states will surrender more sovereign control over banking regulations, depositor insurance and equity requirements and whether Germany will permit the ECB to expand its mission beyond inflation fighting. Mario Draghi became the new ECB President in 2011 and immediately rescinded the ECB's policy to raise interest rates from 1% to 1.5% Instead, he lowered rates as close to zero as possible. He also greatly expanded LTFO, or Long Term Financing Operations, which increased both the size and maturity of bonds borrowed by nations from the ECB. His repeated emphasis on 'doing whatever it takes to preserve the EURO' (as cited in Blinder, 2013: 425) demonstrated strong leadership commitment to defending the euro, and his willingness to campaign openly for sustaining the EU, something his predecessor was reluctant to do, seems to have renewed member states' and the global community's confidence in the euro. However, Draghi is also defending an ideology or a peculiar way of conceiving of or seeing the world, rooted in the odd utopian amalgam of Adam Smith's free market, Catholic morality in a secular guise and Saint Simon technocracy that profoundly contradicts traditional European nation-state ideas. The rising political power of populist nationalist parties across the continent, the passing of the post-war generation, who experienced first-hand the horrors of World War II, the declining support for traditional party elite governance, the rise of regional separatists such as the Scots and Catalonians, who seek smaller, not larger, governing units, the complacency of many accustomed to two generations of growth and prosperity at least within the northern tier of the EU and the dissatisfaction with nameless, faceless, unelected Brussels bureaucrats raise serious questions regarding the EU's future or whether nation-state members will continue to concede the necessary power to the ECB to prevent future economic crises from reoccurring.

Conclusion: Does Administrative Reform Make the State, or do States Make Administrative Reform Possible?

Both the US and the EU originated from deliberate attempts to escape from the traditional nation-state, but the unique combinations of values that shaped their current development and operation remain conceptual opposites. Their decidedly different foundational norms are profoundly important for determining the respective directions and contents of administrative reforms. The Lockean-Jeffersonian-Calvinist mix embedded in America's framing documents, The Declaration of Independence and US Constitution, inspired the dream of a better tomorrow built upon individual effort free from government interference. Without this belief, as Gunnar Myrdal once observed, what would Americans have in common? Americans are a product of what they believe (Myrdal, 1944: 1–3), or as Richard Hofstadter succinctly said, 'It has been our fate as a nation not to have ideologies but to be one' (as quoted in Kohn, 1957: 13). Thus, in the New World, where 'men are born free', as Alexis de Tocqueville so insightfully wrote long ago, the state became an object of hatred and distrust because it was regarded as a constant barrier to individual initiative. Present-day administrative state institutions, therefore, had to be built from the ground up, incrementally, without a plan, often quietly and only as empirical necessity required, yet somehow always in accord with the dominant 'stateless' constitutional doctrines. Thus, Americans, whether they admit it or not, in fact live in, are governed by and govern the globe as the last superpower thanks to a massive, complex administrative state that is always undergoing change, reform and even constitutional challenges to its basic legitimacy. However, the Founders also ensured maximum citizen involvement throughout all aspects of its governing arrangements such that popular support for the entire edifice could be questioned but never denied. Its system similarly fosters excessive individualism and polarized partisanship that at times stymies public action that would benefit the majority and even bring it to the brink of disaster as in the case during World War II, when adequate military preparations and defense were delayed due to skillful isolationist minorities. Nonetheless, the American administrative system is also remarkably open, flexible, adaptive and amazingly stable, as evidenced by its performance throughout the recent Great Recession.

If the Lockean-Jeffersonian-Calvinist normative framework of the US appears antique to the modern world, its fundamental elements are strikingly compatible in that their ideals/ideas all derive from the protestant reformation and altogether emphasize 'negative liberty' to advance human freedom. The EU's normative foundations are far less compatible. Collectively they composed a dash of protestant free market idealism, catholic morality in secular guise, and a technocratic vision, design and direction to promote human freedom and a continent-wide good society by ultimately transcending nation-states. Here was 'positive liberty' to force the individual to be free in the tradition of great European state builders such as Machiavelli, Hobbes and Rousseau yet targeted against the modern nation-state to end its monopolistic, cruel, and destructive five-hundred-plus-year reign. EU administrative reform became one of many competing ideologies on the continent that focused upon smashing the old pre-World War II order of state power politics and replacing it with a new humane, democratic, open 'model society' dedicated to promoting 'positive freedom' in the most extensive and encompassing utopian manner yet witnessed in recorded human history. As did America, the EU laid a unique normative groundwork for administrative reform, but one forged from the horrific circumstances of total war, designed top-down by the consensus of national elites, governing through non-political positive law, with far broader, more holistic and idealistic ambitions. Like America, the EU's ultimate aim was to escape the political state. However, if America's escape route led to numerous concrete negatives preventing state action and over-idealizing individual protection, which often frustrate majority preferences on issues from gun control to abortion rights, irrespective of how beneficial the results might be for society, in Europe, as the last decade vividly demonstrated, the nation-state is hardly a dead letter but is even more potent in deciding the EU's fate. The failed ratification of the draft EU Constitution in 2005 came from no votes in referendums in two of its founding members, France and the Netherlands. Certainly, as the recent financial crisis reflected, Berlin, not Brussels, makes the decisions on the Greek bailout and the euro's survival. Thus, if American administrative reform succeeded in constructing the modern American administrative state, based on piecemeal administrative reforms that often frustrate the will of majorities, it remains unclear whether the EU's administrative reforms can advance and successfully smash the old order and create something new, whatever it may be called, to realize humanity's greatest ideals.

References

Blinder, A. (2013). *After the music stopped: The financial crisis, the response, and the work ahead*. New York: The Penguin Press.
Croly, H. (1909). *The promise of American life*. New York: Macmillan.

Goodnow, F. (1900). *Politics and administration*. New York: Macmillan.

Irwin, N. (2013). *The alchemists: Three central bankers and a world on fire*. New York: Penguin Press.

Judt, T. (2005). *Postwar: A history of Europe since 1945*. New York: Penguin Books.

Kohn, H. (1957). *American nationalism: An interpretative essay*. New York: Macmillan.

Myrdal, G. (1944). *An American dilemma*. New York: Harper Brothers.

Price, D. (1982). *America's unwritten constitution: Science, religion, and political responsibility*. Baton Rouge, LA: Louisiana State University Press.

Taylor, F.W. (1911). *The principles of scientific management*. New York: W.W. Norton.

White, L.D. (1926). *Introduction to the study of public administration*. New York: Macmillan.

Wilson, W. (1887). The study of administration. *Political Science Quarterly, 2*(2), 197–222.

Wood, G.S. (1969). *The creation of the American republic, 1776–1787*. Chapel Hill, NC: University of North Carolina Press.

17 Becoming a Student of Reform

Frans-Bauke van der Meer, Christoph Reichard and Arthur Ringeling

Introduction

Public managers and other public administration professionals and, increasingly, managers and professionals in societal and private organizations, are occupied with or confronted by governmental reform processes. In this contribution, we consider *public sector reforms* (see Kickert, 2000; Kickert, 2005; Kickert, 2007) from an educational perspective. We will argue why it is important for students who are or wish to become public managers, professionals or academics in the field to study public reforms. We ask how they can be supported in this learning process. We attempt to answer this question by exploring reforms as an object of investigation and learning and by analyzing how academic degree programs can and do support future professionals and scholars in becoming students of reform. How do they learn to gain insight into the intended or unintended impacts of reform processes and react and effectively direct these processes? We present our views and findings against the background of our experiences in teaching Public Administration over several decades in various university programs.

We understand public sector reform as intended comprehensive change in the structure and functions of public organizations and networks. The concept of change in the public sector encompasses different levels of aggregation. We can study a single reform measure, a reform policy, administrative reform targeting different policies and reform movements. We can study reforms from an ex ante, concomitant or ex post perspective. We can study various issues in reforms, e.g., the underlying problems, triggers and causes, the reform strategies and policies, the actors and their aims, interests and powers, the intended and unintended results and impacts and, not least, the different values involved. Finally, the study of reform can focus on different stages of a reform process: on the design and decision-making, on the implementation, on intended or unintended impacts and on the evaluation of a reform. However, it is not possible to demarcate precisely the scope of the study of public sector reform. The qualification 'comprehensive transformations', often used as an indicator for public sector reform, depends on the perspective adopted: what may be a minor matter for reformers may represent shifting from one world to another for members of the target group (or, perhaps, vice versa).

In the next section, we argue why studying reform is important for both practitioners and academics in the field of public administration. Then, we devote attention to what should be studied and how by reflecting on different analytical perspectives and normative dimensions of reform processes. Then, we discuss how (future) practitioners and academics can (be educated to) become students of reform, along two lines. Second, we provide some empirical evidence concerning efforts to educate students of public sector reforms in academic Public Administration programs. Third, we identify a number of challenges in such learning processes and suggest options for addressing them, where possible illustrated with examples from practice. We conclude with a brief reflection.

Why Become a Student of Reform?

Governments frequently are occupied with designing and implementing reforms as a means of improving their functioning, of saving money or of realizing substantive changes with respect to existing societal problems. Reforms can be initiated by political, administrative and/or academic stimuli. Public sector reform can be—and generally is—the result of political decision-making, both in the sense of deciding on conflicting values and as the product of institutionalized politics. This role of political decision-making appears consistent with the classic distinction between politics and administration (Goodnow, 2010). However, there are two reservations. First, public managers and professionals play their role in shaping and implementing administrative choices. They can do so because they possess considerable amounts of discretion (Davis, 1971; Ringeling, 1978). Second, because of their increasing professionalism, public managers play a key role in policy formation, especially when it concerns their own organization. The reform measures of the last cabinets in the Netherlands, for instance, are based heavily on an effort by public officials to reduce the budget begun a few years earlier. Thus, public sector reform is fueled not only by political decision-making but also by administrative and professional logics. Academics also play a role in the reform movement. Some are the intellectual godfathers of certain reform movements or contribute considerably to them. Others study reforms and offer advice based on their analyses. Still others engage in prescriptive statements and provide recommendations for how to design reforms and how to manage the implementation of reforms (see Savas, 1987; Kettl, 2000). Public sector reforms imply extensive changes in organizational structures, procedures, strategies and/or personnel policies.

Generally, high costs are to be expected. Often there are also benefits, although not always to the extent expected. Moreover, unintended effects are common. For all of these reasons, the study of reform is important both for understanding the functioning and dynamics of government and for steering reform processes. Therefore, study of reform is not only relevant for Public Administration as an academic discipline but is equally important for politicians, administrators, professionals and managers in the public domain.

There are a number of considerations to support this normative claim.

First, because professionals in the public domain play a key role in shaping and implementing strategic policy choices, changes in service delivery and new approaches to public-private and societal cooperation, they should be able to effectively engage in, design and manage reform processes. This requires insights into the dynamics of reform processes: how do relevant societal and governmental actors anticipate, interpret and react to a given reform initiative? How are reform impacts (intended or unintended) socially constructed? Which power mechanisms play a role, and how are these related to conflicts of interest or values? It also requires skills to develop effective and adaptive strategies in such complex contexts.

Second, public administration professionals and public managers who are or become involved in the design or implementation of reforms are, by definition, simultaneously addressing both goals and means and normative and analytical aspects. They should, therefore, be able to distinguish these aspects, and (re)connect them in a reflexive way. Additionally, they should be able to identify values that are (or may be) affected by the reform, even if this is not intentional. Only by studying these aspects and reflecting on them can sensible goal attainment strategies and measures to prevent undesired effects be developed and applied.

Third, because the success of reform processes is not self-evident, professionals and managers in the public domain should be able to reflect on the design and development processes of reforms and implementation processes and be prepared to contribute to the improvement of ongoing or consecutive reform strategies. This requires that they be able to evaluate reform processes in different stages (ex ante, in process and ex post). Doing so involves answering questions such as the following: which problems should the reform solve? How likely is it that the reform goals will be achieved? What unintended outcomes may emerge? How can the course of the process and its results be explained?

Fourth, insights from monitoring and evaluation may be used to learn, to adapt strategies or to develop new ones, for both current and future reforms. To realize this, public professionals should reflect on what is necessary to learn from experiences and evaluations.

Finally, academic research on reforms is necessary, on the one hand, for a valid picture and explanation of the dynamics of governmental processes and societal problem solving in relation to reforms and, on the other hand, to enable academics to fulfill their societal role in contributing insights, concepts and tools for the improvement of reform design and management.

Aspects of Studying Public Sector Reforms

In becoming a student of reform, one is engaged in learning to understand reform processes and reflecting on them. This involves a number of key analytical questions: how does a reform come about? What is its rationale? What are the impacts of the reform and how can these be explained? However, normative aspects are also important for understanding and addressing reforms: what values and normative choices are involved in the design of a reform? Against what standards can a reform and its intended and unintended impacts be evaluated?

The various theoretical perspectives discussed in the first part of this volume help students (to be) to answer the first two analytical questions (the genesis and rationale of a reform). These questions refer to the presuppositions or policy theory underlying a reform and, thus, to the dominant logic of the reformers. The theoretical approaches discussed in part one may also be helpful in predicting and explaining reform impacts, but not in a straightforward manner. That is, the theoretical argument underlying a reform should not be accepted without discussion as a valid framework for understanding its impacts. The dynamics and impacts of reform processes are generated by the actual behaviors of the actors involved, which are socially constructed through sense-making in interaction (Weick, 1979) and influenced by actor repertoires (Van der Meer, 1983), cultures and power processes (see Allison, 1971; Heyman, 1987).

Thus, students of reform should learn to identify all actors involved, map their interests, resources, repertoires[1] and interdependencies, and study their strategies and interactions. Each of the theoretical perspectives on reform may help to illuminate some actor perspectives and/or characteristics of their interactions, thus supporting a more comprehensive understanding of reform processes. The same holds for other taxonomies of approaches such as that of Hemerijck (2003) (see also Rosenbloom, 2011), the consequential approach (referring to rational analysis and argument or a 'logic of consequence' in Scharpf's (1997) terms), the power approach (cf. Allison, 1971; Heyman, 1987), the institutional approach (cf. March & Olsen, 1989; Lynn, 1996) and the normative approach (see next section). The latter three partly overlap with approaches discussed in this volume. In addition to these theoretical perspectives, actors' accounts of their own vision, philosophy and strategy are useful to answer the analytical questions.

The normative questions are also relevant, both in the analysis and in considering reforms. We will address these questions in the next section. It is possible to analyze these values in specific reform proposals because every reform measure is an expression of public values connected in a certain way to one another. However, a normative analysis can also be conducted for reform movements as a whole, as we will discuss in the next section.

Reform as a Normative Choice

Students of public sector reform should know that reform is a buzzword: reform is 'good', just as innovation is 'good'. These are notions that everyone favors. We are involved in a word game with terms that are attractive and others that are repelling. Perhaps that should be the first lesson for would-be reformers. Reform can lead to improvement, but it can be attractive to some and a disaster for others. There can be disastrous consequences in the sense of unintended and undesired effects. In addressing the issue of public sector reform, we are at the center of a political-administrative discussion. It does not particularly concern technical or politically neutral affairs, but it is certainly related to reform movements that are initiated or promoted by political and value-laden processes.

Public sector reforms are always the result of normative choices (although they are usually also based on analytical insights or practical experiences). All reform movements have a normative core: political and societal values are central. Hood (1991), therefore, characterized these reform movements as doctrines, stressing their normative character. We can refer to their political character, as politics is understood as addressing conflicting values. In the history of Public Administration, there have been many reform movements. In the study of reform, they also must be analyzed. Each author has his or her own typology of movements. Jann (2003) is an example. He distinguishes five movements: the democratic state, the active state, the lean state, the societal state (originally the activating state, but an active and an activating state is perhaps too much of a subtlety) and the regulatory state. Specific movements such as New Public Management and Reinventing Government are part of this typology, organized by their particular view on the state.

The normative foundation of the *democratic state* is the combination of citizenship and the rule of law as a normative standard for governing. Its institutionalization is the democratic *Rechtsstaat*, that historical compromise between liberty and equality, as Mouffe (2005) called it. Considerable time was necessary before it was adequately developed, but from the second half of the twentieth century, it has become robust in Western countries.

The *active state* is the normative consequence of a vision for the role of government in society. Its normative foundation concerns an orientation toward the future, economic welfare and social justice. The role of the state is central to serving these values. Pro-active planning, welfare-focused direction and the intensive coordination of policies and administrative procedures are used as instruments. The state has to play a pivotal role in the humanistic project, in creating decent societies, in creating greater welfare and in distributing it. For these purposes, a public administration organization of a high intellectual and professional level is a necessity.

The moral foundation of the *lean state* paradigm concentrates on economic rationality. The lean state movement is closely related to the New

Public Management doctrine and affiliated with 'lean production' strategies in the private sector. Its main argument is to shrink the public sector and budgets and to transfer public services to the markets to the greatest extent possible. To some extent, it was a response to an excessive and no longer financially sustainable welfare state regime in the decades preceding its development. In a way, this approach expresses the philosophy of utilitarianism: the greatest benefit for the greatest number.

Contract theory can be considered the moral foundation of the *societal state* doctrine. The focus is on the gain of individual rights, offered by the state but also applied against the state. The state offers rights and provisions to citizens, including the right to oppose governmental decisions. However, there is a misunderstanding of its quid pro quo character: a citizen contributes money to the state and should receive goods and services in return. In the individual calculation, government is a matter of taxpayers' money. On the organizational level, contracts determine the relationships among public, private and market organizations. These organizations collaborate in case of a win-win situation. One problem is, however, what these organizations do when there is no feasible win-win outcome. To be able to contract externally, it is preferable for governments to be minimally hampered by rules and regulations. The compilation of contracts, however, does not reduce the number of rules.

The *regulatory state* is to an important extent the consequence of earlier movements. Its need for better and smarter regulation and for structures and procedures that enable these phenomena in a post-modern state is the consequence of reducing the role of government and leaving more public tasks to the market (see Majone, 1996). It enables new forms of co-production among public, private and civil society actors. It is a phase in which parts of the market have to be organized and reorganized. It leads to a new rationality typified as 'more markets, more state', without abolishing all of the previously adopted reform elements such as the rule of law, welfare state protection, the stimulation of privatization and outsourcing. Its moral foundation is to an important extent attributable to instrumental rationalism. When other philosophic considerations are not present, it will be confronted with the same problem as the original instrumentalism: what values is it serving?

Students of public sector reform should be conscious of the different value patterns that underlay measures for reform. They are a result of normative preferences and choices and not neutral instruments for change.

The question of how academics and professionals become capable students of reform gives rise to two further questions: how well are they equipped by their training? How can their process of ongoing learning during their professional career be facilitated? To respond to these questions, we begin by presenting in the next section some findings on the actual attention to reforms in academic instruction on Public Administration. Then, we identify remaining challenges, both in academic programs and with respect to lifelong learning in professional practice, and we suggest possible answers to these challenges.

The Issue of Public Sector Reforms in Academic Degree Programs—Some Empirical Evidence

In this section, we explore to what extent and in which way attention is given to the issue of reform in academic education programs. We wonder whether and to what extent 'reform' plays a role in competence descriptions of programs and whether this issue is listed as a topic in the curricula of such programs. Recently, competences, as a description of the knowledge, skills and abilities expected of graduates have become more relevant in higher education (Lokhoff et al., 2010). First, we examine the competence domains defined as relevant accreditation standards for American Public Administration programs by NASPAA (NASPAA, 2009). However, none of the five listed domains, which are rather general and abstract, directly concerns reforms. Even the examples that NASPAA provides for programs to support the formulation of more concrete competences do not directly focus on the issue of reform.[2] They only emphasize that graduates should be able to 'manage projects' or to 'recognize the social construction of problems', which goes far beyond the issue of reform.

Even if reform is not recognized as a major competence in competence listings, it may be interesting to determine the substantive attention given to this issue in European Public Administration curricula. We therefore analyze the results of a survey of European programs. In 2013, 66 universities were invited to respond to an online questionnaire. In total, 46 programs at 35 universities in 21 countries responded about existing competences and learning outcomes in their curricula. Additionally, nine programs that were recently accredited by EAPAA were evaluated with regard to their competences and learning outcomes. As a result, an inventory of Public Administration-specific competences was established. However, the picture this creates is not much different from the American case: the issue of public sector reforms does not play an important role in that inventory. Very few Public Administration programs include this issue in their competence descriptions, mostly in a quite broad and rather indirect way (e.g., by referring to competences to address change in policy or governance or to make judgments). We can conclude that competences considered relevant for graduates in Public Administration focus more generally on skills such as analyzing, collecting and assessing data, formulating advice, contributing to change and problem solving. The reform issue is not explicitly mentioned in the majority of European Public Administration programs, at least not at the (quite general) level of competences (Reichard & Van der Krogt, 2014).

Based on the NASPAA competence domains and on the survey discussed above, an inventory of PA-specific competences was developed, structured along six subdomains (Reichard & Van der Krogt, 2014). Within these subdomains, four competences with some reference to the issue of reform can be found:

- Knowing how to design, plan and implement a project.
- Developing a positive but critically realistic attitude with respect to changes in policy and governance.
- Judging the performance of public organizations.
- Comparing and evaluating different systems of public administration.

Thus, of the comprehensive list of competences, no single competence directly refers to public sector reforms. The listed competences focus either on reflecting on change in public organizations or on managerial practices.

We therefore assume that the reform issue is more present at lower levels of Public Administration curricula. To verify this assumption, we inspected the module descriptions of various Public Administration programs at German and Dutch universities. Indeed, the majority of such programs include public sector reforms as a theme in one or more of their courses. Below are some examples of postgraduate master's programs for Public Administration professionals offered by German universities: the master's program in Administrative Sciences of the German University for Administrative Sciences Speyer includes reform as a theme in several modules. In the Executive Master in Public Administration of the Hertie School of Governance Berlin, reform appears in some courses, e.g., in 'Managing Organizational Change'. The University of Kassel offers an entire module on administrative reforms and change management in its Master of Public Administration. Finally, the Master 'European Governance and Administration' of the University of Potsdam includes the issue of public sector reforms in two of its four modules.

In the Netherlands, the master's specialization Public Management at the University of Twente is the only program that offers a module named Public Sector Reform. However, as we have seen, the phenomenon goes by many names. The Public Management Master of the University of Utrecht offers a module on innovation in the public sector, and Leiden University offers a module on Organizational Change. Erasmus University Rotterdam also uses the term 'change' in conjunction with 'organization' in a number of modules but also offers in a comparative module on Public Management that devotes considerable attention to public sector reforms in different countries (taught, it can hardly be a coincidence, by Walter Kickert). Moreover, many assignments address aspects of reforms. Finally, we estimate prudentially that at least one in six master's theses is devoted to reform issues. At other universities in the Netherlands, the subject is hardly found in general descriptions, including in broader terms, but it is found when we scrutinize the descriptions of the modules.

Interestingly, a review of German and Dutch Public Administration programs at the bachelor level reveals that the topic of reform appears to attract less attention in curricula. Although a few bachelor programs cover at least some aspects of administrative reform, the majority of such programs do not devote considerable attention to issues of reform. This can be explained by the positioning of the learning process in the professional career of a trainee. Whereas bachelor's programs are typically pre-service programs (pre-entry training) for inexperienced school graduates, large proportions of master's programs in Germany and the Netherlands are directed toward public servants or other variants of professionals in their mid-career stage (in-service training). It is possible that reform processes are considered overly complex and specific to be suitable for inexperienced students. If this is the case, a key question is whether this is a sensible argument and whether it holds more for reforms than for other issues in policy and management. We will return to this theme in the section on challenges below.

For the present, we conclude that the topic of reform has a more prominent position at the more concrete level of module and course descriptions. The salience of this subject, however, differs across the investigated curricula: it varies from a whole program module to a rather modest theme in some courses. It appears to be more common in in-service than in pre-service programs. In summary, we observe that the subject of public sector reforms is not particularly prominent in Public Administration program descriptions, at least not at the level of competences and intended learning outcomes. In part, this can be explained by the ubiquity of the term 'reform'. This term encompasses nearly everything in Public Administration, from 'grand reforms' of a whole government system to rather limited and technical changes in administrative procedures, from 'policy reforms' to internal management reforms. Thus, curriculum designers may argue that certain issues are in fact a subject of instruction but in a different—e.g., more functional—context. Furthermore, certain 'reform'-related issues may be addressed by using similar but different terms such as change, improvement, innovation, modernization, transformation and adjustment. Consequently, 'reform' is often replaced by synonyms. Finally, 'reform' is occasionally part of larger subjects such as government structures or policy fields and is taught in the more extensive subject. In this sense, 'reform' is predominantly a perspective to address a certain subject (e.g., the reform of a ministry, a policy, a law). In other words: students learn to adopt different views on Public Administration subjects, including the change or reform of the respective subject.

However, there seems to be room for improving academic curricula to make them more supportive for (future) Public Administration professionals and public managers to become students of reform and to be able to appropriately address reforms.

Challenges for Teaching and Learning

Didactic approaches and techniques to support students in becoming skillful students of reform, and meeting the challenges formulated in the preceding section, need not be altogether different from effective didactical methods in academic and professional teaching in general. We know that active learning is generally more effective than more or less passively consuming lectures (Healey, 2005; Trigwell, 2010). Nevertheless, because of the diverse and specific nature of public sector reforms, as outlined in this book, a focused discussion of challenges in the process of becoming a student of reform and of possible solutions is useful.

Both students and teachers are confronted with various challenges in the study of public sector reforms. We identify five key themes.

Knowledge, Competences and Attitude

First, studying the topic of administrative reform has—as is the case for other Public Administration topics—several learning dimensions. First, there is a *cognitive* dimension: a student needs to acquire sufficient knowledge on the subject of reform. He or she has to know about various aspects of administrative reforms (e.g., types, approaches, strategies, triggers, actors, interests, change processes and expectable results). He or she has to be familiar with different perspectives to address a certain reform issue, e.g., how to analyze and theoretically explain reforms. Studying scientific literature and attending lectures by academics and practitioners engaged in reforms can fulfill this cognitive need, especially when combined with case studies.

In addition to the analysis of reforms, students should learn to be able to act in reform processes: how should one manage reform processes or address reforms initiated by other actors? Depending on the specific learning objectives, answering such questions also demands relevant *skills*.

First, a student of reform should become able to *analyze* a new reform initiative and to *diagnose* the context in which it is (to be) implemented: what are the key problems to be solved? Why this reform? What are the presuppositions? Which actors are involved? What are their interests, preoccupations, resources, strategies, attitudes, interdependencies, etc.?

Based on a well-founded diagnosis, students of reform should become able to develop options for shaping (or reshaping) a reform (*design*) and exploring its potential impacts (*ex ante evaluation*). Moreover, there is the challenge of gaining insight into and skills for designing and implementing effective *interventions* and *management strategies* intended to realize or adapt reforms. The skills of *monitoring*, *evaluation* and *making comparisons* with experiences elsewhere contribute to the learning processes of students of reform.

Apart from the cognitive and skills-based aspects, there is an *attitudinal* dimension of becoming a 'reformer' or a 'student of reform': students have to be equipped with values and attitudes that ensure that they are not only capable but also willing to undertake (reflect and act on) reforms in practice (see also the concept of Public Service Motivation, e.g., Perry and Hondeghem, 2008). A basic attitude in this context is 'openness to reform', i.e., to engage as a professional in necessary reforms and not to behave as a passive bureaucrat. The development of values that support 'reform-minded' attitudes on the part of students is, however, difficult: it implies that students possess a solid foundation of ethical positions and core values (e.g., the rule of law, democracy, loyalty, accountability). 'Becoming a student of reform' does not mean that students should engage in any change that is simply on the agenda of the consultancy industry or follows the latest fashion of reform apostles (recall some reform waves surrounding the NPM doctrine). To develop reform-mindedness on the part of students implies helping these students to be able to critically assess reform projects and to engage only with reform issues that are in line with their core values and ethical foundations.

Moreover, students of reform need a research-oriented approach to thinking and an appropriate research attitude, not because professionals in the public domain are to be(come) researchers in the academic sense of the word, but because it is vital that they realize that the complex processes surrounding reforms have to be investigated and explored at all stages to identify the intended and unintended impacts and how these are produced. Being directly involved in research on reforms may be helpful to learning to critically reflect on the rationales, strategies and impacts of reform. Reform processes are change processes that need to be managed, not only in terms of implementation but also to realize the goals (which may not be shared by all actors and/or may change during the process) and to prevent undesired effects for some actors. Thus, attention to theories and strategies of change and practices of monitoring, shaping and adapting strategies and directing actual or desired communication processes is essential. Social simulations (Van der Meer, 1983; Vissers & Van der Meer, 2000) may be a means of learning to address these management aspects in practice. In-service students may also use their own work context as object of reflection and as a site for experiments. Perhaps devoting attention to this attitudinal dimension is even more important for this target group than for pre-service students because we often encounter rather cynical attitudes toward reform and its outcomes in this group. If there are reforms, administrators, professionals and managers should be able to find ways to *use* these reforms to realize change for the better.

Reflexivity

These latter considerations with respect to attitudes give rise to a second, more general challenge. It refers to learning reflexivity and how to embed this in the program or courses (Van der Meer & Marks, 2013). One step is to make tacit notions (as a residual of reading books and listening to lectures or of experience and interaction in 'real' contexts) explicit. This process may be called 'freezing': isolating and preparing these ideas for further scrutiny. Next, the evidence and presuppositions on which these notions are based should be made explicit and put to question. We may call this 'unfreezing':

questioning self-evidence. Then, from the unfreezing stage, new interpretations, research questions and hypotheses may be developed. Finally, ways to test the new ideas, either in research or by experimenting in personal practice, should be developed. The challenge here is how should one facilitate the different stages of such comprehensive reflection processes by didactical approaches and techniques?

A research attitude supports reflexivity because it facilitates not taking rationales, presuppositions and ideologies as self-evident. However, reflexivity also involves keeping an eye on goals and values involved, giving due weight to unintended effects, and finding new perspectives, approaches and ways of 'framing'. Making ideas explicit, discussing them (preferably in heterogeneous groups), and experimenting in, e.g., simulations may be of help in this regard.

Life-Long Research and Learning

Third, it should be realized that there is no such thing as 'reform'. Not only are there alternative labels (as mentioned above), but the label is also applied to substantially different forms of change, as other contributions in this book and the work of Kickert extensively demonstrate. Contents, contexts, strategies and rationales differ across reforms. This has profound implications for 'studying reform' or for 'becoming a student of reform'. It means that insights derived from a certain reform process, be it practical lessons or theoretical explanations of its dynamics, cannot be applied without further reflection on other reform areas. Thus, students of reform should be reflexive and develop their insights not only during the process of becoming a student of reform but also in their subsequent practice. The challenge, then, is how should one equip students of reform to continue researching, learning and reflection? They should not only learn and reflect when they are becoming a student of reform (by participating in a formal program or in other ways) but also learn to learn and reflect in their further practice. Studying different reforms and becoming aware of different aims, contexts and impacts may help students to notice that a reform process is always situation specific and path dependent. Being a student of reform is a life-long process of becoming one.

Socializing and Organizational Learning

This gives rise to a fourth challenge. Students being motivated to be open to reforms and to be committed to them depends not only on their personal values and on a successful academic learning process but also on the impact of professional *socialization* (Reichard, 2012). This is particularly the case for students with a practical background (e.g., in-service training). Professionals and managers are subject to intensive socialization processes during their jobs: they adjust their attitudes and behavior to the prevailing behavioral patterns of their working environments, which are in many cases quite conservative and bureaucratic. Employees particularly adapt to the attitudes of their superiors and colleagues. If the attitudes in their job environment are distant from or dismissive of reform projects, employees may be inclined to take on such attitudes and also behave in a more reform-resistant way. If the group attitude is positive with respect to a reform, employees may be tempted to follow this attitude uncritically. Hence, the impact of training that resulted in openness and active commitment to certain reform initiatives may be counterbalanced by the opposing effects of a reform-resistant organizational climate in a trainee's job environment given its socializing impact on the attitudes of the trainee or vice versa. Often, there may be a tradeoff between certain attitudinal effects of training and opposing effects of bureaucratic socialization. Studying the dynamics of reform processes and self-reflection by students engaged in reform processes themselves may help to recognize these mechanisms, reflect on them and act in sensible ways.

Linking Theory and Praxis

Finally, there is the issue of learning to link theory and real-life reform processes in sensible and fruitful ways in both directions. We know that the ability to link theory and practice is key and should generally be the subject of intensive training in Public Administration programs. In such programs, devoting attention to designing reforms, developing strategies and managing implementation and change is self-evident. However, specific characteristics of reforms and related challenges identified in this and other chapters in this book demand specific emphasis on the skills and attitudes to be developed and on ways to make links between 'theory' and 'practice'.

Reforms involve comprehensive changes within a relatively short period of time. This implies that reform dynamics and outcomes cannot be easily understood on the basis of more or less stabilized patterns, at least to a lesser extent than, e.g., the management of a going concern. Moreover, the role of the context is less evident. The description and analysis of existing patterns and trends alone is, therefore (compared to other administrative and managerial issues), not sufficient to reflect on the design and management of reform. This underlines the need for direct links with real-life settings, plans and developments in the learning process. There are numerous ways to insert this element into academic programs.

Moreover, we believe that effective methods to make theory-praxis connections also help to meet the previous four challenges: sensible strategies are shaped through interaction among theory and praxis knowledge, skills, reflection and learning.

In considering how to facilitate the linking of theory and praxis, it is important to note the different starting positions and learning demands between pre-service and in-service students. We have already touched on this topic above. To a somewhat lesser extent, there may be a similar question with respect to pre-service students without any experience in relevant contexts (mainly in the bachelor stage) and those with some experience from internships or projects. The latter group will mainly be found in some pre-service master's programs. The target group without real-life experience in public organizations and reforms may have difficulties in imagining and understanding the intricacies of reform processes. They may be overburdened by detailed knowledge and skills training concerning administrative reforms, particularly as they are usually unable to judge the relevance of contexts. However, this feature is not unique to reform processes. Understanding organization and management processes, the challenges of intergovernmental or public-private cooperation, for example, also demands a valid imagination of real-life contexts in which such processes take place. Students lacking relevant experience may be inclined to develop simplified images and/or to think too straightforwardly about the application of (normative) theories in design, management and steering. The challenge, therefore, is to find didactic ways to introduce relevant contextual and 'experiential' knowledge. This also holds, by implication, for the study of reform.

The pre-service target group that had internship experience or participated in projects conducted in real-life contexts offers at least one additional entrance to develop valid images of real-life settings, viz., reference to their own practical experience and knowledge. Although knowledge and experiences are fragmented and limited and may have produced perhaps even more simplified images, they also provide material to study. If the experiences involve (elements of) reforms, these may be directly scrutinized as reference material for the study of reform. However, other real life knowledge and experience may help—if accessed intelligently—to develop a better sense of (the relevance of) contexts in which reforms take place. The challenge is to find ways to make this knowledge/experience explicit and to analyze it critically.

One element of a fruitful approach is confronting students with real-life experience in multiple ways. This can be achieved by working on well-documented cases or through guest lectures by practitioners involved in a reform process. Practitioner lecturers may present puzzles, dilemmas and challenges that the lecturers encountered during in a reform process. In associated group discussions, students can discuss how they, inspired by theoretical knowledge and practical information, would address or advise on those dilemmas and challenges. Finally, students could present their solutions/strategies to the practitioners and receive feedback. This procedure may also be of interest to the practitioners involved because 'stupid' questions and suggestions by the students may be helpful to find new approaches to the reform process and, thus, for the practitioners in becoming students of reform (again). This model has been successfully used in the Public Administration bachelor's program at Erasmus University Rotterdam.

Case studies can also provide a lively picture of a reform project. Students can better understand the content, processes and results of reforms if they receive an illustration of a 'real-world' project. In such a case study, the student has the opportunity to analyze certain features of a project, to identify possible problems and deficits and to suggest improvements.

Another option is student participation in project studies concerning reform issues: in this form of learning, students have the opportunity to study certain practical problems in a detailed empirical manner and to identify possible problems and deficits (e.g., Reid & Miller, 1997). A project study (often also called a capstone project) is a form of research-based autonomous learning whereby a student team under the supervision of a lecturer undertakes field studies, explores certain problem areas, analyzes and interprets possible causes and proposes solutions for improvement. The study of administrative reforms can be regarded as one of the favorite areas for such studies. Students can, e.g., study a reform project that has just been implemented in a certain governmental environment; they can conduct interviews and document analyses, interpret their empirical findings and summarize their results in a project report that can then be presented to government representatives. The results of project studies can eventually become part of a student's final thesis.

A sense of real-life context and relevance and applicability to theories can also be gained by internships in a reform context, in combination with regular reflection sessions on students' observations and experiences during such an internship: this exposure to administrative practice will be particularly relevant for *pre-service* students. If students become well-prepared before their internship (e.g., how to study reforms) and if the program is monitoring and evaluating the experiences gained by the students during the internship, then a direct encounter with a reform project and its results in practice may be a very valuable learning experience for the students. Under certain circumstances, students can play an observer's role and accompany some steps of reform processes in a real-world context.

Finally, simulation exercises and debriefing may be helpful. In a simulated setting, students can occupy different positions and roles in relation to a (proposed) reform and take the responsibility for its shaping, implementing and impacts (to the extent that these become visible in the simulation), develop and adapt their strategies, etc. (Vissers & Van der Meer, 2000). It is essential here to reconstruct and analyze the processes as they took place in the simulation and how the intended or unintended impacts arose. On this experiential and reflective basis, lessons for real-life reform processes can be drawn.

All of these inputs, experiences and reflections may be used to animate theoretical insights from an earlier stage of study and as reference material to critically evaluate and interpret new theoretical material.

Post-experience programs for professionals offer other opportunities concerning reform issues. Here, students can analyze and reflect on parts of the contents to be learned with reference to existing individual experiences in the field of administrative reforms. It can be expected that such students can understand certain reform concepts, change strategies and reform problems, as they can interpret them by comparing them with previous experiences. Not only can they serve as useful cases from practice, but students can also transfer reform-oriented learning results to their own jobs, which may intensify and contextualize their learning process. However, such students may have negative experiences with administrative reforms (e.g., because of critical experiences with failing reforms or unintended negative effects). Such critical positions may result in cynicism, frustration or other types of disapproval of reform-oriented subjects in training. Moreover, they may be inclined to take their knowledge obtained from practice for granted, which may hamper their critical learning process. Thus, here too are challenges: how to help experienced students reflect critically on reforms (or on their own assessment of them) and to consider them from other perspectives.

In-service students, therefore, also need to be assisted and stimulated to connect theory and (their own) practice. Theory may help to understand their own practice in new ways, and their experience may help them to critically review theory. Both learning processes require freezing and unfreezing. This may be stimulated in diverse ways.

Students should be asked to express their implicit explanations for phenomena in their working experience and their presuppositions of what works (or not) and why. These notions should then be made the object of debate and research: is there evidence for these ideas, how can they be tested, and what can be learned about them?

Moreover, theoretical ideas presented in the literature or in lectures can be compared with a student's own reform experiences and ideas. The results of such comparisons can inspire students to raise new research questions or to identify options for their practice.

A working method in this regard that we found very valuable is intervision. In intervision groups, students present their experiences/puzzles/dilemmas to a few peer students. The *other* students in the small group reflect on the case and come to well-argued suggestions to which the problem owner may respond. By this method, both the presenter of the puzzle and the other group members are actively engaged in linking theory and practice and in giving one another feedback on this linking process.

Moreover, students can be asked to explicitly compare the goals, strategies, processes and outcomes of different reforms or similar reforms in different contexts. If there is diversity in experiences or roles within the student groups, this exercise can be conducted in a similar manner as the intervision groups. An alternative would be to invite guest lecturers to present cases to compare.

In-service students also have or can create the opportunity of experimenting in (their own) real-life context with new approaches or interventions, derived from experiences obtained elsewhere and/or from theoretical insights. Reactions and effects can be registered and analyzed in class or in (intervision) groups.

In so doing, group simulation exercises to experiment with different roles and strategies (Vissers & Van der Meer, 2000) may also be useful, as such exercises provide the students with the opportunity to gain experience in an unknown context, position or role, thereby broadening the realm with which theory can be confronted.

Final Reflection

In this chapter, we discussed why not only academics but also public administration professionals and (public) managers should become students of reform. Public sector reforms tend to have profound impacts, at least for some stakeholders, both intended and unintended. Responsible professionals, therefore, should acquire insight into reform processes and the steering and problem-solving strategies related to them and become able to translate these insights into situation-specific interventions. Because many reforms are unique in character, at least in some respects, and/or occur in different contexts, the *study* of reform should be a continuous process. Managers of reform should become learning professionals equipped with a solid research attitude.

We identified a number of requirements that need to be fulfilled to realize this ambition. We suggested some ways to give due attention to learning to connect theory, research and practice and to acquiring the required skills and attitudes in academic Public Administration programs.

The intended result of all this is not only to train students to become good reform managers but also to remind students of reform throughout their careers, which is a necessary—if not sufficient—condition for successful reforms.

Notes

1. By 'repertoire', we refer to ways of thinking and acting that characterize an actor. These are presumed to be the result of previous experience and sense-making (Van der Meer, 1983).
2. The National Association of Schools of Public Affairs and Administration (NASPAA) is an important quality assurance body in the PA field in the US. A few years ago, this organization introduced competences into their accreditation standards. For examples of describing competences, see NASPAA Self Study Instructions from 05.21.2014 (http://accreditation.naspaa.org/?s=Self+study+instruction).

References

Allison, G. (1971). *Essence of decision: Explaining the Cuban missile crisis*. Boston: Little, Brown and Company.

Davis, K.C. (1971). *Discretionary justice: A preliminary inquiry*. Urbana: University of Illinois Press.

Goodnow, F.J. (reprint 2010). *Politics and administration: A study in government.* Lexington KY: Forgotten Books.

Healey, M. (2005). Linking research and teaching: Exploring disciplinary spaces and the role of inquiry-based learning. In R. Barnett (Ed.), *Reshaping the university: New relationships between research, scholarship and teaching* (pp. 67–78). Buckingham: Open University Press.

Hemerijck, A. (2003). Vier beleidsvragen. In V. Bekkers and A. Ringeling (Eds.), *Vragen over beleid: Perspectieven op waardering* (pp. 33–48). Utrecht: Lemma.

Heyman, P.B. (1987). *The politics of public management.* New Haven: Yale University Press.

Hood, C. (1991). A public management for all seasons. *Public Administration,* 69(1), 3–19.

Jann, W. (2003). State, administration and governance in Germany: Competing traditions and dominant narratives. *Public Administration, 81*(1), 95–118.

Kettl, D.F. (2000). *The global public management revolution: A report on the transformation of governance.* Washington, DC: Brookings Institution Press.

Kickert, W.J.M. (2000). *Public management reforms in the Netherlands: Social reconstruction of reform ideas and underlying frames of reference.* Delft: Eburon.

Kickert, W.J.M. (2005). Public governance: The context of administrative innovations in Southern Europe. In M. Veenswijk (Ed.), *Organizing innovation* (pp. 173–191). Amsterdam: IOS Press.

Kickert, W.J.M. (2007). Public management reforms in countries with a Napoleonic state model: France, Italy and Spain. In C. Pollitt, S. Van Thiel and V. Homburg (Eds.), *New public management in Europe* (pp. 26–51). Basingtoke: Palgrave Macmillan.

Lokhoff, J., Wegewijs, B., Wagenaar, R., González, J., Isaacs, A.K., Donà dalle Rose, L.F., and Gobbi, M. (eds.). (2010). *A tuning guide to formulating degree programme profiles—including programme competences and programme learning outcomes.* Bilbao, Groningen and The Hague: TUNING Association.

Lynn, L. Jr. (1996). *Public management as art, science and profession.* Chatham, NJ: Chatham House.

Majone, G. (Ed.). (1996). *Regulating Europe.* London and New York: Routledge.

March, J., & Olsen, J. (1989). *Rediscovering institutions.* New York: The Free Press.

Mouffe, C. (2005). *The return of the political.* London and New York: Verso.

NASPAA. (2009). *Accreditation standards for master's degree programs.* http://www.naspaa.org/accreditation/ns/naspaastandards.asp. Last accessed 30 March 2014.

Perry, J.L., & Hondeghem, A. (Eds.). (2008). *Motivation in public management: The call of public service.* Oxford: Oxford University Press.

Reichard, C. (2012). Individualisierung und bürokratische Sozialisation in der Verwaltungsausbildung. In S. Armutat and A. Seisreiner (Eds.), *Differentielles management* (pp. 242–252). Wiesbaden: Springer.

Reichard, C., & Van der Krogt, T. (2014). Towards a set of specific competences for academic degree programmes in Public Administration in Europe. Paper at the NISPAcee Conference, 22–24 May. Budapest.

Reid, M., & Miller, W. (1997). Bridging theory and administrative practice: The role of a capstone course in P.A. programs. *International Journal of Public Administration,* 20(10), 1513–1527.

Ringeling, A. (1978). *Beleidsvrijheid van ambtenaren.* Alphen aan den Rijn: Samsom.

Rosenbloom, D.H. (2011). Public administration's legal dimensions: Three Models. In D.C. Menzel and L.H. White (Eds.), *The state of public administration* (pp. 368–387). Armonk and London: Sharpe.

Savas, E.S. (1987). *Privatization: The key to better government.* Chatham, NJ: Chatham House.

Scharpf, F.W. (1997). *Games real actors play: Actor-centered institutionalism in policy research*. Boulder, CO: Westview Press.

Trigwell, K. (2010). Promoting effective student learning in higher education. In P. Peterson, E. Baker and B. McGaw (Eds.), *International encyclopedia of education, 4* (pp. 461–466). Oxford: Elsevier.

Van der Meer, F.B. (1983). *Organisatie als spel*. PhD thesis. Enschede: University of Twente.

Van der Meer, F.B., & Marks, P. (2013). Teaching and learning reflection in MPA programs: Towards a strategy. *Teaching Public Administration, 31*(1), 42–54.

Vissers, G.A.N., & Van der Meer, F.B. (2000). Social simulation and polycentric policy making: Ex ante assessment of administrative reform in the region of Rotterdam. In D. Herz and A. Blätte (Eds.), *Simulation und Planspiel in den Sozialwissenschaften: eine Bestandsaufnahme der internationalen Diskussion* (pp. 231–257). Münster, Hamburg, London: LIT-Verlag.

Weick, K.E. (1979). *The social psychology of organizing*. 2nd edition. Reading, MA: AddisonWesley.

Index

Note: Italicized page numbers indicate a figure on the corresponding page. Page numbers in bold indicate a table on the corresponding page.